German Women for Empire, 1884–1945

German Women

for Empire, 1884–1945

LORA WILDENTHAL

Duke University Press   Durham & London 2001

© 2001 Duke University Press

Printed in the United States of America on acid-free paper ∞

Typeset in Carter & Cone Galliard by Keystone Typesetting, Inc.

Library of Congress Cataloging-in-Publication Data

appear on the last printed page of this book.

For Q

CONTENTS

This book has benefited from the knowledge and helpfulness of many people and the resources of several institutions. It began at the University of Michigan's Department of History under the guidance of Kathleen Canning, Geoff Eley, Laura Downs, and my fellow graduate students. A fellowship from the Berlin Program for Advanced German and European Studies of the Social Science Research Council and the Free University of Berlin, a Rackham Graduate School Research Partnership, and a Mellon Dissertation Fellowship supported the research and writing of the dissertation from which this book developed. In Berlin, I attended the seminars of Adolf Rüger at the Humboldt University, and he provided much encouragement and key archival leads. Doris Kaufmann also gave sound advice. Karin Hausen gave me the opportunity to speak in her women's history seminar at the Technical University of Berlin. In Ann Arbor, Adjaï Oloukpona Yinnon drew my attention to several valuable leads. Fred Cooper and Patricia Simpson read the dissertation and made many suggestions.

At Pitzer College, I benefited from the help and encouragement of the Marching and Chowder Society; the reading group in the disciplines organized by Jim Bogen, Betty Farrell, and Dan Segal; and the WAR group at the Claremont Colleges, especially Audrey Bilger, Karen Goldman, Claudia Klaver, and Cynthia Humes. Pitzer College supported further research with a Summer Research Fellowship in the Humanities, and a German Academic Exchange Service (DAAD) Study Visit grant supported another summer of research. I benefited from comments from the audiences at talks arranged by Robert Moeller, Liisa Malkki, and Jim Ferguson at the University of California at Irvine; Barbara Duden and Adelheid von Saldern at the University of Hanover; Rudolf Boch and Kathleen Canning at the University of Chemnitz; and

Rolf Winau, Johanna Bleker, and Pascal Grosse at the Free University of Berlin. At Pitzer I had the great pleasure of teaching and talking with Dan Segal. He has always been ready to discuss my work and has done more than any other person to help me rethink this project and many other scholarly matters besides.

One version of the manuscript was completed with the support of the James Bryant Conant Fellowship at the Minda de Gunzburg Center for European Studies at Harvard University. Widener Library, along with several other libraries at Harvard, allowed me to track down many leads gathered from the Zentrales Staatsarchiv in Potsdam (later the Bundesarchiv in Berlin), the Landesarchiv Berlin, the Landes- und Universitätsbibliothek in Frankfurt, the Hoover Institution's library, the National Archives II in College Park, and the archive of the Vereinte Evangelische Mission in Wuppertal, whose staff were especially helpful. My thanks to Dorothee Pfeiffer, who allowed me to use the Lou-Andreas-Salomé-Archiv. I am particularly grateful to the family of Else Frobenius for graciously receiving me and for their generosity in allowing me to use their private family archive. Eleanor Alexander directed me to the Leo Baeck Institute, which supplied me with some material by mail.

At MIT, the members of the History Faculty reading group read a new, very long chapter and offered encouragement. I thank especially John Dower, Elizabeth Wood, and Harriet Ritvo for their advice. Dean Philip Khoury generously granted me a research allowance that made MIT an even more ideal place for research and writing.

Several individuals sent references and suggestions all the while: Tina Campt, Marcia Klotz (who shared her own unpublished work), Pieter Judson, Krista O'Donnell (who also shared her unpublished work), Karen Smidt (who gave me not only a copy of her dissertation but many hard to find sources as well), and above all Pascal Grosse. I can't begin to quantify his help with this project.

Most recently, Timothy Burke, Antoinette Burton, Roger Chickering, Glenn Penny, Jessica Riskin, and two anonymous readers read the entire penultimate manuscript and made comments that helped me come up with the present, more manageable version. I appreciate the hours they spent to help me over the last hurdles. Valerie Millholland, Miriam Angress, Raphael Allen, Justin Faerber, Mindy Conner, and others at Duke University Press turned it into a book. I am grateful to Lewis Bateman, who provided encouragement and the book's title, and to Julia Adams and George Steinmetz for including it in their series.

I thank Felicia, Jürgen, and Felix Kübler for years of learning about the German language and much else. I deeply appreciate the love and loyal support of my family in California, Colorado, Michigan, Oklahoma, and Texas. Carl Caldwell has overtaken and surpassed all standards of editing, tact, and patience.

The statements and conclusions in this book are mine and not necessarily those of any of the granting agencies, institutions, or persons mentioned here.

I n 1869 John Stuart Mill wrote that "the surest test and most correct measure of the civilisation of a people or an age" is its "elevation or debasement" of women.[1] Charles Fourier, Friedrich Engels, Karl Marx, and many European feminists shared the feminist and radical maxim that a society's level of advancement can be measured by the condition of its women.[2] The meanings of that maxim extended beyond feminism and radicalism and served European advocates of empire equally well as a description of the superiority of their own societies over others.[3] It posited a relationship among the condition of women, progress, and hierarchical cultural comparison, linking women's fate to nineteenth-century Europe's civilizing mission. The maxim presented women as symbols of their respective societies' backwardness or advancement. This book is about women in the German imperial metropole who sought to be both symbols and agents of their society's advancement. Among them were conservatives, centrists, and radical liberals, as well as feminists and antifeminists.

Between the 1870s and 1914 European states annexed territories in Africa, Asia, and the Pacific at an unprecedented rate. This "new imperialism" was no longer the business only of explorers and their royal patrons; it was an enterprise shared between royal or republican rulers and the citizens of nations, women as well as men, who were demanding rights of political participation. The late nineteenth century was a high point not only of European imperial expansion, but also of feminist and socialist activity. In Germany, Bismarck, Emperor William II, and other leaders hoped that imperial expansion would unite Germans divided by region, class, religion, and political persuasion.[4] Between 1884 and 1900 Germany gained a colonial empire of about one million square miles and about twelve million inhabitants. In 1884 and 1885 Germany claimed four colonies in Africa — German Southwest Africa, German East Africa, Togo, and Cameroon — as well as German New Guinea in the Pacific.[5] In 1888 the island of Nauru was annexed and added to German New Guinea. In the late 1890s Germany undertook a second series of annexations that included the 1897 occupation and lease of the Chinese city of Qingdao (which Germans called Tsingtau) and its hinterland on the Shandong Peninsula and the 1899 purchase of the Mariana Islands, Caroline Islands, and Palau Islands from Spain, which were added to German New Guinea. In 1900 conflict among the United States, England, and Germany over Samoa led to Germany's annexation of the islands Savaii and Upolu as German Samoa.[6] Before the First World War, the German colonial empire was third in territorial size and fifth in population among the British, French, Dutch, Belgian, United States, Portuguese, Italian, and Spanish empires.[7] When Germany lost the First World War, it lost the colonial empire as well. But the colonialist movement — an assortment of geographical, radical nationalist, missionary, and other voluntary associations — remained. Colonialist men and women agitated for the recovery of empire between 1919 and the Second World War, when a second, profounder defeat dashed their hopes.[8]

Formal overseas empire was important to German women, but German women were not initially important to the men who dominated that empire. Women's legal inequality meant that they could not participate in politics as men did; apart from some local elections, they could not vote until 1918. Their enforced lack of academic credentials — most universities were closed to them until 1908 — prevented them from participating in academic "colonial sciences" such as geography and linguistics. Nevertheless, colonialist women managed to institutionalize their presence in the colonialist movement. To do so, they had first to convince colonialist men that German women were necessary to empire. At the time of the first annexations German women were not expected to go to the colonies, except perhaps as Catholic missionaries or as wives of male Protestant missionaries. In both cases, struggles with male authorities awaited them.[9] Many missionaries were ambivalent about the nationalist and secular projects of empire. The colonialist women who are the subject of this book wanted to promote the colonies not primarily for religious reasons, but rather for reasons of Germany's national prestige. They specifically sought out opportunities outside missionary societies for women's participation in German colonialism.

Chapter 1 presents the women's first successful strategy as secular agents of empire: as the organizers and staff of medical nursing in the colonies. After detaching the occupation of nursing from male nurses, male missionary authorities, and religious justification, colonialist women made a niche for secular female nursing in the colonialist movement and the colonial state. They founded the first colonialist organization run by and for women, and oversaw the dispatch of women nurses to all parts of the empire to work in the name of the state and conservative nationalism. Nurses, supposedly desexualized by the rule against marriage, served a limited term in the colonies under the strict discipline of the colonial administration's doctors. Like frontline nurses in wartime, they were permitted to bring certain feminine qualities to an intensely masculine space.

Yet nursing could not contain colonialist women's ambitions, even in the early years of the 1880s. Chapter 2 illustrates the breadth of that ambition through the life of Frieda von Bülow, the first German woman to make an independent colonialist career. Although she helped found the women's organization that administered colonial nurses, her insistence on personal autonomy, radical nationalism, and feminism led to her expulsion. She had a love affair with the infamous colonial adventurer Carl Peters, attempted to become an independent planter in German East Africa, endured Peters's highly publicized trial for the execution of an African woman he kept in sexual servitude, and all the while built a career as a novelist. Her novels depict the predicaments of German women in the new colonies as well as in Germany. Bülow had firsthand experience of almost all dimensions of colonialism then available to women — and also of the difficulties facing women who tried to become agents of Germany's colonial power.

These difficulties arose from men's and women's conflicting aspirations for life in the colonies. Both saw the colonies as spaces where a new, freer German society could be created far from Germany's social strife. But while colonialist women hoped that colonial freedom would offer them new opportunities, some colonialist men envisioned the colonies as a place of freedom *from* German women. In the colonies, German men were able to represent German civilization yet leave "civilized" relations between the sexes behind. Sexual and other forms of coercion that were unacceptable in Germany were part and parcel of the apparatus of rule in the colonies. Men accused of rape and other cruelty toward colonial subjects defended themselves by claiming that their behavior was necessary and even proper in colonial spaces such as Africa or New Guinea. Colonialist women, who were committed both to colonialism and to "civilized" gender relations, found it troubling that a special standard of colonial sexual morality had taken hold.[10] Yet they did not want African and Pacific Islander women to be treated as their equals, for that would threaten their own authority as agents of colonial power. Colonialist men and women, each for their own reasons, produced misleading images of African and Pacific Islander women: as obedient, sexually willing or deviously seductive, and not yet influenced by supposedly civilized — in some men's eyes, overly civilized — doctrines of feminism. Colonialist women faced the larger question of the extent to which the colonies and metropole should be the same moral, sexual, and legal spaces. Emphasis on differences between colonial space and metropolitan space tended to exclude German women from colonialism. For example, even those colonialist men who did not defend rape and brutality as tools of rule nevertheless repeated the received wisdom that the climate, material hardship, and threat of warfare made the colonies too dangerous for white women. Colonialist women were seen as superfluous, or even as liabilities, in the very colonies they promoted.

Chapter 3 discusses the role played by some colonialist men in propelling the acceptance of German women as necessary to colonial life and politics. As German colonists increased in number, had more intensive contact with the metropole, and sought greater rights of political participation through self-administration, a confrontation between "imperial patriarchs" of precolonial and early colonial days and "liberal nationalists" emerged. The liberal nationalists wanted to expand political participation, but also to draw sharper distinctions between colonizer and colonized. Families that crossed racial lines, once considered a normal part of precolonial and early colonial societies, were now described as threats to white German supremacy. In three colonies — German Southwest Africa, German East Africa, and German Samoa — marriages between Germans and colonial subjects were banned. However, the bans on intermarriage aroused fierce opposition from the men in such marriages and had no effect on so-called race mixing outside marriage. In fact, the campaign against race mixing clashed with male colonizers' interests. How could German men's right to choose sexual and marital partners be balanced with the imperative of clear racial hierarchy? Colonialist men came to see white German women as the solution: if more German women were made available to male colonists, the men would of their own accord choose them over local women, and the difficult task of legally restricting men's sexual choices would be obviated. The plan did not work as smoothly as hoped, but it did give colonialist women a fresh opportunity to show German women's importance to colonialism.

Chapter 4 discusses a new cohort of colonialist women who advocated a role beyond nurse and missionary for German women in the colonies: the woman settler as cultural, economic, and political partner of the male colonist, wherever he might go. This group founded the second organization run by and for colonialist women in order to arrange the settlement of specially chosen German women in German Southwest Africa. The preferred destination for these women settlers was the colonial ranch, plantation, or farm. As a site of both economic production and family reproduction, the farm blurred the gendered division of labor between unpaid work at home and paid work outside the home. In that idealized setting, German women were to create economic value, raise white German children, and participate in local German communities without coming into conflict with men. As farmers, women could even take the place of men, yet never leave the farm's extended household. The role of woman farmer-settler appealed both to men who sought a solution to race mixing and to women who likewise opposed race mixing and wanted new economic and cultural opportunities. Among this second cohort of colonialist women were feminists who sought to increase the influence of feminine morality, or "spiritual motherhood" (*geistige Mütterlichkeit*), in public life.[11] Feminists had long argued that there were particular "women's cultural tasks" (*Kulturaufgaben der Frau*) without which civilization would remain incomplete.[12] Colonialist women carried versions of these ideas to the colonies. Their motto became: "The *man* can conquer and subjugate territories in the world for the German idea; but only the persistence of *woman* can implant and preserve the German idea abroad over the long term!"[13] In the wake of the debate over race mixing, their male allies agreed with colonialist women that German women were essential to colonial life.

Feminists and other commentators on the "Woman Question" (*Frauenfrage*) fretted over a supposed surplus of women who remained unmarried, lacked careers appropriate to their social station, and would waste their maternal energies.[14] Feminists called for greater access to education and meaningful careers; marriage and motherhood, they pointed out, could not fill all women's lives. Colonialist men and women referred ironically to this aspect of the Woman Question when they, in turn, spoke of a "colonial Woman Question" that referred not to a surplus of women in the colonies, but to a shortage of white women. The colonial Woman Question sidelined feminist demands for social change by emphasizing numbers of German women rather than the conditions of their existence. It promised that unmarried middle-class women could be converted from a social problem in Germany into a solution for the colonies. But the colonial Woman Question was never just about numbers; after all some six million women lived in the German colonies. The colonial Woman Question was about race. While feminists and social reformers in Germany were able to pursue their projects in law, education, and employment regardless of whether racial distinctions were drawn, drawing racial distinctions was the whole point of the colonial Woman Question. As it happened, the colonial Woman Question opened up opportunities for women in the colonies beyond marriage and motherhood. As in Germany, colonialist women argued that German women made cultural and economic contributions to society other than motherhood, and as in Germany, independent colonialist women found ways to live in the interstices of heterosexual social norms. Nevertheless, the presence of all German women in the colonies was beholden to the racial justification that underlay men's new acceptance of German women in colonial space.

Because women's ability to sustain racial purity was the basis for their political participation in colonialism, colonialist women were preoccupied above all else with German-ness.[15] That might have changed as German colonial societies grew and differentiated. As it happened, the loss of the colonies after 1919, which the Entente powers justified in terms of Germans' civilizational deficiencies, only reinforced colonialists' obsession with the qualities of German-ness. As chapter 5 shows, colonialist women's focus on Germans rather than colonial subjects served them unexpectedly well after 1919. Their concentration on nursing, the household, and the farm as loci of German culture was suited to the conditions of reconstructing German colonial communities that had been uncoupled from German rule. After 1933, colonialists' basic claims about white German women's importance for racial purity did not require very much alteration to conform to the National Socialists' official doctrine of racism. Nazism gave a prominent ideological place, though not much real power, to "Aryan" women as special exemplars of German culture and racial purity. The joining of colonialism with Nazism took place in part because colonialists and Nazis alike were obsessed with race, expansion, and German prestige, and in part because of the antidemocratic political inclinations of some, though certainly not all, colonialists. Nazi leaders gave greater priority to an empire in eastern Europe than overseas, however, and Germany never came close to regaining its old colonies during the Second World War. All colonialist organizations, including women's, were taken over by Nazi party organizations in 1936 and dissolved altogether in 1943 as part of the mobilization for total war. One colonialist women's project survived until the last weeks of the "Third Reich," however: a school for colonial housekeeping and farming located in northern Germany. Into the 1940s, the school attracted women who dreamed of working on tropical farms in Africa or South America.

Colonialist women's activism thus traversed three regimes and two world wars. It coexisted with the expansion of feminism into a mass movement, the institution of women's suffrage in the Weimar Republic, and the destruction of liberal democracy, including suffrage, under Nazism. Some of the women involved were feminists, although many others distanced themselves from feminism. Apart from a shared social privilege — most came from middle-class and aristocratic families with ties to the military, civil service, professions, business, and landownership — colonialists were a diverse group. They were Protestant, Catholic, and Jewish; their political allegiances ranged from archconservative to left-liberal; and they hailed from East Prussia, the Rhineland, southern Germany, and points in between, as well as the colonies.[16] Even the distinction between metropole and colony was blurred by travelers' and colonists' mobility between the two, and by the brevity of the colonial empire, which prevented the formation of lasting German communities in Africa except in Namibia. Germans' ideas of gender and hierarchy shaped colonial practices, and colonial practices raised questions about the nature of Germany. The history of German colonialist women is therefore hard to sum up in a single formula. It is also hard to reduce to a specifically German history. Overseas empire was a project that Germany self-consciously shared with other European and Europeanized states. This book uses German sources to tell its story, but readers familiar with other modern colonial empires and European women's movements will see many points of comparison.

Over the last decade, historians, literary scholars, and anthropologists have reexamined the ways empires shaped European society and culture. Recent work on the colonial empires of Britain, France, the Netherlands, Belgium, and Spain has revealed great complexity in agents, intentions, and effects.[17] Until recently, Germany tended to be left out of these English-language discussions, although a considerable German-language literature on German colonialism, with different points of emphasis, exists.[18] The German colonial empire has often been described as too late and too brief to be really comparable with other modern colonial empires. At the same time, Nazi imperialism and racism complicate efforts at comparison, and they certainly complicate a research agenda that emphasizes political ambiguity. As a result, much literature on German colonialism, whether in English or German, has chosen one of two relatively unambiguous approaches to interpretation: *either* German colonialism was a clear prelude to Nazism, *or* it had little or nothing to do with Nazism and the Holocaust.[19] Each approach has obvious problems. The former suggests that imperial racism was proto-Nazi when expressed and implemented by Germans, but not when it was expressed and implemented by other European or European-descended imperial powers. The latter neglects the importance for Nazism of decades of racialist mobilization, as well as, for example, continuities between colonial empire and Nazism at the level of individual careers. German colonialism cannot be subsumed into Nazism, but neither can the two be treated in complete isolation. Moreover, it is necessary to avoid constructing a mythical unity of a given colonial empire on the basis of nation-state distinctions or even national character. Not everything that took place in the modern colonial empires was informed by a national order of things. The racism of German colonialism must be approached at several levels.

Colonialism's connections to Nazism and the Holocaust are both obvious and extremely difficult to specify historically.[20] That may be why recent English-language scholarship on German colonialism has turned to work on imaginative representations of the colonies.[21] Such work seeks to broaden and deepen the understanding of race in the German past by turning to sources produced outside the chronological or geographical limits of Germany's formal empire. It often refuses conventional periodizations, delving instead into brief moments or imaginative works of art, and juxtaposing diverse situations. Indeed, only a small fraction of Germans' encounters with the extra-European world took place under the auspices of formal German rule. Individual German sailors, businessmen, missionaries, scientists, doctors, and explorers had long worked overseas in precolonial societies, in other European states' colonial empires, and in the independent Latin American states. Race, empire, and exoticism figured in German creative works long before formal empire, and have persisted after it.

Nevertheless, formal colonial rule remains an important subject of study because it ranged individuals, groups, and images in relation to state power. Formal rule, after all, means access to the goods and services of the state: military support, allocations of funds, representation in state institutions, and rights defined by citizenship. The years before 1914 saw new opportunities for colonists to define their access to state power, just as the years after 1919 saw colonialists' efforts to pressure the state into recovering the lost empire. At a time of extensive feminist agitation in the metropole, defining citizenship in the colonies necessarily raised the question of what role women played in the German *Kulturnation*. This book examines how self-defined colonialist women used ideas of race and gender in the context of formal empire both to gain new freedoms as women and to assert German superiority over "backward" societies.

The tendency to collapse German colonialism into other German racisms, notably anti-Semitism, probably arises from a quest for a comprehensive interpretation of German racism. Yet the very power of race lies in its ability to produce myriad new distinctions. This book argues, along with much of the critical literature on race, that race has always been a historical matter: something created, changing, and contextual.[22] Indeed, to seek a definition of race beyond historical context would be to treat race as a transcendent truth, to try to understand it using the terms of racism. Among Germans generally between 1884 and 1914, colonialist men and women were the ones who dealt most explicitly with ideas of race and enjoyed the most widespread agreement for their racial ideas. For Germans as well as most Europeans of the day, differences between "whites" and Africans, Asians, and Pacific Islanders seemed to be naturally "racial" differences. The idea that Jewish and non-Jewish "white" Germans formed distinct races was, notwithstanding its dreadful future, a controversial notion in the era of the German formal empire. The fact of empire allowed colonialists' ideas about race to be put into practice to an extent unusual for pre-1933 Germany. That said, the German colonialist movement did not evolve in a world apart from Nazism; both arose from the same world.

Turn-of-the-century Germany saw several competing quests for new kinds of polities, led by radical nationalists, left-liberals, feminists, and conservative nationalists; women participated in all those groups. Such new polities were invoked through the closely interrelated modern political discourses of feminism, liberalism, and nationalism.[23] All served to individualize political subjects, unify them with common interests, and incite their participation in new kinds of public space. Colonialist women invoked race as a natural collectivity prior to any voluntary one in order to avoid exclusion from full participation in the actual polity of Imperial Germany. Colonialist women claimed membership — even leadership — in the extralegal, biologized polity of the white and German race, which they argued had a substantial reality behind the existing legal and social order of the German state. The words *national* or *cultural* were often substituted for *racial,* but with much the same effect; the point was to invoke an alternative polity. Race was a powerful language with which to argue for inclusion. The feminist Ika Freudenberg made this kind of argument for women's inclusion in a book on women and public life published in 1911. In it, she presented feminism as the latest innovation of Western civilization, that pedigree of recognized predecessors to what feminists and others commonly called the "civilized countries" (*Kulturländer*). Western civilization had prized individualism, yet heretofore had applied it only to men and had neglected women. Freudenberg argued that "race means both sexes . . . and it has to mean both, because it needs both for its purposes."[24] Freudenberg, herself a lesbian and concerned with increasing women's participation in public life, was referring not to pronatalism but to what she saw as the gender complementarity basic to civilization itself. It was important for colonialist women that extensive formal education, high state office, and other trappings of middle-class and elite male privilege were not necessary to perceive race. Race, on this view, was democratically available expertise. Drawing on a posited feminine authority about culture and race, colonialism women moved from seeing themselves as men's partners to acting as independent representatives of German culture. However, none of the colonialist women was able to escape presenting German women as means to an end instead of as ends in themselves. Rather, they substituted race or nation for men. Race and hierarchy were tools for mobilization, but they ended up also defining the people who used them.

This book, as a feminist history of gender and race, privileges the sources that German colonialist women, its primary subjects, produced: travel and fiction books, articles in the periodical press, records of women's voluntary organizations, and private correspondence. Since these women sought to alter the policies of the state and of men's voluntary organizations, this book also draws on much published and unpublished material written by men on the subject of German women's participation in colonialist projects and voluntary organizations. This book is the first to incorporate a large selection of the copious published and archival sources on German women and Germany's colonial empire. Finally, the implications of the inclusion of German women in the colonial project extended beyond empirical data on settlement, employment, and fertility to affect how German culture and society was itself imagined and disputed. Therefore, this book reveals new facets of historical figures and sources familiar to historians from other contexts so that we can better reconstruct today what empire meant to German women and men then.

CHAPTER ONE

Colonial Nursing as the First
Realm of Colonialist
Women's Activism, 1885–1907

The first voluntary association to be run by and for procolonial women was devoted to providing nurses to Germany's colonies. Nursing was second only to missionary work as a social role for German women in the colonies, predating even marriage and motherhood. Years before colonialists urged German women to become wives and mothers of settlers, nurses and the women who raised funds to dispatch them had a secure place in the colonialist movement. Colonial nursing long dominated procolonial women's activism: for the first twenty years of Germany's colonial empire, that first association remained the only organized outlet for colonialist women outside church or other male-run auspices.

Nursing is, at first glance, a curious focal point for colonialist women's interests. It would seem to be a technical occupation rather than a venue for politics or ideology. Yet in nineteenth century Europe, the religious, maternalist, and patriotic meanings of nursing overshadowed its technical aspect. Nursing drew on two traditions. First, Christian nursing orders — at first Catholic, later also Protestant — in which women and men pursued nursing as a religious calling, had been active for centuries. (Because nursing among Christian Europeans was so intertwined with Christian institutions, Jewish nursing had a distinct history.)[1] Second, women traditionally performed nursing duties in the home for ill family members. As secular nursing developed over the course of the nineteenth century, an emerging modern ideology of nursing combined religious traditions with the concurrently developing ideology of motherhood.[2] In German-speaking lands, nursing became associated with military glory and nationalism during the Napoleonic Wars and the wars of unification in the 1860s. Furthermore, nursing was economically vital to German women. As one of the very few paid occupations open to middle-class women, it was an important livelihood for those living outside marriage. The charitable support of nursing also offered women an opportunity for unpaid public activism. Neither as paid work nor as charity did nursing challenge conservative notions of women's place in a hierarchical social order; in fact, nursing met the strictest standards of feminine respectability.

During the latter half of the nineteenth century, nursing in Germany was transformed by secularization (the increasing prominence of secular nursing orders such as the Red Cross), embourgeoisification (displacement of working-class nurses by middle-class or upwardly mobile women), professionalization (increased training and certification standards), and feminization (displacement of men by women from most nursing posts).[3] Doctors argued that women were more obedient and flexible than men (i.e., they protested less when given unpleasant tasks), and that middle-class women were the best at learning repetitive precision techniques. The nursing labor force was evenly split between men and women around 1800 but by 1909 was about 80 percent female.[4] Advocates of "female nursing" (*weibliche Krankenpflege*) never tired of asserting that femininity was itself the main qualification for a nurse: as one doctor put it, "even more than knowledge and experience, a whole woman with a brave heart and a loving disposition is needed."[5] The transformation of nursing in Europe also affected colonial nursing. The feminine self-sacrifice that was part of the ideology of nursing served not only to justify bad wages and working conditions for nurses at home, but also to permit respectable women to travel as nurses to the new colonies. And the charitable support of colonial nursing opened the way for the participation of women inside Germany in the male-dominated colonialist movement.

Even though nursing was more than merely a set of technical skills, it was still a narrower realm than colonialist women had originally hoped to occupy. When the first voluntary association of colonialist women formed in 1886, it included nonmedical as well as nursing projects; Protestant, nonconfessional Christian, and secular nationalist goals; and men as well as women. Only after a series of conflicts over personalities and principles did the group emerge in 1888 as exclusively nursing-oriented, secular, and female. The genesis of the first colonialist women's organization demonstrates what became a recurring pattern in the colonialist movement: struggles over authority—between women and men and among women—led to more sharply gendered divisions of labor, or "cultural tasks." Colonialists resolved conflicts by marking out distinct tasks for men and women. The new, gendered division of tasks always meant a narrower realm for women; men were never excluded on the basis of their sex from joining branches of the colonialist movement, and of course men still dominated the wider movement within which colonialist women acted. But women did exercise increased authority within their narrower realm. And even if tensions with erstwhile male antagonists remained, the women's new goals gained the attention of different men with different interests. Nursing offered a conservative resolution to conflicts raised by women's efforts at participation. Until 1907, women's public colonialist interests were channeled into a single voluntary association, the German Women's Association for Nursing in the Colonies (Deutscher Frauenverein für Krankenpflege in den Kolonien). Given the fractious, splintering tendencies of other colonialist organizations with male members, that was a remarkable demonstration of consensus building—but also of the limitations placed on the women. Colonialist women did not foresee these developments; it was only after struggles among themselves and with colonialist men that they drew these conclusions about the importance of nursing.

RELIGION AND NATIONALISM IN MEN'S AND WOMEN'S
EARLY COLONIALIST ACTIVISM: GERMAN EAST AFRICA

In November and December 1884, Carl Peters and his small expedition made their way through the East African mainland across from the island of Zanzibar. They used bribery, deception, and terror to conclude so-called treaties with local village leaders. These lands had belonged either to people living in acephalous societies or to local rulers loosely allied with the sultan of Zanzibar, Barghash ibn Sa'id (r. 1870–1888). Peters returned to Berlin and in February 1885 persuaded Chancellor Bismarck to grant a charter to Peters's German East African Company (Deutsch-Ostafrikanische Gesellschaft).[6] German East Africa, nicknamed the "German India," soon drew more attention in Germany than any of the other new colonies Germany had annexed. Colonialists hoped to profit from its thriving spice and ivory trade. Along with other

Europeans in a late-nineteenth-century antislavery campaign combining Christian zeal with a drive for colonial annexations, they also hoped to halt its internal, Muslim-dominated slave trade.[7] German East Africa had in Carl Peters a publicity agent who was also Germany's best-known colonialist. Peters fueled the enthusiasm of colonialists in Germany with partly fictitious reports of his chartered company's power and prosperity. In fact, Peters had no effective control over the regions he claimed, which were in any case only a small part of what later became German East Africa. Peters's real achievement was inducing Bismarck and others in Germany to take his treaties seriously. The annexation existed mostly on paper until the coastal war of 1888–1890, when the German military conquered an augmented territorial expanse and direct state administration replaced company rule.[8]

Between annexation in 1885 and the coastal war in 1888, German East Africa became the first setting for German women's colonialist activism. In 1885 Countess Martha von Pfeil of Berlin decided to establish a Protestant church for Germans on Zanzibar, which Carl Peters hoped to add to his new colony. Martha and her sister Eva von Pfeil, who soon joined her efforts, were Protestant, archconservative, and intensely nationalistic noblewomen. Unmarried, they lacked a family fortune and patched together a living from work as teachers, private nurses, and lady's companions, and from taking in boarders.[9] Even though they never left Germany, Martha and Eva were no strangers to overseas colonization. One brother, Bernhard, was a coxswain for Sultan Barghash ibn Sa'id, and another brother, Hugo, settled permanently in the Dutch East Indies (today Indonesia).[10] A cousin, Count Joachim von Pfeil, even belonged to Carl Peters's expedition party in 1884, but he quarreled with Peters on that expedition, remained in Africa for the rest of the 1880s, and played no role in his cousins' activism.[11] The initiative lay with Martha and her sister.

In June 1885 Martha von Pfeil published an appeal for donations in *Kolonialpolitische Korrespondenz,* the organ of Carl Peters's Society for German Colonization (Gesellschaft für deutsche Kolonisation).[12] Several pastors signed the appeal, including Ludwig Diestelkamp, an early follower of Peters who had urged Pfeil to act.[13] So did women connected to Germany's social elite of aristocratic military officers such as Countess Waldersee and her daughter Helene. (Count Alfred Wal-

dersee became head of the Prussian General Staff in 1888 and commanded the German troops in the Boxer War in China in 1900.) In
October 1885 Martha von Pfeil held her first meeting.

The surviving minutes of that meeting indicate disagreement over
whether the new organization should minister to German colonists,
missionize "heathens," or both.[14] This debate was to recur frequently.
The balance shifted in favor of serving German colonists when two not
particularly religious colonialists began to attend Martha von Pfeil's
meetings in March 1886: Carl Peters himself and Baroness Frieda von
Bülow.[15] Peters, a master agitator, soon dominated the meetings. He
had great powers of persuasion with both men and women, and he
consciously cultivated the latter as supporters.[16] Peters had a strategic
interest in fostering new organizations that would offer him personal
loyalty. Joachim von Pfeil was not the only old comrade-in-arms to
break with him; so did Friedrich Lange, a radical nationalist publicist.[17]
In fact, many people who had direct experience with Peters became
disillusioned with him. Some of his contemporaries and most historians
have judged him to be unscrupulous, paranoid, filled with delusions of
grandeur, and given to acts of cruelty.[18] The German government and
his opponents within the colonialist movement distrusted his judgment; Bismarck, for example, limited Peters's powers in the German
East African Company after granting its charter because he feared that
Peters's brusque and erratic behavior would deter investors.[19] Even
though Peters still retained a leading position in the company, he was
gradually losing his grip on it. In an effort to strengthen his power base,
Peters brought some of his remaining allies to Pfeil's meetings and installed them on her group's board. These men were radical nationalists
who definitely preferred rapid exploitation to missionary work: August
Leue, the general secretary of the German East African Company; Fritz
Bley, a pan-German journalist who argued that races were in perpetual
conflict; Count Felix Behr-Bandelin, who bankrolled far-right-wing ini-
tiatives; and Friedrich Schröder, a company official charged with plantation administration.[20]

If Peters was Germany's best-known colonialist man, Frieda von
Bülow soon became its best-known colonialist woman. Like the Pfeil sis-
ters, Bülow had family connections to "exotic" locales. Her father, Baron
Hugo von Bülow, was the Prussian consul at Smyrna (now Izmir, Tur-

key), and her uncle Baron Thankmar von Münchhausen, to whom she was close after her father's death, was likewise at Smyrna and then served as the imperial consul in Jerusalem.[21] In Smyrna Frieda attended a school run by the Kaiserswerth Deaconessate, a Protestant nursing order that combined medical and social work with religious counsel and was well known for its work in the Middle East.[22] When Frieda was nine, her widowed mother, Clotilde von Bülow, née von Münchhausen, moved the family from Smyrna to Germany, into the Herrnhuter pietist community in Neudietendorf, Thuringia. The Herrnhuter pietists ran the oldest German overseas Protestant mission, having begun evangelical work in the Caribbean, Surinam, and western and southern Africa in the 1730s.[23] Bülow retained strong childhood memories of Neudietendorf: of a shop that sold handicrafts from Africa to support the missionaries and a collection box in the form of an African man who "nodded in thanks" when coins were tossed into his carved mouth.[24] A religious skeptic, Bülow nevertheless viewed Protestantism as an important part of German national identity.[25]

In early 1885 Bülow was casting about for a new direction for her life. She had trained as a teacher at Berlin's Crain Institute but disliked teaching.[26] She was despondent over the 1884 death of her sister Margarete, her inseparable companion and a gifted young novelist, who drowned after saving the life of a boy who had fallen through the ice while skating on Berlin's Rummelsburger Lake. Margarete's heroism, and male bystanders' failure to come to their aid, deeply impressed Frieda and apparently helped form her views of female strength and male weakness.[27] Soon after the accident Bülow wrote in her diary: "Sometimes I have a wish . . . to be among utterly foreign people and join a powerful struggle. As long as I live, I want to be master, not slave."[28] She traveled, rejected offers of marriage, and seemed to be well on her way to becoming one of the so-called surplus women about whom commentators on the Woman Question debated. Then she glimpsed in Carl Peters's accounts of East Africa a new possibility for a "powerful struggle."

Bülow's fascination with the German colonies began in March 1885 when she read Peters's reports from his first expedition in the *Tägliche Rundschau,* a Berlin newspaper edited by Friedrich Lange.[29] Bülow already knew Lange, for her sister Margarete's novellas had appeared in his newspaper, and she had met him in 1884 to discuss Margarete's literary estate. Lange recalled his first encounter with Bülow: "I perceived the high-spirited, well-bred vivacity of her character as a masculine tinge to her femininity; in her there was something like the singleness of purpose of an arrow laid upon the string of a bow."[30] In 1884 Lange and Felix Behr-Bandelin had helped Peters to found the Society for German Colonization. Now, in 1885, Bülow arranged for Lange to introduce her to Peters. She asked Peters if her brother Albrecht might join the company and go to German East Africa, and also proposed going to East Africa herself to set up facilities for medical care of the Germans there, most of whom were company employees. Like Peters, Bülow had great powers to impress and persuade. Peters agreed to both plans. Not long after they met, the two began a love affair. For Bülow, high romance and colonial adventure became intertwined; Peters, she later recalled, promised to build her a city in East Africa.[31]

These were the two personalities who joined Martha and Eva von Pfeil, various pastors, and other supporters at a mass meeting in May 1886 to announce the formation of the Evangelical Missionary Society for German East Africa (Evangelische Missionsgesellschaft für Deutsch-Ostafrika). Martha von Pfeil and Frieda von Bülow took seats on the board, along with eighteen men.[32] The women's presence there was highly unusual, as Gustav Warneck, a leading mission figure and critic of nationalist missionary work, disapprovingly noted.[33] The new missionary society announced an impossibly ambitious list of goals: church services for German colonists, missions and schools for Africans, a hospital, care for freed slave children, hostels for convalescing or vacationing Germans in Africa, and "other such German sources of Christian culture."[34] One of its statutes signaled its willingness to aid the company in setting up plantations: "In training the baptized heathens in culture and customs, the missionary is to be mindful primarily of training them *to work.*"[35] In the face of criticism from Warneck and other missionary leaders who preferred to keep missionary work independent of state influence, the men and women of the Evangelical Missionary Society for German East Africa openly wanted to serve nationalist and colonialist ends.[36]

Neither Pfeil nor Bülow took a leading role at the early meetings, at least according to the minutes. From June 1886 on, however, they began to speak out. Pfeil announced that she had obtained a major donation: a wealthy Catholic man had willed his entire estate to them.[37] Bülow, who saw herself as the real leader among the women, urged the board to respond more aggressively to Warneck and other critics of the Evangelical Missionary Society.[38] In preparation for her trip to German East Africa, she attended a nursing course at Berlin's Augusta Hospital, where Empress Augusta bestowed on her a few words of approval.[39] She held theater evenings, balls, and bazaars to raise funds. She also hosted meetings of the Evangelical Missionary Society at her family's house in 1886 and 1887. Along with the pastors, Martha von Pfeil, and Peters's circle, a number of prominent or soon-to-be-prominent figures attended these meetings. One was Helene Lange, one of Germany's most important feminists and Bülow's teacher at the Crain Institute in the 1870s. Lange was soon to publish her famous "Yellow Brochure," a petition to the Imperial government that women be allowed to take the entrance examination (*Abitur*) and attend university.[40] Several of the men who gathered there were or soon became active in far-right and anti-Semitic politics. Among them was Friedrich Lange, who would remain Bülow's friend for the rest of her life. Between the 1880s and the First World War, Lange agitated constantly against Catholics, socialists, and Jews, even calling for the complete exclusion of "Bazillus judaicus" from Germany, public censure of Jewish-Christian marriages, legal treatment of German Jews as foreigners, and boycotts against Jewish-owned shops.[41] Like Peters, Lange also took women seriously as political allies for his radical nationalist projects.[42] Other men in attendance were Diederich Hahn and Hans Wendland, who were active in the Kyffhäuser League (Kyffhäuserverband), an anti-Semitic student organization.[43] One more figure at these meetings deserves mention: the literary critic and satirist Fritz Mauthner, who later wrote on the philosophy of language and the history of atheism.[44] Margarete von Bülow had been his literary protegée. After Margarete's death, he and Frieda edited her writings for posthumous publication, and Frieda turned to him for publishing advice.[45] Mauthner can also be described as anti-Semitic, yet his Jewish family background, which he repudiated but never sought to conceal, differentiated his opinions from those of Friedrich Lange, Wendland, or Hahn. Describing himself as a pan-German nationalist, he was scathing about Jews who converted to Christianity in their quest for assimilation in Imperial Germany.[46]

Bülow wanted the Evangelical Missionary Society to pursue a strongly nationalist program focused on aiding German colonists, and she was not shy about communicating her views. At one meeting, her mother recalled, there was a "hard battle in which Frieda fought against five pastors and had only Uncle Thankmar and Count Behr for help."[47] By September 1886 Bülow and Pfeil had convinced the missionary society to make nursing rather than missionizing its top priority, and to send Bülow and two nurses to German East Africa. The plan was to set up a small hospital in Dunda, a coastal village where Bülow's brother Albrecht had founded a company station. Peters's ally Karl Grimm penned the new appeal for hospital donations: "It will be women's hands and women's hearts to which this work of charity and love, which carries within it a true German character, is entrusted."[48] This nominally religious society was planning to send the three women as nurses before it had dispatched a single missionary.

In October 1886 the Pfeil sisters, Bülow, and eleven other women formed their own group, the German-National Women's League (Deutschnationaler Frauenbund).[49] Its statutory goals echoed the Evangelical Missionary Society's program, except that the German-National Women's League's program demoted Christianity from an overarching reason for Germans to go to Africa to merely one of several aspects of German culture that deserved support. Martha von Pfeil and Bülow retained their positions on the Evangelical Missionary Society's board, and the two organizations planned to cooperate in establishing the first German hospital in German East Africa. Peters continued to patronize the Evangelical Missionary Society while supporting the new German-National Women's League as well. In an 1887 speech to the latter he proclaimed: "Once German women have for their part fully and completely grasped the genuinely nationalist ideal, then men for their part will no longer be able to evade it."[50] Peters specified German manners and customs as women's particular forte; women were to exemplify and promote a truly national (rather than regional) cuisine, dress, and art. Yet Peters also urged the German-National Women's League to "choose the widest possible area of work."[51] Women no less than men faced, in Peters's characteristically apocalyptic phrase, a "choice between victory or the destruction of their nationality."[52]

The reason for the formation of the German-National Women's

League was conflict over authority. The clergymen did not "harmonize" well with Martha von Pfeil, her sister Eva recalled, because they "did not find it proper that a lady should be the leader."[53] Meanwhile, the women wanted to control the money they were raising. Bülow's suggestion to separate the funds for the hospital in Dunda, for which the German-National Women's League was working, from other donations to the Evangelical Missionary Society raised the question of how to distinguish between nursing and religious work.[54] While Bülow believed that charity work for the hospital could be separated from Protestant charity, the pastors did not.

The German-National Women's League's purposefully nonconfessional nature meant that its female leadership could refuse the authority of the missionary society clergymen — and also accept donations from Catholics. Martha von Pfeil hoped that the separate existence of the German-National Women's League would reassure Catholics that their contributions for the Dunda hospital would not be spent on Protestant missionizing. At the same time, she privately reassured Protestant supporters that the German-National Women's League would have a "Protestant character" and that only Protestant schools and hospitals would be built.[55] Her nonconfessional agitation strategy had a larger political significance in the 1880s. Catholic Germans had suffered a public battering at the hands of Bismarck and liberals during the *Kulturkampf* of the 1870s, a campaign to remove Catholic influence from public life. After 1884, Catholics asserted their credibility as nationalists through their conspicuous support for missionary work in the new German colonies. French Cardinal Lavigerie's antislavery campaign, which aimed to halt African Muslim slave trading, helped persuade Catholic Germans that German colonial rule would be beneficial to eastern Africa.[56] Nationalist and procolonial Protestant pastors such as Friedrich Fabri favored a nonconfessional emphasis in the antislavery movement in order to gain Catholic support for a German military intervention.[57] Bismarck finally assented to Fabri's urgings and took up the antislavery cause because it allowed him to represent the conquest of German East Africa in the coastal war of 1888–1890 as a humanitarian deed.[58] At the same time, these men's high political strategy of nonconfessional mobilization had the effect — no doubt unintentional — of creating an opening for women's organizational leadership, as nonconfessional religious charity had done in the past.[59] By the spring of 1887 the German-National Women's League had about 350 members.[60]

Although the German-National Women's League emphasized aid for German colonists, it did not exclude work with Africans, and it also benefited from the antislavery enthusiasm. The league also tried to revive old worries about Germans' high rates of emigration and assimilation. One appeal for funds claimed that German emigration to foreign lands would shrink now that emigrants could go to Germany's own colonies. Yet even there it would be necessary to prevent "foreign elements" (such as British settlers) from co-opting Germans. German women could help. One pamphlet noted, for example: "It is a beautiful task of the German woman to act as protectress of German manners and morals toward foreign elements."[61] The German-National Women's League proposed the creation of hospitals, schools, and churches in the colonies as the "most effective means" of upholding "Germandom."[62] Martha von Pfeil saw these institutions as a nationalist mission to both Germans and Africans: "With them, we will make it easier for our colonists to remain thoroughly German and offer an opportunity to the natives, who have trustingly placed themselves under German protection, to become Germans and Christians."[63]

At the moment of the German-National Women's League's formation, yet another strong personality, Carl Büttner, joined the Evangelical Missionary Society's board and reasserted its religious goals. Büttner, who became the society's first mission inspector in September 1886, personified the fusion of missionary and colonialist ambitions. As a missionary of the Rhenish Missionary Society (Rheinische Missionsgesellschaft) during the 1870s, he had lived in precolonial Namibia and had translated the New Testament into the Herero language. More recently, in April 1885, he had served as Bismarck's special envoy, using his local influence as a missionary to conclude treaties with local leaders and secure the hinterland of newly annexed German Southwest Africa. He thereby directly mixed missionary influence and state power.[64] As the new inspector of the Evangelical Missionary Society, Büttner joined Friedrich Fabri in confronting Warneck and other critics of nationalist missionary work.[65] To procolonial missionaries like Büttner and Fabri, the absence of German missionaries in German colonies seemed to signal a failure of national pride. After 1885, Germans in mission circles became somewhat more willing participants in the colonialist movement.

While Mission Inspector Büttner had at first found the "ladies' circle" benign—after all, missionary societies usually had women's auxiliaries—he soon became irritated with it.[66] Büttner objected to Pfeil's and Bülow's decision to make the German-National Women's League a nonconfessional rather than an explicitly Protestant organization. He complained that the league's statutes "intentionally avoided the words 'Evangelical' and 'Christian,'" which in his view made its cooperation with a Protestant missionary society impossible.[67] In addition, he loathed his Catholic rivals in missionary work and was outraged at the possibility that the German-National Women's League might dispatch Catholic nurses to German East Africa.[68] Büttner accused Bülow of exploiting the missionary society to pursue secular nationalist aims—which was what Warneck had earlier accused Büttner of doing. Büttner pointed out that missionary work had a definite origin in Jesus' commands and scolded Bülow: "If you think, as you seem to, that you can attain similar success with the motto 'German-national,' and can find the same patience and strength to overcome even the greatest suffering . . . you have to find out for yourself that it will *not* work that way."[69] Religion does not seem to have been the only issue here, however; Büttner's authority as a man was also threatened. The two were intertwined because, in both Protestant or Catholic missionary societies, ultimate authority always rested with men.

By February 1887 Bülow was demanding, not merely suggesting, that the Evangelical Missionary Society pay over the funds that the women had raised before the formation of the German-National Women's League. The missionary society continued to insist that the donors had given the funds for Protestant, not secular, purposes, and that the German-National Women's League was not a Protestant organization; it finally did turn over a few thousand marks.[70] In effect, the pastors were pushing the German-National Women's League in the same direction in which Bülow was pulling it: toward a more complete secularization than Pfeil, who originally had wanted to build a church, had ever envisioned.

Now that the Women's League had control of its finances and leadership, and had deemphasized religion in favor of its secular nationalist justifications, Bülow and Pfeil asked for a division of labor as well: they asked the Evangelical Missionary Society to change its statutes to cede nursing at the Dunda hospital entirely to the German-National Women's League. The pastors, along with a majority of the society's board, refused.[71] Büttner and Diestelkamp rejected nonconfessional nursing, with its implication that nursing care could be detached from the spiritual counsel of German and African patients. They wanted to adopt the Kaiserswerth model, in which medical services helped missionaries to reach potential converts.[72] Kaiserswerth nurses were expected to aid missionary work as Saint Paul urged: silently. Büttner expressed the "hope that our *deaconesses,* through their quiet, faithful work, will also have some effect on the *mission,* if heathens and Arabs merely *observe* their way of living."[73] Even if women had provided much of the money and effort behind the missionary society, Büttner and Diestelkamp considered church officials (men, without exception) to be the appropriate authorities over the dispatched nurses. Clearly, women — either as organizers of nursing or as nurses themselves — would not have much authority or autonomy in this version of female nursing. The pastors hired a nurse named Marie Rentsch to accompany Bülow to German East Africa. Rentsch was experienced at her work, pious, modest, and strictly obedient to Büttner.

Bülow, who wanted to detach nursing from missionary work — and indeed from any religious oversight — did not mention religious goals even when she appealed in the name of the Evangelical Missionary Society for support to Johanna von Bismarck, the very pious wife of the imperial chancellor.[74] Bülow was interested in female nursing as a form of feminine patriotic expression for women and as a potential solution to the problem of suitable paid employment for unmarried middle-class women. She abhorred the notion that nurses ought to work out of pious self-denial and in utter subordination to authority. Bülow was influenced by two nonconfessional nursing orders: the Rittberg order, to which her cousin Else von Keudell belonged, and the Victoria Sisters (Viktoriaschwestern), which her sister Sophie later joined. Both orders sought not only to care for the ill, but also to provide worthy careers to women.[75] Bülow's interest in innovative scientific nursing techniques such as maintaining patient charts and teaching preventive medicine (*Hygiene*) to all colonists also reflected those organizations' concerns.[76]

Bülow correctly perceived that the nursing ideology of feminine self-sacrifice allowed hospitals and motherhouses (the conventlike institutions in which nurses were trained and housed) to work nurses to the point of exhaustion. The metaphor of nursing as a mother's labor of love not only made nursing respectable work for middle-class women, but also allowed employers to ask nurses to exceed the labor owed by paid employees. Much of nursing work was menial "women's work": cooking, cleaning, and laundry, with twelve- to fourteen-hour workdays and rotating all-night duty. (These conditions finally led to a Reichstag inquiry into nurses' high disability and mortality rates in 1912.)[77] In Bülow's view, nursing had to draw on the woman's personal convictions, not her exhaustion and fear, if it was to be meaningful as a form of patriotism and as a career. She therefore advocated shorter hours, higher pay, and fewer physically taxing duties for nurses. Bülow could not abide the pious Marie Rentsch and refused to allow the Evangelical Missionary Society to send Rentsch to German East Africa as her aide.[78]

Although Bülow saw no place for Protestantism in nursing, she did believe it could foster national cohesion among colonists. That is a major theme of her 1891 novel *The Consul.* Its heroine remarks to a missionary that back in Germany she felt just as close to God under a starry sky as in a church, but in Africa she had come to appreciate that "the common church service is almost the only unifying bond among us compatriots."[79] Bülow saw colonialism frankly in terms of its benefits for Germans, including German women. Missions and schooling for Africans were, for her, afterthoughts. In fact, she reveled in the exoticism of the Afro-Arabs and Swahilis of the East African coast and evinced no desire to Christianize or Europeanize them.

Martha von Pfeil's views differed from those of the pastors and from Bülow's as well. Pfeil saw nursing as a voluntarist national service of German women, but she was also a serious Protestant who insisted on a distinctly Christian atmosphere. She wished to continue the tradition of Prussian noblewomen who sewed bandages and nursed the wounded during the Wars of Liberation against Napoleon. Pfeil's own appeal to

Johanna von Bismarck, on behalf of the German-National Women's League, exemplifies her conservative nationalism:

> Whose heart does not beat faster at the thought that Germany also has its colonies now, like other countries — God grant that they grow and flourish, to the honor of the German Empire.
>
> How many dangers, how many strains the brave champions of Germandom there have to struggle against, and so we hoped, with God's help, to offer relief to those out there by caring for them when they are ill, being able to offer them a place to rest when they are flagging and weary from the strenuous work. Along with that, Christian charity for the blacks is to be practiced, medicines given them, their wounds cared for, their children instructed in the Christian faith, and they are to be thus allowed to grasp our faith's sublime doctrines. In this way we hoped to be able to collaborate in the undertaking of making the blacks into loyal German subjects; and to do beneficial work, with God, for Emperor and fatherland.[80]

For Pfeil, colonial nursing was military self-sacrifice, women's counterpart to men's colonial soldiering. Demands for personal autonomy — women's or anyone else's — were anomalous in that context.

Büttner and Diestelkamp refused to relinquish nursing to Pfeil and Bülow. In April 1887 the pastors and their allies outvoted the women's faction on the Evangelical Missionary Society board on the question of whether to send Marie Rentsch to German East Africa. Rentsch was now ordered to go to Africa and to report directly to Büttner instead of to Bülow.[81] The vote provoked Pfeil and Bülow into resigning from the board of the Evangelical Missionary Society, along with Bülow's uncle Münchhausen and Peters's associates Behr-Bandelin and Leue. No women remained on the board of the Evangelical Missionary Society, and no men were on the board of the German-National Women's League (although Peters, Münchhausen, and other men continued to support it).[82] The two organizations were now rivals in the establishment of colonial nursing in German East Africa.

Martha von Pfeil fell ill soon after the final break between the Evangelical Missionary Society and the German-National Women's League. According to Eva von Pfeil, Bülow took that opportunity to usurp authority within the German-National Women's League.[83] In May 1887 Bülow and Bertha Wilke, a young woman who was to assist her with nursing, departed for German East Africa. The two women traveled by train to Venice, by ship to Alexandria, by train again to Suez, and then sailed down the eastern coast of Africa, arriving on Zanzibar about a month after leaving Berlin. Bülow stayed for almost a year, until April 1888.

The main record of Bülow's first stay in German East Africa was also her literary debut, a book entitled *Travel Sketches*. It is a lighthearted account of adventurous encounters with exotic peoples, romantic ruins, festivities, and experiences with medical care of Europeans and locals. While Bülow was far from the first German woman to visit Africa, she was quite aware of her status as one of the first German women to see a German colony. She saw herself as an ambassador of German culture and national pride. While still on the ship, she sternly told an irreverent British man that "the topic of German colonization would from now on be off limits between us, since I could and would not accept mockery on this subject."[84] She also sought to bring back into the national fold a German-born man on the ship who had lived for years in India and held British citizenship. She discussed his birthplace in Eastern Frisia, induced him to drop his English mannerisms, and finally had the satisfaction of persuading him to sing German folk songs to the other passengers.

Bülow believed that Germans abroad always got "the short end of the stick."[85] Peters had arrived on Zanzibar in May 1887 as the chief representative of the company, and she wanted him to be shown the appropriate respect. He had instructions to negotiate with Sultan Barghash ibn Sa'id for the transfer of the coastal towns Dar es Salaam and Pangani to the company.[86] On her arrival in German East Africa, Bülow, who saw elegant entertainment as her national duty, joined Peters's social whirl of official receptions, ceremonies, and excursions.[87] Peters and his entourage were jockeying with the British, Italians, Portuguese,

French, and Belgians for influence in Zanzibar, although the British clearly dominated. For years they had kept the sultan of Zanzibar under their influence, and now Peters wanted to displace them. Bülow shared Peters's and many other nationalist Germans' sense of inferiority to and rivalry with the British.[88]

Apart from Europeans, Zanzibar society comprised Afro-Arabs, including the sultan's Omani family; South Asians, including Hindus, Muslims, and Christian Goans; and also Swahilis, Persians, and Egyptians. The colors, faiths, and languages of people in Zanzibar did not correspond in simple ways to levels of wealth, although the wealthiest tended to be Afro-Arabs and Indians who had made their fortunes with cloves and other trade.[89] Individual Germans in the area served non-Europeans in various capacities, as in many places around the world both before and after Germany's own colonial annexations.[90] For instance, all but one of the ship captains in Sultan Barghash ibn Sa'id's employ were Germans.[91] Bülow could not take German power for granted, and for all her thin-skinned national pride she appreciated the intelligence, beauty, and taste of certain Afro-Arabs, Africans, and Indians she encountered. She even acknowledged the efficacy of non-Germans and non-Europeans in her own field of endeavor, praising creole French-Mauritian nurses, Greek nurses, and a Persian doctor.[92]

Bülow spent much of her time on Zanzibar exploring Zanzibar Town and walking by the sea with Peters and his colleagues Baron von Gravenreuth, Friedrich Schröder, Baron Walter von St. Paul Illaire (who soon became one of the biggest landowners in German East Africa), and the Hamburg-based merchant William O'Swald. She was entranced: *Arabian Nights,* a favorite childhood book, now "came to life" before her eyes.[93] With Gravenreuth and O'Swald she went on a day trip to see Mtoni, a palace known to German readers as the childhood home of Emily Said-Ruete.[94] Said-Ruete, born Salme bint Sa'id, was the daughter of Sultan Sa'id Majid of Zanzibar, and had eloped in 1866 with Heinrich Ruete, a German businessman. The German public knew of her through her brief role in diplomatic maneuverings between Bismarck and her brother, the new sultan, Barghash ibn Sa'id, and through her 1886 autobiography, *Memoirs of an Arabian Princess,* the first German-language insider's account of harem life.[95] Bülow hoped to visit a harem but never received an invitation; however, she did receive a formal visit from some elite Afro-Arab women at her hotel. Bülow described her visitors as very beautiful but appearing "as if they were mentally asleep."[96] She contrasted her own mobility among men with their lack of it, noting with humor how her walking companion Friedrich Schröder awoke from a nap startled to discover that he had been locked in his hotel room for the duration of the visit. Bülow shared her excitement at Oriental exoticism, and Peters's imminent mastery of it, with German readers by sending back sketches of her experiences to periodicals such as the family magazine *Daheim* and the Society for German Colonization's journal *Kolonialpolitische Korrespondenz*.[97] Although her official purpose was to organize nursing care, these pieces emphasized her encounters with adoring African children and local notables. She had a colorful, deft writing style and soon gained a readership in Germany.[98]

Amid the elegant receptions and boat excursions, Bülow observed British and French mission nurses at work and performed nursing herself for some German, Indian, Afro-Arab, and Swahili patients.[99] Bertha Wilke, who spoke no English and was of lower social status — and therefore did not attend Bülow's formal festivities — did more nursing work.[100] On one occasion Wilke cared for a malarial Austrian woman for four days, with only one hour of rest each day, while Bülow departed with Carl Peters on a trip to the mainland to visit sites for future company plantations.[101] Since British-German border negotiations in November 1886 had allocated Dunda to the British, Bülow had to revise her plan for nursing clinics. After her first month in East Africa Bülow decided that the main nursing clinic should be on Zanzibar, the gateway to the colony, rather than on the mainland, where there was too little housing and overland transport was poor.[102] From this base on Zanzibar Bülow hoped eventually to supply a string of coastal clinics.

By late September 1887 Bülow had left Bertha Wilke at work in spartan and crowded accommodations on the mainland in Dar es Salaam and set up her own household just outside Zanzibar Town. Relatively urban and cosmopolitan Zanzibar was an altogether more livable place. She hired Frau Glühmann, a Greek woman born in Jerusalem who spoke Arabic and Swahili and relieved Bülow of her communication difficulties. Herr Glühmann, a German hospital orderly whom Frau Glühmann had met and married in Cairo, also lived there. The house on Zanzibar was the site of Bülow's happiest times in East Africa.

She had her privacy and saw Peters frequently. Now that Bülow had arranged things as she liked, she was eager to show that she was prepared to take in patients. She envisioned her house as a convalescents' hostel rather than a hospital for the seriously ill, which meant less strenuous work for her. She responded to news of potential patients with such alacrity that Peters teased her, saying that the illness of others made her happy.[103]

Bülow was confident that she had made a good start on organizing colonial nursing in East Africa. She had also made a series of undiplomatic moves, however, and her reputation suffered. Her romantic attachment to Peters was the subject of gossip in German East Africa and Zanzibar. Peters was having problems of his own. He tried to play the Evangelical Missionary Society off against the Catholic missions, and Büttner and Diestelkamp became irritated and ceased cooperating with him.[104] Then Peters gained the entire coast for Germany in an 1887 treaty with Sultan Barghash ibn Sa'id instead of only, as planned, the towns of Dar es Salaam and Pangani. Although he and Bülow saw that as a brilliant diplomatic stroke, the Foreign Office pronounced it disastrous. Peters's actions and his open intention to annex Zanzibar were undermining the Foreign Office's efforts to preserve British goodwill. The Foreign Office was also alarmed at reports of unprovoked violence by Germans against the sultan's subjects.[105] The company board, for its part, wanted to develop trade, not plantation agriculture, and it abrogated Peters's arrangements for a network of coastal plantations.[106] Since Bülow intended to base her network of nursing clinics on Peters's plantations, her plans were also ruined. In fact, Bülow had committed herself and the German-National Women's League to Peters at just the moment when his opponents in the Foreign Office and the company were edging him out once and for all. The company was furious that Peters had overrun his budget by almost 100,000 marks (much of it unaccounted for) by the end of 1887.[107] Peters persisted in ignoring the Foreign Office's instructions for dealing with the sultan of Zanzibar until it recalled him altogether in December 1887. He left for Germany in January 1888 and continued his colonialist agitation there.

Perhaps most dangerous for Bülow's reputation was her unwillingness to conform to the image of the pious, self-sacrificing nurse. The German consul in Zanzibar sent negative reports about her to the Foreign Office. "Miss von Bülow herself admits she knows nothing about nursing," he sniffed (probably Bülow had told him that she intended to make arrangements for future nursing clinics rather than attend to patients herself full time), and he disapproved of her plan to care for convalescents in her home when the most urgent need was care for the seriously ill.[108] The German-National Women's League board was displeased with Bülow's mounting expenses and the stream of travel writing that she was publishing in Germany, in which she depicted herself doing everything but spending long hours at patients' bedsides. Bülow's decision to live and work on Zanzibar further exasperated the league. Its statutes provided for nursing only on the mainland, inside the boundaries of German East Africa. In November 1887 Pfeil and the rest of the board ordered Bülow to leave Zanzibar immediately and set up a clinic in the coastal town of Pangani.[109] Bülow responded that the monsoon season made it impossible to travel there, and that there were no suitable living quarters there in any case, but she would await a report from Peters and visit it in the spring.[110]

By this time the Pfeils were too suspicious of Bülow to accept her proposals. As Eva von Pfeil saw it, Bülow "became very friendly with the gentlemen and demanded from the little Women's League ever more money, in order to spend it with the gentlemen on her pleasure."[111] The Pfeils learned of Bülow's activities from her published travel pieces and from hostile informants such as Marie Rentsch and Brother Greiner, the Evangelical Missionary Society's first missionary.[112] Greiner and his wife and niece had shared Bülow's ship passage to Africa; Rentsch arrived about a month later. Bülow rarely mentioned them in her writings, but the pretense of their absence was difficult to uphold. Bertha Wilke and briefly Bülow herself were forced to share the Greiners' quarters in Dar es Salaam before Bülow arranged for her own house on Zanzibar. The German community in East Africa was far too small for these rivals to avoid each other.

Rentsch, like Bülow, soon saw that Zanzibar was the best place to base medical care. She began to make arrangements for the Evangelical Missionary Society's long-planned hospital, but unlike Bülow she acted only on orders and with permission. She solicited advice and promises of aid from Carl Peters, the German consul, and other prominent figures in the German community.[113] Rentsch very much conformed to the image of the self-sacrificing nurse; she worked hard at nursing and the care of freed slave children, and claimed to dislike drawing attention to herself. She even asked Büttner to promise that her letters and diary would not be published in her lifetime (missionary societies often published extracts for supporters at home to read), adding in an apparent jab at Bülow that "it is never good if women are made too noticeable."[114]

Bülow confronted Rentsch and tried to browbeat her into submission, insisting that she, Bülow, had priority as the first German organizer of nursing in Zanzibar. Bülow also demanded that Rentsch reveal whatever promises of aid Peters had made, which suggested that Bülow already had reason to lack confidence in him. If Rentsch refused to fall into line, Bülow threatened to have her sent back to Germany. Rentsch responded that Bülow should mind her own "scribbling" and ask Peters herself what he and Rentsch had agreed to, since "you know him very well, better than I do" — a reference to their love affair.[115] Reporting the confrontation in a letter to Büttner, Rentsch quoted herself telling Bülow: "Furthermore you should know that I did not come out here on my own. I know what I want here & what I can accomplish and create here for, as Miss von Bülow puts it, the good of the whole cause of Germany."[116] Rentsch had the backing of established male authorities and of mission and nursing tradition, while Bülow could rely only on herself and the undependable Peters.

Peters demonstrated just how undependable he was at a decisive moment for Bülow's project. In mid-October 1887 the German community in Zanzibar met to elect a committee to oversee the Evangelical Missionary Society's German Hospital.[117] Although Peters had promised Rentsch his cooperation, he now sent his friend St. Paul Illaire to announce that the company would not send any patients to the planned German Hospital, but rather only to the old French mission on Zanzibar and to Bülow's future clinics. Since company employees made up most of the potential hospital clientele, this was tantamount to blocking the German Hospital altogether. The German consul and others among the German community were baffled and outraged, all the more so when it turned out that the company had not authorized Peters to make that decision.[118] Peters then claimed that Rentsch must have misunderstood his earlier promises of cooperation.[119] He sent a message to Rentsch asking her to try to cooperate with Bülow, then another message offering to pay for a clinic for Rentsch in Pangani, on the mainland. Rentsch reported that Peters told her that in Pangani there was a "man who often beats the natives until they are crippled, and maybe he can use me to cure them again."[120] The man was Friedrich Schröder, Peters's friend and Bülow's walking companion, who directed the notorious Lewa plantation of the German East African Company and later received a five-year prison sentence for cruelty to workers there.[121] Rentsch, repelled, refused to go. When a second hospital meeting was held in December 1887, Peters sent a more conciliatory message: the company would not boycott the hospital, but neither would it give it an exclusive contract.[122] Finally, Peters declared that he had all along intended to persuade the French mission to become a German hospital (which was rather unlikely), and thereby save the money that would have been spent in Zanzibar for the German-ruled mainland.[123] It was typical of Peters that he advanced multiple and rather unconvincing explanations for his actions. Bülow did not appear at any of these meetings, but rather remained, upset, at her house.[124]

Rentsch, meanwhile, related her experiences on Zanzibar in increasingly outraged letters to Büttner. She criticized Bülow's extravagance and excursions with Peters (which, according to Rentsch, elicited general astonishment), and mentioned Bülow's brazen request for an audience with the sultan (it was denied).[125] Rentsch accused Peters and Bülow of telling lies in the descriptions of a flourishing colony that both published in the German press. There was nothing in Dar es Salaam, Rentsch wrote, but patients who "lay without any kind of comfort, they did not even have pillows"; a couple of potatoes in a dismal garden; and "two men who hunt, swear at Negroes, etc."[126] As for Bülow's travel writing, Rentsch spluttered: "Neither what she writes about the English mission nor about Dar es Salaam is true. She was not the first to go to the patients' bedsides in Dar es Salaam and she did not go to help at the English mission. Her entire work consists *up to today* of staying at the French hotel with two servants, running around observing the inhabitants, and entertaining and amusing the gentlemen of all nations."[127] As for Bertha Wilke, Rentsch reported that she was "wild," lazy, knew nothing about nursing, and flirted so much that the men made off-color jokes about colonial female nursing. "Everyone here laughs when they hear that female nurses are to work at the [company] stations," Rentsch wrote.[128]

Rentsch gave Büttner her own version of Peters and Bülow's trip to the mainland to plan sites for future company plantations and nursing clinics. Rentsch had accompanied them on the trip, although that was scarcely evident in Bülow's picturesque account in *Travel Sketches*. When the traveling party reached Dar es Salaam, Rentsch immediately began to treat malarial company employees. Bülow was supposed to relieve Rentsch on the second night but never appeared; "the gentlemen wanted to celebrate on board ship, and [Bülow] could not absent herself from that."[129] Heading back to Zanzibar on the steamer, Peters fell into one of his manic fits. He ranted about Pastor Diestelkamp "in as loathsome a manner as possible," the Foreign Office, and others, then insisted that everyone drink a toast to what he had said.[130] Rentsch, disgusted, left the gathering. Peters followed her, shouting that he was the only one who had ever accomplished anything in East Africa and that it was a pity that only a fool like Rentsch was there to hear him say it. It was a few days after these events that Peters made his promise to support Rentsch's German Hospital, perhaps he did so in an effort to undo the damage his behavior had caused.

Although Peters's behavior was, to say the least, unpleasant, he was not as vulnerable as Bülow to gossip and public opinion. It was she who suffered the greatest damage on that trip. The steamer captain obtained a love letter of hers and Peters's, and it found its way into Diestelkamp's hands. Now, Diestelkamp gloated to Büttner, the rival German-National Women's League "would be very willing to make the greatest concessions to us."[131] Bülow's effort to establish colonial nursing as an autonomous women's career, independent of missionary or state support, had been difficult enough before; now, with evidence of her love affair in her foes' hands, it was all but impossible. Nevertheless, Bülow hung on stubbornly to her post. By December 1887 Peters and Bülow had broken off their affair, but Peters remained the most important person in her life, apart from her dead sister Margarete.[132]

In January 1888 Bülow lay ill at her house on Zanzibar with her first serious bout of malaria. Wilke, in Dar es Salaam, was also ill. Yet Bülow still felt so strongly about staying in Zanzibar that she threatened the German-National Women's League board with resignation if they did not allow her to decide where and how to establish clinics.[133] The board called her bluff and dismissed her, even asking the Foreign Office to ensure Bülow's departure from Zanzibar.[134] After having sufficiently recovered her health, Bülow left for Bombay in April 1888. She convalesced further there, then joined her family, who now lived in Freiburg im Breisgau. In the summer of 1888 Bülow traveled to Berlin to meet with Pfeil and the German-National Women's League board, but they failed to reach any agreement and her connection to that organization ceased permanently.

Bülow's demands for freedom and independence, above all for herself, led first Büttner and Diestelkamp, then Pfeil, to repudiate her. Earlier conflicts over money and religion had taken place between the women and men; now conflicts over sexual respectability divided the women. Bülow never accepted what she saw as the pettiness and lack of nationalist vision of the pastors, Rentsch, the Foreign Office, and her colleagues in the German-National Women's League.[135] She certainly never believed that she had acted less than respectably. From her perspective, she had offered her personal bravery and literary talents to a great national cause, only to be stymied by short-sighted organizations. From that point on, she would act independently for the colonialist cause. Chapter 2 examines her later life and her fiction, which dramatized the social and sexual dilemmas of German women who confronted their own strong will, their duties to the German nation, and the unreliability of German men.

Büttner and Diestelkamp, as unrepentant as Bülow, continued to see themselves as the proper authorities for colonial nursing. Well aware that Pfeil and other women had founded the Evangelical Missionary Society, they nevertheless wrote the women out of a leading role in the society's official history.[136] Women continued to belong to the Evangelical Missionary Society after the departure of Pfeil and Bülow, but they no longer participated in decisions at the highest level. A few years later, on the verge of financial collapse, the society placed itself under the charge of Pastor Friedrich von Bodelschwingh, who was famed for his work with the poor and mentally ill at Bethel bei Bielefeld. The Bethel Mission, as the society was now known, continued to combine medical care with missionary work. It narrowed its older, controversially nationalist project by directing its medical care to colonial subjects, not colonists, and it employed only nurses who belonged to a distinctly Protestant nursing order.[137]

The events of 1886–1888 taught Martha von Pfeil that her organization required absolute respectability. The German-National Women's League, held hostage to radical nationalist agitation and Bülow and Peters's love affair, had lacked that. She purged her organization of all traces of Bülow and in April 1888 gave it new statutes and a new name: the German Women's Association for Nursing in the Colonies (Deutscher Frauenverein für Krankenpflege in den Kolonien). The official histories of this new association consistently named Martha von Pfeil as the sole founder, even when they inconsistently gave 1886 or 1888 as the year of its founding. They never mentioned Frieda von Bülow.[138]

NURSING FOR THE STATE:
RESPECTABILITY AND CONSERVATIVE NATIONALISM

The difficulties of sustaining an organization by and for colonialist women continued beyond Bülow's departure. With no other female presence in the leadership of the colonialist movement, Pfeil needed to seek the support of men. So far, only two male constituencies had expressed interest in the women's cooperation. One was the Evangelical Missionary Society men, who expected the women to subordinate nationalism to their own Protestant clerical authority. The other was the radical nationalists around Peters, who were too controversial to ensure widespread support for the women. Pfeil's response was to make the German Women's Association for Nursing in the Colonies simultaneously more feminine, secular, and conservatively nationalist. Like the Evangelical Missionary Society, it narrowed its statutes, in this case to the provision of secular nursing, primarily for German colonists.[139]

Pfeil invited Countess Clara von Monts de Mazin, a prominent Berlin socialite, to become the association's chairwoman.[140] Monts, in turn, attached the association to Germany's most successful institution for women's public activism: the Patriotic Women's Leagues (Vaterländische Frauenvereine).[141] The federated leagues, which traced their origins to Queen Luise of Prussia and other German princesses during the Wars of Liberation against Napoleon, were conservative, nationalist nursing charities. Their official aims were "to participate in the care for the wounded and ill in the field and to support the apparatus for that purpose" in wartime, and in peace "to ease extraordinary emergencies and to promote and improve nursing care."[142] Prussia in particular was a leading advocate of the Red Cross movement, and the Patriotic Women's Leagues joined the Red Cross in 1878.[143] The Patriotic Women's Leagues had already confronted the problem of how to maintain female leadership without flouting male authority. Far from questioning the ideology of nursing, the Patriotic Women's Leagues elevated it to a principle of organization. The women in the Patriotic Women's Leagues who organized charitable support for nursing claimed a uniquely feminine caring role, yet carried it out in a larger context of male authority. That authority was male doctors in the case of nurses; in the case of the Patriotic Women's Leagues, it was the state. The rewards of conservative feminine behavior were great: collectively the Patriotic Women's Leagues constituted by far the largest women's organization in Imperial Germany, the result not only of its members' energy, but also the state's patronage.[144]

Like the Red Cross of which they were a part, the Patriotic Women's Leagues won the state's favor with their efficiency and willingness to place themselves under military command. The putatively neutral Red Cross groups agreed to obey the army's military medical rules (*Kriegs-sanitätsordnung*), which were not at all neutral. Over the long term, war and preparation for war catalyzed the expansion of the Patriotic Women's Leagues and the rest of the Red Cross. The only wars Germany fought between 1871 and 1914 were in the colonies, and the German Women's Association for Nursing in the Colonies expanded over the course of four major colonial campaigns — the East African coastal war of 1888–1890, the Boxer War in China in 1900, the German Southwest African war of 1904–1907, and the Maji Maji war in German East Africa in 1905–1906 — as well as smaller conflicts in German East Africa during 1891–1892, German Southwest Africa in 1893 and 1896, and Cameroon in 1896 and 1905.

As the Patriotic Women's Leagues' embrace of nationalist war suggests, their members affirmed Imperial Germany's social and political order. These women hated Social Democracy, supported the authoritarian monarchy, embraced militarism, and offered conservative responses to the Woman Question. Their organizations therefore contrasted politically with those of socialist, radical, and even moderate feminists of the day. The conservative apoliticism of the German Women's Association for Nursing in the Colonies represented not only the political opinions of many of its members, but also a strategic response to its past experience of conflicts with men over women's participation in nationalist activism. Nursing in the Tropics, where illness was the leading cause of death among Europeans, was of great practical use, but it also carried with it the potential for feminist and other political disputes.[145]

Not all contemporaries of the Patriotic Women's Leagues saw the leagues as distinct and distant from the "women's movement." Two early German feminists, Louise Otto-Peters and Lina Morgenstern, saw the leagues as contiguous with, or even part of, the women's movement.[146] Lina Morgenstern is herself hard to classify: a moderate feminist who advocated women's suffrage and a Jew who belonged to the Protestant-dominated Patriotic Women's Leagues, she is best known today for organizing low-cost mass meals in "people's kitchens" (*Volksküchen*) in 1866 and 1870. She also published a major survey of women's paid work in Germany (which included the German Women's Association for Nursing in the Colonies).[147] She had a personal connection to the German colonies: her son, an engineer, was a railroad director in Usakos, German Southwest Africa.[148] While feminists, who are better known to historians of German women than conservative nonfeminist women, accepted or even embraced an oppositional stance, conservative women in the Patriotic Women's Leagues sought to remain publicly active while evading the accusation of opposition. The Patriotic Women's Leagues and the German Women's Association for Nursing in the Colonies were not feminist organizations, but they shared with feminists the challenge of responding to a male-dominated society.

The German Women's Association for Nursing in the Colonies made itself indispensable to colonialist men by subsidizing, in effect, German colonization.[149] Using funds raised through charity benefits and dues, the association sent nurses and supplies to government hospitals, remote clinics, and chartered company headquarters. In return, the secular state agencies of the Foreign Office (after 1890, the Colonial Department) and the Naval Office became enthusiastic patrons of the association. (Clara von Monts was herself the widow of a navy vice admiral.) The civilian and military doctors these agencies employed were especially strong supporters. After the association's reorganization, the first nurses arrived in German East Africa in 1888, in German

New Guinea in 1891, in German Cameroon in 1892, in German Southwest Africa in 1893, and in Togo in 1894. The association began work in the city of Qingdao in 1902, and in German Samoa in 1905. Soon its secular nurses overshadowed mission-based medical care in the colonies.[150]

The German Women's Association for Nursing in the Colonies was refounded just in time to benefit from the culmination of the nonconfessional and colonialist German antislavery movement. Women were allowed to attend the most important antislavery assembly, which took place on 27 October 1888 at the Gürzenich hall in Cologne, and they packed the gallery.[151] In December 1888, with the help of Ludwig Windthorst and his Catholic Center Party, the Reichstag approved appropriations for a special armed force led by Hermann von Wissmann for the East African coastal war. Wissmann's forces won in early 1891, after some very bloody fighting. The antislavery movement lost momentum in national politics after 1890, but it never died out altogether. Women's Association for Nursing members continued to send gifts to Africa for "industrious German negro children,"[152] slave children who had either escaped their masters or been purchased, and thereby "freed," by Germans. (Some freed slave children even became the godchildren of Ludwig Windthorst.)[153] The fact that these children were often passed from German to German and apparently always worked for their "liberators" indicates the relative nature of their freedom.[154] The German Colonial Society ran an "antislavery lottery" during the early 1890s and used the money to send Wissmann back to German East Africa in 1893 with a steamship to monitor slave trading, further militarizing the colony's interior.[155] Antislavery activists continued their work in the Africa Association of German Catholics (Afrikaverein deutscher Katholiken), the Evangelical Africa Association (Evangelischer Afrikaverein), the German Congo League (Deutsche Congo-Liga), and the German Society for the Protection of Natives (Deutsche Gesellschaft für Eingeborenenschutz). As cynically manipulative as Bismarck's and colonialists' appropriation of the antislavery issue was, their manipulations would not have worked had the fight to end slavery not genuinely captured Germans' imagination. The naval agitation of the late 1890s, a mass campaign in favor of building a navy that could rival Britain's, likewise aided the growth of the Women's Association for Nursing.

While the Women's Association for Nursing benefited from popular enthusiasms for colonial wars and naval expansion, it was by no means an organization of or for the common people. It was marked by the active involvement of the very wealthiest and the very highest of the titled nobility. Empress Augusta, the wife of Emperor Wilhelm I, was a friend of Clara von Monts and served as the association's patron, as did Empress Auguste Viktoria, the wife of Wilhelm II. Queens, princesses, and archduchesses of Imperial Germany's federated states likewise served as "protectresses" of the association's regional federations.[156] The wives of some of Germany's largest landowners were members, such as Princess Solms-Baruth, the duchess of Ratibor, Countess Stolberg-Wernigerode, and Princess Henckel von Donnersmarck (whose husband was both a landowner and an industrial magnate). Women from the Hoesch and Stumm families — Germany's most important industrialists — also belonged. About 14 percent of the membership belonged to the nobility, and about 12 percent to the overlapping group of the military. Families of the civil service and the educated middle class (*Bildungsbürgertum*) were also prominently represented.[157] The clubwomen were by and large far wealthier and more socially prestigious than the nurses they sponsored. Given the requirement that nurses be unmarried or widowed, marital status often also distinguished clubwomen from nurses. The association therefore encompassed two very different groups of women who encountered colonial space in very different ways.

NURSES IN COLONIAL SPACE

The German Women's Association for Nursing in the Colonies substituted nationalism, service to the state, and a generic Christian humanitarianism for the specifically confessional motivation of religious nurses. Colonial nurses shared the usual reasons of nurses in Germany for choosing that occupation. Some had faced a precarious personal or financial crisis such as the death of a father; others did not wish to marry or could not find a suitable husband. Colonial nursing carried some of the same burdens and rewards of nursing in Germany. It made private life all but impossible and endangered women's health, but it also offered job security and increased social status for women from humble backgrounds. The ideology of nursing offered women a rare chance to claim status as brave heroines, skilled professionals, and paragons of selfless femininity.

The first motherhouse to supply nurses to the association was the Clementine House (Clementinenhaus), founded in 1875 in Hanover by Olga von Lützerode.[158] It accepted as prospective nurses only "unmarried women and widows of Christian confession from the *educated classes,* between 20 to 40 years of age."[159] As the exclusion of Jewish women indicates, religion was never absent from such motherhouses; their secular nature consisted only in the fact that they were not part of a church bureaucracy.[160] The stricture about class shows the embourgeoisification of nursing then under way. The father or guardian of a prospective nurse had to give his permission for the woman to enter the motherhouse, even if she were an adult. Once in the motherhouse she owed complete obedience to the matron (*Oberin*).[161] After training, the hiring process reflected the overall chain of command from the state to the nurse. First, the Colonial Department—or, in the case of Kiao-Chow, the Naval Office—requested nurses and equipment from the Women's Association for Nursing. Then the association contracted with a motherhouse to hire nurses—never dealing directly with the individual nurses—and finally the nurses were dispatched to the colonies.[162] The nurses owed obedience first to the doctors with whom they worked, then to the association and the motherhouse. The association did not want to transform nursing in Germany, but rather wished to export conservative, authoritarian nursing to the colonies. It distanced itself from the image that Bülow had created of colonial nursing as an independent women's adventure.

Yet the promise of adventure in the colonies was an irreducible lure for the nurses. Their work was extraordinary. Apart from missionaries, they were practically the only European women in the regions where they were posted. Until the late 1890s, colonial doctors and bureaucrats advised men against bringing European wives to German Southwest Africa, German East Africa, German Samoa, and Kiao-Chow, and did the same until around 1910 regarding Togo and Cameroon. Soldiers, and in some cases even officers, were forbidden to bring their wives from Germany at all, especially in the early years of empire.[163] Nurses often decided to work for the Women's Association for Nursing in the face of family opposition. One nurse-recruit was ready to depart for New Guinea when her mother's veto put an end to the proceedings.[164] Another nurse, Anna Meyer, was dispatched with her parents' "initially only hesitant and displeased . . . permission."[165] On another occasion, a fiancé prevented the dispatch of his prospective wife, even though she planned to complete her service in German Southwest Africa before their wedding.[166] One of the first nurses the association sent to German East Africa after Frieda von Bülow was Countess Lilly zu Pückler-Limpurg. At the prospect of her departure, her distraught father appealed to no less an authority than Bismarck. "This risking of life and death is quite too adventurous," Count Ludwig zu Pückler-Limpurg wrote; "my wife . . . is in despair about it."[167] He pleaded with Bismarck to "use everything in your power to render the journey to Zanzibar impossible for my daughter."[168] The Clementine House matron was dismayed at the idea of sending Lilly, who was twenty-six years old, against her parents' wishes, and replaced her in 1889 with a nurse who had no living parents to protest.[169] But the Pückler Limpurgs' attempt to prevent the dispatch of their daughter ultimately failed; she departed for Africa in June 1890. As it turned out, Pückler-Limpurg was one of the hardiest and most successful nurses to be sent by the association. She stayed abroad much longer than other nurses, leaving her post in German East Africa only once in six years.[170]

Colonial nursing was undeniably dangerous. Of the 178 nurses the association dispatched between 1888 and 1907, 12 (or about 7 percent) died at their posts. Practically all nurses, regardless of the colony where they worked, reported suffering from malaria or "fever," and dysentery was common.[171] Ill health compelled many to return to Germany before their contracted terms expired. During the early years nurses' contracts lasted two years; later, the association matched the nurses' contracts to those of the colonial and naval civil service: nurses served for eighteen months in Togo and Cameroon; two years in German East Africa; three years in German Southwest Africa, German New Guinea, and German Samoa; and four years in Qingdao.[172] Although the association tried to prevent nurses from being stationed alone, in practice illness and delays meant that they often did work alone.[173] When that happened, the already physically hard work became exhausting. Nurse Anna Bäss-ler wrote from Cameroon: "We trot from early morning, often already at five in the morning until evenings at ten o'clock, without interruption."[174]

The nurses were eager to go in spite of such risks, and they wrote about their experiences in detail, mostly in letters that appeared regularly in the association journal, *Under the Red Cross*. Most had never left Europe or even seen people of color in Germany, so their first encounters with non-Europeans occurred on the voyage out. For nurses bound for German East Africa, the first stop they described as exotic was Port Said, Egypt; for nurses headed to German Southwest Africa, it was Liberia. The women reacted with fear and disgust at aggressive peddlers and the poverty and shabbiness of the first ports. Mathilde Knigge called the people who came up to the ship at Port Said "intrusive and repulsive" and fled back onto the ship.[175] Margarete Leue complained that Liberians were "repulsively ugly."[176] Helene von Borcke described a sense of unreality: "At first everything seemed to me altogether too foreign and bizarre, so that I often had to ask myself, 'am I dreaming or awake?'; it is as if one really is in another world."[177]

Soon after their arrival, however, the nurses became accustomed to the people and landscape. Leue reported: "On the first day the blacks seemed to us quite sinister. . . . Now we are so used to the blacks that we are astonished when we see an unexpected white face."[178] Nurses produced sightseeing accounts of the Africans, Pacific Islanders, or Chinese whom they glimpsed on walks through town, much as Bülow had. But nurses also dealt with colonial subjects directly and practically: they were medical caregivers, employers, customers, and sometimes foster mothers to colonial subjects. To romantic notions of the exotic, nurses added experiences of affection, irritation, and outright fear. Nurses evinced an interest in the antislavery movement by adopting and schooling slave children, and they often shared their quarters with the children. This was true mostly of German East Africa, but also of Cameroon, where nurse Margarete Leue wrote that she was "given" a four-year-old girl who was to be her "daughter."[179] The association focused on medical care for German colonists, and nurses cared for patients in quarters segregated by race and wealth. Yet it was impossible to decide priority of treatment completely on the basis of race or colonial subject status, for the simple reason that Germans' servants, manual laborers, soldiers, and overland porters, who originated from all over Africa, also required medical help if Germans were to proceed with their own work.

The early nurses in particular often discovered on arrival that their clinic had still to be built or renovated. Most had not envisioned themselves in the role of employer and overseer, but in order to do their nursing work effectively they had to form working relationships with local laborers and merchants. Nurses were responsible for hiring local people as cooks, launderers, janitors, and errand boys. Leue reported that twenty Africans greeted her on her arrival in Cameroon and immediately asked for work, news having spread quickly that two European women were to arrive and set up a clinic.[180] Nurses often wrote of their efforts to impose labor discipline, and of the intense irritation and impatience such efforts generated. Their first letters home already reflected frustration with colonial subjects who, in the nurses' opinion, did not work fast enough or skillfully enough, or refused to work altogether. In some cases the women became philosophical about obtaining labor that met their specifications. Helene von Borcke reported: "One also gradually learns the great art of being patient."[181] They often analyzed their predicament in racist terms that they understood as ethnographic truths. Borcke, like many other nurses, adopted the point of view that adult Africans were childlike; her superior, Carl Büttner, had described Africans to her in the same terms before she had ever left Germany.[182] Nurses' concrete experiences and opinions about individual workers did not necessarily reflect such maternal condescension, however. Borcke, for instance, bemoaned the incompetence of African and Indian clinic workers in general, but in her descriptions of individual workers, she praised the skill, humor, and helpfulness of each one.[183]

Anger and paranoia sometimes crept into nurses' descriptions of workers' failure to respond to the incentives of wages and penalties that were standard for European workers. Many nurses turned to physical blows to enforce their orders. While beatings were hardly uncommon in European factories and mines, they were not openly lauded as appropriate methods of labor discipline. Nurses tried to justify blows with the image of the workers as children. Borcke ordered a German male lazarette aide to administer a beating to one worker in order, as she saw it, to further the worker's moral development.[184] Like colonists, nurses depended on colonial subjects' labor and vented their frustration at that dependence with physical force. Nurses were often quick to adopt local colonists' notions about colonial subjects' inferiority.[185]

Nurses were also plunged into an intimate — and sometimes highly political — knowledge of the colonists' lives. As medical personnel for both Europeans and colonial subjects, they were in a privileged position to know about cases of severe physical abuse. In 1894, for example, the acting governor of Cameroon, Heinrich Leist, a promoter of the Women's Association for Nursing, was accused of forcing African women into prostitution with himself and other Germans, and of whipping the women in an exceptionally cruel way.[186] As news of Leist's crimes spread in Germany, the association leadership insisted in the pages of *Under the Red Cross* that their nurses would have said something if the accusations contained any truth.[187] Leist himself protested along similar lines: "The nurses Bässler and Leue, who lived with me on the Joss plateau, have repeatedly stated to Colonial Director Kayser and the board of the Red Cross that they had never heard anything objectionable about me."[188] Among his character witnesses, Leist cited none other than Alexander von Monts, son of the association chairwoman, Clara von Monts.[189]

Leist's and other Germans' brutality toward the Cameroonian "pawned women" precipitated an uprising in 1893 in which Margarete Leue herself was embroiled. Leue wrote to the association that she had first heard shots while working in her apothecary. "I resolved, if the rebels came, to approach them, in order at least to be killed as soon as possible."[190] A male employee of the Woermann trading company named Hesse escorted Leue and her patients to the governor's house, where Leist chivalrously offered Leue his room as a place to rest. The Germans hid there until a rebel siege forced them to run to the shore, where they boarded a boat to reach a ship waiting offshore. Just before this last dash to safety, Leue wrote, she grabbed a revolver, "in order, in case it came to the last, to protect myself from falling into the barbarians' hands alive."[191] Running to the ship, she lost a shoe, bent to pick it up, and heard a bullet pass just over her head. Reminiscing with evident pleasure at this point, Leue remarked: "It must have been a pretty picture, by the way: in one hand the shoe, in the right hand the revolver, the dress covered with blood from top to bottom. On my head a big hat that belonged to the black lazarette aide!"[192] Leue's bravery in caring for her patients under fire earned her a medal and an audience with Empress Auguste Viktoria.[193] She credited Hesse with saving her life and, implicitly, her honor. They married in Germany later that year and soon afterward returned to live in Cameroon.[194]

While nurses often displayed racial anxieties, nursing did not depend on drawing sharp boundary lines of race. Though fundamentally conservative, colonial nursing nevertheless permitted a range of motivations, political commitments, and opinions. In 1910, for example, when white supremacy was at its height in German Southwest Africa, the Women's Association for Nursing protested against the compulsory examination of all African women prisoners there for venereal disease.[195] This admittedly unusual instance of a confrontation between the association and male colonial bureaucrats suggests that even though nursing had established itself on narrowly respectable terms, it did not necessarily determine nurses' or, as we will see, clubwomen's ideas of race. Nursing remained a task that women performed, rather than the racialized essence that white German motherhood in the colonies was soon to represent.

Most nurses returned to Germany and lived out their lives there, probably as unmarried women. Others, like Leue, married men they met in the colonies. Auguste Hertzer, in contrast, made an independent career as a nurse in the colonies. One of the very first nurses sent by the association, she arrived in German East Africa in 1888 and hardly ever returned to Germany after that.[196] She fell ill in 1889, but insisted on staying in order to be able to care for Emin Pasha, a German-born official of the Egyptian government who had been cut off from European contacts by the Mahdi uprising in the Sudan. Carl Peters and the British explorer Henry Stanley had competed to find him, and Stanley won and brought him to the coastal town of Bagamoyo. Having survived the rigors of the African interior for years, Emin Pasha almost died of injuries he sustained from falling out a window while celebrating his return with other Germans in Bagamoyo.[197] Hertzer returned to Germany in 1890, then departed for German New Guinea the next year. She worked there for the Women's Association for Nursing for eight years, often unaccompanied. In the mid-1890s she obtained a special contract from the association to run a hospital single-handedly at Beliao, German New Guinea. When she terminated her contract with the association in

1899, she did not leave New Guinea but instead became an independent health care worker on the remote western Gazelle Peninsula of the New Guinea mainland. There she applied Robert Koch's new quinine method of malaria prevention, having been trained by a military doctor to perform the necessary microscope work.[198] Clearly, Hertzer preferred to work under her own authority and feared neither colonial subjects nor the climate.[199] She managed to turn a short-term posting as colonial nurse into a lifelong overseas career. Her example, though rare, indicates that even though nurses led generally very restricted lives, colonial space — especially if remote from other colonists — offered the possibility of autonomous action.

CLUBWOMEN IN COLONIAL SPACE

Most members of the German Women's Association for Nursing in the Colonies lacked the nurses' experiences of traveling to the colonies, or even making a living by paid work. Typical association members were wives of locally prominent men. The women's interest in colonial nursing stemmed from their existing charitable work, the desire to help their own relatives in the colonies, or the desire to promote a nationalist project. Colonial exoticism added fascination and vicarious adventure to the middle-class and elite feminine charity of nursing. Like the nurses, the clubwomen saw themselves as sacrificing for the sake of faraway men and women and for a nationalist cause. *Under the Red Cross* published accounts of clubwomen hastening to sew and pack supplies in time for a ship's departure alongside the nurses' letters describing their work in the colonies. The clubwomen also claimed a special authority over the nurses: as women, they declared themselves best suited to overseeing the training and work of other women.[200]

While a few association chapters formed in the colonies, most clubwomen's colonial encounters took place in Germany: at ethnographic shows (*Völkerschauen*) where people whom Europeans considered exotic were put on display, at balls and other festive occasions of the colonialist movement, and in private homes. Such events created a kind of colonial ambience through decorations and the use of Africans as performers or party servants. Clubwomen also had imaginative colonial encounters in the pages of *Under the Red Cross,* which featured ethnographic articles about courtship, marriage, and motherhood among the various peoples under German colonial rule.[201] Colonial subjects appeared in caricature, too, such as a carved figure of an African at a Christmas fund-raising bazaar in 1891 similar to the one Bülow remembered: a "so-called 'Toss-Man,' a Negro dandy . . . into whose wide-open mouth a ball had to go, in order to yield the remarkably valuable prizes to the skilled thrower."[202] These added a fascination that most other charitable nursing work in Germany lacked, and it was in these exotica that clubwomen perceived colonial space.

For clubwomen, colonial space was entertaining, never threatening. They never faced masses of Africans at a marketplace or confronted Pacific Islander workers in their home. The colonial subjects clubwomen saw were isolated individuals who were virtually always peripheral to the women's own everyday lives and needs. The sexual fear that sometimes surfaced in nurses' accounts was replaced by pity, curiosity, or even flirtation in the accounts of clubwomen. For example, the Cameroonian Paul Zampa, who belonged to the Guard Fusiliers (Gardefusiliers) in the garrison of Potsdam, was described in affectionate terms.[203]

Clubwomen also found endearing the African children who had been "rescued" from slave traders and brought to Germany. One of these former slave children, Kanza, had been bought from slave traders in 1891 in Witu (in what is now Kenya) when she was about eight years old. Her new de facto owner was Friedrich Schröder, the old friend of Carl Peters and Frieda von Bülow. When Schröder's sister-in-law Clara Schröder-Poggelow visited German East Africa, Schröder "gave" her Kanza to take back to Germany with her. Thereafter Kanza lived on the family estate in Poggelow, Mecklenburg. Clara Schröder-Poggelow took Kanza to the association's Christmas bazaar in 1891, where she served as a program salesgirl.[204] Soon she was speaking the local dialect of Plattdeutsch, underwent baptism, and was attending school happily and with success. In 1893 *Under the Red Cross* reported that "Kanza has become completely German."[205]

A similar case concerned a Cameroonian war orphan named Titia. Albert Plehn, a doctor employed by the colonial administration there and a supporter of the German Women's Association, brought Titia to his family's estate in Lubochin, West Prussia (today Lubocien, Poland), where his sister Maria Plehn raised her. According to a family friend, the feminist and social policy expert Marie Baum, "For some years she was a lovingly spoiled plaything, did light housework and amused everyone with her naïvely clever questions and opinions."[206] Although Titia apparently also became quite German, the Plehns decided that she could not remain in Germany after reaching, as Baum put it, "marriageable" age.[207] The Plehns arranged a marriage with a mission pupil in Cameroon and sent Titia to the colony. It is impossible to know what Titia thought of their decision to return their "plaything" to Cameroon; she died there while still a young woman.

The leaders of the Women's Association for Nursing themselves tried to adopt and train two adult African women. In 1893 the explorer Franz Stuhlmann brought two Aka Pygmy women to Berlin from central Africa, where he claimed to have freed them "from the hands of cannibalistic Manyema."[208] Stuhlmann claimed that the women, named Asmini and Chikanao, who were in their mid-twenties, were the first of their kind to enter Europe. He promptly put them on exhibit as a fundraising event for the German Colonial Society, which in turn invited the Women's Association for Nursing to share in the arrangements and proceeds.[209] *Under the Red Cross* explained that in this instance Stuhlmann was making an exception to his rule of exhibiting Africans only to scientific audiences. Ethnographic shows were a popular form of entertainment in Germany in the 1880s and 1890s, and although there was no public advertising for the exhibition of Asmini and Chikanao, crowds filled the museum for the duration.[210] The German Colonial Society men who organized the exhibition invited Martha von Pfeil; Clara von Monts; and the association's secretary, Clara Müseler, to meet Asmini and Chikanao before the exhibition. Monts recorded her and the other clubwomen's impressions in several subsequent issues of *Under the Red Cross*. The three clubwomen arrived expecting to be charmed by the Aka women. However, Asmini and Chikanao ran away and stuck out their tongues at the visitors. Monts persevered in trying to approach them, claiming that such genuine, uncivilized nature won her heart. The Aka women sometimes argued and struck one another, and that too Monts ascribed to their savage nature. Even on such occasions, Monts insisted, the Aka women remained "graceful and discreet," although she also described them as stupid and childish.[211] The Colonial Society men explained that the Aka women were "tribeless and homeless," and that none of the German explorers or Africans in Berlin could speak their language.[212] The women could communicate only in a second language with one of Stuhlmann's African male servants, a mission-educated Myao and former slave whom Stuhlmann had "bought into freedom" in 1880 in Zanzibar.[213] Clara von Monts reacted more positively toward the African male attendants. They were, she reported, of a very dark black color and "strikingly beautiful specimens of their race."[214] The clubwomen were intrigued by the anecdote that Stuhlmann had once received a blood transfusion from one of them.

A curious dispute developed between the clubwomen and the German Colonial Society men when the Aka women rejected the Germans' effort to look beneath their clothes. Monts reported that "the attempt to make visible even only a small part of the delicately formed shoulders failed due to their energetic resistance. The gentlemen were inclined to attribute this very striking peculiarity to a well-developed natural sense of modesty [*Schamgefühl*]."[215] The clubwomen had perceived the Aka women as exemplars of unspoiled, primitive nature; yet Monts refused to accept the men's idea that the Aka women might share a fundamental femininity, and innate modesty at that, with women like herself. The Aka women were suddenly too close for the clubwomen's comfort. Monts would have none of the men's notion of a feminine modesty shared across racial and civilizational divides: "The present writer cannot wholly agree with their views. She cannot believe that creatures who until 16 months ago wore *string* as their only dress, and two or three grass stalks pulled through a hole pierced in the upper lip as their only jewelry, can have *artificially* appropriated within the short time mentioned such a feeling of exaggerated decency."[216] Instead, Monts concluded, the Akas had learned to see clothes as "the essence of the higher *race*," and they refused for that reason to yield to the Germans' efforts to bare their shoulders.[217] "To give up even only the smallest part of this new attainment may have meant the same to them as being obliged to give up their elevated status."[218] Modesty, for Monts, was thus a quality inculcated in women by a high level of civilization. The Aka women might clumsily imitate it, but they could not really share it. Against the supposedly natural unity of womanhood that the men invoked, Monts invoked the supposedly natural barrier of race. This became a recurring pattern in colonialist women's approach to race: while German men might opt to see all women as fundamentally alike, colonialist women saw themselves first as Germans, then as female. They could not express, nor apparently imagine, a raceless femininity.

Even though the encounters between the clubwomen and the Aka women continued to be hostile, the association developed the "pet idea" of training the women to be nurses' assistants and dispatching them along with the nurses to Africa.[219] Asmini and Chikanao were sent for training to a sanatorium in the provincial town of Blankenburg, where the local German Colonial Society chapter and two former colonial nurses, Amalie Steins and Helene von Borcke, took them over. Even bringing the Akas from the railroad station to the sanatorium was a problem because "already on the first day of their arrival in the pretty little Harz town, they aroused the interest of all the children to such a lively degree, that they soon had a crowd probably numbering in the hundreds behind them."[220] Because the locals mobbed them every time they appeared, Asmini and Chikanao were not permitted to walk beyond the park of the sanatorium where they were being "trained," the first step of which was assigning them to clear away dishes. The experiment was not successful. Monts mentioned that the women threw tantrums at the sanatorium. In August 1893 Asmini and Chikanao were sent to Bagamoyo in German East Africa. The German Women's Association did not relinquish them even there, however; they stayed with the nurse Lilly zu Pückler-Limpurg, who was to continue their training. Monts still expressed the hope that they could be trained as "perfectly useful little women, so that we can report good things about them from time to time!"[221] The association finally released Asmini and Chikanao from their involuntary duty in early 1894, apparently in response to Pückler-Limpurg's skeptical letters to Monts. Franz Stuhlmann took them to Dar es Salaam, where they lived with Stuhlmann's former caravan leader.[222] The fact that the clubwomen persisted so long in attempting to mold the Aka women into a sort of toy version of themselves suggests a desire to control, in their own way, colonial subjects. The clubwomen understood their own actions toward colonial subjects as affectionate and benign, even though the effects of the clubwomen's casual adoptions of African children and of the hobbylike effort to train the Aka women were often quite the opposite.

Between 1888 and 1907 the German Women's Association for Nursing in the Colonies was the sole colonialist women's organization outside church auspices. It wove together various threads of German women's colonial interests: conservative nationalism, antislavery, and female nursing as nonconfessional Christian mission and as paid career. The secularization of nursing, specifically its detachment from clergymen's leadership, opened up possibilities for women's leadership, helped make colonialism a women's cause, and secured cooperation with the colonial state. Colonial nursing installed German women in official capacities in all the German colonies, a remarkable achievement in a colonial administration and colonialist movement that otherwise overwhelmingly excluded them. The association did its best to repress two especially difficult issues that Bülow would or could not ignore: German women's emancipation and German men's sexual violence in the colonies. Bülow's experiences and writings foreshadowed the sexual and gender conflicts that arose by way of colonial sexual scandals and debates over intermarriage between German men and African and Pacific Islander women. Eventually, these conflicts unraveled the ability of the Women's Association for Nursing to act as sole mediator among women's and men's secular colonialist interests.

Although Frieda von Bülow had appeared in the roles of club-woman, nurse, travel writer, and romantic heroine by 1888, her career had scarcely begun. Still before her was a second sojourn in German East Africa, where she ran her own plantation, and a career as a successful novelist—the first, male or female, to use the German colonies as a setting for fiction. She maintained an independent career, living by her pen, for the rest of her life. No other colonialist woman gained public attention in so many different roles. Bülow was unusual not only in the range of her activities, but also in the frankness and depth of her explorations of conflicts with German men. Dissatis-fied with the few conventional realms available to middle-class and aris-tocratic women (marriage, nursing, or teaching), she sought meaning in radical nationalism, colonialism, and feminism. None provided the answer.

Three themes pervade Bülow's writings.[1] The theme of radical na-tionalism, which this chapter discusses first, would appear to be the most straightforward, but the two other themes, women's freedom and men's violence, reveal how little radical nationalism or colonial space could solve the problem of how German women were to carry out colonialism together with German men. Bülow had a troubled relation-ship with feminism. She simultaneously advocated female freedom and feared the effects of that freedom. A similar ambivalence emerges in her confrontation with men's, especially Carl Peters's, violence.

Bülow's fictional worlds were closely related to her personal experi-ences. Countless parallels between her life and fiction indicate that close-ness, as does her own statement that she saw her fiction as a set of political ideas, not as art, and that she chose the medium of fiction because it was "unostentatious [*unaufdringlich*]."[2] Her contemporaries read her novels as romans-à-clef; one man actually sued her over an unappealing character in her novel *Tropical Rage* who, he thought, resembled him.[3] Bülow sketched her fictional characters with economy, often with cutting wit, and with a high degree of determinism. As her plots unfold, each character confirms the hopes and doubts planted by early clues of posture, facial profile, and political views. A remark by the poet Rainer Maria Rilke, who knew Bülow well in the 1890s, suggests a similar determinism in her real-life relationships: "It was Baroness Bülow's nature to assume her friends to be as she had developed and authoritatively completed them."[4] For all this verisimilitude, however, her novels and short stories remained imaginative fiction, and she reworked those sources of inspiration to create widely varying scenarios of strong women's and men's erotic obsessions and conflicts.

FRIEDA VON BÜLOW'S RADICAL NATIONALISM

Bülow held classically radical nationalist views. In her opinion, Imperial Germany was failing to be vigilant about the depredations of materialism and moral inferiors, and an immoral softness and pursuit of comfort was spreading. Conventional conservative nationalism had become an unthinking reflex; a more deeply felt attachment to "Germandom" and "German-ness" (*Deutschtum*) was needed. Bülow mocked Germans who mouthed chauvinistic phrases without giving them serious thought.[5] Her criticism was therefore directed not only at those whom she saw as the source of Germany's problems — capitalists, Jews, and Slavs — but also at those whom she felt ought to be Germany's best representatives, such as the nobility, feminists, and Christian Germans generally.[6] The critical nature of radical nationalism has led some scholars to see in her writings instances of ambivalence about nationalism and colonialism.[7] While the meanings of a fictional text cannot be completely delimited, however, the historical and political context of her writing should be kept in mind. Radical nationalists did question and criticize, but they did so to deepen national essentialisms, not to disintegrate them. Bülow understood her nationalism to be not only a political position, but also a moral and ethical imperative.

Radical nationalists formed a national opposition roughly when Bismarck fell from power in 1890. From the political far right, they challenged the imperial government to pursue, for example, a more aggressive foreign policy and a stronger Germanization policy in the Polish regions of Prussia.[8] Radical nationalists believed that the existing political system was too formalistic, and that it was oppressing a genuine but silenced German nation. Their extreme rhetoric and references to a supposed German racial essence as a source of authority for their ceaseless demands have reminded many historians of the later Nazi movement. As it happened, the reputations of Bülow (who died in 1909) and Carl Peters (who died in 1918) were revived during the Nazi period as officially approved forerunners of Nazi imperialist and racist ideology. Certain of Bülow's ideas made that revival easy, although she had to be bowdlerized and simplified for official Nazi tastes, for she had questioned male authority, female submission, and conventional sexual virtue.[9] The meanings of scenarios of race and sexuality in her fiction cannot be easily summarized or controlled. And as a woman who rejected marriage and motherhood, accepted lesbian sexuality, and always earned her own living, Bülow conformed less to a Nazi model of womanhood than did many other colonialist women before the First World War.

Bülow's own experiences and those of Carl Peters fed her radical nationalist convictions. Both saw the events of 1887 and 1888 in terms of distant bureaucratic authority having confounded them just as they were vindicating German national power. Peters's recall from Zanzibar in December 1887 was one of several setbacks for the "conquistador" of German East Africa (as some contemporaries sarcastically called him). Peters gained the limelight again in 1889 by leading an expedition to reach Emin Pasha in the Sudan.[10] The explorer Henry Morton Stanley reached Emin Pasha first, but Peters took the opportunity created by the expedition to make new treaties in regions to the north of German East Africa, once more against the wishes of the German Foreign Office. On his return to the coast in July 1890, he learned that his new treaties were worthless because the new imperial chancellor, Leo von Caprivi, had concluded the Heligoland-Zanzibar Treaty of 1890, and among its provisions was the repudiation of all German claims to Zanzibar and the African mainland north of Lake Victoria. Peters, incensed, returned to Berlin and helped found the radical nationalist Pan-German League in 1891.

Bülow shared Peters's frustration when the government rejected his "bold, truly heroic deeds."[11] In a letter to Peters's sister Elly Peters, Bülow compared Germany in the 1890s to the defeated Prussia of 1806, and Peters to the Prussian generals Yorck and Blücher who defied their king in order to take up the fight against Napoleon: "Through them and through them alone, Prussia, trampled to the ground and disgracefully humiliated, raised itself. Men with such a strong sensibility in matters of national honor, like your brother (fortunately, also mine) are the ones who preserve and support the nation, *in spite of* the feeble politics of retreat that comes from above. . . . These days I am so completely preoccupied with these things that I cannot and do not want to write of anything else."[12] Her comparison of Prussia's defeat and humiliation to the situation in Imperial Germany was rather strained, given that the 1890s were a period of unprecedented economic and military expansion in Germany. Yet such images were common at that time among radical nationalist critics of the state.[13] For Bülow, "Germany" was not the emperor, the government, or the state; it was a nation whose aggressive political will lacked a spokesman. A few years later she confided to Elly Peters that she hoped Peters would emerge as a great leader in Germany, again comparing him to the Prussian reformers and generals of the Napoleonic Wars: "What we *need* is a man who knows what he wants and who is *not afraid,* but rather determined to enforce what he wants, with or against the government, as Stein, Blücher, Gneisenau, Bülow, and York [*sic*] did in 1812! I wish now with my whole heart that we may celebrate your brother as this kind of liberator and *man*."[14] Bülow wholly subscribed to the radical nationalist vision of a Germany in bonds awaiting its "liberator."

She also subscribed to standard radical nationalist notions of who or what was oppressing Germany. Britain, with its dominance in foreign policy and its condescension, was high on the list. So was capitalism, with its lack of moral values and its promotion of parvenus. Closely related to such anticapitalism was political anti-Semitism, which described Jews as the particular agents and beneficiaries of capitalism. Some radical nationalists saw Jews as a race, a fundamentally different and distinct people who could never become German. Bülow and other radical nationalists presented Jews as infiltrators into positions of influence in "real" German society, from where they cynically promoted the degradation of German values. Bülow expressed her fear and distrust of Jews' supposed power in a 1902 letter to Peters in which she warned him that accepting Jews' financing would make him "one of the marionettes that the hate-filled Jew, smiling coldly, holds on a string."[15] Her novels include an array of caricatures of Jews.[16] There are a few passages in her writings that offer a more thoughtful and historicized account of Jews' place in German society, consistent with Bülow's habit of presenting political ideas in the context of fictional debate scenes; but the overall presentation of Jews in her writings, both fiction and nonfiction, makes Bülow's racism clear.[17] She presented Slavs, especially Poles, in much the same fashion. Although Slavs lacked, in her view, Jews' chameleonlike adaptability, they were still dangerously resentful of German virtue and power.[18] While Bülow evidently felt deep ambivalence about German women's emancipation and German men's violence, her racism toward Jews and Slavs was neither complex nor ambivalent.

Colonial Africa, Bülow believed, offered the "Germany" that radical nationalists sought, a "Germany" that was detached from the actual German state and social order.[19] In contrast to the German Women's Association for Nursing in the Colonies, which sought to export a feminine version of conservative nationalism to the colonies, Bülow wished to import a new German nationalist sensibility from them. In her novels and short stories set in German East Africa, which appeared between 1890 and 1899, she inaugurated the theme of men's nationalist renewal through colonial experience.[20] Her narratives depict strong German men rediscovering their gifts for courage and hard work, and even generous love, far from decadent, industrialized Germany.[21]

Bülow often portrayed the renewal of noblemen, suggesting that the conflict between the Prussian nobility's traditional hierarchy of honor and service and industrial capitalism's cash-based hierarchy could no longer be resolved within Germany's borders. Like the nobility itself, Bülow insisted, the value of German culture could not be appraised in terms of mere capitalism. Marcia Klotz has aptly described this theme in Bülow's fiction: "The colonies must be pursued no matter what the cost, not because they make money, but because they make real men."[22] Although the colonies could not recoup men who were inherently flawed, they set free virtues that had been languishing and suffocating in Germany, and they punished flaws that had been flourishing unchecked.

Bülow gave her fullest account of the colonial education of a German man with the character Baron Ludwig von Rosen, whose story extends across three novels.[23] At the opening of the eponymous novel, Rosen is living as a kept man in Berlin, in "humiliation and enslavement."[24] Rosen's escape from materialism and moral weakness is complete by the end of the novel: he has regained his full manhood. The narrator exclaims: "Before him lay a new life that had nothing in common with the old one: a life of faith and hope! A life of privation, daily struggle, of work and of duty!"[25]

Bülow inaugurated not only the theme of the colonial education of the German man, but also that of the German woman. Indeed, in her view the radical nationalist struggle required the efforts of both women and men. Yet the way she portrayed the colonial education of the German woman reveals her ambivalence about women's freedom. Bülow's fiction offers multiple imaginative resolutions to a problem that was close to Bülow's lived experience: the strong woman who must find moral meaning in a materialistic and unjust society. Bülow's boilerplate heroine bears more than a passing resemblance to Bülow herself. She is vivacious, strong-willed, outspoken, and unconcerned with conventional limits on female behavior. She is pedigreed, though not wealthy, and a father or husband is either weak or absent. She is dark-haired, slightly exotic, and attractive, but not conventionally beautiful. A certain gender ambiguity draws men to her: they talk to her as they would to a man, then realize that they have plunged themselves into casual intimacy with a woman. While she is often the center of male attention, she is innocent of any motive to seduce. What she does want is independence, power, and a meaningful mission in life. She is unable to deny her nature, settle for less, and become like other female characters, who are portrayed as more harmonious but, it is hinted, are weaker and more superficial. Bülow's typical heroine has, like Rosen, inherent virtues, but her quirky status could easily tempt her toward ill.

Bülow offered three resolutions to her heroine's predicament, and all of them contrast starkly with that of men's colonial education. If German men escape "humiliation and enslavement" through a colonial education, German women find a master who tames them in romantic, happy endings.[26] Only two of Bülow's novels have conventional happy endings in which the hero and heroine unite at the height of their passion: her first novel, *At the Other End of the World* (1890), and *Tropical Rage* (1896).[27] In both, the hero gradually establishes his authority over the stubborn heroine, who in turn battles her own strong desire for independence. In the case of *Tropical Rage*, Rosen impresses the headstrong Eva Biron with his sternness and discipline. In *At the Other End of the World*, the character of the hero, Bothmann, is not as well developed. Something else helps tame the heroine, Monika von Uffeln: the realization of her own superfluity in the colony. The love and bravery she has proven by making a secret journey to German East Africa to join her fiancé at his plantation are not enough, she learns, for a German woman in Africa. She is not very useful to her fiancé. Unlike his friend, the cheery merchant Danbruck, she does not know how to cook or how to run a tropical household. The example of Danbruck makes Monika fear that German women, at least of a certain class, are superfluous "luxury objects" in the colony.[28] A scullery maid, she exclaims, would be more suitable than she, a "spoiled young lady of the castle who was so helpless, so useless."[29] Ultimately, she discovers that she can nurse the wounded and ill better than the men. Even though she knows she must leave the war-torn colony, she begins to learn all the other humble tasks of the colonial housewife, thereby proving that the miseducation of the elite German woman can be put right. She emphasizes repeatedly that she has learned her lesson: following her fiancé's wishes is the only safe course. A German woman, then, could be a good helpmeet to a male colonist if she were brave, capable of hard work, and obedient.

But problems interested Bülow far more than happy endings. A second type among her narratives explores the consequences of unlimited male and female power. Some of these take up the failure of any man to tame the heroine; in others, a woman is destroyed by male tyranny.[30] Sinister forces, usually represented by Jewish, Slavic, or lower-class characters, undermine the victims' few chances at redemption. None of these stories takes place in the colonies, and indeed they would not have made good colonialist propaganda. They suggest a lasting pessimism about women's ability to be independent, moral actors.

The third and most frequent type of narrative in Bülow's fiction traces what happens when the female character plays the part of a proper heroine but is disappointed by the weakness of her intended hero. In Bülow's second novel, *The Consul* (1891), it is the Berlin Foreign Office, not the hero, Max von Sylffa, who is at fault; the Foreign Office wrong-headedly recalls him and thereby stymies his romantic happy ending with the heroine, Nelly Donglar. Yet Nelly Donglar has undergone a colonial education and becomes an exponent of the best kind of German nationalism, and so a nationalist happy ending is substituted for personal erotic gratification. Later stories show heroes whose flaws cannot be traced to government institutions: Ralf Krome of *In the Promised Land,* who cannot control his sexual appetites or temper, and Joachim von Bruckring of *Kara,* who toys with naïve young women and openly commits adultery.[31] This type of narrative focuses on the predicament of strong women in a patriarchal society, doomed to betrayal by weak or immoral men. After the failure of the heroine's romance, she is a painfully disappointed woman who faces the future without illusions. She has achieved self-control and a lonely victory only after the greatest struggle with her infatuation. Flirting, gossip, and men's manipulations no longer affect her. She is isolated, for only people who have been through similar soul-searching could understand her. She becomes a desexualized caregiver to both flawed men of her own class and her needy social inferiors.[32]

Though the endings to these novels are hardly happy ones, they do display some optimism about women. Bülow presented the experienced, disillusioned heroines as genuine moral actors (usually nationalists), not deluded or weak figures. They have dealt in passions so strong that lesser women would have broken down completely. They have also pushed beyond the limits of petty conventional morality. Indeed, some of Bülow's heroines are immoral in some ways, yet are held up at the narrative's end as courageous and admirable figures. For example, Maleen Dietlas, of *In the Promised Land,* marries her husband although she does not love him, allows him to spoil her, dreams of leaving him for the Peters-like character Ralf Krome, and even commits adultery. Kara, of the eponymous novel, is so obsessed with her lover that she disgraces her family with a premarital affair, allows her now-husband to persuade her not to breast-feed her baby in order to preserve her looks, and then deserts the newborn to accompany him on a trip (the baby dies in her absence) — and still believes that she made the only choices possible.

Real emancipation for women, Bülow suggested, came from final escape from the romantic life course prescribed for women and entry into a realm of comradeship with men and a social life in which women represented themselves as they served their nation. The plots of her colonial novels suggest that radical nationalism was not only a struggle shared by men and women, but also a struggle between them.

FRIEDA VON BÜLOW'S QUEST FOR FREEDOM

Bülow knew from personal experience that the terms of cooperation between radical nationalist men and women were difficult. Her affair with Peters combined in ideal fashion nationalism and personal passion.[33] But by late 1887 in Zanzibar, at the same time that the pettiness of the German-National Women's League and the Foreign Office was fostering her own radical nationalism, Bülow had to confront the fact that her own colonial hero was failing her, and their affair ended. After returning from Africa in 1888 she faced public curiosity about her attitude toward Peters, and responded with confident declarations of his heroic qualities. She urged her old friend Fritz Mauthner to tell his journalist colleagues that "my enthusiasm for Peters has *in no way* cooled. I mourn now in him one of the most brilliant and, in any case, the most determined and bravest people I have ever encountered. The friendship I maintained with him in Zanzibar was already worth the price that I have had to pay for it."[34] Now began a period of her life in which she lived more or less free of Peters but with the knowledge of the intensity of her obsession. After 1888 she attempted to come to terms with sexuality, emancipation, class, and race, not in colonial space but rather inside Germany.

On returning to Germany, Bülow lived briefly with her family, but her mother's death and sister Sophie's entry into the Victoria Sisters nursing order meant that she was soon on her own again. Bülow set up an apartment in the house of her uncle Thankmar von Münchhausen and his wife, Anna, in the Berlin suburb of Lankwitz. For much of the 1890s she traveled, met writers and artists, and wrote in rural retreats in Thuringia. She published at least one book each year from 1889 until her death in 1909, with the exception of two years of personal crisis: 1893, when both brothers died in quick succession, and 1907, when Peters was facing a new round of scandal, and when she may well have discovered her final illness, cancer.

During the 1890s Bülow maintained her old friendships with Helene Lange, Fritz Mauthner, and Friedrich Lange and also joined a new circle of friends and acquaintances who were poets, artists, bohemians, and feminists. The most important of these for Bülow was Lou Andreas-Salomé, a critic, philosopher, and novelist known for her friendships with Friedrich Nietzsche and Paul Rée.[35] In 1887 she married Friedrich Carl Andreas, the son of a German father and a German-Malay mother, who taught at the Seminar for Oriental Languages at the University of Berlin. However, the couple lived apart for several years between 1891 and 1903, when Andreas-Salomé was romantically involved with the Social Democratic Reichstag delegate Georg Ledebour and the poet Rainer Maria Rilke. It was during these same years that her friendship with Bülow was the most intense. Bülow met Andreas-Salomé in 1891 through a mutual friend, the writer Johanna Niemann. At the time, Andreas-Salomé was living with her husband in Schmargendorf, on the western outskirts of Berlin. Bülow and Andreas-Salomé soon became close. They traveled together to Paris, Vienna, and Russia in 1894 and 1895, and lived together for several months in Munich in 1897.[36]

Both made much of the contrasts between them, especially in temperament and worldview.[37] Each modeled fictional characters on the other and penned fictional debates about love, pain, and independence that echoed their real-life discussions.[38] They even debated publicly in the pages of *Die Zukunft* about whether there was, or should be, a specifically feminine style of writing.[39] They also argued about Bülow's continuing obsession with Peters.[40] Yet Bülow and Andreas-Salomé also shared a great deal in common. Both led unconventional lives, rejecting the marriage and motherhood expected of women. Both were involved with men with strong personalities, and both maintained their own strong identities in the wake of those relationships. Biographers of both have speculated that each had romantic relationships with women.[41] Each displayed her unconventionality through a gender-ambiguous self-presentation.[42] Over years of conversation and correspondence about the emotional and intellectual experiences of women and their own experiences of autonomy and subordination in relationships with men, they forged a deep friendship.

In the midst of her new friendships with Andreas-Salomé and others, Bülow experimented again with colonial life. In 1892 her brother Albrecht was killed in battle against the Chagga near Mount Kilimanjaro. Albrecht left behind a plantation in German East Africa, near the coastal town of Tanga. After Albrecht's death, Frieda's other brother Kuno considered running it, but he had already accepted a position in German Southwest Africa working for the land concession company of Julius Scharlach, a wealthy colonialist and speculator. On returning to Berlin briefly in 1893, Kuno committed suicide over an unhappy love affair. Kuno's death affected Frieda deeply; apart from Margarete, he was the family member to whom she was closest, and she identified his struggles with passion's "demonic power" with her own.[43] Now Sophie was Bülow's only surviving family member. Bülow, who had helped Albrecht to purchase the plantation, decided that she would run it to earn an independent livelihood in German East Africa.[44] While instances of widows continuing to operate the family farm were not unknown in the colonies, Bülow was probably the first never-married German woman to own and run her own colonial plantation.

Bülow left Berlin in June 1893. Sophie, Lou Andreas-Salomé, and Carl Peters (who had just been recalled from a post in German East Africa, in a third rebuke by the state) saw her off from the train station in Berlin. As on her first trip, Bülow sent back accounts of her colonial experiences for publication in periodicals such as *Die Frau*. These published accounts, her private letters, the information she gave to her biographer, and her 1899 novel *In the Promised Land* all suggest that she faced initial alienation from the other German settlers. Poisonous gossip surrounded her as the lover of Carl Peters, himself no longer an unblemished hero. She made it a point of honor to defend him, which only increased the disdain of her fellow Germans.[45] Her former social circle was gone or now snubbed her.[46] However, Bülow apparently overcame the objections of old acquaintances and gained new ones, including a navy doctor named Ehrhardt, with whom she had an affair, and the Women's Association nurse Countess Lilly zu Pückler-Limpurg.[47]

Bülow was fascinated with the romance of colonial farm life. She wrote Elly Peters that she preferred life in German East Africa; she was isolated at her plantation, but found the solitude healing: "The colony is a fountain of youth for my morale."[48] To Andreas-Salomé she described herself happily marching about her fields like a man, in boots.[49] Bülow's pleasure at her agrarian idyll was by no means uncommon among feminist and colonialist women; indeed, the woman farmer was to become a powerful image in later colonialist women's activism.

Although Bülow did not provide much detail about her interactions with Africans, she apparently was successful in finding laborers to build a kiln, dig wells, and plant crops on her land.[50] She was ultimately satisfied that she was a model colonist, enjoying the respect of her fellow German colonists and obedience from the African colonial subjects under her control. Bülow was not able to solve other problems, however, including ill health, insufficient capital, and bureaucratic opposition to her landholding. Already in 1891, the Colonial Department had decided to discourage small-scale, private landownership in favor of company landholding.[51] Bülow returned to Berlin in early 1894 and attempted to float the "Tanga Company" with Friedrich Lange and Julius Scharlach.[52] The venture failed, and she finally had to sell her plantation to the German East African Company.[53]

The fact that Bülow had lived in Africa twice and pursued independent projects there attracted people to her for the rest of her life. Her biographer, the novelist and activist for gay and lesbian rights, Sophie Hoechstetter, saw Bülow's struggle to gain the respect of her fellow colonists as typical of what women faced if they dared to flout convention: "Now Frieda von Bülow had to experience how hard a single woman had to fight in order to succeed in public life."[54] To artists and intellectuals in Europe whom she encountered in the 1890s, Bülow represented courage and the exotic. Rainer Maria Rilke saw in her elements of the primitivism to which many modernists were drawn. According to Rilke's biographer, he was "fascinated . . . by Frieda's connection with East Africa" and "touched by Frieda's colonial model of the primitive life as a guide to an improved existence."[55]

Bülow and Andreas-Salomé met Rilke in Munich in May 1897, where Bülow was giving a colonialist lecture. That summer and again in 1899, the three of them spent several weeks at a vacation cottage they had named "Loufried," in Wolfratshausen, a small town in the countryside outside Munich, "walking barefoot, wearing peasant clothes, and eating vegetarian food."[56] They were joined in 1897 by the architect August Endell; Akim Volynsky, a Russian friend of Andreas-Salomé; the photographer and feminist Sophia Goudstikker; and her sister Mathilde Goudstikker. Sophia Goudstikker owned her own studio, the Atelier

Elvira, located in a house of Endell's fanciful design that was a *Jugendstil* landmark of Munich. The Atelier Elvira was a hub of gay and lesbian social life and intellectual and artistic life in Munich.[57] Goudstikker was the first unmarried woman to obtain a royal license as a photographer.[58] In the late 1890s Bülow became friends with Goudstikker's romantic partner, Ika Freudenberg, a writer, chairwoman of the Munich Association for Women's Interests (Münchner Verein für Fraueninteressen), and cofounder, along with Goudstikker, of the first legal advice center for women in Munich.[59]

Between 1894 and 1900 Bülow took up feminism as part of her quest to understand the fate of women in Imperial Germany. She wrote essays that addressed the exploitation of women factory workers, defended feminists from accusations of deficient patriotism, and advocated a year of national service for young women as a way of earning full citizenship analogous to young men's military service.[60] In a public exchange with Andreas-Salomé over the relationship between a writer's sex and writing style, Bülow insisted that women, far from seeking to conceal their femininity in their writing, should embrace the idea of writing specifically *qua* women.[61] She also produced several stories that directly addressed how social institutions and men's power oppressed women, such as "The Stylized Woman" (dedicated to Goudstikker) and the collection *Lonely Women*.[62] The problem of how unmarried bourgeois and elite women could support themselves touched Bülow personally. Her inheritance did not suffice to support her, and she always had to live by her writing.[63] Bülow's feminist short stories and essays express the feeling of entrapment that many women of her class shared around the turn of the century.

Feminists were among Bülow's readers and admirers from the beginning of her writing career. The radical bourgeois feminist Marie Stritt, for example, reviewed *Lonely Women* positively, noting that Bülow was a "*modern* writer in *our* sense."[64] But, like Rilke, feminists seemed to appreciate Bülow more for her deeds than for her ideas. They praised especially the realism of her portrayals of colonial life and of women of the rural nobility in Germany. According to the leading feminist Gertrud Bäumer, *Tropical Rage* and Bülow's other colonial novels offered women salutary political lessons:

[They] show, in a way that is not at all to be presumed of a feminine sensibility, a passionate interest for the [colonial] cause. Colonial life is not only the background for psychological events and inner situations; it is very much the main point. Colonial policy questions and conflicts are at issue, and the work out there is grasped in a thoroughly generous, brave spirit, as a service to the national cause, to Germany's world economic tasks. We feel how the author, along with these pioneers of German power and culture, struggles through the unspeakable difficulties that beset them: the narrowness and bureaucracy at the green baize table back at home and the unfavorable conditions abroad.[65]

Bäumer saw Bülow as an example of female courage worthy of feminists' admiration. Sophie Hoechstetter likewise focused on Bülow's nationalist politics: "Patriotic enthusiasm is certainly not a common feature among the intellectual women of our time. Since women are as good as excluded from any *political* life and are entitled only to indirect influence through husbands or sons, they could only remain inactive or engage themselves in unimportant matters. Frieda von Bülow had the chance to place herself in the direct service of a great national cause. And she did so with all the passion of her nature."[66]

Bülow's own relationship to feminism was somewhat uneasy. She felt a generational divide between herself and many younger feminists of the 1890s and 1900s, who gravitated toward Nietzsche and other cultural critics.[67] Bülow knew that she did not fit the expectations of any of the groups with which she was associated; she told Andreas-Salomé: "That is what always happens to me: for the conservatives I am too modern, for the moderns I am too conservative. For the old Africa hands I am too much of a literary type, and for the literary types I am too much of an old Africa hand, so that I don't belong anywhere and must always work in obscurity [*Fledermaus sein*]."[68] Bülow also suspected feminists of egotism and selfishness.[69] The liberal individualism underpinning much of German feminism was too distant from her own political views, leaving her uncertain of what overarching ideal ought to motivate feminism. Focused as she was on duty and sacrifice, feminism ultimately made sense to her only as part of subordination of the self to a larger national project.[70]

In 1904 Bülow moved permanently with her sister Sophie to the picturesque Thuringian town of Dornburg an der Saale. Living in the town's castle, which belonged to a friend, she embarked on a new way of life: in relative seclusion, she wrote and visited poor townspeople's homes and helped convalescents.[71] She had finally taken up the traditional role of the rural gentlewoman. Only a few friends saw her regularly. In 1907 she had a rapprochement with Peters and at least one private meeting. Not long thereafter, however, she was hurt to learn from the newspaper of his engagement to a wealthy young woman, Thea Herbers.[72] Bülow was convinced that Peters had married for money and not for love — a final betrayal. She died of cancer in nearby Jena in 1909.

In her last years Bülow turned away from writing feminist stories with characters based on her friends Andreas-Salomé, Goudstikker, and Helene Lange, and back to her central theme of women disappointed by men and the social order in Germany. This late fiction presents feminist struggle as an inadequate response to the predicament of women. *The Daughter* (1906) and *Woman's Loyalty* (1910) concern women who achieve independence through painful disappointment at the hands of men. Feminism is depicted here as a well-meaning but ultimately unsatisfying answer to women's dilemmas. The main female character in *The Daughter*, Hilma, briefly engages in feminist activism, but soon reconsiders where she ought to direct her energies and turns to caring for her aged mother. In *Woman's Loyalty,* the feminist character Alida Studt energetically promotes the rationalization and professionalization of time-honored activities of women such as gardening and housekeeping. However, the heroine, Wilhelma, chooses to continue to perform that work in a traditional mode, and the reader is given to understand that her expertise derives from devotion and morality, not superficial training. In other novels Bülow replaced such relatively gentle criticism of feminist ambitions with unflattering, even repellent depictions, putting demands for female freedom in the mouths of selfish and tyrannical female characters.[73] In these novels, women's insistence on greater autonomy is poisonous because they already are suffering — and making others suffer — from an excess of female freedom.

Even as the radical nationalist Bülow waxed enthusiastic about men finding freedom in the colonies, she held a deep ambivalence about freedom for women. In an 1891 letter to Elly Peters she made one of her strongest statements about the danger and pain of female freedom. Elly had expressed regret that her brother Carl preferred the freedom of Africa to having a family of his own in Germany. Bülow responded: "But I believe that for men of brilliant qualities, the value of freedom well compensates them for family happiness, which would burden them with a thousand chains. Not so for us women! For *us*, I think, 'freedom' is a gift of the Danai that we find heavier to bear than beloved chains."[74] Bülow compared freedom for women to the Greeks' gift of the Trojan horse, which, once accepted into the city gates, destroyed its unsuspecting recipients. The question of freedom was the subject of a long-running debate between Andreas-Salomé and Bülow. Andreas-Salomé asserted that freedom to follow one's impulses and passions was necessary to women's sexual and emotional lives. Bülow gave a haunting negative response in her 1909 story "Free Love," in which a husband and wife decide after much rational discussion to grant each other the freedom to form friendships with others and even to pursue affairs. At the end of the story both wife and husband are isolated, and the husband reflects that "in love that has been freed . . . the soul freezes."[75] To Bülow, love was inextricable from bonds of duty, nation, and authority. Her lived experiments with radical nationalism and women's freedom uncovered more problems than answers.

THE PROBLEM OF GERMAN MEN'S VIOLENCE

In 1897, in the midst of Bülow's most feminist phase, she entered into an exchange with the gynecologist and antifeminist publicist Max Runge, who argued that men needed to be strong in order to protect naturally frail women. Bülow retorted: "Today's culture opposes brutality with all its energy and will thereby protect the female much more securely than has been accomplished by the erection of unnatural walls and barriers. What does the female have to fear from male brutality in America, for example? And even we are past the stage of the law of the club," she concluded sarcastically.[76] Comparisons between the United States and Germany that favored the former's freedoms for women were common among German feminists. Unremarked in this passage by Bülow was the role of racial hierarchy in underpinning those freedoms for white American women. In her response to Runge, written in the wake of several colonial scandals caused by the violence of German men, including Carl Peters, she presented the extremes of male brutality and female vulnerability as something uncivilized and an obstacle to German men's and women's egalitarian relations. But those scandals posed the question of whether male violence really was at odds with what colonialists embraced as progress and civilization.

The colonial scandals of the mid-1890s and after forced the German public, both male and female, to debate the extent to which "European," or "civilized," standards of behavior were applicable in the colonies. Especially controversial was violence of a sexual nature. Some of the cases of violence have already been presented. Friedrich Schröder, recall, was found guilty in 1896 of "crimes against morality, . . . unlawful detention and . . . repeated deliberate, [both] mild and dangerous bodily injury" committed at the German East African Company plantation of Lewa, which he founded in 1887 near Pangani.[77] Schröder also intruded into the harem of the Afro-Arab Abushiri bin Salim, who took revenge during the coastal war of 1888–1890 by ordering the destruction of Lewa.[78] Acting governor Heinrich Leist was found guilty in 1894 of forcing Cameroonian women into prostitution. The lightness of his initial sentence exemplified the double standard of sexual morality that led feminists in Imperial Germany to demand the abolition of state regulation of prostitution, which allowed men access to supposedly healthy prostitutes while subjecting prostituted women to demeaning physical examinations and other violations of personal freedom. Married women, in contrast, were still condemned for the slightest infidelity.[79] In 1906 Governor Jesco von Puttkamer was recalled from office after the exposure of his, and several of his civil servants', sexual practices. At least two of them, Government Councillor von Brauchitsch and Superior Court Judge Meyer, had forced young women already engaged to African men to become their concubines, terming the transaction a purchase. They insisted that their practices were commonplace — an assertion belied by the Akwa people's petition to the Reichstag in 1905 that specified that complaint among many others.[80]

Bülow knew of these cases not only through the newspapers but also through personal experience. On the basis of available sources it cannot be determined with certainty what she saw while she was in German

East Africa and Zanzibar; however, it seems impossible that she was wholly ignorant of the actions of Schröder and others. Moreover, if the scenes of German men's violence against African men and women that appear in her novels were modeled as closely on experience as many other aspects of her fiction apparently were, then she must have been privy to at least some actual scenes of her friends' violence.[81] Peters's circle in East Africa during 1887–1888 was no average group of colonists; many were men notably quick to violence. Immediately before Bülow's arrival in Zanzibar in 1887, the gratuitously violent behavior of Peters and his men had been the subject of a complaint to the German consul.[82] Baron von Gravenreuth, who was probably Bülow's closest friend among Peters's group, participated in Peters's exploits in eastern Africa (and later in Cameroon) and, like Peters, was not averse to summary executions.[83] Bülow's brother Albrecht was also no stranger to violent outbursts. Bülow herself described him as having a dangerous temperament.[84] In a letter to his family, published in the Society for German Colonization's journal, he jovially recounted his expedition experiences during his first months in Africa in 1885. Africans, he wrote, were "in actuality apes that can speak."[85] Faced with some Africans' reluctance to give directions, Albrecht von Bülow responded with immediate force: "So I took my Mauser gun and shot up the *kraal* well and proper."[86] After that, he noted with satisfaction, the locals fed and sheltered him attentively. Emil von Zelewski, another early employee of the German East African Company, was held hostage in August 1888 by angry residents of Pangani because of his acts of cruelty. It was one of the first events of the East African coastal war of 1888–1890.[87] Bülow defended him in a letter to Elly Peters.[88] While colonizers, especially early explorers, were hardly known for their gentle ways, the tactics and behavior of Carl Peters and others in the German East African Company disturbed even other colonialists.[89]

For the German public, these cases of colonial violence, especially sexual violence, raised the question of whether the perpetrators were individual sadists or normal people acting in justified, even necessary ways. The accused and an array of metropolitan defenders claimed that the latter was the case. Leist, for example, deflected sole responsibility for his actions in two typical ways: first, he claimed that sexual violence (specifically, coerced prostitution) was normal in Africa; and, second, he emphasized that he was far from the only German colonial official to participate in it. Leist cited as an example his own superior, Governor Eugen von Zimmerer, who, Leist claimed, had watched with pleasure and interest as one "well-known explorer" whipped an African woman accused of sexual infidelity. Zimmerer even recorded the scene in a sketch and gave it the title "Love in Africa."[90]

Carl Peters, who was at the center of the most prominent colonial scandal concerning sexual violence, also defended himself with arguments that sexual exploitation was the norm in Africa.[91] In 1890 Peters had returned to Germany from his well-publicized Emin Pasha expedition hoping to receive an appointment as the first governor of East Africa. However, the director of the new Colonial Department of the Foreign Office, Paul Kayser, had no intention of entrusting him with such a delicate position. Instead, he appointed Peters imperial commissar and stationed him at Marangu, a remote post near Mount Kilimanjaro, in 1891. Peters was quietly recalled from that post in 1893. Once more in Germany, he attempted to use his colonialist prestige as a springboard for a more generally radical nationalist political career. He placed himself at the head of yet another radical nationalist movement, this one with a mass appeal far greater than the Pan-German League's: the agitation for a German navy to rival Britain's. He maneuvered the Berlin chapter of the German Colonial Society into a schism along radical nationalist lines and ran as a National Liberal for a Reichstag seat. His election campaign was unsuccessful, but his opponents on the left, the Social Democrats August Bebel and Georg von Vollmar, took no chances and began to air lurid details of Peters's tenure as imperial commissar at Marangu during Reichstag sessions.

Among other things, Reichstag members learned that in 1892 Peters had ordered the execution of an African man named Mabruk who worked at the Marangu station. Mabruk's crime, Peters recorded, was breaking and entering. In 1893 Peters ordered the execution of Jagodjo, an African woman at Marangu, for treason. Bebel and Vollmar revealed further details. They claimed that Jagodjo and other women at the station had been forced to serve as Peters's concubines, and that Mabruk had been executed because he had dared to have sexual relations with Jagodjo. Jagodjo then tried to escape, but was held prisoner at the station. When she did manage to escape, a village headman returned her to

Marangu, and Peters ordered her to be whipped, under his observation, over several days. She survived and managed to escape once more, but Peters recaptured her and then ordered her execution. The Colonial Department decided to hold a trial in order to try to halt the Reichstag accusations.

Peters never denied ordering the executions. Rather, he argued that such drastic punishments were warranted because of the precarious security of Marangu station, which adjoined the lands of an African community hostile to German rule. Mabruk was stealing supplies, Peters claimed, and Jagodjo was a spy. Outside the courtroom and especially when drunk, however, Peters said much more. He told associates that Jagodjo was his concubine, and indeed that according to "African marriage custom" she was actually his wife.[92] He also told people that Mabruk had indeed slept with her, and that he, Peters, refused to be *Lochbruder* (literally, "hole-fellow") with an African man and therefore had executed the two.[93]

Peters was found guilty (the specific offense was the submission of false reports) and dismissed from colonial service, whereupon he moved to London. He viewed his trial as an example of the treachery of bureaucrats and the hypocrisy of the German public, who wanted colonies but refused to give true colonizers the necessary free rein. Like Leist, von Brauchitsch, and Meyer, Peters argued that he had merely participated, indeed had to participate, in the normal African sexual order. The falsity of their claims about African sexual norms need not detain us; African men and women's protests against German men's treatment of African women give the lie to such claims. In effect, Leist and Peters were expressing the radical nationalist notion that Germany and the colonies were fundamentally different moral realms and that it was impossible and disastrous to apply "German" standards of procedure, morality, and mercy in Africa. Yet radical nationalists' sharp distinction between metropolitan space and colonial space was not sufficient to reassure Germans, even colonialists, about the scandals.

Peters's critics, who included not only declared opponents of colonialism but also missionaries and some colonialists, argued that he had displayed weakness, not strength, in keeping order at his station with executions. In their view, he allowed sexual and sadistic motives to affect how he ran his station and how he conducted relations with nearby

African leaders. They argued that brutal behavior was un-German and undercut the German civilizing mission in Africa. While Peters's supporters depicted the two executed Africans as immoral and as threats to military security, Bebel described them in the Reichstag almost as noble savages engaged in an innocent romance that Peters cruelly smashed out of brutish jealousy.[94] The scandals publicized the uncomfortable fact that German colonial rule rested not only on superior firepower, economic domination, and strategic diplomacy, but also on the sexual coercion of African women. Peters's "reason of state" — protecting the military security of his station — had become entangled with officially acceptable rape. And even those colonialist Germans who accepted sexual coercion as a tool of political rule faced the troubling implication of defenses such as Leist's and Peters's that Germans, far from bringing civilized mores to primitive Africa, were themselves exhibiting brutality.

Would they bring that brutality back to Germany? A 1904 cartoon in the satirical journal *Simplicissimus* posed that question. Entitled "The Power of Habit," it depicts a German male colonist or soldier caressing his African mistress under a palm tree. In the next frames, he is back in Germany with his German wife. Watching his wife apply blacking to the kitchen stove, he is struck by an idea. He seizes her brush and covers her with the blacking instead. In the final frame, the cartoon takes an even more startling turn: he is shown lashing his wife with a long whip. The man thereby displays two simultaneous desires: to make his white wife black and to take pleasure in beating her. To its contemporary viewers, the cartoon raised the question of whether German men were spreading German civilization in the colonies or returning to Germany having themselves been changed. Or perhaps this husband was expressing something already in him that his colonial experience had merely served to uncover? The cartoon depicts the women in geographically separate spaces. German men may have taken for granted the possibility of moving between those two spaces, but what did it mean to German women that German men could live in both spaces? What would happen if African and German women were to occupy the same social and moral space? These were important questions for colonialists. For others, perhaps the biggest question was why Germans and other Europeans so readily appropriated African women as figures in scenes of sexual sadism.

The questions raised by the behavior of Leist and Peters and other

Die Macht der Gewohnheit

Figure 1. "The Power of Habit." From *Simplicissimus,* 1904. This photograph taken from Jürgen Petschull and Thomas Höpker, *Der Wahn vom Weltreich: Die Geschichte der deutschen Kolonien* (Hamburg: Stern-Buch / Gruner & Jahr, 1984), 122.

colonial sexual scandals were troubling in the extreme to German colonialist women. But while most reacted with silence or indirect formulations, Bülow again was exceptional, for she did address these questions, in novels such as *Tropical Rage* as well as in nonfiction. Bülow was torn over Peters's actions. On the one hand, she was committed to the radical nationalist vision of the colonies as a space different from Germany. She admired Peters's talents as a conqueror and despised his critics as hypocrites who were happy to benefit from Peters's achievements but refused to accept what was necessary to achieve them, and she defended Peters privately and publicly.[95] To Peters, she wrote in 1897: "You know that I am not stupid, and that I know you too well to idealize you. I know you can be brutal, and I certainly don't love brutality. But I also know that this brutality is almost inseparable from certain qualities that are rare and of the highest value, and that it is necessary in some situations."[96] Bülow's colonialist convictions were in tension with her views about progress and the attenuation of male brutality. The resolution, for her, was a racial division between German or white women, on the one hand, and African women, on the other. Through racial hierarchy she organized in her own mind the problem of German men's—even or especially colonial heroes'—violence toward women.[97]

Although she was troubled by Peters's violence, she was also drawn to it. For her, violence organized not only the racial difference between German and colonized women, but also the erotic relationship between German men and German women. Her portrayals of violent men are sometimes critical, sometimes ambivalent, and sometimes outright admiring.[98] Both Bülow's fiction and contemporaries' recollections of Peters suggest that violence gave him pleasure.[99] How was a German woman who valued her own freedom and power to make herself the object of such a man's desire? At certain points in her life, Bülow seems to have decided that it was worth it to place herself at his mercy. She remained emotionally dependent on him, at least at intervals, for the rest of her life.[100] Even after the end of their love affair Bülow apparently liked to imagine herself at his mercy. In 1893, while Peters was still at Marangu, Bülow wrote to Elly Peters that his "qualities of character permit one to hope and to fear so *much*! In the case of most men, *both* are much more limited, and therefore much less exciting."[101]

Bülow's friend Lou Andreas-Salomé interpreted Bülow's behavior as a form of masochism. In her 1921 novel *The House,* Andreas-Salomé created portraits of Bülow and herself in the characters Renate and Anneliese. In one scene Renate tells Anneliese that she, Renate, has seen "him" again. Anneliese regrets the renewal of Renate's affair, thinking to herself that the object of Renate's obsession is "in his soul a sort of racehorse–stable boy, familiar only with the whip." But Renate speaks effusively of "this delirious appeal of subordination!" When Anneliese expresses sympathy over how he has made Renate suffer, Renate responds: "I've suffered, you said a moment ago. No, Liese: enjoyed — that is far truer. Because even to be trod upon: if we love the one who does it, then we wanted it from him. He only seems to be the subjugating master, but in truth [he is] our tool, — passion's servant — who knows!"[102] Andreas-Salomé was in all likelihood drawing on one of their many exchanges about Bülow's relationship to Peters and the nature of erotic obsession. Her vignette suggests Bülow's emotional masochism in the years after the affair, and also her fantasy of some kind of control over her tormentor and lover.

In practice, Bülow was not masochistic enough to subordinate herself to anyone for long, even Peters. And once she had decided that Peters was not worthy of being her master, then no man was. She preferred to ponder German men's violence and German women's subordination in retrospect, from a position of independence and peace. As she wrote to her friend, the writer Toni Schwabe: "To overcome passion appears to me more beautiful than the passion itself — which, however, if one is to be able to speak of overcoming, must be as strong as possible in the first place. . . . In place of desire there comes to be understanding. . . . This is the most profound experience of *my* life and underlies in one way or the other each of my books."[103] The predicament of a strong-willed woman could be resolved only in solitude, after great suffering.

Bülow wrestled with issues of lasting difficulty for feminists and other women in Imperial Germany: careers, freedom, sexuality, and violence. She differed from other colonialist women not so much in her opinions on race and feminism as in her unusually frank treatment in her fiction of sexuality and violence and her public defense of Peters. Colonialist women in later years almost always refused to examine German men's sexual attraction for African women or the erotics of violence.[104] Those who wrote in Bülow's genre, the colonial novel, depicted violence in a clumsily self-righteous manner that attempted to close off moral ambiguity.[105] In fact, colonialist women, as activists and authors, sought to bury the issues Bülow had raised as deeply as possible. Bülow's discussion of German men's sexuality and violence raises another issue, however: the extent to which colonialist men were themselves disunited on the question of sexual morality in the colonies. Since men controlled the colonialist movement, including German women's place in it, the struggles among German men over race and male morality helped shape colonialist women's activism in the years after Bülow's debut on the colonial stage. These struggles are the subject of the next chapter.

CHAPTER THREE

A New Colonial Masculinity:
The Men's Debate over
"Race Mixing" in the Colonies

C ontemporaries and historians alike have observed that as more white women settled in colonies, racial separation and hierarchy became more marked.[1] Many white women in modern colonial empires did oppose sexual relations between white men and women who were colonial subjects; however, white women's opinions had never yet determined colonial policy, and there is no reason to assume that they did in this respect either. In the German case, colonialist women gained a hearing only in the course of a debate among male colonialists and colonists over "race mixing" (*Rassenmischung*).[2] This debate offered women a new opportunity for colonialist activism. Between the mid-1890s and the First World War, male colonists and colonialists came to see a tension between colonial racial hierarchy and their masculine sexual prerogatives over African and Pacific Islander women. These men were not necessarily feminist, but they did envision marriage as a partnership in terms of companionship, culture — and race. Although male colonists had once expressed patriarchal and racial dominance through their unions with local women, now those unions seemed to challenge the institution of racial hierarchy (if companionate marriage was chosen) or the institution of companionate marriage (if racial hierarchy was emphasized). At the same time, men resisted legal measures limiting their sexual and marital choices. As they struggled to balance sexual rights of autonomy with what they called "race purity" (*Rassenreinheit*), German men came to agree that white German women were the solution. If more white women lived in the colonies, race mixing would disappear of its own accord without any troubling restrictions on men's rights. The men's debate thereby helped colonialist women claim a new importance in matters of colonial sexuality and race.

The men's debate focused on the legal manifestations of race mixing:

marriage between Germans and colonial subjects, adoption, and paternal legitimization of children born outside marriage.[3] These legal statuses defined kinship, citizenship, and property. The vehemence of the debate was not due to the number of such marriages alone, for these were few.[4] Nor was it due to the much higher number of German men cohabiting with female colonial subjects outside marriage. There was relatively little debate about race mixing in Togo, for example, in spite of one missionary's calculation that there was practically one mixed-blood child for every European man — including missionaries — in the colony.[5] Rather, the vehemence of the debate over race mixing was due to the fundamentality of propertied male citizens' rights. The debate was most intense in the three colonies with the most German settlement and the most politicized colonists: German Southwest Africa, German East Africa, and German Samoa. In all three, male colonists campaigned for increased political rights while settlement simultaneously put pressure on colonial subjects' land and labor and destabilized earlier patterns of negotiation and accommodation between colonizer and colonized. Although other conditions varied — after all, the peoples in those three colonies shared nothing more than their confrontation with German colonial power — the debate over race mixing and male colonists' rights took broadly similar forms in all three and revealed a conflict between two models of masculinity: "imperial patriarchy" and "liberal nationalism."

The residency of the "imperial patriarchs" in the German colonies often dated from precolonial and early colonial years. They acquired their land, cattle, or trading connections before such wealth became scarce and regulated, often through marriage to women from locally prominent indigenous families.[6] These German men usually spoke a local lingua franca, such as English, Pidgin, Swahili, or Afrikaans (Cape Dutch), and they applied local agricultural or commercial methods. Their masculine authority rested on wealth in land and livestock, military valor, and skill at manipulating colonial social networks. They saw relations between colonizer and colonized in terms of negotiation and unequal integration into a German-dominated political structure. The imperial patriarchs prized their sense of a personal autonomy that was limited only by their own strength and skill. They had created a way of life that would have been impossible to duplicate in Germany.

In colonial surroundings, the European idea of patriarchal authority over an extended household of social inferiors came to include authority over racial inferiors.[7] Max Buchner, who served as Germany's first representative in Cameroon after annexation in 1884, exemplified the imperial patriarchal view of Africans in an 1887 book. Buchner invoked, in a tone of noblesse oblige, the "human dignity of the Negro, which I will always defend." But he insisted that "the Negro" did not possess "full legal maturity in the European sense." Such immaturity was not a matter of "the lasting inferiority of his entire race," he said, but rather "that immaturity which marks the lower strata of our own people, and which likewise makes them as demanding as they are useless when under the influence of the calamitous apostles of equality."[8] He compared African colonial subjects to Germany's working classes and implicitly compared German colonists to the ruling classes at home. Political hierarchy was at least as important, on this view, as a biologically imagined racial difference.

For imperial patriarchs, political authority over Africans in general was entirely congruent with sexual relationships with African women in particular. Buchner illustrated this in another passage of his book, in which he recommended concubinage:

> As for free social intercourse with the daughters of the country, it is to be seen as more helpful than harmful to health. The eternal feminine, also under dark skin, is an excellent charm against low spirits, to which one is so vulnerable in the solitude of Africa. Apart from these values for the soul, there are also practical advantages of personal safety. Having an intimate black girlfriend protects one from various dangers. One can debate the morality of such relationships. But what the pious missionaries so often claim, namely that their female lambs are exposed to the pursuit of immoral company employees who use devilish arts of seduction, is usually the other way around.[9]

Buchner saw taking an African mistress as a German man's personal decision and denied any need to answer for it to missionaries or other critics. He clearly saw no conflict between German rule and German men's sexual access to Cameroonian women. For imperial patriarchs, racial hierarchy did not require racial purity; sexual relationships with colonized women, far from damaging German authority, expressed that authority.

Some German men experienced the colonies as a more naturally patriarchal order than Germany. The tropical doctor Albert Plehn praised the helpfulness and obedience of African women, who became "indispensable as willing servants" of German men.[10] German women, by contrast, could be spoiled and demanding. According to the geographer Karl Dove, who visited German Southwest Africa in 1892 and 1893, the only sort of German woman needed there was the obedient housewife; the exigencies of colonial life required women to fulfill that supposedly natural role first and foremost. "I recommend a study visit in Southwest Africa to all those who defend the equal treatment of women in every area of life," he declared confidently; an "emancipated personality" was out of place there.[11] Dove was less voluble than Buchner with regard to sexual opportunities with African women, confining himself to a few appreciative remarks about Rehobother Baster women, Christians of mixed Boer and Nama descent whose forebears had migrated from the Northern Cape.[12]

More than a few male colonists saw sexual access to local women, including by force, as their prerogative.[13] The most extreme exemplars of this aspect of imperial patriarchy were Carl Peters, Heinrich Leist, and others involved in the colonial scandals of the 1890s. Peters and Leist did not think that they contaminated themselves or damaged white prestige when they raped African women or entered into concubinage with them. When Peters and Leist found themselves on trial for allowing their passions to interfere with their political judgment and endanger other Germans' security, they defended themselves in true imperial patriarch style: refusing to be subjected to what they saw as superficial morality, they insisted that matters of sex and corporal punishment be left to the judgment of the experienced man in the colonies rather than imposed from distant Germany. The scandals juxtaposed their arrogation of personal power with the limits on personal behavior that German laws imposed, and helped turn public opinion against the imperial patriarch model of masculinity.

The "liberal nationalists" challenged the imperial patriarchs' insistence on that kind of personal autonomy. Colonists who took the liberal nationalist position had generally arrived too late for the military glory and land grabs of the early years. Their hopes for land and a compliant, cheap labor force depended on state-ordered expropriation of colonial subjects, not on political alliances and intermarriage with them. They argued for the proletarianization of colonial subjects and greater upward mobility and equality for deserving German colonists. In their view, sex was not a man's private decision, but a social marker of status.[14] Sexual relations between German men and African women were no longer mere sex, but rather "race mixing," a threat on the scale of Buchner's feared doctrines of political equality. The liberal nationalists included self-described left-liberals and progressives. While the center-right National Liberals had long supported colonial empire, many left-liberals became enthusiastic only in the years between 1904, when the German Southwest African and German East African wars began, and the First World War. They seized the opportunity of postwar colonial reform under the new, left-liberal colonial secretary, Bernhard Dernburg, to install their model of a more uniform, formally egalitarian membership in an idealized German community overseas.

Germany itself was an empire in which peoples of diverse traditions and statuses were united only at the highest levels. Its various federal states retained such prerogatives as royal houses, some military powers, and citizenship.[15] While conservative advocates of this imperial arrangement did not find the diversity of traditions and statuses among Imperial Germany's subjects problematic, liberal nationalists did. They sought a more unified German identity and citizenship status, and they valued institutions and territories that superseded the traditions of the federated states: the navy, the Reichsland Alsace-Lorraine (annexed from France in 1871), and the colonial empire. Such spaces were mirrors for a more uniform German identity in which the particularism that German nationalists had so opposed throughout the nineteenth century might be left behind.[16]

Both metropolitan left-liberals and colonists embraced the characteristically liberal language of self-administration as they struggled against the metropolitan state and the imperial patriarchs, respectively.[17] In fact, however, the colonists' goal of increased political participation ran counter to metropolitan liberals' efforts to strengthen the Reichstag. The Reichstag, elected by universal, equal male suffrage, was the most democratic institution of unified Germany. The extent to which the emperor was to share authority over the colonies with the Reichstag and Federal Council (Bundesrat, or upper house) was one of the most basic questions of colonial law.[18] In 1892 the Reichstag gained an important right:

the power to review colonial budgets. Each year, anticolonial delegates such as the leader of the left-liberal Progressive Party (Freisinnige Partei), Eugen Richter, and the Social Democrat August Bebel sought to strengthen the Reichstag's say in colonial affairs by staging lengthy debates in which they questioned various subsidies. In order to avoid their criticism, the colonial administration governed by decree (*Verordnung*) whenever possible rather than by law (*Gesetz*). The promulgation of laws required Reichstag approval and hence opened up more possibilities for plenary debate.[19] This reliance on decrees irritated the left-liberals. Colonists, for their part, resented the Reichstag's opposition to colonial subsidies and scorned the delegates' unfamiliarity with the colonies. The colonies sent no delegates, and colonists could not vote in Reichstag elections. The colonial administration was no better as far as colonists' political participation was concerned; they complained about the Colonial Department's tendency to govern from behind closed doors.[20] The colonists' quest for greater self-administration meant eluding the control of the Reichstag — which, of course, conflicted with the metropolitan left-liberals' drive for parliamentarization.

Colonial self-administration also meant defining who was eligible to exercise political rights, in anticipation of the augmentation of those rights. Liberal nationalists tried to force persons into sharply demarcated groups of rulers and ruled. They claimed to be preserving supposedly natural racial differences, but in fact they intervened in political and personal relationships on an unprecedented scale. Women and men of African or Pacific Islander descent found themselves detached from their locally recognized sexual, familial, or political ties to German imperial patriarchs. Liberal nationalism's impact on colonial societies was therefore at once equalizing for some and racializing for all. Liberalism served to create new categories of rights-holders but also new ways to organize exclusion from those rights.[21] Both the patriarchal and liberal models were racist, and both entailed male domination, but racism and sexuality interacted in distinct ways in each model.

Colonial officials sympathetic to these ideas even banned marriage between German citizens and colonial subjects in German Southwest Africa (1905), German East Africa (1906), and German Samoa (1912).[22] These bans were unique in all the European colonial empires of the day, although similar to bans on "miscegenation" in the United States.[23] If the bans were unique, however, the wider context of intervention into patterns of colonial sexuality was not. The existing literature suggests that Germany's interest in intervening in sexual and familial relations between colonizers and colonized came about slightly earlier than or at the same time as that in other colonial empires.[24] Given widespread European interest in curbing or monitoring interracial sexuality, it is then necessary to ask which political and organizational factors led to formal measures in the German case, and what the sources of support and resistance to these measures were. The bans on "racial mixed marriage" (*Rassenmischehe*) were legally questionable because they assumed the validity of race as a legal concept in German citizenship law, while in fact neither the 1870 citizenship law nor its modified 1913 version made use of a concept of race. (No Reich-wide German laws did so until the Law for the Restoration of the Professional Civil Service [Gesetz zur Wiederherstellung des Berufsbeamtentums] in April 1933.) While the child of a white German and a colonial subject was often termed a "mixed-blood" (*Mischling*), the term had no legal meaning because citizenship could not be mixed.[25] Moreover, the form of the bans was controversial: they were administrative decrees issued by either a colonial governor or the colonial secretary, not laws that had received the approval of the Reichstag.

The following three sections examine conditions in each of the three colonies where bans on intermarriage were decreed. In spite of considerable differences, there were struggles in all three between local colonial political authority and the metropolitan authority of the colonial administration and Reichstag. The greatest controversy concerned not whether intermarriage was objectionable, for soon almost all German participants were at pains to insist that it was, but rather the bans' intrusion into German men's rights to marry and to father children as they wished. The colonial bans never found full legal acceptance and were at no point valid inside Germany. The obstacle to their acceptance was the difficult legal question of how German male citizens could have one set of rights in metropolitan space and other—indeed, lesser— rights in colonial space. Metropolitan conditions therefore affected the colonial politics of race mixing. Yet colonial conditions also affected metropolitan politics, albeit in a more diffuse way that was not captured in legal measures in the era of formal empire. Once the issue of racial difference was raised, it was not easily laid to rest. If race mixing was accepted as problematic in one locale, then it was hard to argue that it was irrelevant in another. Race purity advocates' emphasis on supposed underlying, inescapable, natural racial truths militated against such flexibility. By 1914 the colonial administration accepted the principle that race mixing was a problem in the entire colonial empire. The racial order of colonial space was not legally imposed on the metropole in the era of formal empire, but the question of whether or not the same racial order ought to pertain in both did arise. Thus did colonial politics affect the metropole.

GERMAN SOUTHWEST AFRICA

The first ban on intermarriage took place in German Southwest Africa. Yet colonialists and colonists had not always criticized intermarriage there. The missionary Carl Büttner, who knew precolonial Namibia from his time there as a Rhenish missionary in the 1870s and his assistance to Imperial Commissioner Heinrich Goering in treaty-making in 1885, strongly advocated intermarriage. Writing from Berlin in mid-1887, several months after he had accepted a new post as mission inspector for the Evangelical Missionary Society for German East Africa (see chapter 1), Büttner listed the advantages of intermarriage between German men and African women for the Foreign Office. As Germans' in-laws, Africans would "feel secure and happy as genuine subjects and denizens of the German Empire."[26] The children of such marriages would be good workers (*tüchtig*), consider themselves white, use the German language, and consume German-made products.[27] Büttner argued that intermarriage would aid German rule by strengthening the ties between colonizer and colonized.

Büttner waxed enthusiastic as he recounted the family history of the Rhenish missionary Heinrich Schmelen, who, "to no little horror of his acquaintances," married a "Hottentot" (i.e., Nama) woman named Anna.[28] Anna Schmelen helped her husband to alphabetize the Nama language. The Schmelens had a daughter who married another Rhenish missionary, Franz Heinrich Kleinschmidt, founder of the mission station at Rehoboth. Frau Kleinschmidt was "*highly respected* by whites and natives . . . her household could be a *model* for all the whites living in

Damaraland [central Namibia]."[29] The Kleinschmidts had four daughters, each of whom also married Rhenish missionaries, and three sons, two of whom were traders in the colony; the third was a teacher in the German federal state of Westphalia.[30] Büttner summed up: "In short, this entire family, descended from a mixed marriage, has had an *important* role in the development of this land and one can only wish that there be more like it."[31]

Büttner wanted the state to support intermarriage in order to protect Christian African women and their families from sexual and material exploitation by German men. He explained that long-term cohabitation was common, and that the women's families viewed it as marriage. Furthermore, the male colonists gained "considerable advantages in their business through the support of their wives' relatives."[32] But too often, Büttner complained, the white man left the colony after acquiring a fortune and abandoned his wife and children.[33] Such exploitative concubinage threatened political relations between Germans and Africans, Büttner pointed out, because the German men tended to choose their companions from the "most refined and educated colored families."[34] African leaders who had treated with Büttner in 1885 expressed their hope that German rule would help regularize such relationships.[35] Marriage would give these women and children rights in case of desertion. Büttner sought, and soon received, a specific practical remedy from the Foreign Office: special authorization for missionaries to perform civil as well as religious marriages.[36] Missionaries were likelier than civil servants to reach couples living in remote areas who had not formalized their unions.

Over the next twenty-five years, colonists in German Southwest Africa and colonialists in Germany rejected every point Büttner had raised in favor of intermarriage. They deemed intermarriage a danger to German rule and claimed that children of mixed parentage were inferior both to white Germans and to Africans. Marriage between "whites" and "natives and Rehobothers" was banned in the colony in 1905. In 1907 the colony's superior court pronounced a principle known in the United States as the "one-drop rule": the discovery of any African descent whatever rendered a person a "native," regardless of the person's existing legal citizenship.[37] In 1909 a charter granted local self-administration to colonists but denied the new municipal suffrage to men living with or married to women of African descent. In 1913 the one-drop rule was applied to two of the Schmelens' progeny: their great-grandson Ludwig Baumann and great-granddaughter Mathilde Kleinschmidt, who found themselves legally recategorized as "natives" when they attempted to bring a court case and to marry, respectively.[38] By 1914 German Southwest Africa had become highly stratified by race. Who began this process of reversal, and why?

The earliest criticisms of intermarriage came from colonial military commanders who invoked the anticipated rights of army veterans (land grants and political rights) as well as class-specific sexual norms. Curt von François, Heinrich Goering's successor as chief administrator of the colony, announced to his soldiers in October 1892 that anyone who married or lived with a native woman would lose his veteran's right to a free homestead.[39] Another commanding officer, Ludwig von Estorff, complained a few years later that local women "encouraged [the soldiers] to waste their pay and lead a dissolute life. The number of crimes against manly discipline was high."[40] Estorff's solution was to evacuate his men to another region and keep them hard at work building roads. Officers with the social status of Estorff and François — aristocratic or upper-bourgeois Germans with military or academic backgrounds — were the most likely to bring white German wives with them to the colony. The enlisted soldiers under their command, by contrast, were the most likely to intermarry with local women.[41] Indeed, a number of François's men ignored his order and married Rehobother women (and none had to forfeit his homestead in the end).[42] The soldiers were mostly working class; in Germany they would have remained, as Dove put it, "little-esteemed members of society."[43] Class antagonism persisted even when some of these soldiers became successful farmers. Dove explained that from the veterans' point of view, "as whites, here they and their superiors were, up to a certain point, of equal birth; here they were lords . . . solely on the basis of their color."[44] In other words, the veterans insisted on social recognition from Germans who would have been their social superiors back in Germany. Aristocratic or upper-bourgeois Germans did not necessarily agree.

Büttner's successors in the Rhenish Missionary Society opposed François's attempt to ban intermarriage and continued to worry about the soldiers' exploitation and abandonment of women and children. A fresh influx of four hundred German soldiers in 1896 moved the missionaries to appeal to the colonial administration for clarification of German men's right to marry local women.[45] The Colonial Department and the new head of the colony, Theodor Leutwein, assured the missionaries that the right to marry was secure; François's ban could not be legally enforced because it was in contradiction with Reich civil law. At the same time, however, Leutwein referred to intermarriage as a "necessary evil" preferable only to nonmarital cohabitation, and he fretted over the extent to which the children of such marriages were to be treated as "whites."[46] Leutwein still pursued an imperial, as opposed to nationalist, policy of integrating various African groups on unequal terms into the German ruling apparatus. He also still perceived important social distinctions within each status group of Africans and Germans, referring to the refinement of some Rehobother families and the wide range of respectability among the German soldiers.[47] Within a few years, however, Leutwein no longer bothered to distinguish among intermarried couples, at least for the metropolitan public; all intermarriage, he claimed, had ill effects.[48]

Conscription, instituted for German male colonists in 1896, brought these early disagreements about intermarriage to a head because it raised the question of who was to be drafted for which kind of service.[49] When Henning von Burgsdorff, the officer in charge of training the African conscripts, attempted to draft sons of German men and their Reho bother wives, the young men protested that they were German citizens.[50] Burgsdorff and Leutwein insisted that these sons were not Germans, but rather Rehobothers like their mothers; their parents' marriage ceremonies had been performed by missionaries and so had only religious, but not civil, validity.[51] According to German citizenship law, a man's wife and legitimate children acquired his citizenship, and illegitimate children acquired the mother's citizenship — in this case, the status of colonial subjects.[52] But some of those marriages had been performed by missionaries whom the Foreign Office had specially authorized at Büttner's request. The Colonial Department therefore instructed Leutwein that the sons in question were German citizens.[53]

Leutwein had to yield in those cases, but he still believed that he should be the final arbiter of the validity of German-African and, for that matter, German-Boer marriages.[54] He systematically misinformed colonial army veterans by telling them that marriage between German men and African women was illegal.[55] The Colonial Department learned of Leutwein's tactic in 1899 and instructed him curtly that even if the civil validity of the early religious marriages might be questioned, civil marriage was available at all times to any German man. A German man had the legal right to marry any woman he pleased; only the usual restrictions of, for example, age, close kinship, or mental incapacity applied.[56] Citizenship status (a status recognized in law) and race (a status not recognized in law) were not among these restrictions. A tedious legal debate ensued, the essence of which was that German law neither confirmed nor denied the legality of marriage between German citizens and those with the citizenship status of "natives."[57] "Citizen" and "native" (*Eingeborene/r*) were two distinct citizenship statuses governed by distinct systems of law: "German law" and "native law." The new field of "colonial law" concerned itself with the relation between the two.[58] The juristic gap regarding intermarriage could be resolved only by a new, positive law promulgated at the Reich level. After 1900, when a new colonial code applied the 1870 citizenship law to colonial subjects "only to the extent decided by imperial decree," fresh uncertainty emerged because the decree mentioned in that law was never issued.[59] The Colonial Department was internally divided on the issue and postponed taking an official position for as long as possible.[60] To those who argued that civil marriage could not be denied to German men on the grounds of the prospective wife's citizenship status or race, the status of the woman was irrelevant. To those who argued that intermarriage was not legally permissible because the law did not expressly apply to the "native" partner, her status could not be overlooked.

The conflict over German soldiers' marriages to Rehobother and other African women came to the attention of colonialists in Germany almost immediately. In 1896 the German Colonial Society held a meeting at which they discussed the phenomenon of colonial army veterans' intermarriage.[61] The speakers did not differentiate among the various communities from which veterans drew their partners; they saw any kind of creolization as disastrous for the German Colonial Society's self-consciously nationalist project of investing in settlement there.[62] One member proposed sending marriageable white German women to the colony as an antidote to intermarriage. The German Colonial Society made the idea the basis for a new project. It allocated money for selected unmarried women's free ship passage to German Southwest Africa, where they would work as domestic servants for colonist families until bachelor colonists married them. Women in Germany who were already engaged or married to German colonists were also to receive free passage. The first women who traveled to the colony under the German Colonial Society's auspices were two fiancées, in 1897. In 1898 the society sponsored twelve domestic servants. By 1907 it had given free passage to 111 unmarried German women.[63]

The notion that increasing the number of white German women in German Southwest Africa would reduce the number of German male colonists who intermarried or cohabited with African women became an article of faith for the rest of the German colonial era.[64] That notion was nevertheless false. Although white women were indeed scarce in the colony, German men generally did not substitute the more numerous African and mixed-descent women for scarce white German women.[65] Rather, a pattern had become established in which marriages between men and women of equal social status coexisted with men's marriages and cohabitation with women who were their inferiors in class and racial status. German and other European or white men made distinctions among themselves based on the sexual partnerships they maintained.[66] The women were not interchangeable; male colonists either did without white women, did without women of color, or engaged in marital and sexual relations with both. As the maverick colonialist economist Moritz J. Bonn put it when discussing the high numbers of mixed-descent children born outside marriage, "the main cause of bastardization in Africa was not the absence of white women but the presence of black ones."[67]

German male colonists who did try to substitute African wives for German ones, such as the upwardly mobile colonist Wilhelm Panzlaff, encountered lasting opposition from settler society. Panzlaff arrived as a soldier in German Southwest Africa in 1891. After his discharge from the colonial army he planned to bring his fiancée from Germany to join him in the colony, but she absconded with the money he sent her and married someone else. Lacking the money to travel to Germany and find another bride, Panzlaff instead married Magdalena van Wyk, who belonged to the respected Diergaard family of Rehoboth. A missionary performed their wedding ceremony in 1894.[68] Panzlaff was one of the first to notice Governor Leutwein's reluctance to recognize German men's marriages to Rehobother women. He inquired in 1898 about the status of his marriage, which had meanwhile produced two children, but received no clear answer.[69] Panzlaff became even more determined to confirm his own marriage when a fellow veteran, a trader named Johr, died in 1899 and the colony's court awarded the estate to relatives in Germany instead of to Johr's Rehobother wife.[70] He ceased his attempts to clarify the tangled legal question of whether his original 1894 wedding had civil validity and decided to remarry his wife in a civil ceremony and legitimize his children. By 1899, however, Leutwein opposed intermarriage so stubbornly that no civil servant in the colony would agree to perform the ceremony. Finally the Colonial Department ordered Leutwein to permit the ceremony, and the Panzlaffs were remarried.[71]

Most German men in mixed marriages lived near Rehoboth or on isolated ranches in the south of the colony. Panzlaff was apparently the only German man legally married to an African-descended woman who lived in Windhuk, the colony's capital and the district with the densest German settlement.[72] He and his wife moved in German circles, and his children attended the same school as other German colonists' children. Panzlaff and his family faced a long series of local measures against people in mixed marriages and against mixed-descent children. The Colonial Department in Berlin responded to his petitions with repeated assurances that his children were German citizens. Panzlaff and a few other colonial army veterans in mixed marriages were exceptional for their degree of success in preventing their exclusion from the full rights and status of successful German male colonists.[73] In contrast to several unsuccessful petitioners, these men could boast of prosperity and spotless morality. Panzlaff's own social ascent was remarkable: a housepainter in 1894, he owned his own farm by 1912.[74] However, Panzlaff and his family were unable to force other colonists to treat them as Germans with full rights. The Panzlaff children were educated in Germany, but when they visited their increasingly segregated home they were treated as colonial subjects in public accommodations and faced new legal insecurity with each new race purity measure. When Panzlaff petitioned the Colonial Office about these matters in 1913, the Colonial Office refused to uphold his children's right to be treated as the social equals of white Germans. The Colonial Office was willing to protect white German men and their patriarchal rights, as it had in 1899 when it ordered Leutwein to allow Panzlaff's marriage, but it refused to come to the aid of "colored Germans"—men and women who had both legal German citizenship and known African ancestry.[75]

One of Panzlaff's opponents was Hans Tecklenburg, an official in Governor Leutwein's office who ushered in the next phase of the debate. Tecklenburg fumed about the Panzlaffs' marriage: "Now Panzlaff's Hottentot wench struts about at the veterans' and marksmen's club gatherings, next to our German women."[76] He admitted that "she still does not find much of a reception there," but he wanted to make sure that no other German wife of color joined her.[77] Tecklenburg was one of the first colonial officials to describe intermarriage and concubinage not as mere sex or as a lapse in discipline but as race mixing: a social phenomenon with dire economic, cultural, and biological consequences for all Germans. Tecklenburg argued that the colonial administration's current approach of keeping informal lists of children of mixed parentage was inadequate because it merely recorded what he saw as racial contamination rather than preventing it.[78] In 1903 he drafted a decree that would place all people of mixed descent in the legal category "natives," regardless of whether or not they were legitimate children of German men. If German men wished to avoid that outcome, they had to act before marriage: they were to apply to the governor for certification that their brides might hold status equal to whites. Minimum conditions for such certification were three quarters "nonnative" blood and an appropriate upbringing.[79] Tecklenburg thus introduced blood percentages into a debate that had so far focused on morality, rights, upbringing, and appearance. Since Tecklenburg was proposing that German men apply for a right that German civil law already had given them—the right to pass on their citizenship to their wives and children—it was obvious that the Colonial Department would not accept it. Even the governor's office in Windhuk was divided. Leutwein supported Tecklenburg, but the highest judge in the colony, who was aptly named Richter and who defended Panzlaff, consistently held that there was no legal basis for withholding marriage from German men who wished to marry female colonial subjects.[80]

The major anticolonial war that broke out in German Southwest

Africa during the last days of 1903 and early 1904 and lasted through 1907 allowed Tecklenburg to overcome the resistance to his plans.[81] In June 1904 General Lothar von Trotha arrived in the colony, put it under military dictatorship, and began a disastrous policy of extermination against the Herero and other combatants.[82] Leutwein resigned and left the colony in late 1904, as did Judge Richter, who had served as Leutwein's deputy. Tecklenburg, as Trotha's civilian deputy, became the highest ranking civilian in the colony. After Trotha was himself recalled on 2 November 1905 amid controversy over his policy of extermination and revelations of other Germans' war profiteering, Tecklenburg continued to serve as the interim deputy. Soon Oskar Hintrager, the deputy of the new civilian governor, Friedrich von Lindequist, arrived to assist Tecklenburg; Governor von Lindequist did not arrive in the colony until 19 November 1905. Tecklenburg, Hintrager, and Lindequist were all advocates of white supremacist land and labor policies and of race purity.[83] Tecklenburg and Hintrager put their ideas about race mixing into action during Trotha's military dictatorship and the chaotic hiatus between it and the reestablishment of civilian administration under Lindequist. On 23 September 1905 Tecklenburg and Hintrager instructed marriage registry officials that, effective 1 January 1906, they were no longer to perform civil marriage ceremonies between "whites" and "natives, including Basters."[84] Lindequist approved the ban upon taking office as governor.[85] This was the first administrative decree in the colonial empire to ban intermarriage, and it was effective only in German Southwest Africa.

Once again it was soldiers' plans for intermarriage that had irritated colonial civil servants. About a thousand veterans of the 1904–1907 war planned to remain as colonists, and two of them had applied to marry Rehobother women in July 1905. Hintrager claimed that he and Tecklenburg could not wait for Berlin to send instructions; they had to act quickly in the face of the "danger" of the soldiers' imminent marriages.[86] They knew, of course, that the Colonial Department would not have approved their action in advance. The colony's superior court, no longer headed by Judge Richter, upheld their ban, and its decisions were not subject to review by any higher court in Germany.[87] The Colonial Department was powerless to reverse the ban, which it learned about in a letter from Tecklenburg dated a month after his instruction to marriage registry officials. His and Hintrager's objections to intermarriage revolved around men's military duties and anticipated political rights. They pointed out that the male children of German men in mixed marriages "will be obligated to do military service and will be eligible for public office, the suffrage that is to be introduced someday, and other rights derived from citizenship."[88] They added the conventional wisdom of opponents of race mixing: that experience showed that native wives never Europeanized, but rather that husbands "went native" (*verkafferten*), and that the children always displayed the bad qualities of each parent and never any good qualities. Finally, they cited political interests, claiming that "not only the preservation of German racial purity and German civilization, but also the white man's position of power, are altogether endangered."[89] While he admitted that sexual unions between German men and African women would not cease, he was satisfied that they would now "stand outside the law, as contradictory to the state's interest."[90]

Many colonialists interpreted the 1904–1907 war as a "race war" (*Rassenkrieg*). That is, they saw it as one manifestation of an underlying, inevitable conflict between two well-defined groups of people rather than a political struggle over rule and resources with diverse constituencies on various sides.[91] The ideas of race war and race purity supplanted the older imperial vision of crisscrossing agreements among various groups under German rule. Under the new circumstances, race mixing was practically treason—even in the case of Rehobothers, who had remained loyal allies of the Germans throughout the war. Germans who refused to interpret the conflict in those terms, such as some Rhenish missionaries, found themselves accused of aiding the insurgents.[92] Some German soldiers realized the idea of race war by targeting dark-skinned people regardless of whether or not they were combatants.[93] Moreover, the Native Regulations of 1905, 1906, and 1907 engraved white supremacy in property relationships. The regulations forbade Herero and Nama people to own land or cattle, to travel without permission of their employer, or to settle in groups larger than ten families; all persons over eight years of age had to carry identity cards, and all adults had to hold a labor contract or face prosecution as vagrants.[94] Herero and Nama political and social structures were dismantled. By 1908 even the Rehobothers had become impoverished.[95] The old relationships and proportions among various language groups, as well as the old imperial network of alliances between African groups and the Germans, were gone.

The war likewise transformed settler society by expediting its transformation from a gaggle of soldiers, officers, civil servants, traders, farmers, and adventurers of diverse nationalities, languages, and colors into a white German national polity that contained representatives of all social classes and whose bourgeois members claimed to speak for the whole.[96] Local militias and clubs formed; newspapers were established.[97] Even before the war German male colonists had been demanding greater latitude in running the colony through some form of self-administration; during the war Trotha's military dictatorship and policy of extermination — which threatened their labor force — mobilized them further.[98] Colonists demanded their own representative institutions that would rescue them from Reichstag and Colonial Department tutelage.

The political climate in the metropole itself was changing fast as well. During 1904, 1905, and 1906, Social Democratic and Catholic Center Party delegates in the Reichstag cited the mounting evidence that German colonists' own exploitative trading practices, land hunger, and acts of violence had precipitated the war, and that the colonial administration was unable to control profiteering and other scandals. In late 1906 these critics managed to persuade the Reichstag to use its budgetary approval powers to refuse additional credits for the German Southwest African war.[99] Imperial Chancellor Bernhard von Bülow dissolved the recalcitrant Reichstag in December 1906, gambling on the power of nationalism and colonialist enthusiasm in wartime, and the new elections in January and February 1907 proved him right. They produced a solidly procolonial parliamentary coalition, the so-called Bülow Bloc, that lasted until 1909. The Bülow Bloc excluded the Catholic Center Party and the Social Democratic Party but included the left-liberals.[100] Colonists in German Southwest Africa now held the attention of the metropole. Through popular fiction and memoir, including Gustav Frenssen's best-selling novel *Peter Moor's Journey to Southwest,* Germans came to see the colony as more romantic and attractive than ever, and the new availability of expropriated land accommodated a dramatic increase in new settlers.

Chancellor von Bülow appointed the banking expert Bernhard Dernburg colonial secretary in 1907, to head a Colonial Office made newly independent of the Foreign Office. Dernburg's mandate was to clear up the wartime scandals and to draw up a program of colonial reform and rational economic development. He and his allies denounced adventure for adventure's sake.[101] Much to the colonists' irritation, Dernburg stressed the importance of "native protection" (*Eingeborenenschutz*). He implemented reforms in economic, land, labor, and legal policies in the entire colonial empire, although his policies cannot easily be summarized as favorable to Africans.[102] If colonial reform eased Germans' consciences, it did not really change Germans' domination of Africans. On the contrary, it extended the control of the colonial state in new and more intensive ways, rationalizing rule over the African survivors.[103] Dernburg was considered close to the Progressives, but he was no democrat: he preferred the three-class, curial suffrage of Prussia to the equal and direct suffrage of the Reichstag.[104] Dernburg discussed the dangers of universal male suffrage with the colonists at length, citing the power of the Social Democrats in Germany and of the workers of color who held suffrage rights in the neighboring Cape Colony. He wanted industrial development for German Southwest Africa, but he also wanted to prevent the white working class there from gaining political power through any universal white male suffrage. Nor did he want to give the farmers and merchants more power; indeed, he considered most of the colonists to be politically immature.[105]

The colonists soon learned that Dernburg meant something different by self-administration than they did. Dernburg wanted self-administration only at the municipal, not the colony-wide, level. He envisioned a few leading local figures raising local revenue through self-administration organs and using that revenue to pay for local improvements. That would unburden the colonial budget and reduce Reichstag interference without inviting colonists' criticism of high-level colonial policy. Dernburg, in other words, saw self-administration as a way for colonists to achieve some economic independence from the colonial administration. The colonists, by contrast, had hoped that self-administration would bring them the political power to decide how to spend funds allocated by the Reich budget. They did not want economic self-sufficiency at all; in fact, they insisted that their sufferings during the war entitled them to more subsidies than before. They did want political self-sufficiency, insisting that only those who lived in German Southwest Africa could grasp its conditions and needs, and that they ought "to receive a state and communal administration similar to home conditions as soon and as much as possible."[106]

At the same time that the colonists were confronting the metropole, they were also carrying on a fierce internal debate over who was entitled to speak for the whole of settler society. Large-scale farmers considered themselves the most prestigious members of settler society, and they disliked the colonial administration's land and labor policies. Their rivals were the civil servants of Windhuk and the merchants there and in Swakopmund. Those groups — farmers, civil servants, and merchants — tended to see themselves as the only whites who counted in the colony, but in fact there were also numerous white market gardeners, traders, artisans, miners, and construction workers. In fact, wage laborers in construction and mines whose origins lay in the Cape Colony, Italy, Germany, or elsewhere in Europe comprised, after civil servants and the military, the third largest occupational group of Europeans in the colony.[107] Some settlers therefore began a discussion of elections by *Stand,* a word that variously indicated occupation, class, or status.[108] Like liberals in Germany, they opposed indiscriminate universal male suffrage. In typically liberal style, colonists zigzagged between claiming to support what was good for all and what was good for the "productive" members of society.

Even as the colonial administration and colonists clashed over self-administration, they worked in tandem to promote white supremacy in the postwar era of colonial reform.[109] Dernburg supported the 1905 ban on intermarriage, and even though he allowed some exceptions, he insisted that those be kept to a strict minimum.[110] He was the first head of the colonial administration to try to reconcile policy on interracial sexual and familial relations in various colonies instead of merely stalling and hoping things would work themselves out; for example, he asked all colonial governors to send in proposals for a uniform policy.[111] The most vocal members of settler society also approved of the ban on intermarriage. The Government Council, a new self-administrative organ comprising civil servants and lay members, approved the ban unanimously at its first meeting in October 1906. The council furthermore specified that only "white" children were permitted to attend the new government-funded school in Windhuk.[112] Local voluntary associations joined the campaign against race mixing: the Windhuk gymnastic club refused membership to men married to "native" women, and farmers' associations in Windhuk and Gibeon barred farmers who "had relations with black women in a manner causing public offense."[113] A new kindergarten in Windhuk organized by Protestant missionaries and the local chapter of the Women's League of the German Colonial Society refused admittance to mixed-descent children.[114] In October 1906 Governor von Lindequist expanded the ban on intermarriage so that not only civil but also religious ceremonies were forbidden.[115] In 1907 the colony's superior court declared that all existing mixed marriages, even those concluded before the 1905 ban, were invalid.[116] Some missionaries, especially Catholics, protested the ban and the accompanying measures; however, there were supporters of the ban among both Protestant and Catholic missionaries.[117] When Germans in the metropole and especially the Reichstag protested against the ban on intermarriage, the colonists and their colonialist supporters likened themselves to Boers rebelling against the British and to Confederates in the United States — both examples of republics legally organized by race. They accused their critics of wanting to impose conditions like those of Spanish America, the Portuguese colonies in Africa, and the Cape Colony, all of which they saw as efforts at world empire doomed by lax racial morality.[118] Their historical examples illustrate the colonists' shift away from an imperial conception of the colony and toward a liberal and national one.

The rhetoric of colonial reform and the mobilized, self-consciously German polity of colonists attracted the interest of metropolitan left-liberals. Colonists presented their society as a utopia of individualism far from the frustrating world of party politics in Germany. As one colonial newspaper editorialist proclaimed, "Here in the pure, sunny air of the African highlands . . . there is only *one* party, and its program reads: a warm German heart, love for the new fatherland and a healthy, free, practical view for real life that does not allow itself to be narrowed by doctrinal orthodoxy or dogmas of any kind."[119] Such criticism of partisan thinking was an old liberal theme. Paul Rohrbach and Wilhelm Külz, two left-liberals from Germany, became fascinated with German Southwest Africa and, in their capacity as special representatives of the colonial administration, left their imprint on the colony. These two men supported colonists' struggles for political rights and a liberal, national, and distinctively white German masculinity.

Paul Rohrbach was a Baltic German who had moved to Germany to escape Russification policies. Educated as a theologian, he belonged to the Evangelical-Social circle of the left-liberal theologian and social imperialist Friedrich Naumann.[120] He became an immensely popular journalist of *Weltpolitik*, focusing on geographical and economic questions with a rapid succession of travels to Turkey, central Asia, China, and Africa. In later years his reputation rested on his proposals for aggressive First World War aims. At the time of his appointment as settlement commissioner for German Southwest Africa in 1903, he was best known for his advocacy of the Baghdad Railway. As settlement commissioner he was charged with planning and overseeing future settlement of the colony. Almost immediately after his arrival, however, the outbreak of war made settlement planning moot. Rohrbach became commissioner for war damages compensation, but resigned in early 1906 out of frustration with both Trotha's military regime and the colonists.[121] Rohrbach came to see German Southwest Africa as a unique and irreplaceable setting for the creation of a new "overseas type of German" who could bring fresh virtues of love of freedom, self-reliance, and national community to metropolitan Germany.[122] He rhapsodized that "in the colony every individual has his own importance; at home he is only a number."[123] The liberal idyll that Rohrbach found in German Southwest Africa was surprisingly similar to Carl Peters and Frieda von Bülow's radical nationalist one: individual German men could prove their mettle as masters in colonial space, as they could not in stifling, decadent Germany.[124]

The lawyer Wilhelm Külz was the mayor of Bückeburg in Lower Saxony between 1904 and 1912. Today he is best known for his role as a founding member of the Bloc of Antifascist-Democratic Parties in 1945 and of the Liberal Democratic Party of Germany (Liberaldemokratische Partei Deutschlands) in the early German Democratic Republic.[125] His scholarly work before the First World War focused on liberal and social reform issues such as the constitutional provision for a peacetime army and the support of abandoned children at public expense.[126] An authority on municipal self-administration, he was best known at the time of his dispatch to German Southwest Africa as the author of Germany's most progressive self-administration charter, for the district of Lippe.[127] In 1906 Dernburg appointed Külz imperial commissioner for self-administration in response to demands from lay members of the Government Council and assigned him the task of drawing up a self-administration charter for the colony. To that end Külz stayed in German Southwest Africa from late 1907 until late 1908. Like Dernburg, Külz favored restricting colonists' power to the most local level and opposed universal, equal manhood suffrage. Külz saw the introduction of self-administration as the beginning of a process of political education for the settlers: education away from their "selfish interests" and toward the "common good." The freedom and independence of the old patriarchs was to give way to "public spirit."[128] Külz treated the colonists with greater tact than did Dernburg, and gently criticized the farmers even as he advocated their cause.[129] He shared, for example, the farmers' views on labor policy, finding harsh measures justified to overcome Africans' "laziness."[130] The farmers returned Külz's favor, respecting his views and praising his charter as "imbued with a *sensible* liberal spirit and completely suited to the particular qualities of the colony."[131]

Both Rohrbach and Külz arrived in German Southwest Africa without any prior experience of a German colony — or, indeed, of Africa. Both crisscrossed the colony tirelessly to gather information because they placed great importance on incorporating the knowledge and wishes of the people into policy. Külz declared that the knowledge of individuals in the colony ought to be put to public use, and rule from the "green baize table" in Berlin replaced by government as close to the people as possible.[132] But who were "the people"? Rohrbach and Külz talked and listened mostly to German officials and colonists, and usually the prosperous ones at that. In contrast to Leutwein and other early colonial officials, Rohrbach and Külz did not see themselves as administering a native population or even balancing the interests of all people in the colony. Rather, they saw themselves as the political preceptors of a white, national polity of Germans. Their vision of German Southwest Africa as a "Neudeutschland" placed white German colonists at the center of all colonial policy.[133]

In spite of their emphasis on learning only from practical, objective experience, what Rohrbach and Külz learned from their encounters with

German, Boer, and other white colonists and with African leaders, workers, and servants conformed to colonialist clichés. Traveling "alone" (i.e., accompanied by one or more Africans) across the vast landscape of Namibia, they saw an "empty" land waiting to be developed by German colonists.[134] Namibia, Rohrbach said, had no history, and he planned to give it some.[135] Külz was fascinated by his opportunity to draw up a charter from "scratch."[136] They both became entranced with, as Rohrbach put it, the "incomparably greater freedom of the general way of life in colonial country."[137] Colonial freedom also meant acting without compunction against those who would never be part of the national polity. Külz felt so free in colonial space that he fired his gun into a group of peacefully encamped Bushmen (San) merely in order to obtain a souvenir of one of their crafts.[138] Rohrbach and Külz reiterated the clichéd formula of "strict but fair" treatment of Africans, a precept that proved very elastic in practice.[139] They conflated economic motives with civilized and civilizing ones: both insisted that Africans had to be transformed into faceless, cultureless wage laborers in the service of Germans; their value was to be viewed strictly in economic terms and relative to Germans' needs.[140]

Rohrbach and Külz also concluded from their colonial experience that the best colonist was a male head of household with plenty of capital. The gentleman farmer who arrived in the colony with at least twenty thousand — preferably fifty thousand — marks and owned at least five thousand — preferably ten thousand — hectares of land deserved the greatest political voice. Rohrbach and Külz knew that colonists for German Southwest Africa were not plentiful and that rich ones were the rarest of all, but their pleasure at drawing up the criteria for an ideal German polity prevailed over realism. Their model colonist possessed not only material prosperity but also certain domestic tastes and mores. Prizing a racially pure "German" family life, he was to bring his white wife and children with him from Germany. Rohrbach conceded that a white German wife required a greater initial outlay than camping indefinitely in African-style dwellings.[141] But as an invaluable partner in colonization with her husband, she was worth the investment. Apart from providing worthy companionship, she helped save money by helping her husband plan, running a thrifty household with home-raised food and home-cooked meals, and preventing the alcoholism that often accompanied isolation and carousing with bachelor companions.[142] Rohrbach and Külz emphasized that the model colonist would never "go native," a term Rohrbach used with confidence within weeks of his arrival.[143] Both insisted that intermarriage, which they saw as a social phenomenon of race mixing and not an individual matter, was disastrous, and both defended the bans on intermarriage.[144] In 1912 Külz lectured in Germany against race mixing with a slogan he coined: "No black woman, no yellow one! Only the German woman is to be our culture-bearer [*Kulturträgerin*]!"[145] Rohrbach and Külz claimed that their understanding of the ills of intermarriage likewise came from first-hand colonial experience. In or out of marriage, German men were ruined, Rohrbach claimed, by "keeping a filthy house with the lazy, ignorant, indolent, in a word barbaric and in almost every respect base colored wenches."[146] The idea disturbed him that German men "for years and years have no other contact with women besides this intercourse that is down-dragging, demoralizing, and nothing but coarse sensuality."[147] Such vehement language was typical among advocates of race purity in the years just before the First World War.

Rohrbach and Külz practiced what they preached. Each went to some lengths to ensure that his wife would be able to follow him to the colony and spend a considerable period of time there. Rohrbach insisted that a house be built specially for his wife, Clara, and their children, and he urged every married civil servant to insist on the same sort of family accommodation.[148] Put off by the carousing of the unmarried white men of Windhuk, he took obvious pleasure in his family's domestic life.[149] Likewise, Külz's wife, Erna, and their young child joined him three months after his own arrival in the colony.[150]

Rohrbach and Külz differed from earlier opponents of intermarriage in the role they foresaw for white German women. For them, white German women were not merely symbols of their husband's wealth or status, or sexual objects whose presence might dissuade men from race mixing, but indispensable partners of German men who helped create a joint prosperity. Liberal nationalists like Rohrbach and Külz developed an innovative colonial gender politics. They also became members of a core group of male supporters of the new Women's League of the German Colonial Society after 1907.

The companionate role Rohrbach and Külz saw for white German women was not necessarily intended to make the women equal to men. Rohrbach and Külz were typical of liberals of many states and generations in that they saw no contradiction in upholding egalitarian rights for individuals while excluding whole categories of people from the status of "individual." Liberal feminists in Germany also saw municipal suffrage and self-administration as a political training ground for women, and they were also attracted by the rhetoric of colonial freedom.[151] The Silesian Association for Women's Suffrage (Schlesischer Verein für Frauenstimmrecht) seized the moment of the promulgation of Külz's self-administration charter in 1909 to petition the imperial chancellor to extend municipal suffrage to German women in German Southwest Africa. Külz responded that it was premature to grant female colonists the vote because there were too few of the right kind of women there: "We do not yet have any fully developed type of German woman at all in the colony."[152] He did not bother to specify what the proper type of woman for female suffrage might be. Just as Dernburg had told male settlers to mind their private business and not meddle in politics, Külz told the Silesian Association for Women's Suffrage that the best contribution German women could make in the colony was to care for their families and engage in charitable projects. Külz's perceptions and beliefs shaped the self-administration charter. Voters had to be male, at least twenty-five years old, resident in the colony for at least two years, and "economically independent."[153] Germans who were bankrupt, on poor relief, or "married to or living in concubinage with a native woman" could not vote.[154] When lists of voters were assembled in 1910, only 2,000 of the 6,999 German men in the colony held the right to vote in local elections for their municipal council (*Gemeinderat*).[155]

While the charter evaluated white German men on the basis of their economic status and sexual behavior, women of color (or of merely questionable whiteness) who had ties to white men experienced drastic violations of their liberty and dignity. Tecklenburg's 1903 suggestion for racially certifying a prospective wife foreshadowed a pattern of placing the onus on the woman in mixed relationships to prove her legal status, and to do so in the face of ever more hostile and legally problematic requirements. Two key court cases demonstrated the strategy of preserving the autonomy of white German men as far as possible while penalizing women of color in mixed relationships. In each case, a woman of mixed African and European descent who was married to a German man attempted to gain legal satisfaction in the colonial courts for wrongs done her by her husband, including physical abuse. The women sought divorces, but the colony's superior court refused to grant them (and the property settlements that would have come with them) on the grounds that the couples had never been married in the first place. The judgments ruled that racial difference was, a priori, a bar to legal marriage, regardless of the legal circumstances at the time of marriage.[156] This retroactive application of racial difference to existing marriages effectively denied the women any rights or recourse against abusive husbands — in a manner even more unfair than what the missionary Carl Büttner had feared.

Colonists and administrators discussed and enacted various measures to monitor and coerce female colonial subjects in ways that, they hoped, would discourage German men from entering into relationships with them in the first place.[157] As of 1912, any African woman who gave birth to a mixed-descent child was compelled to register that birth on pain of losing her job.[158] The measure was intended to discourage women from bearing such children, but since the white father was not to be named during the registration process, it did nothing concrete to discourage German men from fathering them. African women also felt the impact of the Native Regulations in distinctive ways. Along with compulsory pass carrying and labor service, for example, African women known or thought to be prostitutes faced compulsory physical examinations for venereal disease. The governor's office had originally planned to carry out examinations of all African women detained for any reason, and only protests from the Women's Association for Nursing Care in the Colonies deterred it.[159] As in Europe and other colonies such as India, white men were understood to be victims, not agents, of the spread of sexually transmitted diseases, and prostituted women became, in effect, the state-certified sexual instruments of the men.[160] In 1912 the Territorial Council (Landesrat) considered placing all African women under a curfew after nine o'clock in the evening and establishing state-approved houses of prostitution employing African women or white women, but neither plan was carried out.[161]

The older pattern of marriage, long-term cohabitation, public liaisons, and rape was replaced by the new system of prostitution, secret liaisons, and rape; however, the cultural importance of sexual access to women of color did not change. African and African-descended women were dealt with harshly while white German men were left largely with their liberties intact and allowed to follow their own consciences. Although the idea of criminalizing sexual relations between Europeans and Africans was aired in 1910, it too was dropped.[162] And in 1912 the colonial administration in Windhuk flatly rejected the notion of publishing the names of men who fathered illegitimate children and forcing them to pay child support.[163] The plan was rejected because it would require that a female colonial subject's oath be given greater weight than a German man's. There were never any positive penalties for German men who engaged in sexual relations with African women with no issue. Instead, advocates of race purity hoped that German men would choose of their own volition to avoid female colonial subjects who were legally second-class wives and state-monitored lovers. The debate over race mixing was, in fact, a struggle over how to preserve white German men's patriarchal sexual liberties while pursuing the goal of race purity.[164]

The desire even among advocates of race purity to defend men's sexual rights emerges in a final series of measures intended to moderate the "harshness" of the 1907 superior court ruling and Külz's 1909 self-administration charter. The 1905 ban and these additional measures were quite disruptive to white men, and even to some white women who were married to men previously considered to be white.[165] In March 1912 the Territorial Council decided to recognize those mixed marriages concluded before 1905, but only in cases in which the district council — note the choice of arbiter — decided that "the parents' life and the raising of the children" corresponded to "general requirements of custom and morality."[166] In such cases, the 1912 measure provided for a certificate that the relevant person was "considered to be white."[167] The civic rights of those men in mixed marriages who were prosperous and of sound moral reputation were restored, and the men in question, including Wilhelm Panzlaff, now supported the ban on intermarriage.[168]

Like any provision for certifying people to be white, the measure implied a recognition of the fictive, legally constructed nature of race. However, the year after the Windhuk colonial administration decided to allow race mixing to be recertified as race purity under certain circumstances, the colony's superior court upheld its principle once more that race was real and not a juristic fiction. In 1913 the superior court remanded the case of the Schmelens' great-grandson Ludwig Baumann to the native court on the grounds that since Baumann had some African blood, however little and however legitimated through marital German paternity over generations, he was a colonial subject. The conflicting legal interpretations of race and citizenship of the German Southwest African superior court, on the one hand, and the Colonial Office in Berlin, on the other, was now out in the open. The superior court in Windhuk stated: "Whether a person is a native or a member of the white race is a question of fact."[169] The Colonial Office in Berlin, which generally found existing citizenship law to be adequate for distinguishing colonizers from colonized, responded: "The question of who is a native or member of the white race is not merely a fact, but rather primarily a legal question."[170] In the wake of the Baumann case, the Territorial Council renewed its call for racial certification, demonstrating even more clearly how the campaign for race purity and the notion of racial certification produced chaotic legal reasoning.[171] The discussion of race had come full circle: legal certification was needed to decide who was to be seen as white or black, citizen or colonial subject—although it was precisely legal, as opposed to intuitive, definitions that had been found wanting in the first place. The only real changes that the campaign for race purity in German Southwest Africa had wrought were to augment the rights of "white" men and to change the arbiters of a person's racial status. No longer did distant Reich law decide; now, local entities comprising individuals with "colonial experience" did. While many in Germany, and especially the Reichstag, opposed the bans on mixed marriage because they were undemocratic decrees, colonists and their supporters in Germany liked to say that the legal bans as well as voluntary associations' expulsions of German men in mixed marriages showed the genuine voice of the German colonial community.[172]

GERMAN EAST AFRICA

German East Africa was the second colony to ban mixed marriage. There were several similarities to the situation in German Southwest Africa. The governor's office decreed the ban during an anticolonial war, the Maji Maji war, which began in July 1905 and lasted through 1906. Colonists, especially in the region of Mount Kilimanjaro where German plantations were concentrated, wanted to make the colony into "white man's land" and interpreted the war as a race war.[173] Although German settlement was much sparser than in German Southwest Africa, it increased steadily just before the First World War; in 1912 more European planters lived there than in neighboring British East Africa (today Kenya).[174] The war catalyzed colonists' demands for self-administration, and they eventually gained rights second only to those of the colonists in German Southwest Africa.[175]

Colonists in German East Africa encountered greater opposition from their governors than those in German Southwest Africa did, however. Governor Adolf von Götzen, who was in office from 1901 until 1906, openly sided with the planters and other German colonists, but his predecessor, von Liebert, and his successors, Albrecht von Rechenberg and Heinrich Schnee, did not. Götzen purged Indians and Africans from the colony's district councils, turning those local institutions into all-white entities that served only the colonists' interests. During Götzen's term of office, German East African society became increasingly polarized along white and nonwhite lines.[176] Götzen was in office when the Maji Maji war began and had to take responsibility for failing to maintain peaceful German rule. Before resigning, however, he decreed a ban on marriages between persons in the categories of "Europeans" and "natives" in March 1906.

The new governor, Baron Albrecht von Rechenberg, a conservative and paternalistic agrarian, Catholic, and Baltic German, reversed many of Götzen's policies. In the context of the colony, his political views produced an imperial style of rule that sought to counterbalance the diverse groups of Arabs, Indians, and Africans through unequal inclusion.[177] Rejecting the colonists' demands for enfranchisement at other groups' expense, Rechenberg developed instead a self-administration scheme that brought people of varying statuses — including non-German European men and, he briefly proposed, German women — back onto the district councils.[178] As in German Southwest Africa, however, suffrage for German women was not enacted. Rechenberg's policy of "native protection" pitted him against the colonists, especially planters. For example, he encouraged Africans to increase their agricultural productivity and market their crops competitively, while German planters wanted

Africans to labor instead on German plantations and refrain from competing with German producers. Planters also sought preferential treatment over town merchants and traders. Like German Southwest African farmers, they used a language of individual autonomy and rights together with nationalist language that described the colony as an especially pure German space. After years of bitter attacks on Rechenberg, they ousted him in 1912. Rechenberg's successor, Governor Heinrich Schnee, attempted to tread a middle path. He sympathized with their goal of settlement, and on the matter of intermarriage and race purity he sided firmly with the colonists.[179]

German East Africa also differed from German Southwest Africa in its lack of early intermarriages between colonial subjects and German missionaries, settlers, and soldiers. At the height of the debate over race mixing, between 1905 and 1914, the Colonial Office found only one case of intermarriage inside the colony, and the husband in question was a non-German European.[180] Romance, concubinage, casual sexual contact, and prostitution appear to have been as widespread in German East Africa as in the other German colonies — but not marriage.[181] No group had the characteristics that made Rehobother women, for example, potential brides for German men: Christian faith, political alliance with the Germans, elite status relative to other groups under colonial rule, and property in land. The local elites in German East Africa were Muslim and Hindu, and they did not seek intermarriage with Christian Germans. The only Christians were a small community of Goans, who were allied politically with the Germans but whose modest prosperity in civil service and trade was not easily transferable through marriage.[182]

German East Africa nevertheless saw a full-blown debate over race mixing and especially intermarriage. The Government Council deliberated, the colonists' press waxed indignant, missionaries pointed out the problem of paying to raise abandoned children fathered by Germans, and the legal difficulties of the ban were once again aired. The German East African version of the debate over race mixing shows how, even in the virtual absence of intermarriage, the issues of race, family, and sexuality provided a language for German colonists' self-constitution as free and autonomous political subjects.

Intermarriage was so rare that the sources record only two cases; Götzen's 1906 ban stymied a third.[183] The two cases differed from German Southwest African ones in that the first, precolonial marriage concerned a royal daughter, and the second was actually concluded in Berlin and became part of the debate over race mixing in German East Africa only when the couple attempted to enter the colony. The latter case also concerned the unusual constellation of an African husband and German wife, which only heightened the condemnation by advocates of race purity. The basic trajectory of opinion about intermarriage was similar, however: from Germans' early positive response to a sweeping condemnation of intermarriage as a source of political disorder.

The precolonial case was in its day a famous romantic love match. In August 1866, Salme bint Sa'id, the daughter of Sultan Sa'id Majid of Zanzibar and sister of his successor, Barghash ibn Sa'id, eloped with Heinrich Ruete, a businessman from the Hamburg trading firm Hansing & Company. They carried out her adventurous escape from her father's palace after a series of secret trysts. After the birth of their first child in December 1866 and her conversion to Christianity, they married in Aden in May 1867, then lived in Germany. Only three years later, Heinrich Ruete died in an accident. Widowed with three children, Emily Said-Ruete, as she was now called, renewed her efforts to gain control of the inheritance her brother had denied her since the elopement. Bismarck and Heinrich von Kusserow of the Foreign Office decided to underwrite her journey back to Zanzibar in 1885 to petition her brother as part of their diplomatic maneuverings with Britain.[184] Emily Said-Ruete never succeeded in regaining her wealth, but she did find important patrons, including Empress Frederick, the mother of Emperor William II.[185]

Said-Ruete also made an impression on the German public with her autobiography, *Memoirs of an Arabian Princess,* which appeared in 1886, immediately went through four editions, and was translated into English and French.[186] Her book gave German and other European readers one of their first accounts of harem life from an Arab woman's perspective. Said-Ruete attempted to counter Europeans' prejudices about the harem, Muslim women, and slavery as practiced by Muslims in eastern Africa. While living in Germany she became exasperated with people's constant curiosity and ignorance about her background. On one occasion, for example, "a very naïve lady became engrossed in [Said-Ruete's] so-called negro-hair and took the peculiar freedom to even touch it."[187] After her husband's death she did not feel at home in Germany. She revisited Zanzibar in 1888, residing with her daughter Rosalie in the German Hospital run by Marie Rentsch, then lived in Jaffa and Beirut between 1889 and 1914.[188] Her two daughters married German men and made their lives in Germany, however, and she returned there in 1914 and stayed until her death.

While Said-Ruete had a mixed experience of Germany, colonialist and other Germans had a positive impression of her. Her marriage was popularly perceived as high romance. Indeed, it was suited perfectly to an Orientalist narrative according to which a Christian man liberates an oppressed Muslim woman from her cruel family and introduces her to marriage based on romantic love.[189] Said-Ruete and her children apparently did not experience any (intentional) public criticism of their background. The children married white Germans, and one, Antonie Brandeis, lived in German Samoa as the wife of a colonial official.[190] For German colonialists, the Said-Ruetes were a reminder of the thrilling old days when German colonial expansion was just beginning.

The second case of mixed marriage associated with German East Africa was different in almost every way. Mtoro bin Mwinyi Bakari was a Swahili man of modest but respected social station from the coastal trading town of Bagamoyo, and not, like Salme bint Sa'id, a member of a royal family. Bertha Hilske was a working-class woman from Berlin, not a successful bourgeois man from the port city of Hamburg, with its long tradition of tropical trade. The couple confronted special opposition when they attempted to travel from Germany to German East Africa — thereby crossing the divide between metropolitan space and colonial space. Finally, the configuration of the couple aroused particular outrage. Marriage between a male colonial subject and a female German was virtually unheard of in the German colonies, and rare though not unique inside Imperial Germany.[191] This marriage did not conform to the Orientalist narrative according to which a man liberated a woman from backward oppression and initiated her into the pleasures of romance. Rather, advocates of race purity considered it racial anarchy.[192] The few Germans who spoke out on the couple's behalf defended Mtoro bin Mwinyi Bakari's intellect and hard work, not his loyalty to his wife and certainly not the power of romance. In fact, although neither one of the couple was a white German man, the primacy of men's rights continued to organize the discussion of whether and how the marriage was to be tolerated. No one went on record defending Bertha Hilske except her husband and mother.

During the 1890s Carl Velten, a German linguist living in German East Africa, asked Mtoro bin Mwinyi Bakari and several other Swahili men there to write about Swahili traditions and everyday life. Velten wanted both to record Swahili culture and to produce language manuals for German colonial administrators. This was not Mtoro bin Mwinyi Bakari's first contact with the German colonial bureaucracy; he had already worked as a tax collector for the German East African administration.[193] He had an extensive Muslim education and a fine writing style, and he edited the entire collaborative manuscript that he and the other Swahilis produced. The book, considered today a masterpiece of Swahili prose, appeared in both German and Swahili editions in 1903.[194] Velten next invited Mtoro bin Mwinyi Bakari to work with him as a lecturer in Swahili at the Seminar for Oriental Languages at Berlin University. In 1900 Mtoro bin Mwinyi Bakari moved to Berlin, where he was apparently a model teacher and colleague.[195]

In 1904 Mtoro Bakari, as he called himself in Germany, told Velten and Eduard Sachau, the director of the Oriental Seminar, of his plans to marry Bertha Hilske, a factory worker and the daughter of his landlady. One of Mtoro Bakari's supporters later speculated that the example of Na'arber, an Arab at the Oriental Seminar who had married a German woman without facing any criticism, may have encouraged him in this step.[196] Velten and Sachau argued and threatened, but they were unable to dissuade him. When the news spread at the Oriental Seminar, the students (mostly candidates for the colonial civil service) insulted him constantly, making further teaching impossible. Mtoro Bakari confronted Sachau and asked him either to defend him against the students or to accept his early resignation from his post. Neither Sachau nor Velten would defend him. Hilske and her mother complained to Sachau, who angrily responded that Mtoro Bakari had caused all of his troubles himself.[197] He resigned in August 1904 and married Bertha Hilske in Berlin the following October.

Mtoro Bakari obtained the necessary papers for his marriage through the Colonial Department — including a document signed by Governor von Götzen — and the couple married without any bureaucratic difficulty.[198] Life in Berlin was difficult, however, because Mtoro Bakari was now unemployed. It was impossible for him to obtain a post as a language teacher without Sachau's or Velten's help. In 1905 he decided to return with his wife to Bagamoyo, where his family owned some land. His original contract with the Oriental Seminar included free passage for himself; he purchased passage for his wife and shipment of their belongings with his savings.[199]

When their ship stopped in Tanga, the first port in German East Africa, in September 1905, the couple was forbidden to disembark for undefined "security" reasons. The same thing happened at the next port, Dar es Salaam. The Colonial Department in Berlin had given advance warning of the couple's arrival to Governor von Götzen and asked him to use his own discretion in dealing with them.[200] Götzen ordered that Bertha Hilske be prevented from leaving the ship anywhere in German East Africa. Mtoro Bakari was told that he could either proceed alone to Bagamoyo or return with his wife to Germany. According to an old Swahili acquaintance of Mtoro Bakari, colonial officials told him that if he stayed in Africa he could return to Germany for visits with his wife, but they could not live together in the colony.[201] Colonial officials promised to pay for the return passage to Germany and to restore his old position at the Oriental Seminar; they also threatened Mtoro Bakari with twenty-five lashes if he dared to go ashore with his wife.[202] He refused to leave his wife, and so the couple was forced to return to Germany without ever disembarking in Africa.

The colonists strongly supported Götzen's order to bar the couple. The *Usambara Post* shrieked: *"Do we want to preserve our racial prestige or not?"* The colonists' "instinct for self-preservation," the *Post* insisted, would make them reject a fellow German who was married to a "nigger [*sic*]."[203] African servants would lose respect for their European bosses, teasing them with the prospect of becoming in-laws. In trying to back up these claims, that article narrated the case in terms that were particularly ill-chosen for this couple. It depicted Mtoro Bakari as someone only very recently accustomed to civilized ways: only five years before, it was claimed, he had subsisted by climbing palm trees clad only in a loincloth. In point of fact, of course, he was holding Friday sermons in Bagamoyo and working on the book that Velten published.[204] The article claimed that the Oriental Seminar's high salary and life in Europe had turned his head. Yet even before going to Berlin, Mtoro Bakari, as a tax collector, slaveowner, and local religious leader, had belonged to a relatively privileged class, and in any case Germans had described him as modest and hardworking. The article described Bertha as downwardly mobile: Did she really, the article asked with horror, intend to flail rice dressed in a cloth wrap and to hoe fields for her husband? Were the children of a white woman really to be sighted someday "on the rubbish heap of a bush village"?[205] Ironically, Bertha Hilske's choice of a husband should have made her upwardly mobile. He was more educated than men of her class, held a position at the Berlin University, and according to his own remarks he intended to support her. Had she married a working-class man in Germany she probably would have labored after marriage, even if it were in a factory and not a rice field. It was even conceivable that her children might be seen in the vicinity of one of Berlin's rubbish heaps. The parting shot in the *Usambara Post* article was aimed at the Colonial Department for allowing the marriage to happen at all.

The Colonial Department member who brought the article to the attention of his colleagues rushed to condemn the marriage: "Nothing can undermine the prestige of the Germans more than a white woman's devotion to a negro," he wrote indignantly next to the clipping.[206] The Colonial Department unearthed the old paperwork and set about trying to hide its participation. It is not clear from the sources whether Governor von Götzen was challenged directly over his equally routine participation. Since a German East African newspaper had only praise for his "strictness" in the case, he was apparently able to hide his own initial role in the marriage from the public.[207] The Colonial Department had the law on its side; at the time of the couple's marriage in October 1904, not even German Southwest Africa had banned intermarriage. Yet the Colonial Department did not defend itself by citing the law, as it had in the years of discussion of German Southwest African intermarriage. Probably because this marriage involved a black man and a white woman, some special measures seemed necessary. The Colonial Department at first proposed that all marriage license bureaus in Germany obtain permission from the colonial administration before performing mixed marriages of Germans and colonial subjects.[208] But one Colonial Department member argued that such a uniform procedure was "out of the question." Each case would have to be handled not with general principles, he continued, but internally, like this one. He explained, "In Samoa it is an everyday occurrence that whites marry Samoan women. Should permission also be required there? Or only for marriages of colored *men* with white *women*? Clearly, this matter cannot be handled through laws."[209] He assumed that his colleagues found intermarriage between German men and Samoan women so acceptable that an extra piece of documentation would be an excessive hindrance. And the likelihood of creating separate marriage laws for German men and women at the Reich level was even smaller than reaching agreement on intermarriage in the colonial empire, for there was almost no support for legally banning racially mixed marriages inside Germany, and such a gender-specific legal change would only draw attention to the continued lenience toward German men's intermarriage. The highest priority was to protect the right of white German men to marry, even if that meant leaving open the formal possibility of a white woman's marriage to a man of color. If necessary, extralegal means could be used to restrict the rights of mixed couples, as in the present case. The Colonial Department officials agreed among themselves that Götzen's deportation of the couple was just and necessary for political reasons.[210] They also agreed that the marriage itself could not have been stopped legally. They decided that the best thing was to shelve the matter. After all, the couple was back in Germany.

But that was not a satisfactory solution for Mtoro Bakari and Bertha. They had invested his savings in the trip in order to start a new life in Bagamoyo, and had lost everything. Mtoro Bakari appeared at the Colonial Department and demanded compensation. He pointed out that there was no indication beforehand that there would be any obstacle to his marriage or his return to German East Africa. Now further debates took place within the Colonial Department: some wanted to pay him back in full; others, such as future governor of German Southwest Africa Theodor Seitz, insisted that the state owed him nothing. Members of the Colonial Department also argued over whether an unimpeded marriage in Germany implied the right of the couple to reside in a colony. Finally it was decided to compensate Mtoro Bakari, which then raised the question of how to hide the payments from other state agencies that might ask why the Colonial Department did not stop the couple from going in the first place.[211] The answer to that last question remains unclear.

The compensation paid for the retrieval of the couple's possessions from freight storage, but Mtoro Bakari and Bertha still faced hostility in Germany. The promise of his old job was not fulfilled — Sachau refused to see him — and he had no prospects for any other steady work and no savings. The university-educated bureaucrats he spoke with seemed unable to understand his occupational predicament. He was a writer, translator, and lecturer, but they envisioned for him the jobs of shoe-shine boy, furnace stoker, temporary employment at a current colonial exhibition in Berlin, manual craft apprenticeship — in fact, "any kind of wage labor."[212] They became impatient when he refused the one firm offer they negotiated: to work as an errand boy in a colonial supply house. Instead he chose to continue teaching Swahili at a mission society headquarters in Lichterfelde, a suburb of Berlin, for half the pay of an errand boy. Perhaps it was growing curiosity, or suspicion, about how the couple survived at all that led Dernburg's undersecretary at the Colonial Office, former governor of German Southwest Africa Friedrich von Lindequist, to order the police to spy on them in 1907.[213] The police could only corroborate what Mtoro Bakari had protested all along, however: that he only sought a position that would allow him to support his wife, and that they would "soon be quite desperate."[214] Later, during the First World War, he worked as an itinerant lecturer, although he faced abuse in the streets from Germans who took him for a French occupation soldier.[215]

A few people were concerned about what was happening to Mtoro Bakari. A Reichstag delegate and father of head of the Lichterfelde mission house, H. C. Gluer, asked Governor von Rechenberg about the case. An official of the German Young Men's Christian Association (Christlicher Verein Junger Männer) appealed to the Colonial Department. A prominent linguist at the Oriental Seminar, Carl Meinhof, also defended him, praising his abilities as a language teacher.[216] All three portrayed Mtoro Bakari as a wronged man. They did not see Bertha as a wronged woman, however. The records offer no information about her difficulties coping with insults or finding work. Everyone, even those who found Mtoro Bakari's expulsion from German East Africa wrong, thought that hers justified. In fact, Götzen himself made a distinction between them from the beginning: technically, only Bertha had been barred from the colony; her husband had been given the choice of disembarking without her.

Mtoro Bakari described his plight to Emperor Wilhelm II in 1906: "When we wanted to go ashore in Dar es Salaam, we were simply expelled — for what reason, we still do not know today. But in any case the officials there had no reason to expel us, as German subjects standing on German territory."[217] He wrote to the soon-to-be colonial secretary, Bernhard Dernburg: *"Because I concluded a legally valid marriage in accordance with German law through the organs of the German government, I have been expelled from my homeland and made destitute here in Germany."*[218] His logic rested on the legal uniformity of Germany and the colonies: what was legal in one location ought to be accepted in another. His position that he had behaved as a responsible man and husband echoed the claims of white German fathers of mixed-descent children in German Southwest Africa.

In early 1906, only a few months after Mtoro Bakari and Bertha's trip to the colony, a German man in the northern coastal town of Tanga named Werner Thiel attempted to marry an African woman. Thiel managed the business branch of a Protestant mission station in Tanga (most missions sold crops or crafts to obtain income), and his partner, whose name did not appear in the colonial administration's records, was a member of the mission station's congregation. Thiel approached the district office and district court in Tanga but was told that his planned marriage was against those agencies' wishes and might even result in his deportation from the colony. The German East African ban on intermarriage therefore originated even more locally than the German Southwest African ban: among district officials in the northern coastal town of Tanga rather than in the governor's office in Dar es Salaam. When Thiel appealed to Governor von Götzen, the latter upheld the local officials' statements.[219] In a March 1906 letter to Thiel, Götzen wrote that "political reasons speak against permitting marriages between Europeans and natives," and that "a married couple, one of whom was of the European race and the other of whom of the native race, if they settled in the colony after concluding their marriage, would always face the possibility of expulsion."[220] This was a step beyond any measure in German Southwest Africa, where no one broached the expulsion of mixed couples. In German East Africa, however, marriage (as opposed to cohabitation or more casual sexual relations) between German men and African women was rare enough that, apparently, such persons could be treated as pariahs with political impunity. Apparently Götzen saw the case of Mtoro Bakari and Bertha Hilske as a precedent for all mixed couples. At the same time that Götzen informed Thiel of the rejection of Thiel's application, he instructed the district judge in Tanga not to perform the marriage and sent the same instruction, along with an order to report any application for a marriage between "Europeans" and "colored" to the governor's office, to judges and district officers in the areas of white settlement.[221] This March 1906 document constituted the German East African ban on mixed marriage. Governor von Götzen did not bother rehearsing any of the possible legal arguments against intermarriage; he cited only political reasons for his decision.[222] As in German Southwest Africa, the Colonial Office was not informed until after Götzen's instruction, which had the effect of a decree, had been circulated within the colony.[223]

Götzen did not face protests from colonists in German East Africa, or from local missionaries who might have been expected to prefer marriage to cohabitation; in fact, Thiel was forced to resign from his job because the missionaries at his station opposed intermarriage.[224] German East African voluntary associations barred persons of mixed descent from membership.[225] However, Götzen had to leave office about a month after the March 1906 ban, when the Maji Maji war broke out.

Governor von Rechenberg, Götzen's successor, was far less sympathetic to the colonists' demands on Africans' land and labor. As for policy on intermarriage, Rechenberg neither augmented the 1906 ban nor attempted to reverse it. But he had to take a position in August 1907 when the new colonial secretary, Bernhard Dernburg, asked him to draft a regulation on the rights of children fathered by "white" men with "colored" women.[226] In a memo to Berlin, Rechenberg's assistant Winterfeld conceded the existence of race mixing but argued that it was not a problem: "The few offspring of whites with colored women . . . have not stood out in any way. *Usually* they have a predominantly black skin color, are raised by their mothers as native children, and, even in later years, are hardly aware of their part-European extraction."[227] No regulations would be needed, Winterfeld claimed: "A case in which the descendant of a European and a native woman felt himself to belong to a higher race and correspondingly attempted to adapt his way of life to that of a European is so far unknown. It is also not to be assumed that this will change in the foreseeable future."[228]

Most colonists actually agreed with Rechenberg that German East Africa did not have a race mixing, or more precisely a race hierarchy, problem. As one of the local newspapers put it, "A mixed blood question is altogether nonexistent in German East Africa, since the number of mixed-bloods is so negligible that they merge completely into the black population and disappear."[229] But the Reichstag was threatening to "artificially cultivate a mixed blood question here where there had been none," according to the colonists, by refusing to uphold the ban on intermarriage and trying to protect the rights of persons in mixed families.[230] In May 1912 the Reichstag passed a resolution that asked the Federal Council to draft a law "which secures the validity of marriages between whites and natives in all German colonies, and makes legal provision for illegitimate children not currently covered by the Civil Code."[231] The colonists vowed to demonstrate their own opinion through spontaneous boycotts: "each person for himself, every social, economic, or political association, as well as every commercial or other enterprise, will refuse any economic, social, business or personal intercourse with a European who enters into a mixed marriage."[232] The Reichstag, they claimed, was autocratically forcing unwanted measures on the German colonial community.

Just a month before that Reichstag resolution was passed, the German East African planters finally succeeded in ejecting Rechenberg. The new governor, Heinrich Schnee, wanted to defuse the high drama of the planters' struggle with Rechenberg, and that meant appeasing them on the now well-publicized issue of race mixing, as well as on native protection policies. Governor Schnee took a bureaucratic approach to race mixing, instructing his district officers in September 1913 to draw up the colony's first local reports on the "mixed-blood question" (*Mischlingsfrage*) according to a standard format. The reports were to note how many mixed-bloods lived in the district, how they were being raised (specifically, whether at mission stations or in "colored" families), and whether their white fathers voluntarily contributed toward their upbringing. The district officers were also to suggest an age at which each child would be considered too old for further support, and to note criteria for appointing guardians for the children. Finally, Schnee asked whether the district officers recommended the adoption of the 1912 German Southwest African measure against African women that required the reporting of all births of mixed-descent children.[233] Now race mixing had become an official problem for all of German East Africa.

The ingredients for the new consensus over how to protect German men's rights in a liberal, national, and racial order were soon in place. A new white colonial masculinity emerged among advocates of race purity that permitted German men's sexual access to African women while avoiding the troubling family and property issues that ordinarily accompanied long-term sexual relationships. Karl Oetker, a medical doctor in German East Africa and a strong opponent of race mixing, offered this solution in 1907, just one year after the ban was imposed: "I can very well imagine for myself the situation of an unmarried man who buys himself a negro girl for a shorter or longer period of time. . . . It is very obvious, but nevertheless can be emphasized here, that every European who has relations with black wenches must take care that the relationship remains sterile, to prevent a mixing of races. . . . Such liaisons can and ought to be seen only as surrogates for marriage that are to be forbidden any of the state recognition and protections granted to marriages between whites."[234] Oetker was proposing a strict distinction between German men's sexual acts, on the one hand, and their social relationships, on the other. German men's sexual prerogatives were to be protected as far as possible. As a German East African newspaper put it in 1912, "the *European woman alone can solve the problem* [of race mixing]. Only she can *accomplish something positive,* all so-called disciplinary measures belong to the realm of *prohibitive and negative decrees,* in which no real value resides: nature cannot be driven out with a pitchfork."[235]

The case of Mtoro Bakari and Bertha Hilske added a particular twist to the rhetoric about race mixing in German East Africa. Advocates of race purity argued that the ban on intermarriage was necessary to ensure German women's safety: "The tolerance of mixed marriages would deeply degrade the *prestige of the white race* in Central Africa and would severely endanger the white woman. *Mixed marriages* would then be permissible for *white women as well,* with native men. The white woman would thereby lose the only thing that offers her an unconditional protection from attacks in the colonies today, the respect of the colored."[236] This argument was rare in German Southwest Africa. The *Usambara Post* reported that there had been "repeated" cases in which "a white woman has thrown herself away on a negro," and opined that such women ought to be deported from the colony. If such behavior continued unchecked, German women might have to be barred from the colonies altogether for their own safety.[237] These fulminations inverted the usual relationship between the emphasis on white German women and race purity: white women could appear as the solution to race mixing or as the reason race mixing had to be stopped. In either case, the focus on German women shifted the public's attention away from the German men who were responsible for race mixing in the first place.

GERMAN SAMOA

The social context of intermarriage in Samoa differed from that in both German Southwest Africa and German East Africa. In terms of numbers of colonists, German Samoa trailed a distant third behind those two colonies. Moreover, intermarriage was not as rare. In 1913 there were about 227 German men, about 63 German women, and 76 couples recorded as mixed in German Samoa.[238] Like German Southwest Africa, German Samoa had a tradition of intermarriage with local, relatively elite women that brought property and trading connections to German men. Unlike in German Southwest Africa, Samoans did not experience extreme proletarianization under German rule, and so remained desirable financial matches. Samoan and German habits facilitated intermarriage. To Germans, Samoan marriage looked like simple long term cohabitation or concubinage because no Christian or state ceremony marked it. German-Samoan couples often married "Samoa-style," then added a German civil and perhaps religious marriage a few years later. Compared with German Southwest Africa and German East Africa, intermarriage in German Samoa remained relatively free of stigma until the First World War. Individual colonists were known to taunt mixed-bloods, such as the children of the German ethnographer Richard Parkinson and his Euroamerican-Samoan wife, Phoebe Coe Parkinson, but it was also true that the Parkinsons were widely respected, and Governor Albert Hahl of New Guinea, where the Parkinsons' plantation was located, considered Phoebe Parkinson a close personal friend.[239] That would have been unthinkable in German Southwest Africa. Finally, Germans' racism toward Samoans differed qualitatively from that toward Africans. Germans and Europeans imagined the Pacific islands, but not Africa, as an Edenic paradise. While Germans considered Samoans to be an inferior race, they also found them beautiful, especially the women, and (what was practically synonymous for them) European-like.[240]

The German Southwest African and German East African bans were local measures that defied the Colonial Office's authority. The Samoan ban, by contrast, came from the Colonial Office. Wilhelm Solf, governor of Samoa from 1900 until 1911, became colonial secretary in December 1911. Only a few weeks later, on 17 January 1912, he ordered the new governor of German Samoa, Erich Schultz-Ewerth, to permit no new marriages between nonnatives and natives there.[241] It was the first occasion on which the Colonial Office had publicly sided with opponents of intermarriage. Solf's ban received only limited support in Samoa itself. While the Government Council in each of the other two colonies had unanimously upheld the bans, the Samoan Government Council approved Solf's ban with two abstentions. Even Governor Erich Schultz-Ewerth and Solf's subordinate at the Colonial Office Heinrich Schnee opposed banning intermarriage.[242] Solf's ban was all the more surprising because he was reputed to have taken a relaxed approach to mixed unions as governor. Like Governor von Rechenberg in German East Africa, Solf was a paternalist advocate of "native protection" who was committed to reforming colonialism, and his proudest achievement as governor was the establishment of Samoan colonial subjects' — not colonists' — self-administration.[243]

The 1912 ban for German Samoa had roots in both the colony and the metropole. As governor, Solf had frequently confronted angry German settlers who arrived with little capital and found a local labor shortage. The leader of this faction was Richard Deeken, and the two men became embroiled in a personal and political battle. Deeken made his name as a promoter of settlement in Samoa for the "little man." In a 1901 book Deeken urged Germans to settle in Samoa, claiming that anyone could become rich quickly there by planting cocoa.[244] With backing from pan-Germans, Deeken almost singlehandedly brought about a wave of settlement in Samoa by Germans of limited means. But these small-scale settlers did not become as rich as Deeken promised, and they resented the prosperity of large-scale planters of longer standing. Deeken, who came from Germany with his wife to run a plantation, insisted that Solf expropriate more land from colonial subjects and allow a freer hand in the exploitation of Chinese laborers, whom under-capitalized German planters sought in place of Samoan or New Guinean workers.[245] In the course of their very public battle, Solf sued Deeken for libel, had him imprisoned for abuse of Chinese laborers, and tried to expel him from the colony. However, Deeken was expert at escaping responsibility for the rumors he planted, and Solf's evidence fell short of what was needed for expulsion.[246]

Deeken antagonized other planters as well. While the newer, less wealthy settlers around Deeken were Germans, there were a number of British and U.S. citizens among the planters of longer standing. Deeken, who had founded the Planters' Association (Pflanzerverein) in 1903, decided that its meetings were to be held exclusively in the German language. It was a gratuitous insult to the established planters, given that English and Pidgin, not German, were the languages of business in the colony. When Solf criticized Deeken's disruptive actions, Deeken and his allies accused Solf of favoring non-German whites over Solf's own fellow Germans — a typical conflict between nationalist politics and the older imperial patriarchal colonial order.[247]

Solf and Deeken also clashed over the issue of race mixing. Both agreed that intermarriage was undesirable. The debate arose out of dis-putes within the German community over what kind of colonist (or, to use Solf's expression, "bringer of culture" [Kulturbringer]), ought to be favored. Solf insisted that Germans of few means were the likeliest to "go native." He wanted slow settlement, carried out by Germans with plenty of capital.[248] Wealthy planters and company agriculture, rather than capital-poor family farms, would best prevent Germans' racial de-generation, Solf argued, because the wealthy could afford regular con-tact with Germany and German wives, and would not have to depend on Samoans' assistance in economic hard times. And even if prosperous planters did have sexual relations with Samoan women, as they obvi-ously did, they could better afford to keep a Samoan family on the side.

Deeken and his allies wanted rapid, large-scale settlement in German Samoa. They saw the colony as an agrarian, family-based idyll where Germans of modest background could leave the unfair social hierarchies of Germany behind. If only Samoa could be wrested from bureaucratic government control and capitalist speculation, they argued, these plans could be realized. Press items appeared in Germany, probably with Deeken's help, that praised the sexual and racial morality of the newer, smaller-scale settlers and condemned that of wealthy planters, civil servants, and Solf himself.[249] The number of German civil servants in Samoa who lived with Samoan women became a small scandal in Germany, also with Deeken's help.[250] Within a few years Deeken had made Solf appear to be an ineffective administrator who abetted racial and sexual anarchy in Samoa.

In fact, Solf's opinions and actions about cohabitation and intermarriage changed over the years. In his early years as governor he took a laissez-faire approach toward Samoan-style marriages, and definitely preferred them to mixed marriages in the German style. He met criticism for this from Catholic missionaries in Samoa and the Reichstag Catholic Center Party delegate Matthias Erzberger, who frequently criticized colonial policy before 1907. The missionaries insisted that Christian marriage was always preferable to cohabitation and urged German-Samoan couples to marry under German law.[251] In 1900, when the new colonial code came into effect and reopened legal questions about intermarriage, Solf made a first attempt at developing a policy on race mixing in Samoa. He issued a decree that neither banned intermarriage nor upheld it, but rather focused on making sharper distinctions among the children. Persons of mixed Samoan and European heritage were to choose between registering themselves as "living in European style, that is, wanting to be treated as Europeans, or 'fa Samoa' (living in Samoan style) with corresponding treatment as Samoans."[252] A local court examined applicants' property and behavior.[253] Such distinctions were not necessarily easy to make. There were genuinely syncretic individuals, such as Phoebe Coe Parkinson and her sister Emma Coe, who ran one of the most successful commercial enterprises in the region and was married at various times to British and German men.[254] In addition, there were persons who changed categories at different times in their lives. Heinrich Schnee recalled an encounter in a "remote village on Savaii" during his early colonial career under Solf in German Samoa, before he went to German East Africa:

> To my great astonishment, a tall man in Samoan dress, that is, with bare chest, who had a completely European appearance, apart from bronze-toned skin, and with a very intelligent demeanor, presented himself to me as village chief. In the course of our conversation, which was held in the Samoan language, he told me that he was the son of an Englishman and a Samoan woman. He had lived for awhile "faapapalangi," that is, in the European style, but then, when he inherited the chiefship on his mother's side, preferred to live as a Samoan. He was perfectly happy and had no wish to appear as a European ever again.[255]

Samoan colonial society, like other colonial societies, was not amenable to categorization under a few unitary and unchanging identities.

As late as 1906, Solf told the Colonial Department that the political obstacles to banning intermarriage for civil servants in German Samoa were too great, and that banning intermarriage for the rest of the "white population" was out of the question.[256] But he changed his position the very next year. In 1907 Dernburg took office as colonial secretary and, as part of his program of colonial reform, asked each governor to submit a development plan for his colony. Solf dated his decision for a Samoan ban on intermarriage to that moment.[257] It is hard to know whether he actually changed his mind about the importance of race purity or simply decided to try putting the politics of race purity to his own uses.

Solf's development plan for German Samoa condemned race mixing in general and its political implication of racial equality. The fundamental mistake in international racial policy had been slave emancipation, Solf proclaimed; President Abraham Lincoln had doomed the United States by abolishing slavery. This was a bizarre argument, given that the antislavery cause had helped legitimize the annexation of the German colonial empire that Solf now headed.[258] Now, Solf continued, the chaos of the Reconstruction South was about to descend on the German colonies because Reich law unnaturally and unacceptably granted German citizenship to the legitimate children of German men and African or Samoan women. Mixed marriages were "tasteless and an insult to white women" as well as "immoral, because they prostitute[d] the essence and moral value of the marital bond as practiced among civilized peoples."[259] The colonial administration should ban intermarriage in Samoa, Solf concluded, but had to be prepared "to brave the attacks of all those who, out of ignorance, false humaneness, or misunderstood morality, share the standpoint of the missions."[260]

Governor Solf in effect permitted a ban on intermarriage in 1910 when he refused to intervene in the decision of a district judge in Samoa, Adolf Schlettwein, who had denied marriage to two mixed couples.[261] In Schlettwein's legal opinion, the Colonial Code of 1900 forbade intermarriage because the law did not expressly extend German legal forms to the native partner (that was left, it will be remembered, to a future decree). Samoans' relative racial similarity to Germans, Schlettwein wrote, did not justify bending the law.[262] Schlettwein proposed a ban on intermarriage that would allow exceptions for Samoan colonial subjects fluent in a European language and living European style; the governor was to approve each case individually. When Schlettwein attempted in 1910 to deny marriage to a third couple, the plantation owner Dr. Wilhelm Grevel and a Samoan woman named Savali, his actions brought Solf notoriety inside Germany. After Schlettwein and other local judges refused to marry the couple, Grevel appealed to Governor Solf. Solf was irritated that an educated, clearly bourgeois man such as Grevel, who violated Solf's expectation that prosperous planters would bring wives from Germany or at least keep a Samoan partner as an informal mistress, could bring such a "crass" case and told him to await a general ruling on intermarriage from the Colonial Office.[263]

Less than a month later, Solf succeeded Lindequist as colonial secretary in Berlin. In January 1912 he banned intermarriage for Samoa, and his decree contained a specific rejection of Grevel's application to marry.[264] His ban also included new definitions that were intended to align race more closely with citizenship status. All children of mixed parentage born outside marriage and after the January 1912 ban now became "natives." Mixed-descent persons born to married couples or to fathers who later legitimized them became "white." That left mixed-descent persons who had been born before the ban and whose fathers had not recognized them. These were divided into two further groups: those to be "treated as white" and those to be "treated as natives." To be treated as white, these persons had to register in the colony's "List of

Mixed-Bloods" (*Mischlingsliste*). Criteria included fluency in the German language, a European education, and a generally European way of life.[265] If a person included on the list was found unworthy later due to failure to meet the criteria, he or she was to be removed from the list. How knowledge of such a failure would reach the authorities in charge of the list was not specified.

In Solf's version of racial certification, culture was to serve as the swing factor in determining race. His decree appeared more flexible than the German Southwest African measures, and it certainly eased the impact of race purity measures on German fathers. But it was no more compatible with German citizenship law than Tecklenburg's blood percentages or the German Southwest African court's one-drop rule. Solf's decree still amounted to second-guessing existing citizenship law. Nevertheless Solf persevered, even expressing interest in making a unitary policy on intermarriage and mixed-descent persons for all the colonies.[266] His idea for a uniform colonial race policy arose not only from the Samoan context, but also from the interaction between colony and metropole in the debate over race mixing.

Although the groundwork for Solf's January 1912 ban was laid in Samoa, it had a particular metropolitan context as well. It called forth outrage in Germany. Heinrich Schnee, who was now Solf's subordinate in the Colonial Office (and soon to be governor of German East Africa), was surprised at the "storm from the Center and Social Democrats — first in the press, then in the Reichstag" — and noted that Solf "had great difficulty in defending himself."[267] It was in this context that the Reichstag approved the May 1912 resolution on behalf of persons in mixed families. The resolution asked the Federal Council to initiate legislation to clarify the rights of "whites" and "natives" in mixed marriages and of children of mixed sexual unions, whether legitimized through marriage or not. While the Civil Code set forth rules for the children of unmarried female German citizens (they took their mother's citizenship), it did not define the citizenship of children of unmarried female colonial subjects. The resolution showed the influence of missionary societies, whose members argued that banning intermarriage in effect favored the immorality of cohabitation; of jurists who rejected the use of race in citizenship law; and of those who rejected the idea that the colonies were a space so distinct from Germany that they required different rules of law and morality. The Budget Commission passed the resolution on 20 March 1912 with a vote of 21 to 4.[268] Solf was intensely irritated, and his annual speech to the Reichstag on the colonial budget was rude and provoking.[269] On 8 May 1912 the Reichstag passed the resolution in plenary session, with a vote of 203 to 133.[270] However, the Federal Council vetoed the resolution.

The resolution indicated not only the strength of metropolitan opposition to the bans on intermarriage, but also the Reichstag's determination to increase its own role in colonial legislation.[271] When Imperial Chancellor Theobald von Bethmann Hollweg and his foreign secretary, Alfred von Kiderlen-Wächter, resolved the Second Morocco Crisis by changing the borders of German Cameroon without consulting the Colonial Office or the Reichstag, the Reichstag was infuriated at the imperial chancellor's power to order colonial matters by decree.[272] When Solf made use of precisely that controversial power of decree to issue his January 1912 ban, it was "like a spark in a powder keg."[273] Even the procolonial National Liberals in the Reichstag opposed Solf temporarily. The storm over the resolution was at least as much about how to force the government to take responsibility for its chaotic foreign and colonial policy as it was about race mixing.

In fact, in spite of the multifarious opinions and proposals aired over the previous decade or so, there was not much real disagreement over race mixing. As a colonialist periodical summed up, "in the final analysis" the resolution had "nothing to do with the actual race question. On that matter, thank God, there is complete agreement among all parties, Center and Social Democracy included, that race mixing is objectionable [*verwerflich*]."[274] That was true: even the strongest opponents of bans in the Reichstag, such as the Social Democrat Georg Ledebour, made their personal aversion to intermarriage clear in the debates that led to the May resolution.[275] The real debate all along had been over the extent of the protection to be offered German men as their old colonial prerogative of sexual access came to be reformulated as race mixing.

Sexual unions between German men and colonized women were an idiosyncratic set of phenomena stemming from diverse social contexts of each colony as well as from a number of ideological and cultural sources within Germany. Yet once they were grouped under the heading of race mixing in the course of political struggle, it was hard to set them aside again. Colonial administrators committed themselves ever more to systematic, bureaucratic approaches to race mixing. In July 1912 Solf asked all colonial governors to hold a discussion of the "mixed-blood question." It was, he told them, "one of the most important problems of colonial policy," and "its solution, however it turns out, will intrude deeply into the private interests of the white population."[276] In 1913 he carried forward his policy of making distinctions among people of mixed descent. To relieve "hardships that have appeared where a fundamental mixed marriage ban has been emphasized," Solf proposed empowering governors to reclassify certain colonial subjects as having the status of whites. While policy on intermarriage was to be unitary across the colonial empire, the status of illegitimate mixed-descent children could still be handled by each governor according to local conditions. However — and this constituted a new form of oversight from the Berlin Colonial Office — governors were to inform Solf of their intentions before issuing their decrees.[277]

Self-administration never removed colonists from the colonial administration's and metropole's tutelage. Yet the liberal nationalist colonists and their supporters won the right to be heard. Even if race were questionable as a social distinction among Germans in the metropole, Germans readily believed in the factual reality of race in the colonial context. Colonists and colonialists claimed special authority, gained through practical experience, on the latter.[278] And even if a judge, governor, or other civil servant was now empowered to reclassify individuals, the power to bring such cases to their attention lay in settler society itself. The colonists had won the "right" to a mode of political participation, not least via popular denunciation.

By 1914 most colonialists agreed on two strategies for reducing race mixing. One was to restrict the rights of African and Pacific Islander women, which, it was hoped, would dissuade German men from having sexual relations with them, or at least from formalizing the relationship. The other was to encourage white German women's settlement. Colonialist men liked these strategies because they promised to alter white German men's sexual choices while leaving their rights and prerogatives intact. Colonialist women endorsed these strategies because they entailed a vital role for German women as colonizers. While under the older patriarchal system a wife, whatever her ancestry, was not considered important enough to affect a German man's public standing in a colony, the liberal nationalist model of colonial masculinity made the white German woman a necessary partner in colonization.

The debate among men over race mixing offered colonialist women a new opportunity, though not of the women's own making. A number of questions remained, however. What if German women's simple arrival in the colonies failed to halt sexual relations between German men and colonized women? The men's debate ignored the economic basis of German women's travel to and subsistence in the colony as well as the economic basis of many mixed sexual alliances. Would white German women live on paid work there? Only before marriage? Was marriage itself compulsory? Unlike the older female roles of missionary or nurse, the liberal nationalists' role for German women depended on the women's whiteness *and* capacity for maternity—it was highly racialized. It also ignored the political Woman Question of how men's and women's sexual, familial, and social relationships were to be reformed. Colonialist women were overwhelmingly supportive of race purity, but they were uneasy with their assigned role as sexual substitutes for female colonial subjects. The next chapter discusses their efforts to imbue their new role as partners in colonization with cultural and national, as well as racial, meaning.

CHAPTER FOUR

A New Colonial Femininity:

Feminism, Race Purity,

and Domesticity, 1898–1914

The debate over race mixing, and especially the notion of racial citizenship, opened up new opportunities for colonialist women beyond nursing and missionary work. Colonialist women in Germany acted on these opportunities at moments of general nationalist mobilization: the passage of the Navy Laws in 1898 and 1900, and the election of resoundingly procolonial delegates to the Reichstag in January 1907. Members of the government consciously cultivated such popular nationalism, but it also took on a life of its own.[1] Women of a range of political persuasions took part in these waves of nationalist enthusiasm. At the same time, the colonial woman farmer (*Farmersfrau*) came to dominate the imagination of colonialist women. A wave of memoirs and novels by actual women colonists documented and dramatized the abilities of the colonial woman farmer to a reading audience in Germany. Most of these women were married, although a few were widowed or single, but those fundamental markers of women's social existence receded before the all-important recounting of women's productive work on the farm. In colonial space, women's work promised direct participation in the German community: women could become the yeoman farmers of classical republicanism. Colonialist women's fascination with the *Farmersfrau* led them to join the faction of men who upheld settlement colonialism. Since the mid-nineteenth century, German colonialists had been urging emigrants from overpopulated rural areas to go to yet-to-be-established German colonies instead of to foreign lands such as the United States.[2] Such emigration would still serve as a social "safety valve" protecting German lands from revolution, yet would not, it was hoped, drain away population. In fact, the high rate of emigration to the United States and other destinations had fallen by the 1880s, when Germany annexed its colonies; by 1900 Germany had a net labor shortage.[3] And far from offering a refuge from economic uncertainty, colonial farmers were just as vulnerable to the mysteries and instabilities of the international economy as industrial workers.[4] Finally, settlement of the German colonies remained minuscule in relation to the metropolitan population and nineteenth-century emigration to the United States. Yet settlement colonialism retained its influence nevertheless. Even though it was based on circular reasoning and a flawed understanding of economics and statistics, it addressed anxieties about political conflict and industrialization.[5] It also addressed middle-class women's anxieties about their own economic superfluity.

Two political moments were particularly important in colonialist women's activism. The first involved the procolonial feminists of the Women's Welfare Association (Verein "Frauenwohl," founded 1888), who sought to help plan women's settlement in German Southwest Africa in 1898 and 1907. Their failure to obtain men's support for their vision of a feminist transformation of colonial society exemplifies the difficulties German women faced when they sought to become not only objects but also agents of colonial settlement. The second moment, in 1907, concerns a quite different group of women, generally the relatives of military officers and colonial officials, who did enjoy the support of colonialist men. They founded the second secular organization run by and for colonialist women: the German-Colonial Women's League (Deutschkolonialer Frauenbund), which was soon renamed the Women's League of the German Colonial Society (Frauenbund der Deutschen Kolonialgesellschaft). In spite of its name, the organization was formally independent of the male-dominated German Colonial Society. In fact, already by 1910 the Women's League had conflicted with that organization on several issues. Although colonialist men expected the Women's League to be a more congenial working partner than the Women's Welfare Association, the Women's League took up some of the latter's ideas.

Colonialist women did not want to repudiate the roles of marriage and motherhood to which the debate over race mixing had drawn attention. However, they did want to build on those roles in order to claim a larger social and, for the more feminist of them, political role for women. But essentialism about women's reproductive capacity always structured procolonial women's activism between the late 1890s and the

First World War. This was evident in two ways that are discussed briefly at this chapter's conclusion. First, the German Women's Association for Nursing in the Colonies shifted its goals ever closer to the pronatalist, family settlement program of the newer Women's League. Both were converging on the goal of promoting racially defined German reproduction. Second, colonialist men and even some women grew increasingly impatient with the existence of more than one women's colonialist organization. As racial reproduction came to subsume other reasons for women's presence in the colonies, there seemed to be a need for only one agitation organization. Colonialist women gained the attention of the men of the movement, but only by allowing themselves to be the means to an end of racial reproduction. While colonialist women sincerely shared that goal, they also found it limiting.

RADICAL FEMINISTS AND THE "CULTURAL TASKS OF WOMAN" IN THE COLONIES

The Women's Welfare Association was a radical bourgeois (i.e., nonsocialist) feminist organization that worked on issues affecting both middle- and working-class women such as suffrage, employment conditions, the creation of new women's careers, and prostitutes' rights. Its willingness to engage socialist feminists set it apart from other bourgeois feminist groups.[6] Like other bourgeois organizations, however, it upheld nationalism as a basis for progressive social transformation. Its founder, Minna Cauer, who also edited its journal, *The Women's Movement* (*Die Frauenbewegung*), saw the navy debates of the late 1890s as an occasion for educating women politically. She reminded readers of *The Women's Movement* that whenever the "people" of Germany were invoked, women were also meant. She insisted that women had a duty to engage themselves in national and nationalist politics even though they could not vote in statewide elections.[7] Cauer hoped that the women's movement would have a "cultural" influence on conventional party political activity.[8] The Women's Welfare Association saw the possibility of concrete activity in another nationalist project of the late 1890s: settling German women in the colonies. Governor Theodor Leutwein and men from the German Colonial Society were seeking to reduce intermarriage between male colonists and local women in German Southwest Africa.

Governor Leutwein visited Germany in 1898 and publicized a plan whereby single women would receive free passage to the colony and placement in a paying job (usually domestic service) for a contracted period of two years. They would meanwhile form a pool of prospective brides for male colonists.

Cauer saw the plan as yet another opportunity for women's political engagement, but not all of her readers agreed. One protested that the men's financial sponsorship of prospective brides was tantamount to procuring.[9] Another remarked that women ought to be suspicious of such a financially generous offer; it would seem to bode ill for the colony's working conditions and marriage choices.[10] A third, the feminist Gertrud Bülow von Dennewitz, argued that the male colonists did not deserve the women. Sending them "suitable female breeding material from the Reich," as she sarcastically put it, would not prevent the growth of a mixed race because German men's sexual fascination with African women would continue unabated.[11] As an example of the sexual violence present in the colonies Bülow von Dennewitz cited a passage from her distant cousin Frieda von Bülow's novel *Tropical Rage,* in which the heroine's drunken brother and his companions invade Africans' homes and try to rape the women. Bülow von Dennewitz also cited with disapproval a play written by Leutwein's secretary, Max Hilzebecher, that depicted the happy love affair of a German man and an African woman. In its final scene the Nama leader Hendrik Witbooi and Governor Leutwein bless the union. This idealized romance was being staged to great acclaim in Germany, she complained, at the very moment when Governor Leutwein was touring Germany giving speeches about the shortage of German women in the colonies and the ensuing danger to race purity.[12] Here, a long literary tradition of representing German colonization as peaceful and harmonious through the image of sexual union between a German man and an "exotic" woman conflicted with the literal claims of the advocates of race purity.[13] Bülow von Dennewitz clearly disapproved of both the settlement scheme and intermarriage between German men and African women.

Minna Cauer agreed that the men's settlement scheme had the potential to exploit women, but she found it too attractive to dismiss out of hand. The colonies needed women's moral influence, she claimed, noting that "previous experiences have unfortunately shown that barbarism, selfish economic interests, and old-fashioned views have brought about a shocking crudity over there."[14] She and other feminists would gladly help, she wrote, if men would work with them on the "solution of cultural tasks in the colonies."[15] Marriage was a worthy goal, Cauer continued, but German women could not be restricted to a wifely position. They needed a larger role that would permit them to exert positive moral influence. Cauer proposed a number of alterations to the men's existing plan that would better protect the women emigrants.

Not only did the colonies need German women, according to Cauer, but German women needed the colonies. Cauer thought women's emancipation could be institutionalized more easily in colonial space than in the metropole: "Here is a field of activity for women, but it can be taken up only if women are given the same position as men in the colonies — which, after all, do not have to reckon with traditions and old-fashioned prejudices. Women must immediately count as equal-born, equally enfranchised members in the churches, schools, and municipalities that are just now springing up from new beginnings."[16] As the men who advocated race purity overlooked the entrenchment of the existing kinship pattern with its distinctive places for white women and women of color, so did Cauer overlook the fact that German Southwest Africa was already socially formed by particular power relations, including gender relations.

Cauer's aspirations elicited a prompt response from Governor Leutwein: "The so called 'women's movement' might possess some larger kernel of justification in the old fatherland, with its surplus of women. To transfer it to the colonies, with their tremendous minority of women, where the *female*, but only as *such*, is sought and treasured, can only harm women themselves."[17] Like Cauer, Leutwein saw German Southwest Africa as a social space qualitatively different from Germany. But for him, that difference meant the irrelevance of conflict between the sexes there. He believed that feminist activism in Germany was rooted in an excess of women, and he rejected the idea that the colonies could be a more feminist space than the metropole. By "female as such" he meant the reproductive woman who was the wife of a German man and the mother of white babies. It is not clear how he thought feminism would harm German women colonists, but it is clear that he saw no need to share leadership with "surplus" women. Leutwein refused to meet with Cauer, and he and the German Colonial Society proceeded to send the first contingent of single women, who arrived in German Southwest Africa in January 1899.[18]

To help pay for the expensive scheme the German Colonial Society requested a subsidy from the Colonial Department of the Foreign Office. When the Reichstag discussed the scheme in plenary session, Social Democrats and Progressives mentioned Cauer and reiterated her criticism. They accused the German Colonial Society of procuring and pointed to the exploitative labor contract.[19] Now Cauer and Anna Pappritz, another feminist from the Women's Welfare Association best known to historians for her work on prostitutes' rights, appealed once more to Governor Leutwein and the German Colonial Society. They presented a set of proposals prefaced with the declaration: "The women of Germany are thoroughly sympathetic to settling young women in the colonies. . . . However, the maxim that the female, but only as such, is sought for the colonies has to be dismissed." They "hope[d] and expect[ed] that a free and worthy position [would] be granted to women in the colonies, since only thus [could] the cultural task of woman be fulfilled."[20]

Cauer and Pappritz asked that women be seated on the selection committee and that the labor contract include provisions to help women defend themselves against on-the-job sexual and economic exploitation. They also proposed measures aimed at increasing colonial career opportunities for single middle-class women. They suggested hiring a "supervisory matron" to guide young women on their journey to the colony and oversee their employment, and also seeking women with formal qualifications in agricultural management, market gardening, teaching, and secular nursing for positions in the colonies.[21] Evidently concerned that only working-class women would represent German womanhood in the colonies, Cauer and Pappritz cited as their model the United British Women's Emigration Society, which operated on the principle that "above all the *educated* [*gebildete*] woman must be the female pioneer in the colonies."[22]

The German Colonial Society appeased the Reichstag by adding a provision for free return passage if a woman became ill or completed her two years without marrying. But it refused to adopt any of Cauer and Pappritz's suggestions. In mid-1899, after months of seeking to influence the emigration program, Cauer concluded bitterly: "As lowly sexual creatures condemned to slavery by a harsh contract that rests on coercion, women will never be able to fulfill a cultural duty, and under such circumstances hopefully no women's organization will offer to participate in the work for colonization."[23] The difference between her experience and that of the Women's Association for Nursing is instructive. While the Women's Association for Nursing behaved obsequiously toward colonialist men and was offering, in effect, a subsidy, Women's Welfare dared to challenge the men's judgment and to suggest expensive alterations to the men's plans, such as the supervisory matron. And while the Women's Association for Nursing did not seek to change colonial societies, but only to offer aid under the supervision of male doctors, Women's Welfare proposed a role for women beyond male control that was intended to transform colonial society.

In 1906 a second upsurge in popular nationalism and imperialism aroused the German public. Once more Germany's world power seemed to be at stake. After two years of an expensive and scandal-ridden colonial war in German Southwest Africa, the Reichstag became recalcitrant about appropriating further funds for it. Emperor Wilhelm II dissolved the Reichstag in December 1906, and new elections were held. Cauer hoped that the drama of the German Southwest African war would stir women into political action and that the prospect of new elections would induce left-liberals to overcome their disunity and rally around the colonial cause.[24] The Reichstag's dissolution was a "wake-up call," she told readers of *The Women's Movement:* "Is it a matter of indifference to women if the blood of German men flows on the dark continent; are they not sons of German mothers. . . ? Yes, the colonial question is in the final analysis also a woman question, for the new world can become a homeland for German men only when German women are successfully settled there."[25]

Yet Cauer was to see women snubbed once more. A major colonialist assembly was held in Berlin on 8 January 1907. The speakers included Bernhard Dernburg, soon to be colonial secretary of the newly independent Colonial Office, and noted social scientists from the Association for Social Policy (Verein für Sozialpolitik) such as the economist Gustav Schmoller and the historian Max Delbrück.[26] In accordance with the Prussian Law of Association, which had outlawed women's presence at "political" gatherings since 1850, women were refused entry.[27] The Women's Welfare Association protested the exclusion of women with a flier that read in part:

> [We] condemn the shortsightedness of leading men who want to win the wide masses of the people for questions of world power politics, and go about it by excluding the striving elements of working and thinking women from working for the political future of their people.
>
> This manner of proceeding directly contradicts the wish recently expressed by Deputy Colonial Director Dernburg that women emigrate to the colonies, as well as the principle enunciated by Professor Rohrbach and other authorities that the *settlement of the colonies can be carried out only through the immigration of German women.*
>
> Women therefore insist on their right to be included at all times in discussions of the future of our colonies.[28]

Cauer sent a copy of the flier to Dernburg and recounted the Women's Welfare Association's efforts to participate in women's settlement.[29] Dernburg, who apparently had no previous ties to the German Colonial Society, now learned about Cauer's efforts for the first time. Although he refused to criticize the Prussian Law of Association, he was not as dismissive toward Cauer as Governor Leutwein and the German Colonial Society had been.[30] After Dernburg became colonial secretary he added the theme of women's settlement to his program of colonial reform. He took to declaring in his speeches that "railroads, doctors, and women" were what the colonies needed most.[31] He even publicly praised Cauer on one occasion as the one who had first alerted him to the importance of German women's participation in colonization. Cauer's friend and colleague Else Lüders remarked that it was probably the first time a government official had commended the radical women's movement.[32]

Dernburg's support for Cauer and the Women's Welfare Association came too late. The very assembly at which Dernburg praised Cauer had been convened to celebrate the founding of a new colonialist women's organization: the German-Colonial Women's League. The women who formed the league came from military and colonial officials' families, had extensive ties to the German Colonial Society, and did not consider themselves feminists. Cauer joined this new organization, but she did not play any leading role in it.[33] The Women's League participated in the planning of women's settlement, but on an entirely different basis than Cauer and Pappritz had wanted. Far from challenging the men of the German Colonial Society, these women tried to counter public criticism of the scheme by lending it feminine respectability. As one member of the new Women's League recalled, the German Colonial Society thought no one would question the morality and judgment of middle-class ladies in charge of selecting and sending prospective brides.[34] As it turned out, criticism of the scheme as immoral, exploitative, and ineffective against interracial sex continued.[35] And even though the colonialist men had hand-picked the women they now worked with, the issues that Cauer and Pappritz had raised did not disappear.

"RACE WAR" IN THE EARLY GERMAN-COLONIAL WOMEN'S LEAGUE

The German Southwest African war was won militarily, but the peace was being lost to race mixing, claimed Luise Weitzenberg, one of the eleven colonial officers' and officials' wives who founded the German-Colonial Women's League. Baroness Adda von Liliencron later recalled that Weitzenberg had appealed to her for help with the new organization in terms of race war: "The hard-won territory was in danger of going completely to the Boers and Kaffirs . . . because a growing race of mixed-bloods threatened from the beginning to nip German-dom in the bud."[36] Liliencron succumbed to Weitzenberg's plea and agreed to become chairwoman of the Women's League. Under her, it was run by women but on behalf of men, especially men of the colonial military. Liliencron's motivations could hardly have differed more from Cauer's hopes of women's enfranchisement via liberal nationalism. For Liliencron, colonialism offered not civic equality for women but affirmation of German militarism. Her interest in the German colonies dated only to the war of 1904–1907 in German Southwest Africa, but it had deep roots in her lifelong fascination with male military adventure.

Born Baroness von Wrangel, Liliencron came from one of the most prominent and reactionary military families of Germany. Her great-uncle General von Wrangel commanded the forces that crushed the

1848 revolution in Berlin. Not yet four years old at the time, Liliencron claimed to remember how her father, also an officer, had to enter his Königsberg house through the back door to escape a crowd of revolutionaries stoning his carriage.[37] An only child, Liliencron received in full force the conservative Prussian and militaristic upbringing that her parents so valued. She listened entranced to the battle stories of her father's fellow army officers, so that "from my earliest youth an appreciation was impressed upon me for the idea of heroism, the spirit of sacrifice, and loyalty to the death." She penned her own stories of combat from an early age, in spite of her parents' opposition to girls doing any sort of writing: "My father feared that I might become, as he called it, a bluestocking, and my mother was worried for my health."[38] Parents and child compromised after she reached the age of thirteen by allowing one hour each Saturday during which she could put down on paper her military tales.

After her marriage in 1864 to Baron Karl von Liliencron, an officer who served in the Austro-Prussian and Franco-Prussian Wars, Liliencron took part in the usual charitable activities of officers' wives, such as sewing and knitting items for soldiers. More interesting for her was an opportunity during the Franco-Prussian War to serve as a volunteer nurse in a Potsdam military hospital. When a doctor asked her to stand in for his trained nurse during an operation, Liliencron finally saw a soldier's blood flowing and proved to herself that she could be soldierly in her stoicism: "Neither the scalpel nor the wounds laid open had — as I had feared they would — any horror for me."[39] Soon she was able to approach the scene of combat more closely: hearing that her husband was stricken with cerebral typhoid fever, she traveled to the French front to care for him in 1870, relishing the adventurous journey. After her husband retired from the military, they moved to a landed estate in the Oberlausitz region of Saxony. Liliencron often ran the estate alone for months at a time while her husband served as delegate in the Provincial Diet (Landtag). She wrote patriotic plays, rehearsed her servants in the roles in the manor hall, and charged the locals admission in order to raise money for charities. She also taught geography and history at the village school.[40]

After her husband's death in 1901 Liliencron lived with her daughter in Schwerin, performed volunteer nursing at a military hospital, and taught military history to ex-soldiers. She wanted to be, in her own words, "a little bit of mother" for the soldiers.[41] She also continued her writing, churning out more than sixty novels, plays, biographies, short stories, and long poems with themes of past and contemporary military glory and titles such as *Loyal to the End*.[42] She described her oeuvre matter-of-factly: "These dilettante's writings [are] quite simple, without literary value. . . . [They are] intended only to inspire young, warmly beating hearts with the great deeds of the past."[43] She firmly believed that moments of patriotic euphoria created actual unity across classes, and that the more such moments she created, the less class conflict there would be. Her particular causes were "fallen" women, prisoners, and poor Polish laborers in the eastern provinces. She helped run nurseries and kindergartens for the mostly Polish-speaking children of working mothers and taught the children patriotic German songs, to the parents' disgust.[44] Around the time she became chairwoman of the German-Colonial Women's League, she was noted in the German *Who's Who* for her ceaseless writing and organizational work: "Enjoying a rare level of energy and youthful vigor, she is active from early morning until late at night."[45]

In her memoirs Liliencron admitted "with some shame" that the dispatch of troops to German Southwest Africa in January 1904 had escaped her notice. "I knew precious little about the colonies, although my dear little mother interested herself in every bit of colonial news, especially about Cameroon — the only one in our family to do so."[46] Then Liliencron happened on a newspaper account of a recent battle in German Southwest Africa that detailed how German soldiers crawled on all fours through withering fire: "That was undaunted heroism!"[47] Realizing that material for her writing was being lived right then, she sought out men in her own military circles who had volunteered for duty in German Southwest Africa. The war, trumpeted in the colonialist press as "the first war of Wilhelmine Germany," meant a chance for colonialists to escape the sense of being epigones of a more glorious German military past. Liliencron recounted her feelings while watching a ship full of colonial soldiers depart from Hamburg for the colony: "Memories of the war years in the time of my youth appeared before me; like a fleeting vision they marched past in the mind. Thrilling campaigns of heroism and loyalty to the death, stormy advances and exultant hurrahs, tenacious defense at danger-ridden posts, the spirit of sacrifice and comradeship in their finest moment, and at the same time blood and wounds and heroic death."[48] Liliencron's militaristic imagination was so powerful that she seemed sometimes scarcely to distinguish between actual and vicarious experience of war. She now announced her own intention to "enter the service of the colonial army," by which she meant raising charity funds and increasing publicity inside Germany for the colonial troops.[49] With the aid of a colonial army officer and the African servant of Colonel Ludwig von Estorff, a prominent commander in the German Southwest African war then visiting Berlin, she drafted a play entitled *In Africa*. After she polished it with authentic details according to their suggestions, *In Africa* played for three evenings to sold-out audiences.[50] Liliencron had long been producing nationalist verses and plays; now her colonialist writing career began. In quick succession she published a songbook commemorating the German Southwest African war with original verses to be sung to familiar melodies and an anthology of letters she had received from colonial army officers and enlisted soldiers.[51] She selected the letters from among the thirty or so a day that she received during the war. Her verses also appeared on commemorative postcards of the war. In colonialist circles she soon bore the affectionate nickname "Baroness of Africa."[52]

When Liliencron became chairwoman of the Women's League, it gained the services of a successful one-woman colonialist propaganda enterprise. The league's first major fund-raising event was a revival of *In Africa*.[53] Unlike Frieda von Bülow, whose colonial writing reputation rested on the authenticity of her colonial experience, Liliencron produced yards of colonialist text without ever having seen any colony. Liliencron savored her inauthentic yet vivid colonial persona: "Almost without exception, the first questions that strangers ask of me now are: 'How long were you over there? Have you become acclimatized again back here?' etc. Rather than admit that I was never in Southwest Africa, I would prefer most of all to answer: 'In spirit I was over there for years, took part in the entire *orlog* [war] and know perhaps as much about it as some who were personally in the precious, thorny land.'"[54] The German Southwest African war allowed Liliencron to create her own version of the military stories and fantasies that had obsessed her all her life. The colonial soldiers and officers mythologized her as a perfect pioneer and colonist. Fantastical anecdotes about the "Baroness of Africa" reached her ears: "From Southwest Africa, out of the south, I heard lately that they say I was in the colony for years and I possessed a special gift for training the natives to work and for taming the skittish animals of the wilderness. A springbok followed me like a dog, and on my shoulder sat a tame chameleon."[55] The two talents the soldiers attributed to her are telling: the effortless disciplining of African laborers and the ability to commune with and thereby control the natural environment. Apparently they derived comfort from the image of a mythical feminine colonizer who had effortlessly preceded their violent final conquest of the colony.

Liliencron wanted to continue "mothering" the colonial soldiers after the war, and the new Women's League with its administration of the women's settlement scheme provided just such an opportunity. Liliencron saw nothing wrong with sending women to work at temporary menial jobs on the assumption that they would soon marry. She did not see herself as serving women primarily in any case, but rather the male colonists, especially "her" veterans. The Women's League shared Governor Leutwein's opinion that the Woman Question had no relevance in the colonies. As a Women's League promotional flier from 1908 put it: "*The Woman Question in the colonies* arises, quite the reverse from in the home country, from the *lack of German women* out there." The flier pointed out that while almost five thousand German men lived in German Southwest Africa, barely more than a thousand German women did.[56] The Women's League urged German women to leave Germany, where they were supposedly superfluous, and go to German Southwest Africa where they were needed. They would become wives of colonial war heroes and at the same time solve a colonial policy problem: "As a result of this deficient in-migration by German women and girls, the great danger now exists that a mixed race will grow up out of the *natives.* This danger is especially prominent in the parts of the colony where the Hottentots are settled. This odd, yellow-skinned people is, in contrast to the negroes, very receptive to the influences of the whites, and their women are proud if their children's appearance betrays a white father."[57] By drawing attention to the putative characteristics of local African women, the flier suggested that German men had only a passive role in this phenomenon. Moreover, the flier cited Boers as a threat to the Germanness of the colony because of their sheer numbers and their language, which along with English, was commonly spoken in the colony; Rehobothers and British colonists likewise threatened the German character of the colony.[58] German men were in need, and only German women could help them: "The German soldier has conquered the land with the sword, the German farmer and trader seek to develop its economic potential, but *the German woman alone is called upon and able to keep it German*. We must raise a strong German lineage in Southwest Africa. As once in the rough, sandy marches of Brandenburg a capable and militarily strong branch of our people formed, it is certain that the new German lineage that is formed in the big, arid steppes will be far from the worst."[59]

The premises of race war and race mixing underlay the rest of the Women's League program as well. The Women's League aimed "to interest women of all classes [*Stände*] in colonial questions," to improve schools for white children, to "aid women and children in the colonies who [fell] into difficulties through no fault of their own," "to preserve and strengthen the economic and spiritual connections of women in the colonies with the homeland," and "to prepare and preserve a secure place for the cultivation and care of German family spirit and German customs and morals in the colonies."[60] The Women's League called on women to be conduits of colonialist sentiments in the home and community, claiming that women were uniquely capable of making public politics into private ways of living. At the same time, women were sought after as a popular audience for agitation: spectators who would donate, fill lecture halls, and subscribe to periodicals. Unlike the original statutes for the German-National Women's League written by Martha von Pfeil and Frieda von Bülow, the Women's League's statutes made no mention of church-related goals and named only activities with unmistakable feminine associations. Moreover, the Women's League's goals were directed entirely at German colonists; unlike missionary and secular nursing work, its statutes ignored colonial subjects. The goal of winning the supposed race war permeated all of the Women's League's activities.

A year later the German-Colonial Women's League signed an agreement with the German Colonial Society that gave it the right to use the latter's name, and became the Women's League of the German Colonial Society. The 1908 agreement also provided for the Women's League to administer the women's settlement scheme that the German Colonial Society had initiated in 1898.[61] The German Colonial Society still paid the sponsored women's ship passage, was legal party to the women's job contracts, and monitored Women's League board meetings through special delegates; nevertheless, the Women's League was a separate organization, not a branch of the men's organization. Liliencron and the chairman of the German Colonial Society, Duke Albrecht Johann zu Mecklenburg, anticipated harmonious — and hierarchical — cooperation. Liliencron recalled from the celebration of the new agreement: "The Duke's words at the banquet best characterized our position toward the German Colonial Society as it had been envisaged when, after his toast, His Highness clinked glasses with me 'to the young marriage.'"[62]

This "marriage" was burdened with the unspoken but all too obvious question of fidelity, both individual and racial. German male colonists were hardly helpless or passive in their relationships with African women, as men's private photographs of themselves with their lovers showed.[63] It is impossible to know how many male colonists and men active in colonialist politics engaged in interracial sexual relationships, but the men themselves claimed the number was high. What colonialist men did not say was that even those men who spoke out the most loudly against race mixing had done it. Hans von Ramsay, for example, a former colonial army captain who held the office of secretary of the Women's League and remained active in it for years, fathered an unacknowledged daughter with a Swahili woman in German East Africa.[64] The sexual double standard that so irritated the feminist readers of Minna Cauer's *The Women's Movement* was built into the Women's League's program: it was the postulate of men's helplessness, and not feminist principles of parity, that permitted women's participation in planning women's settlement. Women were sought for German Southwest Africa not for their own sake, but for men's. Such distance from feminism was important for the earliest members of the new Women's League, but within a few years the two groups drew closer.

Tensions emerged between the German Colonial Society and the Women's League when their visions of colonialism diverged. The Women's League became a gathering place for men of radical nationalist, prosettler, and anti-big-business political opinions. Meanwhile, it also offered women an active and economic role in the colonies and colonial movement without the stigma of feminist activism. The Women's League sought to become "populist" (*volkstümlich*), or nonexclusive with regard to people of both sexes and all classes. Populist tendencies had existed in the colonialist movement from its beginnings and periodically produced splinter groups. By 1907 such populist splinter groups for men included the German Colonial League (Deutscher Kolonialbund) and German-Populist Colonial Association (Deutschvolklicher Kolonialverein).[65] Both emphasized race purity and policies favoring small-scale family settlement.

The Women's League's partnership with populist men is best demonstrated in the periodical *Colony and Home* (*Kolonie und Heimat*). The brainchild of some men who wished to challenge the German Colonial Society, it was first issued in July 1907, when the excitement at the Reichstag elections of January 1907 was still fresh. It was a novum in the colonialist press. No "dry doctrines" of a "small circle of experts" were to appear in its pages (a dig at the German Colonial Society's publications).[66] It was filled with photographs, puzzles, jokes, serialized fiction, sentimental verse, colonists' and colonial soldiers' memoirs, and articles on colonial policy written at an undemanding level. Its inaugural issue declared that it was the first "colonial family journal": "We *want to gain a place around the German hearth,* here and beyond the oceans. Also, it is precisely the *women* whom we want to attract as comrades in our cause, and to fill *youth* with true-to-life pictures from German distant lands, to form in them a freer and wider vision."[67] The editor, Eduard Buchmann, was committed to keeping *Colony and Home* inexpensive, as befitted a "family" publication. Buchmann emphasized that both men and women from many different social and occupational backgrounds were on his staff.[68] Several had served in the colonial army; others were women colonists who were publishing war memoirs and novels.

Buchmann and his colleagues at *Colony and Home* sought out the Women's League leaders and repeatedly invited them to join their new journalistic project. By contrast, the editor of the German Colonial Society's much older *German Colonial Journal (Deutsche Kolonialzeitung)* did not bother to approach the Women's League at all. Liliencron found the *German Colonial Journal* too expensive and too oriented toward economic and other abstract policy issues, and she liked *Colony and Home*'s populist tone and low price.[69] When Buchmann offered a page in *Colony and Home* to the Women's League at a cut rate, Liliencron agreed to make *Colony and Home* the official publication of the Women's League. She cited the "advantage" it offered of bringing "our cause to wide, varied circles," and its suitability to members of the Women's League, who came "partly from very plain elements, mostly also women," who would be more interested in "pictures and a colonial novel or so."[70]

Colony and Home's formula was successful. Colonial Secretary Bernhard Dernburg and Imperial Chancellor Bernhard von Bülow praised it as evidence of just the sort of colonialist enthusiasm they wanted to promote.[71] Even the secretary of the German Colonial Society, the navy doctor Ludwig Sander, had to concede that *Colony and Home* had outdone the German Colonial Society. Sander, whose wife, Sophie Sander, was one of the original founders of the Women's League, told Liliencron: "We freely admit that the paper is well suited to interest precisely the little people and families in the colonies and colonial issues, and we ourselves would have liked to have created such an enterprise. . . . As it is . . . for just those reasons *Colony and Home* already has such a big head start on our *Colonial Journal* that we must use all our energies and means in order not to allow it to drive our paper altogether to the wall."[72] *Colony and Home* became a forum for snide remarks about the stodgy, older German Colonial Society.[73] A common source of contention was its habit of crediting the women's settlement scheme entirely to the Women's League without mentioning the German Colonial Society's funding. The German Colonial Society repeatedly complained to the Women's League, whereupon the women either blandly apologized or, rather unconvincingly, denied knowledge of *Colony and Home*'s editorial decisions.[74]

Even as the strain between the Women's League and the German

Colonial Society grew, the alliance between the Women's League and the men of *Colony and Home* flourished. Buchmann joined the Women's League board and remained a member through the First World War. His longtime contributor, the former colonial army captain Richard Volkmann, served as treasurer of the Women's League and remained active in it into the Nazi era. In fact, men played an important role generally in the Women's League; by 1914 men had founded 21 of its 134 chapters.[75] The Women's League enjoyed the support of well-known colonial policy experts, including Paul Rohrbach, who contributed regularly to *Colony and Home* and helped the Women's League establish a hostel for its newly arrived women in the German Southwest African town of Keetmanshoop; and Wilhelm Külz, who also contributed to *Colony and Home* and gave public lectures to benefit the Women's League.[76]

Probably the single most important man in the Women's League was the doctor and hygiene professor Philalethes Kuhn. His wife, Maria Kuhn, was one of the league's original founders and remained a very active member for years.[77] She accompanied her husband while he served as a military doctor and district commander in German Southwest Africa from 1896 to 1905.[78] They returned to Germany and stayed until 1912, when he took a post as a military doctor in Cameroon. During that posting Kuhn and another doctor close to the Women's League, Hans Ziemann, organized the racial segregation of the city of Duala in the name of combating malaria. Africans were forcibly expropriated, expelled from their city, and resettled in an unhealthy area some distance away.[79] Kuhn exemplifies several German natural scientists who drew on colonial experiences to make innovative careers in the new fields of racial and social hygiene.[80] A member of the Society for Racial Hygiene (Gesellschaft für Rassenhygiene) since 1908, he became professor for social hygiene at the University of Strassburg (Strasbourg) during the First World War, then professor for social hygiene at the Technical Institute at Dresden and at the University of Giessen in the 1920s, where he was an early Nazi activist. Philalethes Kuhn founded four Women's League chapters, including the major ones of Greater Berlin and Bremen. He also belonged to the Berlin chapter of the German Colonial Society, which had been a radical nationalist outpost ever since Carl Peters had won an upset victory as chairman in the early

1890s. Kuhn's machinations on behalf of the Women's League were so obvious that a German Colonial Society member complained that the Berlin chapter worked more for the Women's League than for itself.[81]

Two other medical doctors and "race hygiene" specialists used the Women's League as a platform to argue that race purity was possible not only in German Southwest Africa but also in the intensely tropical climate of Cameroon and Togo. Ludwig Külz, brother of the municipal self-administration expert Wilhelm Külz, was a doctor employed by the colonial administration in Cameroon and Togo who became a professor at the University of Hamburg after the First World War. In a 1906 collection of his correspondence prepared by his wife, Agnes Külz, he argued that white German women were quite capable of living and reproducing healthily in the Tropics.[82] Hans Ziemann, a navy doctor, medical adviser for Cameroon, and later professor, who had collaborated with Kuhn in the segregation of Duala, likewise argued that women as well as men could live over the long term in the tropics. The key for both, he emphasized, was strict adherence to modern rules of hygiene. In 1907, when it was still widely doubted that German women could live in Cameroon, Ziemann wrote: "Above all we must counteract the development of a mixed population by sending ever more white women. . . . It is our world historical calling to rule in Africa, not over black brothers, but over black subjects."[83] In 1912 he reiterated that "German family life" was the "only and the most radical means" of fighting race mixing.[84] These German discussions of acclimatization and white women occurred several years earlier than or concurrently with those in other European colonial empires.[85]

Men joined the Women's League because of its race purity program, its populist approach to colonial policy, its low cost, and its lack of snobbery, at least compared with other organizations in the colonialist movement. Although the Women's League membership was elite in the context of the whole of German society, it was less aristocratic than the Women's Association for Nursing. None of the original eleven women founders bore noble titles, and even though many aristocrats did join the Women's League, they tended to be less highly titled than those in the Women's Association for Nursing.[86] During its final years, the league was dominated by Foreign Office, colonial army, and navy families of middle and lower rank. Liliencron wished to distance the group from the social elitism of established procolonial circles. When enlisted soldiers who had fought in the German Southwest African war of 1904–1907 hesitantly asked her if people "in their circles" were welcome in the Women's League, Liliencron emphatically affirmed that they were.[87] These connections proved useful to her. In Nuremberg, for example, the local German Colonial Society chapter informed her frostily that "their ladies" were too busy with the Women's Association for Nursing to help Liliencron found a Women's League chapter — and so Liliencron cheerfully accepted the aid of local colonial veterans and their wives, who worked with "true enthusiasm."[88] It was, she told the duke of Mecklenburg, her "great wish that this colonial work and colonial interest penetrate more into the people."[89]

Liliencron's success in attracting men and women to the Women's League irritated the German Colonial Society. By 1909 men made up 10 percent of the Women's League membership; in 1910 they were almost 17 percent.[90] Such percentages were not necessarily unusual in women's organizations; a 1909 statistical survey of women's organizations showed that about half of all women's and feminist organizations had men as members.[91] But in contrast to the Women's Association for Nursing, which allowed only women to be full members, the Women's League gave men full membership rights, reserving only the offices of chair, vice chair, and secretary for women.[92] The bitterest issue for the German Colonial Society was the number of men who belonged to the Women's League but not to the German Colonial Society, contravening the 1908 agreement, which contained a provision that men could not belong to the Women's League unless they were already German Colonial Society members.[93] The German Colonial Society saw the Women's League's recruitment of previously inactive men as poaching, and the society's secretary demanded that the men who belonged only to the Women's League either join the German Colonial Society or be expelled from the league. But the German Colonial Society was helpless in the face of the Women's League's refusal to enforce the rule. Moreover, the German Colonial Society suspected the Women's League of underselling. The secretary of the German Colonial Society reported hearing men say, "I'm going to the Women's League; it's cheaper there."[94] Throughout 1910 and 1911, when the Women's League expanded especially rapidly, complaints flew from the German Colonial Society that the

Women's League represented "unfair competition" and was "digging the ground out from under us."[95] Some members of the society complained that the Women's League competed for members of new chapters by holding recruiting events a few days before the German Colonial Society had planned its own events.[96] Others grumbled that the Women's League behaved too much as if it were an official part of the German Colonial Society; for example, by leading prospective members to believe that Women's League dues would buy entry to all German Colonial Society events. The Women's League chairwoman after 1910, Hedwig Heyl, was unapologetic on such occasions, replying that "on *our* part an effort is made to give ever more life to the great colonial idea and to do propaganda work, also in men's circles."[97] Already by late 1908, the honeymoon between the German Colonial Society and the Women's League was over.

Populist and race-purity-oriented men were not the only sources of authority for women's active role in colonization, however. During the same years when the Women's League was founded and flourished, another source of authority developed: the women who farmed in the colonies (*Farmersfrauen*) and wrote about it. These women renewed Frieda von Bülow's vision of radical nationalist economic and cultural self-sufficiency in colonial space.

THE MYTH OF THE *FARMERSFRAU*

Between 1900 and the First World War a number of diaries and novels written by women who had lived as farmers and housewives in the colonies appeared in Germany. The earliest were penned by women who had experienced colonial warfare. Most of the authors were active members of the Women's League, and excerpts of their books appeared in *Colony and Home*.[98] Like Frieda von Bülow, these women offered firsthand colonial experience and self-consciously feminine nationalism. The books served an important agitation function as evidence of German women's ability to work and thrive in the colonies.[99] They portrayed the life of the *Farmersfrau*, who was usually a wife or widow, or, more rarely, an unmarried, independent woman. The books' drama rested on the narrators' efforts to manage a household and farm, in some cases without any aid from a husband or other male relative. The authors presented themselves as conscientious defenders of national virtue, sexual morality, and race purity.

Agrarian nostalgia in Germany and the colonies fascinated many men in the Wilhelmine era, but it had a special meaning for women.[100] The mystique of the farm appealed to German women in ways that were specific to their situation. Socialist and bourgeois feminists had long recognized that the shift from home to factory production had devalued women's work and accentuated their dependence on men.[101] Family farm–based agriculture rested on a conventional model of the family, yet also granted importance to women's economic contributions. The farm reunited production and reproduction and allowed women to cross boundaries between men's and women's labor, and between public and private activity. Women thereby might avoid men's accusations of unfair competition and escape contemporary conflicts over women's family and economic roles. The colonial farm also promised an escape from the questions of class that had so plagued feminists in Germany, for the racialized economy of German Southwest Africa seemed to convert political cross-class encounters into supposedly natural cross-racial encounters. In the colony, German women would no longer be divided by barriers of class. The *Farmersfrau* mystique offered a displaced sort of feminism that avoided direct demands for equality such as those of Minna Cauer and other radical feminists. While feminists treated the sexual division of labor as a social issue, in these memoirs it shrank to the scale of an isolated partnership of husband and wife on a colonial farm. If the authors were left alone by widowhood, as were Else Sonnenberg and Helene von Falkenhausen, or through divorce, as was Margarethe von Eckenbrecher, the memoirs offered an even more individualistic version of the Woman Question: the colonial woman farmer earning her living alone on the farm.

The *Farmersfrau* memoirs are crowded with generic colonialist propaganda and personal details of daily life, from laundry methods to overland journeys. They retell colonial experiences such as the German Southwest African war of 1904–1907 or confrontations with African servants, in often formulaic ways. They embrace the "race war" interpretation of colonial war: Africans had inexplicably turned on German men and women using duplicitous, unconventional methods, and were never again to be trusted with any notable measure of liberty. It is predictable that the women authors, like other colonists who had experienced the war at first hand, blamed Africans and reflected little on the role of the Germans in provoking the conflict.

The first one of this genre was Magdalene von Prince's 1903 memoir, *A German Woman in the Interior of German East Africa*.[102] The wife of noted colonial army officer and planter Tom von Prince in West Usambara, German East Africa, she was a senior figure in the colonist community until the First World War. Although her book appeared before the Maji Maji war of 1905–1906, it did include her accounts of regional colonial warfare of the 1890s. It saw new editions in 1905, during the war, and in 1908, during the era of colonial reform. Memoirs from the German Southwest African war followed. The first two were penned anonymously, then two more books appeared by the war widows Else Sonnenberg and Helene von Falkenhausen.[103] Falkenhausen left the colony in 1904, published her memoir, and became a successful speaker on the colonialist lecture circuit in Germany. In 1912 she came back to run a "teaching farm" for German female emigrants at Brakwater.[104] Falkenhausen quarreled with the Women's League, and her school was completely separate from the league's similar enterprises.[105] A fifth women's memoir to come out of the war years of German Southwest Africa was Margarethe von Eckenbrecher's *What Africa Gave and Took from Me* (1907), which ran to seven editions.[106] Eckenbrecher experienced the war, but not as a widow; she had divorced her husband, a painter and big-game hunter. In 1904, soon after the war broke out, she returned to Germany and gave colonialist lectures, raising money for the Women's League and founding five chapters between 1909 and 1914.[107] She worked as an instructor in modern languages, economics, and geography at a women's business school in Brunswick and gave courses in social work to women, but still had difficulty making ends meet.[108] In early 1914 she resettled in German Southwest Africa with her two sons and still lived there in 1937 when her memoir was reissued. The new edition covered her life story up to 1936; she also altered the original text to suit Nazi racial sensibilities.

Even though these women took the occasion of colonial war to publish their memoirs, they had no intention of conceding that war made the colonies too dangerous for German women. Rather, they presented the wars as all the more reason for women to settle there. The only way to prevail over Africans in the long term, they explained, was to strengthen the German race in each colony, and that in turn meant increasing white German women's and family settlement and thereby ensuring race purity and white supremacy. Far from excluding German women, colonial war had made them more important than ever before to the colonies' future.

After the German victory in the German Southwest Africa war of 1904–1907, several more women wrote about their experiences. These authors were in some cases merely visiting or recreational farmers, such as Maria Karow, who joined some relatives, and Clara Brockmann, who held an office job while toying with the idea of purchasing some farmland on her own.[109] Both wrote for *Colony and Home* and lectured on behalf of the Women's League. These peacetime authors were if anything more racist, and certainly they were more ignorant of the old political realities of the colonies, than the earlier memoirists. They took up the race war thesis and applied it to peacetime life in the colony. Although they occasionally produced appreciative descriptions of African men's appearance, they were harshly critical of Africans in general and of African women in particular. They were scathing about interracial sexual relations and intermarriage, and indeed about almost all domestic interactions between Germans and colonial subjects, such as those between employer and servant.

The personal colonial experience of these women memoirists added fresh evidence to the debate among male colonialists and scientists over whether white women could live permanently in the Tropics. Not surprisingly, colonialist women intervened on the side in the men's debate that did not consign them to irrelevance: that of the settlement colonialists and white supremacists.[110] Two women who had lived in Cameroon and Samoa insisted that German women were not as fragile as some men thought and that they ought to live in all the colonies. They did not deny that tropical life posed dangers, but instead pointed out that white men and women shared a common vulnerability unless both followed hygienic preventive practices conscientiously, such as sterilizing drinking water, using mosquito nets, and restricting alcohol consumption. They did not live on farms, but they shared with the *Farmersfrau* authors a vision of German women's roles as thrifty helpmeet in the household and moral, cultural, and racial anchor of settler society. Frieda

Zieschank, who wrote a book on her life in Samoa between 1906 and the First World War, when she had to leave, advocated increased German women's settlement there, insisting that German women could thrive in the supposedly dangerous tropical climate of Samoa. Zieschank, whose husband was a doctor employed by the Samoan colonial administration, declared Samoa to be the "healthiest tropical colony, in which not only the European man, but also the white family can make its residence without danger to life and health. And what would be better suited for permeating a new land with our nationality [*Volkstum*] than rooting the German family?"[111]

Grete Ziemann traveled to Duala, Cameroon, to keep house for her brother Hans Ziemann, whose advocacy of female settlement and race purity was noted above, and to assist him in laboratory work. A few years later, when her family asked her to care for other relatives, she returned to Germany, where she published a memoir about her African sojourn. Ziemann wrote her book with the express purpose of dispelling Cameroon's reputation for ruining European women's health. She declared briskly, "We now know that even the coastal climate is no hell on earth for white women."[112] Citing European families who resided for fifteen years at a stretch in the Dutch East Indies as well as her own experience, she argued that it was not nature that set limits on Europeans' health in Cameroon, but rather insufficient investment in proper housing.[113] The key for German men and women alike was to follow hygienic rules — and German women were the best at helping German men do that. German women's settlement was necessary not only for such practical, everyday functions, she added, but also for racial reasons: "The Europeans who take black women may well train good sick-nurses and dog-like slaves for themselves, but we will never conquer Africa with the children. In my opinion, race pride — naturally only in the best and noblest sense — cannot be exercised strictly enough. *If Germany wants to conquer Africa, in no case may a mixed race arise there.* From that follows the compelling demand that, as much as possible, white women in ever increasing numbers be active there as true pioneers of European culture."[114] It is obvious that her views coincided with those of her brother, yet a German woman's testimony of her own experience carried a different weight for a German female audience than a male scientist's medical tract on acclimatization.

Once one accepted the importance of the German woman as the constant sexual, intellectual, national, and health-conscious comrade of the German man, one was hard put to explain why she might be needed in one colony but not in another. A new and more pervasive gender complementarity took hold through the efforts of the Women's League, the populist men around *Colony and Home,* and the *Farmersfrau* literature: wherever German men went, they needed German women next to them. Colonialist women expanded on Governor Leutwein's notion of the necessity of the "female as such" to argue for more comprehensive economic and cultural significance for German women in all the colonies. These arguments never repudiated race and pronatalism, but they also came to encompass tenets of Germany's bourgeois women's movement.

HEDWIG HEYL'S FEMINISM AND PROFESSIONALIZED DOMESTICITY IN THE WOMEN'S LEAGUE OF THE GERMAN COLONIAL SOCIETY

In April 1910 the bourgeois feminist and social reformer Hedwig Heyl became the third chairwoman of the Women's League of the German Colonial Society.[115] Under her expert organizational guidance, the league's membership increased from about 4,500 members in 1910 to about 17,800 members in 148 chapters in Germany and the colonies in 1914.[116] At that point it was as large as the Pan-German League and almost half as large as the German Colonial Society. By 1914 the Women's League's membership had diversified beyond Liliencron's conservative and colonial army circles. While the original founding committee in 1907 was almost entirely drawn from the colonial military, by 1910 only four of the executive committee had such ties. Women teachers were among the first civilian groups to join.[117] Civil servants' and professors' wives, daughters, and sisters were also prominently represented, as were the families of businessmen.

Under Heyl, the Women's League moved closer to the bourgeois women's movement. Heyl had many ties to feminist groups, including an honorary post on the board of the Women's Welfare Association.[118] In 1911 the Women's League joined the Federation of German Women's Associations (Bund Deutscher Frauenvereine), the umbrella organization of nonsocialist feminist and women's groups. The leaders of the German-Evangelical Women's League (Deutsch-Evangelischer Frauenbund) and Catholic Women's Association (Katholischer Frauenbund) joined the Women's League.[119] The Women's League also expanded its work with new projects that were colonial versions of concurrent feminist projects in Germany. These projects reflected Heyl's lifelong goals of the rationalization of housework, the creation of new careers for women, and the public recognition of women's paid and unpaid work. Heyl believed that if the public grasped the scientific principles, hygienic importance, and economic value of housework, women's real importance to the nation would be appreciated. The image of the individual household as a small-scale version of the national economy was not just a metaphor for Heyl; it was literal truth.

Heyl's success in strengthening feminists' influence in the Women's League indicated not only an increase in left-liberal backing for colonialism under Colonial Secretary Dernburg, but also a shift in German feminism in the years just before the First World War. In 1908 the Prussian Law of Association was changed to legalize political activism for the women who lived in Prussia (three-fifths of all German women). That lessened what conservative women had seen as the stigma of feminism in women's groups beyond the Patriotic Women's Leagues. As a result, the bourgeois women's movement expanded numerically and "moderate" and conservative-minded women in it became more vocal. The bourgeois women's movement as a whole shifted rightward.[120] Heyl herself exemplified this reorientation of German feminism.

Heyl's vision of colonial domesticity did not emerge from the German Southwest African war, as was the case for most *Farmersfrau* authors, but rather from her own progressive education and interest in social work. Her alertness to the possibilities of professionalized domesticity for the colonial empire is all the more striking because Heyl in fact knew little about things African or colonial. She never traveled to the colonies, nor did she show any interest in doing so. She seems not to have discussed colonial policy issues beyond the Women's League's own concrete programs. Nevertheless, her belief in the importance of the efficient and hygienic German household for the German nation dovetailed perfectly with the league's orientation toward populist family settlement in the colonies. Heyl went so far as to equate women's domesticity with overseas colonization: "Distant lands cannot truly be taken into possession if domestic economy does not take root there. The first step that the women in Southwest [Africa] ventured, other than nursing, was the establishment of German housekeeping, around which everything will crystallize," she declared at a major feminist conference in 1912, blithely ignoring the history of missionaries.[121] Heyl's professionalized domesticity was, after Cauer's liberal nationalism and Liliencron's conservative militarism, a third path into colonial politics for Wilhelmine women.

Heyl and Liliencron shared a talent for popularizing colonialism, but apart from that the two women could not have been more different. While Liliencron was from the Prussian east, conservative, and belonged to an old aristocratic military lineage, Heyl came from the western German port city of Bremen, was left-liberal, and belonged to the commercial bourgeoisie.[122] Her father, Eduard Crüsemann, amassed a shipping fortune as a founder and the first director of Norddeutscher Lloyd. He arranged for his daughter to receive the most innovative and progressive education then available. Hedwig Crüsemann's first teacher was Ottilie Hoffmann, who was later prominent for her social reform efforts against alcoholism and active in the Federation of German Women's Associations. Hoffmann's father was a missionary in Africa, and Heyl later recalled how she and Ottilie Hoffmann sewed clothes for "naked Negro children."[123] Like Frieda von Bülow and uncounted other women in Germany, then, Heyl first encountered images of Africans through missionary appeals. As a teenager Heyl attended another innovative school, Henriette Breymann's school for girls at Neu-Watzum. This school, inspired by democratic educational ideas of 1848, was known across Germany for its progressive pedagogy. Breymann was a niece of Friedrich Fröbel, the pioneer of democratic education in Germany.[124] Heyl recalled that the most important thing taught there was "the Fröbelian principle of mediating opposites."[125] As an adult Heyl applied that principle to everything from class conflict to women's cultural tasks. Women, she claimed, were specially called upon to mediate between "idea and work," "spirit and body," and "ideality and reality."[126]

At eighteen she married Georg Friedrich Heyl, the owner of a chemical factory in Berlin. The couple joined a circle of liberals and social reformers in Berlin that included Helene Lange; Henriette Breymann; Breymann's husband, Karl Schrader;[127] and Crown Princess Victoria (later known as Empress Frederick in memory of her husband, Frederick, who was briefly emperor in 1888). Heyl's father-in-law, Eduard Heyl, was an 1848 democrat who remained active in Berlin politics.[128] In 1889 Georg Heyl died prematurely, leaving Hedwig to rear their five children. She ran their factory herself for seven years, then her oldest son took it over. All the while she was prodigiously active in social work and feminist organizations.

Heyl first applied the ideas she had learned at Breymann's school and in her political circle to the workers at her factory. Her efforts began, she recalled, after she became a mother and noticed how unfavorably her workers' babies compared with her own. She decided to teach the women factory workers her own newly acquired knowledge of infant care. Soon she had established a factory canteen to prevent workers from imbibing alcohol at nearby lunch stands, cooking classes for female factory workers, parents' evenings to discuss child-raising problems, a factory kindergarten, and an after-school youth center for factory workers' older children, which later took in children from her Berlin suburb, Charlottenburg.[129] Heyl eventually turned the youth center over to her protegée Anna von Gierke, who became nationally famous for her work with youth and her promotion of social work as a career for women.[130] Heyl installed Berlin's first factory showers, and she personally monitored the female factory workers to detect health problems and to make sure that they really washed.[131] In addition to the social reform projects that grew out of the Heyl family factory, Heyl also founded or cofounded the Association for Home Care (Verein für Hauspflege), which provided new mothers with medical care and housekeeping services; the Lyceum Club (Lyzeum-Club), a women's institute where lectures on political, artistic, and scholarly topics were held; and the first gardening school for women, which sought to professionalize gardening as a woman's career.[132] She helped run college-preparatory courses (*Gymnasialkurse*) for women, which Helene Lange had pioneered in the late 1880s, and oversaw the on-site planning of two major events for the bourgeois women's movement: the 1904 International Women's Congress and, along with Alice Salomon, the 1912 exhibition "Woman in Home and Career."[133]

Heyl brought her formidable administrative skills to the task of professionalizing the Women's League's internal affairs. She centralized the league's administration, which helped avert embarrassing differences of opinion among the local chapters.[134] At the same time, she added a middle level of regional associations between the local chapters and the Berlin headquarters, which increased revenue by charging additional dues and sponsoring more events.[135] Heyl kept statistics of clients served and correspondence answered in the central office and converted volunteer jobs to paid positions, in keeping with her promotion of women's careers.[136] She installed a wall map of Germany with red push-pins for existing chapters and blue pushpins indicating places where agitation was necessary, aiming to create a "complete network of the Women's League all over Germany."[137] She increased funding for agita-tion and sent press releases to the newspapers every two or three weeks. Under Heyl's leadership, the Women's League began to use films, post-cards, and slide shows for publicity work.[138]

Heyl was best known for her work in home economics, and she applied its principles to all her projects. Just as she had professionalized gardening, work with youth, and "home care" for new mothers into new careers for certified women, she also professionalized home eco-nomics by creating the first courses in Germany that certified women as home economics teachers. She was not the first to organize housekeep-ing and cooking courses in Germany, but her innovative courses inte-grated a practical knowledge of chemistry, nutrition, and organizational efficiency; and her cookbook, *Kitchen ABC,* included scientific explana-tions of cooking techniques.[139] She founded yet another organization to sustain the courses, the Federation for the Advancement of Women's Home Economics Education (Verband zur Förderung hauswirtschaft-licher Frauenbildung). Heyl belonged to the German Hygiene Associa-tion (Deutscher Hygieneverein), authored nine books on housekeep-ing and child care, and contributed regularly to the *Gazette for Public Health Care* (*Blatt für Volksgesundheitspflege*). Later, during the food shortages of the First World War, the mayor of Berlin appointed her to organize "middle-class lunchrooms" (*Mittelstandsküchen*), where inex-pensive food was served to the impoverished middle classes. Nicknamed the "food general" and the "Germans' female Hindenburg," Heyl was an important figure on the Berlin home front.[140] She founded the League of German Housewives' Associations (*Verband Deutscher Hausfrauen-vereine*) during the war in order to promote efficient housekeeping. In

1925 she received an honorary doctorate in medicine for her work in cooking and nutrition.[141]

Heyl did not fit easily into more radical varieties of feminism because she never sought to distance women's paid work from unpaid work in the home. Rather, she saw them as two sides of the same coin of rationalized housework: wherever women worked, they were or ought to be using the skills of rationalized housework.[142] Heyl prided herself on a certain degree of social egalitarianism; for example, she sent her own children to the Heyl factory kindergarten she had founded. She also insisted on practical knowledge of all tasks, disliking what she saw as the "dilettantism" of traditional women's charities.[143] Heyl insisted that every pupil in her cooking courses, no matter how high in status, had to perform dirty kitchen tasks such as scouring pots, and she even prevailed on Empress Frederick's daughter Princess Victoria to hold a live carp and chop off its head. The princess's friend Marie von Bunsen recalled that when the princess demurred, "Frau Heyl urged her onward with eloquence, saying that it had to be done for the sake of example, that she was setting up large-scale cooking courses and that she wanted to tell the young girls: 'even Princess Victoria did not refuse.' Thus the murder came to pass."[144] Even royal daughters had to possess basic household skills.

But there were limits to Heyl's egalitarianism. Even if she, a commoner, might teach kitchen skills to a princess, the fact remained that in her various organizations and training courses lower-status women did not generally teach higher-status women. Rather, middle-class women converted their knowledge of hygiene and discipline, which depended on middle-class resources and priorities, into paid careers in teaching and monitoring working-class women.[145] Heyl believed that rationalized domesticity would alleviate two major social problems at the same time: working-class families' living conditions and middle-class women's need for paid careers suitable to their social station. Time and again Heyl tried out an idea on working-class women, then realized it would be at least as beneficial for middle-class women and continued the project with the latter. The cooking class for the teenaged Princess Victoria and her friends, for example, was an outgrowth of Heyl's cooking classes for workers at her factory.[146] After Heyl took over the Women's League of the German Colonial Society, the same pattern emerged in the women's settlement program. If it was good for working-class women to settle in German Southwest Africa, would it not be even better for middle-class, educated women to do so?

HEDWIG HEYL AND THE "COLONIAL WOMAN QUESTION"

Heyl wished to create new careers in the colonies that would reduce the "surplus" of women in Germany. She anticipated that educated German women would become teachers in kindergartens, schools, and home economics courses; midwives; governesses; youth center matrons; trained housekeepers; market gardeners; and agricultural overseers in German Southwest Africa. The similarities to Cauer's ideas were not by chance; Heyl conferred with Cauer on developing women's colonial careers.[147] Heyl also succeeded in obtaining one of Cauer's old demands: a clause in the German Colonial Society's contract for the sponsored women settlers that guaranteed free return passage in case of maltreatment on the job.[148] Under Heyl's guidance the Women's League created colonial versions of Heyl's projects in Berlin, including a kindergarten in Lüderitzbucht, German Southwest Africa, that was run according to Fröbelian methods, and a youth center named the Jugendheim, like Anna von Gierke's in Berlin.[149] Unlike the projects in Germany, however, Heyl and the others in the Women's League explicitly justified these colonial versions in terms of racial separation and hierarchy. For example, the kindergarten, which accepted only white children, was intended to aid German colonists by removing their children from the "danger" that African nannies and servants supposedly posed.[150]

The centerpiece of the Women's League's program was the women's settlement scheme for German Southwest Africa. The league's administrative duties included corresponding with prospective women emigrants and their employers, receiving the women's formal applications, and checking their credentials. If the women traveled third class, passage was free (domestic servants typically did this); if they chose second-class passage (the usual option of teachers, governesses, and some housekeepers), 150 marks was provided toward the ticket.[151] Each year after 1908 the Women's League sent a small but growing number of women to German Southwest Africa. While the German Colonial Society had sent only 111 unmarried women between 1898 and 1907, the Women's League sent 561 unmarried women in the shorter span between 1908 and 1914.[152] The league's success depended partly on the general upsurge in colonialist enthusiasm and settlement after the war of 1904–1907. The program had always been successful in terms of its original goal of promoting marriage between German men and women in the colony, for the vast majority of the sponsored women did indeed marry German colonists. There was no shortage of female applicants to the Women's League: between 1907 and 1914 the Women's League received as many as fifty inquiries in a single day.[153] German women of both the working and middle classes expressed interest in emigrating to German Southwest Africa and other colonies.[154]

Conflicts emerged between the Women's League and the German Colonial Society, however, over the sort of women who ought to be sponsored. The German Colonial Society had routinely rejected teachers and other women holding professional certification in favor of domestic servants since 1898, citing the colony's labor market.[155] When the Women's League began to administer the program in 1908, its rejection of some apparently suitable working-class women bewildered Colonial Society officials.[156] The duke of Mecklenburg, the chairman of the German Colonial Society and holder of the purse strings, questioned the league's judgment and insisted on having power of final approval over each application.[157] While Liliencron had acted as patroness of the "little people" and did not complain about the humble backgrounds of the female emigrants, Heyl and other members of the Women's League wished to see more "cultured" (*gebildete*) women among the sponsored female emigrants to German Southwest Africa.[158] The old conflict of 1898–1899 between advocates of the "female as such" and advocates of a larger women's mission to transform colonial societies arose once more. But it now took a new form: middle- and upper-class women were asking whether the colonies most needed working-class women, whom they saw as the lowest-common-denominator "female as such," or middle-class women like themselves, whom they saw as fuller human beings with a wider role to play there. The Women's League had Colonial Secretary Dernburg on its side in this matter. Already in 1909 he had declared to its Berlin chapter: "To supply German farmers with wives cannot and ought not to be the sole purpose of the Women's League.

The Women's League *must promote all which is likely to bring to the colonies that fine and educated sense that distinguishes the German in the homeland.*"[159] That year his wife, Emma Dernburg, chaired the Committee for the Creation of Work Opportunities for Educated Girls in the Colonies in the Women's League.[160]

Margarete Schnitzker, who headed the Berlin chapter's selection committee, explained to readers of *Colony and Home* how difficult it was to find suitable women to sponsor under the settlement scheme. She complained first of all that women applicants approached the Women's League with the attitude that the league needed them rather than the other way around.[161] Apparently the Women's League was unprepared for the effectiveness of its own propaganda about the need for women. Schnitzker rejected the vast majority of applicants quickly. She turned away "those who had no certified qualifications, . . . those who had too many qualifications, or those who — and this is really dreadful — 'absolutely did not need to go, but just wanted to get out a bit.' That is, in plain German, those who hoped to find a man over there after the hope appeared futile here."[162] Precisely the wish to marry could disqualify an applicant from the scheme, even though it had been founded to promote marriages. Schnitzker also turned away women who wanted to make a fresh start in life. Among the applicants were, she wrote, "a bunch of desperate creatures. Women who wanted to get away from their husbands; . . . young girls from good social circles who had gotten into distressing situations, usually because the father had died, and who apparently had the odd idea that work in the fatherland was shameful but work in the colonies was not, and who considered themselves capable, on the spot, of filling the position of servant girl, even though they had heretofore at the very most held a dustcloth in their hands; and finally, those who have lust for adventure of all kinds written plainly all over their face."[163] Schnitzker, like Rohrbach, favored prospective colonists who were already well situated in life. She regretted that she had so little to offer educated women, the applicants she most favored:

> Among the educated [*gebildeten*] girls, who usually held positions here as housekeepers, kindergarten teachers, and companions, the greatest percentage by far consists of very pleasant, industrious young women of good character. . . . I am always terribly sorry to have to

turn them away, as I have the feeling that precisely the emigration of such educated women to our colonies could bring much more advantage to the [colonial] Woman Question than simple girls, in spite of all their good qualities, could do. . . . [I can] only support with all my heart the notion that educated women and girls, if they are industrious and clever, ought to have the way smoothed for them in our colonies.[164]

The Woman Question in the colonies was starting to look like the Woman Question in Germany: neither place made much room for educated women who did not want to marry. In both places, middle-class women faced a lack of demand for their paid work, or to put it more precisely, they were purposefully and explicitly excluded from many kinds of middle-class paid work. The strongest market demand in the colonies for German women continued to be for sexual relations, marriage, and maternity.

The Women's League created two institutions to try to, as Schnitzker put it, "smooth the way" for middle-class women: a women's hostel in German Southwest Africa and a school for colonial housekeeping in Germany. Both were intended to equip middle-class, "educated" women to be more competitive in the colonial labor market. The hostel, called the Homeland House (Heimathaus), opened in 1910; by the First World War, 176 newly arrived women had stayed there.[165] It was located in the southern town of Keetmanshoop where, according to Philalethes Kuhn and others, the threat of German men's intermarriage with Rehobothers and Boers was the greatest.[166] Those women who were sponsored through the settlement scheme but could not be matched with an employer before departure from Germany signed a contract to work instead at the Homeland House for three months.[167] The Homeland House was intended to earn its own keep by offering laundry, mending, baking, and guest rooms for traveling "ladies."[168] A full-time, salaried matron instructed the sponsored women in colonial housekeeping skills and oversaw the African laborers who were hired to do the most unpleasant tasks, such as laundry.[169] In the Homeland House's earliest planning stages, it reflected Liliencron's and the German Colonial Society's expectations that working-class women would be sent to the colony. The hostel was intended "to train female household help and to give farmers and settlers opportunity to make the acquaintance of German girls"; "undemanding, simple girls" would be sent.[170] Under Heyl, when the Women's League sponsored more middle-class women, it became apparent that the latter were less employable: "While the efficient domestic servant finds happy and willing acceptance among the settlers and a girl seldom remains for three months in the Homeland House created for her transitional lodging, the placement of educated, less practical workers is more difficult."[171] Even so, the Women's League had succeeded in transforming the original structure of the female emigration program: while the German Colonial Society in the late 1890s had seen workplaces in colonists' homes as way-stations on women's paths toward marriage, with the Homeland House the Women's League had created a way-station on women's paths toward paid positions in the colony.

The second institution that the Women's League established in order to help middle-class women adjust to the economic opportunities of colonial society was the colonial housekeeping school for women.[172] The league helped found two schools in succession, both of which were financial failures. The Deutsche Kolonialfrauenschule, built next to the older men's colonial school at Witzenhausen an der Werra, near Kassel, and run by Countess Anna von Zech, opened in May 1908. Only four women registered at the school's opening. Zech and the Witzenhausen men's headmaster, Ernst Fabarius, quarreled and the school folded in late 1910.[173] In 1911 the Women's League established a women's colonial school at Bad Weilbach, near Wiesbaden, that remained open until 1914.[174] The school signaled that it sought only middle-class and elite women as pupils by charging a high annual tuition of 1,400 marks (the course of study took twelve to eighteen months) and specifying that only "daughters of educated German families" would be accepted.[175] Only nine women registered as students at Bad Weilbach in 1911, and the annual enrollment hardly ever exceeded fourteen.[176] Some were engaged to colonists and wanted to prepare for their future "house-wifely career," and others "intended to take an independent position in the colonies."[177]

The point of the school was, according to Heyl, to make educated women less academic and more oriented toward housework and women's work, so that they might find a niche in German Southwest Africa.[178] While the men's colonial school at Witzenhausen offered academic training in subjects such as languages and natural science along with the practical skills of agriculture, the women at the Bad Weilbach school devoted almost all their time to practical, even menial tasks such as cleaning out livestock stalls and scrubbing pots. In addition to a three-month course on nursing care, especially maternity care, they were to learn:

> simple cooking, baking of black and white bread and cakes, the carving, efficient use, and storage of meat, corning, smoking, sausage preparation, etc.; preservation of vegetables and fruit in jars and tins in various styles, preparation of fruit wines, laundry and ironing, cleaning rooms, kitchen and equipment; polishing lamps and metal, mending of linens and clothing, plain needlework, dressmaking, all kinds of handiwork necessary in colonial households such as minor repairs, soldering, painting, upholstering, leatherwork, etc.; care of chicken coops, of vegetable and fruit gardens, beekeeping, dairy processing, cattle-keeping and other agricultural tasks; [and] principles of practical bookkeeping.

Only a few hours were spent on "colonial geography and history, economics, and colonial readings."[179] The course of instruction promised to whisk women to a mythical time and place where they would have a central role in the economy that industrialized Germany had denied them. Both of the colonial schools for women offered the odd spectacle of middle-class women paying high tuition to perform the kind of manual labor that usually fell to their social inferiors. Working-class German, Boer, British, and African women in German Southwest Africa were doing much of the same work without certification.

By 1911 the Women's League was planning to extend the settlement scheme to German East Africa, where, it was hoped, educated women would be more employable.[180] German East Africa lacked schools for white children, and so colonists with children created a demand for governesses. Moreover, as one Women's League member noted, white domestic servants were not "necessary" in German East Africa because colonists there typically employed African men as household servants.[181] That meant, in turn, that the German Southwest African race purity efforts banishing African women from households would not apply. The First World War interrupted plans to send unmarried, educated women to German East Africa, but the Women's League resumed its efforts after the war and sent German women to what was then the British mandate of Tanganyika.

The Women's League institutionalized women's participation in the colonialist movement in areas beyond nursing and missionary work. Colonial war, populist settlement, colonial "reform," and German women's continued efforts to participate in the colonialist movement pushed the men to imagine new gender arrangements within the German community. Together, colonialist women and their male allies questioned the political and social primacy of the colonial patriarch, with his prerogatives of property, prestige, and sexual freedom. Colonialist women had even developed a rhetoric of their own primacy in German cultural survival. As one woman journalist put it: "The *man* can conquer and subjugate territories in the world for the German idea; but only the persistence of *woman* can implant and preserve the German idea abroad over the long term!"[182] Yet the limits of men's acceptance of women in the colonialist movement remained visible in two phenomena of the years immediately before the First World War. First, under pressure to focus attention on distinctively "feminine" tasks, the Women's League and the Women's Association for Nursing converged, even collided, in the area of pronatalist work. Second, colonialist men continued to assume that only "feminine" tasks justified the existence of procolonial organizations led by women, and they therefore questioned why the two groups should continue to exist separately.

GENDER AND THE CONVERGENCE OF COLONIALIST
WOMEN'S ACTIVISM ON RACIAL REPRODUCTION

By 1914 both the Women's League and the Women's Red Cross Association for the Colonies (Frauenverein vom Roten Kreuz für die Kolonien, as the Women's Association for Nursing was renamed in 1908) had gravitated toward tasks related to maternity and family health. The list of their projects showed extensive overlap: both funded maternity wards; midwives; milk-supply programs; courses in maternity, infant, and general nursing care; kindergartens; nursing schools; youth centers; and convalescent homes for families who would otherwise have had to return to Europe.[183] Both organizations competed for the same group of clients: white German women *qua* actual or potential mothers.

As the projects of the two colonialist women's groups grew more similar, each retained its distinct history and attitudes. The result was tension and rivalry. Given the rapid expansion of the Women's League, it is not surprising that it came into conflict with the Women's Red Cross Association. With 20,000 members in 1914, the Women's Red Cross Association was still slightly larger than the Women's League, but that membership represented the work of almost thirty years.[184] The elite status of its membership meant that the social basis for further recruitment was narrow. Meanwhile, the Women's League had gained the greater part of its 17,800 members in just the years between 1910 and 1914. In 1909 the Women's Red Cross Association announced that it had secured the agreement of the Women's League to cooperate as far as what it described as the "very different" tasks of the two organizations would allow.[185] In 1913 relations reached a low point. A vice president of the German Colonial Society served as mediator during sessions in which representatives from the Women's League and the Women's Red Cross Association drew up a formal agreement on how to separate their respective endeavors. The agreement expressly noted "kindergartens, convalescent homes, schools," and fund-raising events in small towns as areas of "disagreeable competition."[186] Neither was to undertake any new project without consulting the leadership of the other organization.

Feminine expertise, whether expressed as female nursing, Liliencron's traditional motherliness, Heyl's professionalized domesticity, or Schnitzker's ability to sniff out unworthy German women, justified the acceptance of the Women's Red Cross Association and Women's League into the colonialist movement as separate organizations in the first place. Now, however, men in the German Colonial Society began to question the need for both. If there was a specific feminine expertise or mission for the colonies, was it not the same for both women's organizations? In 1908, only a year after the Women's League was founded, men began to propose that the two women's organizations merge. Quite apart from the men's presumption that they were entitled to direct the internal affairs of two independent organizations (a presumption the German Colonial Society Secretary, Ludwig Sander, pointed out), the proposals showed that the men perceived only one basic "women's interest" in the colonies: the mobilization of women into colonialist activism. The Bamberg chapter of the German Colonial Society announced a motion at the annual German Colonial Society meeting that the two women's organizations should merge.[187] Even many women in the Women's League favored merging with the Women's Red Cross Association. In early 1909 the entire board of the Women's League voted in favor of a merger, with the sole exception of Philalethes Kuhn. Perhaps fearing that his own leading position would not survive a merger, given that the Women's Red Cross Association did not even accept men as full members, Kuhn insisted that the Women's League ought to expand "considerably more" before taking such a step.[188] In March 1910 the Munich chapter of the Women's League submitted a motion for a merger.[189] However, the Women's League never actually proposed it, and in any case the Women's Red Cross Association objected to the idea, presumably sensing that it would lose control of its larger treasury to the more dynamic Women's League.[190]

Back in the very different circumstances of 1888, Martha von Pfeil and Countess von Monts had chosen to strengthen their women's group by narrowing its statutes from the ambitious ones of Frieda von Bülow's German-National Women's League to a strict formula of colonial female nursing for Germans in the colonies. That well-defined, practical endeavor had ensured a place for women in the colonialist movement. Now, however, feminine colonialist work was defined ever more by a racialized feminine essence rather than by a specific task such as nursing. Now nursing was perceived as subsidiary to the Women's League's comprehensive goal of building pure German communities. Race, identified biologistically with women's essence, had become the universal goal, and the skills of medical care were ancillary to racial reproduction. As the Bamberg chapter of the German Colonial Society put it, the Women's League's goals were "more extensive" than those of the Women's Red Cross Association, and "it would be easy for [the Women's League] to take into its area of work the care of patients and new mothers, that special women's area so important to the colonies."[191] Reproduction in all its facets, including racial, now seemed to open the way for women's participation in the national adventure of colonialism.

At the same time, the goal of racial reproduction just as easily provided a pretext for silencing women or reducing their multiple roles in the colonialist movement to one homogeneous category of "women's work." In 1910, despite requests from Heyl and others for greater women's participation, the organizers of the German Colonial Congress permitted the Women's League and Women's Red Cross Association to give only one speech apiece.[192] Both speeches were placed in a session on German emigration and colonial settlement. No women spoke at all in the other sessions of the congress, which mostly concerned policy and scientific questions, even during the open discussions that took place after each session (and were printed with the conference proceedings). The limitation of women's place in the colonialist movement to "women's" topics of settlement, pronatalism, and nursing could not have been plainer.

By 1914 colonialist women had created a place for themselves in agitation and policy; however, they were under constant pressure to define a particular "feminine" role, on pain of being forced to yield authority to the men. That meant that organizational life repeatedly directed the women's diverse colonial interests into the same few channels of racial reproduction. The German woman was to focus her attention on keeping German men and children German. Colonialist women could not know that within a few years the colonial empire would be lost, or that their curious specialization in nationalist and racist solipsism would gain an unexpected usefulness in a new, postimperial Weimar Republic.

CHAPTER FIVE

The Woman Citizen and the Lost Colonial Empire in Weimar and Nazi Germany

In November 1918 the revolutionary government of republican Germany proclaimed the political enfranchisement of women. In June 1919 Article 119 of the Versailles Treaty announced the disenfranchisement of German men and women as colonizers. These were tremendous changes for German women and for the colonialist movement. Yet colonialist women's activism changed surprisingly little during the Weimar Republic and the Nazi dictatorship, at least on the surface. The Women's Red Cross Association for Nursing in the Colonies continued to dispatch nurses, and the Women's League of the German Colonial Society resumed its sponsorship of unmarried women emigrants to former German colonies. These organizations even expanded their membership and the geographic scope of their programs.

The Weimar Republic was, in fact, a vital time for the colonialist movement. Once the hyperinflation of the early 1920s eased, more than a dozen old and new procolonial organizations held mass assemblies; the fourth German Colonial Congress took place in 1924; schools taught colonialist propaganda; universities expanded their offerings in the "colonial sciences"; and colonial monuments were erected in many towns — indeed, most colonial monuments in Germany today date from the Weimar era.[1] Colonialist publishing flourished. Fiction and nonfiction about life in the colonies before the war as well as about Germans' efforts to reestablish themselves in the mandates attracted readers.[2] Hans Grimm's novel *Volk ohne Raum*, about a German man's bitter experiences in South Africa, brief redemption in German Southwest Africa, then disappointment in Weimar Germany, appeared in 1926 and had sold half a million copies by 1939. Images of the lost colonial empire could be found on everything from beer coasters to collectible cards in cigarette packets; they pervaded everyday life.[3]

The unique manner in which German decolonization took place — at the hands of other colonial powers and at the end of the first "total" war — profoundly shaped interwar colonialist activism in Germany. The Entente states' official justification for depriving Germany of its overseas colonial empire was that Germans had been unusually cruel colonizers of Africans, Pacific Islanders, and Chinese, and that Germans' "dereliction in the sphere of colonial civilisation" made it impossible for the Allied powers to "again abandon" millions of "natives" to Germany.[4] The German colonies, most of which had been lost militarily early in the war, were distributed as League of Nations mandates to the victors: Britain and South Africa, Portugal, Belgium, France, Australia, New Zealand, the United States, and Japan.[5] The fact that other imperial metropoles, and not colonial subjects (many of whom had tried and failed to drive Germans from their lands in previous years), had forced Germany to relinquish its colonies meant that German colonialists focused their criticism on those powers. When German colonialists demanded that the Versailles Treaty be revised so that they could once again rule over Africans and others, they were expressing not only a racist claim to rule over supposed inferiors but also a reproach to the Entente powers for betraying fellow white colonizers.

The specific German experience of decolonization also affected how Germans viewed their former colonial subjects. In other cases of decolonization, bitter wars of national liberation dismantled fantasies of affection between colonizer and colonized. In the German case, the absence of an all-out confrontation with colonial subjects nourished colonialists' fantasy that Africans, Pacific Islanders, and Chinese had never wanted them to leave. This fantasy was expressed in the titles of interwar colonialist books such as *Master, Come Back* and *When Will the Germans Finally Return?* and through the frequent invocation of individual Africans' statements of loyalty.[6] Such statements were not difficult to find or embroider. By placing the peoples most affected by German colonial rule under new colonial rulers, the Entente redirected those peoples' political resentments away from Germans and toward the new rulers. In the context of strategic negotiations with the new rulers, former German colonial subjects sometimes invoked the good old days under German rule.[7]

After 1919, then, colonialists thoroughly sentimentalized and romanticized the relationship of German colonizers to the colonized, ignoring the fears of racial contamination that had been prominent in colonialists' prewar debate over intermarriage. To the extent that interwar colonialists reconciled racial sentimentality with racial fears, they expressed fear in nonnational terms of a struggle between all blacks and all whites — "the Negro invasion of the civilized world," as one interwar author put it — while reserving sentimental optimism for relations between Germany and its former colonies.[8] That combination of sentimentality and fear continued into the Nazi period, when officials encouraged former colonial subjects residing in Germany, or "German negroes," to act as propagandists for restoring German colonial rule while subjecting other black people residing in Germany, or "real negroes" — including those of mixed German and African descent — to abusive treatment such as sterilization and internment.[9] In spite of Nazi-era colonial scientists' claims that they would avoid what they saw as the colonial era's Christian or liberal laxness on racial issues, they too instrumentalized race in contradictory ways.[10]

Germany's specific manner of decolonization also affected gender relations among German colonialists. German men could no longer claim the colonies as quintessentially male space. The combat front of the First World War, as direct or vicarious experience, took the place of the colonies as a key site of "male fantasies." And, as in the earliest years of colonial conquest, nurses were the only women allowed into that male space.[11] Colonialist women no longer criticized German men for excluding them from a colonial paradise, but rather joined with the men in criticizing the Entente powers. Colonialist women's fantasies of colonial freedom and independence, as well as their organizational efforts, still sometimes conflicted with men's. Yet colonialist women most often expressed their relationship to German men as maternal solicitude and comradeship in the face of a common victimization.[12] The new, post-1919 German colonialist identity, which was inflected with a profound sense of victimhood, turned out to be well suited to colonialist women.

Women active in the pre–First World War colonialist movement had to emphasize their uniquely feminine expertise in order to preserve their niche. Although the Weimar Republic ended the formal political inequality of women that had produced those strategies, the strategies themselves persisted. Colonialist women used their new political voice to perpetuate their claim to feminine expertise, especially through maternalism.[13] While their rhetoric of unique feminine tasks was a sign of weakness and constrained choices before the war, now that same rhetoric found new salience under conditions of imposed decolonization.

Colonialist women were well suited in several respects to be agitators in the 1920s and 1930s. Colonialist men's channels of high politics and big business, from which women had always been excluded, had become less important. Diplomatic protests to the Entente powers were fruitless. Business between Germany and its former colonies was at first forbidden, then struggled in the mid-1920s before receiving another blow when the world economy collapsed in 1929. Colonialist women, who had developed their projects at a time when women lacked a formal political voice or recognized expertise in statecraft, science, or large-scale business, were less seriously hampered by these new restrictions. The loss of formal political authority over Africans and Pacific Islanders did not affect their programs as much as it did many colonialist men's because secular colonialist women had always directed most of their efforts at other Germans. Several thousand Germans lived in the former colonies, and colonialist women were able to continue their "unpolitical" feminine work in nursing, schools, settlement of unmarried women, and providing aid to needy German families.[14]

Of course, colonialist women were quite aware of the political value of their work. The Women's League and the Women's Red Cross Association argued that the best way to overcome the decolonization imposed by the Entente was a gradual, informal retaking of the former colonies household by household, community by community. Colonialist women's focus on feminine essence and the household rather than formal political boundaries was now a positive advantage, for after the

First World War the household was the only territory that many Germans felt they could still control. Hedwig Heyl, who remained chairwoman of the Women's League until 1920, responded to the Versailles Treaty article that removed the colonies from German rule with the motto: "Wherever Germans are abroad, colonization is taking place, regardless of the territory that may be disputed them."[15] Like much revisionist and antirepublican rhetoric of the interwar years, this motto was both vacuous and extreme. By conflating Germans' mere existence with the power ambitions of colonization, it politicized everyday existence and deformalized the rules and procedures of colonial rule, citizenship, and borders. It also made new alliances possible: older distinctions and rivalries dissolved among advocates of colonial Germans, Germans living in east central Europe, and Germans in places such as Brazil and Canada. Members of all these groups joined organizations such as the German Protection League for Borderlands Germans and Germans Abroad (Deutscher Schutzbund für das Grenz- und Auslandsdeutschtum). Legal citizenship was no longer the main criterion of German-ness for Germans whose homes were now located in Poland and Czechoslovakia, or for Germans in the Southwest African mandate who accepted South African citizenship in 1925 in exchange for the right to remain there undisturbed. The definition of who was a German shifted to "cultural" public enactments such as church attendance.[16] Colonialist women's existing formulas for conjuring feminine and German essence were tailor-made for antirepublican and *völkisch*, or racialized German, agitation.

As historians of German feminism have noted, women who had opposed feminism and suffrage rights before the war were as quick as left-liberal and socialist women to seize their new political rights in 1918.[17] Politically active conservative women in organizations such as the housewives' associations used women's new basic political rights to oppose the republic itself.[18] The rapid rise to prominence of these nationalist and right-wing women is less surprising when seen in the context of their political mobilization in nationalist associations before the First World War. Women gained experience in committee work, agitation materials, and public speaking in the Patriotic Women's Leagues, the German-Evangelical Women's League, the German League against Women's Emancipation (Deutscher Bund zur Bekämpfung der Frauenemanzipation), and women's nationalist and colonialist pressure groups.[19] The First World War intensified that training with its National Women's Service (Nationaler Frauendienst).[20] Else Frobenius, for example, gained journalistic and public speaking skills as the general secretary of the Women's League of the German Colonial Society between 1913 and 1922, then discovered after 1919 that party, state, and voluntary-association posts "fell into my lap."[21]

At the moment when key feminist demands had been realized or seemed within reach, and when increased numbers of women were entering universities and even studying the "colonial sciences,"[22] the older ideology of feminine expertise continued to shape women's colonialist activism. Colonialist women and men reiterated the anti-intellectual, professionalized housewifeliness that Heyl had done so much to promote in the women's movement.[23] A pamphlet from the First World War, for example, sought women's support for the colonial empire by presenting economic problems in terms of a fictional housewife's everyday use of leather, cooking oil, cotton, and chocolate. The housewife, after listening to her teenaged son hold forth about the value of the colonies, concludes: "I confess that *the German colonies now interest me much more,* since I know that they *have to do with my own household!*"[24] The pamphlet conflated "household" with "economy" (both *Wirtschaft*), a slippage that the prewar *Farmersfrau* novels and memoirs had also played on. Colonialists offered the woman citizen of the Weimar Republic similar fare after the war. For example, during the 1925 "Colonial Week" the colonialist and feminist politician Else Lüders addressed "the housewives of Berlin" on the importance of tropical products for running a household.[25] The conflation of "household" and "economy" connected German women's new political role, which required them to be aware of economic issues, with traditional gender roles.

The unmooring of German identity from German institutions also affected colonialist women's conceptualization of race. Both the Women's League and the Women's Red Cross Association came to define German-ness and its propagation in terms of individuals and households, and not by state territory. They saw the individual Germans or German families they supported as outposts of German culture. The Women's Red Cross Association expressed this shift in 1922 when it changed the rest of its name from "for Nursing in the Colonies" to "for

Germans Overseas" (Frauenverein vom Roten Kreuz für Deutsche über See). The organization continued its work among Germans who remained or settled anew in the former colonies (including Qingdao and a new post in Tianjin) and added Germans living in Peru, Argentina, Brazil, Chile, Curaçao, Lithuania, Paraguay, Spain, and the United States.[26] The women's organizations no longer claimed to operate throughout various territories, but rather only among German persons and families in those territories. Before the war the Women's Red Cross Association had never completely excluded colonial subjects from its services; now, it announced that colonial subjects would have to do without the association's help.[27] For the Women's League, the shift in focus from territory to individual persons meant the end of its attempts to change the sexual behavior of the entire population in a colony. If the Women's League or Women's Red Cross Association decided that recipients were deficient in racial or national virtue, they could easily cut off funds and repudiate their former clients as representatives of German culture. Discarding Germans found unworthy had never been so simple under formal colonial rule. Post-1919 colonialism was now almost completely detached from state institutions. Before 1914, and especially in the debate over race mixing, the colonial state's jurisdiction and operating principles sometimes interfered with colonialists' aspirations. Now colonialism belonged to the colonialists. Because the former colonies were no longer the legal responsibility of the German state, Weimar- and Nazi-era heirs of radical nationalism were less constrained than ever before in their selective representation of the former colonies as a pure German space and refuge from the realities of postwar Germany. Colonialist women, as citizens of the Weimar Republic, now had the same formal access to the state as men — but at a moment when the state had lost importance among colonialists of both sexes.

COLONIALISTS IN DEMOCRACY AND DICTATORSHIP

Because colonial revisionism eventually became the property of the far right, and especially the Nazi party, it is easy to overlook its appeal across the political spectrum in the early years of the Weimar Republic. Many Germans referred to Article 231 of the Versailles treaty, which placed complete responsibility for the war on Germany, as the "war guilt lie" (*Kriegsschuldlüge*). Colonialists adapted that slogan to refer to Article 119 and the Entente's accusations of cruelty as the "colonial guilt lie" (*koloniale Schuldlüge*). As the left-liberal colonial expert Moritz Julius Bonn recalled, the manner of German decolonization "made many Germans colonial-minded who before had been in the habit of decrying colonies."[28] Anger at the "war guilt lie" and "colonial guilt lie" smothered domestic discussion of Germany's own annexationist war aims, which had included extensive western and eastern European lands as well as Mittelafrika, a swathe of the continent intended to connect Cameroon with German East Africa.[29]

In 1925 a procolonial caucus formed in the Reichstag. This Inter-Party Colonial Union (Interfraktionelle Koloniale Vereinigung) spanned, from right to left, the German National People's Party (DNVP), the German People's Party (DVP), the Catholic Center Party, the German Democratic Party (DDP), and the Social Democratic Party (SPD). The SPD, originally an entirely anticolonial party, had developed a wing in favor of "reformed" colonialism in the last years before the First World War. Now that wing gained the support of leading SPD women: Marie Juchacz, Wally Zepler, and Clara Bohm-Schuch proclaimed their opposition to Article 119.[30] Even the Independent Social Democratic Party (USPD), which had broken away from the SPD during the First World War out of principled opposition to annexations, briefly joined the revisionists: in March 1919 it voted in favor of a National Assembly resolution that called the anticipated Article 119 "unbearable, unfulfillable, and unacceptable."[31] That was the last time the USPD supported colonial revision, however. The new and small German Communist Party (KPD) rejected all procolonial statements.

Likewise, only a few nonparliamentary political associations spoke out against colonial revision. One was the German branch of the International Women's League for Peace and Freedom (Internationale Frauenliga für Frieden und Freiheit), to which several important German feminists, including the lawyer Anita Augspurg, belonged.[32] The colonialist movement followed the public speeches of the International Women's League with intense irritation. After a speech in favor of self-determination by peoples of color by Magda Hoppstock-Huth, a male colonialist reporter fulminated: "The 'modern' woman is as barren as this chatter. Women without children and nations without colonies —

those are the results of free self-determination!"[33] Helene Stöcker, an important radical feminist and pacifist, participated in the League against Colonial Oppression and Imperialism's famous 1927 congress in Brussels.[34] Opposition to colonial revision could be dangerous in the first years after the war: the colonial soldier turned pacifist and anticolonial journalist Hans Paasche was murdered for his views in 1920.[35] Support for colonial revision, by contrast, posed neither physical nor political risks — which helps explain its ubiquity, including among women's organizations. The Federation of German Women's Associations (Bund Deutscher Frauenvereine, BDF) actively supported colonial revision. In 1920 its general manager, Dorothee von Velsen, and Else Frobenius organized a coalition of women's organizations to agitate on behalf of borderlands Germans and Germans abroad, including colonial Germans, that numbered, Frobenius claimed, three million members. And in 1921 Frobenius and the DVP Reichstag delegate Clara Mende organized the Women's Committee against the Guilt Lie (Frauenauschuss zur Bekämpfung der Schuldlüge).[36] Such responses to Article 119 were far more common than those of Hoppstock-Huth, Stöcker, or Paasche.

Outrage over the colonial guilt lie served to unite Germans more effectively than real existing colonialism had ever done.[37] But new divisions soon arose. Alongside pure colonial revision — the demand for restoration of the colonies in exactly the same form as before the war — emerged proposals for new forms of colonial power. These proposals arose out of pragmatism in the face of the Entente's intransigence rather than from a principled turn away from formal empire. In 1920 former governor of Samoa and colonial secretary Wilhelm Solf suggested that international (white) oversight was appropriate for all colonies, not just the formerly German ones, in order to protect colonial subjects from abuses that had taken place in every modern colonial empire.[38] Reichsbank president Hjalmar Schacht (DDP) proposed in the early 1920s that the European states and the United States form a chartered company for the joint exploitation of lands extending from Africa to Russia.[39] Former colonial secretary Bernhard Dernburg (DDP) suggested in 1926 that Germans should work to increase their trade in tropical products and to improve conditions for German settlers abroad. Formal political rule now looked too expensive and difficult, however, due to "the race problem that ha[d] arisen in Africa" (Dernburg apparently meant pan-Africanism).[40] Wilhelm Külz, now minister of the interior (DDP), favored Schacht's and Dernburg's ideas.

These proposals infuriated the more rigid colonialists. Former governor of German East Africa Heinrich Schnee (DVP), the radical nationalist publicist Wilhelm Föllmer, and Franz Ritter von Epp, a Free Corps leader and Nazi party member since 1928, called proposals such as Schacht's a "colonial policy stab in the back" and proclaimed their unswerving insistence that the former colonies be restored to full German control.[41] Members of the Reich Working Group on the Colonies (Koloniale Reichsarbeitsgemeinschaft, KORAG), a coalition of colonialist organizations founded in 1922, claimed the right to speak for genuine colonial revision. These extreme revisionists, who resisted the stabilization of the Weimar Republic, narrowed the political range of the colonialist movement and, from the mid-1920s, moved it toward the far right.

In the mid-1920s the colonialist movement still included many people whom the Nazis rejected, such as the Reich League of Jewish Front Soldiers member Theodor Freudenberger, who lectured in 1927 on his experiences as one of General Paul von Lettow-Vorbeck's army in German East Africa. Lettow-Vorbeck was colonialists' idol because he led the only German force that was undefeated in the field at the time of the armistice.[42] Freudenberger wished to disprove not only the colonial guilt lie but also two "prejudices": that Jews did not do their share of fighting during the First World War, and that Lettow-Vorbeck had been able to hold out so long because there were no Jews among his colonial force (in fact, Freudenberg noted, there were seventeen, some of whom died in action).[43] The review of Freudenberger's lecture in *Der Kolonialdeutsche,* a periodical that served at various times in the 1920s as the official organ of the German Colonial Society, Women's League, Women's Red Cross Association, and several colonial veterans' associations, indicates that the myth of Jewish underrepresentation on the front in the First World War, exemplified by a census of Jews in the military in 1916, was alive and well.[44] It also shows that while colonial revision was important to Freudenberger, Freudenberger's concerns about anti-Semitism were not important to other colonialists. The review does not comment on how he disproved the "prejudices," but rather only on how well Freudenberger argued against the colonial guilt lie.

As for Lettow-Vorbeck, he took an active part in armed counter-revolutionary activity from the first weeks of the Weimar Republic. The colonialist movement as a whole exhibited a clear antirepublican tendency by 1928.[45] The stock market crash of 1929 brought more support for far-right positions. Under Schnee and Epp, the colonialist movement moved ever closer to the Nazi party (National Socialist German Workers' Party, NSDAP) between 1928 and 1933. It was not necessarily an obvious partnership, for the Nazi party had shown almost no interest in overseas colonial issues between 1919 and 1927, while the right-liberal DVP had established itself as both the most strongly procolonial party and a prorepublican one as well.[46] The colonialists' motive for joining forces with the Nazis was to escape their upper-bourgeois reputation and become a true movement of the common people (*Volksbewegung*). The Nazis, meanwhile, wanted to establish an alliance with traditional conservatives. In 1932 Schnee resigned from the DVP; by then he took for granted that the NSDAP was necessary to any solution to the crisis of the republic. When he joined the NSDAP in 1933, the colonialist-Nazi alliance was already in place.[47]

The existence of the colonialist-Nazi alliance before 1933 meant that Hitler's seizure of power was not a major turning point for many colonialists, at least as far as their activism was concerned. There were some changes: the Reich Colonial League (Reichskolonialbund), a new umbrella organization, replaced the KORAG, and the Women's League affiliated itself with the Nazis' German Women's Enterprise (Deutsches Frauenwerk).[48] Local chapters of the Women's League were required to include Nazi party members on their boards. Nevertheless, the Women's League remained a distinct organization and continued to control its own funds. Certainly there were women with Nazi sympathies already in its ranks, including Else Frobenius, who remained active as a volunteer in the Women's League after leaving her paid position as general secretary in 1922. She joined the NSDAP in 1933 and held posts in it into the Second World War.[49] The Women's League chairwoman after 1932, Agnes von Boemcken, likewise joined the NSDAP in 1933, and remained at the helm of the Women's League even after it was "coordinated" (*gleichgeschaltet*) in 1936.[50] But the Women's League did not depend only on convinced Nazis for its smooth transition into the Third Reich. The aging former chairwoman Hedwig Heyl, a liberal since prewar days, praised Nazism in enthusiastic, if vague, terms at a Lyceum Club meeting just before her death in 1934: "Our time makes demands that are very simple where Hitler's essence and laws are the content. . . . His demand is that we are to desire only the good, the noble. To this purity of desire belongs also trust in one another. The laws that Hitler has established are to be understood in their entire greatness, in their goodness, in their love for the people, in mutual goodwill. Always remember that we face great tasks. We are working not for the present, but rather for the future!"[51] Like Schnee, Heyl was not originally drawn to Nazism, but nevertheless she met it more than halfway. Yet overt enthusiasm was not ubiquitous in the colonialist movement; the early 1933 issues of the Women's Red Cross Association's postwar organ, the *Green Pages,* did not mention the regime change at all.[52]

The Women's League and the Women's Red Cross Association enjoyed unbroken success across the political divide of 1933. The Women's League expanded from a 1925 membership of 6,500 to 20,560 in 1930, 24,000 in 1932, 25,000 in 1933, and 30,000 in 1936.[53] The Women's Red Cross Association expanded from the latter half of the 1920s onward as well, regaining 14,000 members by 1928; in 1935 it reached a longtime goal of founding its own nursing motherhouse.[54]

By contrast, colonialists who were Jews, Christians of Jewish descent, or strong political opponents of Nazism, as well as Germans of African or Samoan descent, certainly found 1933 a major turning point. In March 1933 the German Colonial Society yielded to pressure from Nazis in its midst to remove the liberal Wilhelm Külz, the Catholic Center Party mayor of Cologne Konrad Adenauer (the later chancellor of the Federal Republic of Germany), and the Jewish Social Democrat Max Cohen-Reuss from their posts in the organization.[55] Georg Wunderlich, a lawyer of Jewish descent who had been a prominent member of settler society in German Southwest Africa before the war, was likewise forced to emigrate in 1936 and joined his sister, Prof. Frieda Wunderlich, in New York City. Neither the support of his friend Theodor Gunzert in the tiny Division for Colonial Matters in the Foreign Office nor his plans to publicize the cause of German colonial revision once he reached the United States helped him avoid the confiscation of most of his assets.[56]

The new regime in 1933 also affected people of non-European descent who held German or foreign citizenship and lived in Germany or in the former colonies. The debate on race mixing continued to affect individuals whose legal kinship and citizenship status had been unsettled by the bans on intermarriage. For them, German state power continued to be linked to racial classification. The Nazi regime threw up new obstacles in the path of those people of color whose applications for naturalization were still pending.[57] The German bureaucracy had long put off the application for German citizenship of one plantation owner from Tanga, Tanganyika, who lived in the German community and was of Afrikaner (Boer) and Syrian descent. After 1933 he found himself being questioned about possible Jewish ancestry and photographed from the front and side. He gave up his quest for naturalization in 1936.[58] Discrimination on the basis of race became law inside Germany in April 1933 with the Law for the Restoration of the Professional Civil Service. The first Nazi law to apply the racial categories "Aryan" and "non-Aryan" (defined as those persons with one or more non-Aryan parents or grandparents), it excluded "non-Aryans" from the civil service.[59] In October 1933 Heinrich Schnee and former governor of Samoa Erich Schultz-Ewerth inquired whether persons of German and Samoan descent would be affected by that law. The answer was a typical example of Nazi arbitrariness as a tool of racial persecution: "Since the origin of the Polynesian race has not been completely scientifically clarified," they were told, all cases would be examined individually.[60]

Neither the archival records of the Women's League and Women's Red Cross Association (which are incomplete) nor their official publications, nor even the memoirs of individual figures such as Frobenius, mention the exclusion of Jews or political opponents in 1933. Yet Jews and principled liberals had participated in these organizations. In 1926, for example, the Israelite Women's Association (Israelitischer Frauenverein) had sent a delegate to the Women's League's annual congress.[61] Those Jewish and left-liberal women who had not already resigned by 1933, by which time Boemcken had been chairwoman for a year, were probably pushed out unceremoniously and without debate.[62] Antonie

Brandeis-Ruete, for example, the granddaughter of Sultan Sa'id Majid of Zanzibar and the daughter of Emily Said-Ruete, was active in the Hamburg chapter of the Women's League during the Weimar years and helped establish a new Colonial School for Women in the Holstein town of Rendsburg (Koloniale Frauenschule Rendsburg). She and Boemcken sat on the school's board of directors from its founding in 1926, and she often published pieces in colonialist anthologies and periodicals.[63] After 1933, when she would have been sixty-five years old, her name vanished from the list of school board members, although the sources do not permit the moment and details of her departure to be pinpointed.[64]

Those colonialists who were not jeopardized by race or political opinions and whose excitement at the new Germany was unpunctured by misgivings about Nazi policies experienced 1936 as the real turning point for their colonialist activism. That year, Schnee's efforts to maintain the autonomy of the colonialist movement finally failed and the entire movement was "coordinated." No independent voluntary associations with colonialist interests remained; all were integrated into the refounded, now fully Nazified Reich Colonial League under Epp.[65] Like other colonialist groups such as colonial veterans' associations, the Women's League chose to relinquish its independence "voluntarily" in June 1936 rather than face the alternative of forced liquidation. It became Division IV (Abteilung IV) of the new Reich Colonial League and was to carry out "cultural work" in Germany and the former colonies.[66] Boemcken, who had evidently proven her loyalty to the NSDAP, became the head of Division IV. The year 1936 also saw the incorporation of the Women's Red Cross Association into the Nazified German Red Cross; it became the "Main Division — Overseas" (Hauptabteilung Übersee). Probably even some convinced Nazis among the colonialists regretted the changes of 1936, which confiscated their painstakingly assembled funds and restricted their organizational autonomy.

Despite changes in organizational structure, colonialist women's writings continued to pour forth. Writers of the 1920s portrayed women in the colonies as victims, as mothers, and as emancipated comrades. They reiterated the themes of the prewar colonialist movement, but in a colonial space even more detached from European, African, and Pacific reality.

When Germany was defeated in 1918, mobilized Africans were among the soldiers victorious over it. Germans experienced Africans in military authority over them in two episodes: the French, Belgian, and British occupation of the German colonies, and the French occupation of the Rhineland. France's militarization of colonial subjects, already controversial before the war, now became associated with rumors of sexual violence.[67] This was new: the German colonial empire had not seen any of the racialized rape scares that had occurred in other colonies, like the intermittent "Black Perils" in South Africa between 1893 and 1913 or the rape scare that led to the White Women's Protection Ordinance in British-controlled Papua New Guinea in 1926.[68]

As the Entente powers invaded and occupied the various German colonies, they interned and usually deported German civilians there. Only in Southwest Africa were Germans generally allowed to remain, although male officials were deported, most of them to South Africa.[69] Government officials who interviewed deported colonists on their arrival in Germany asked them leading questions with respect to race in order to assemble evidence of Entente atrocities. "How rapid was the expulsion or escort out of the colony? Who carried it out (colored soldiers?) and how?" asked the official questionnaire. In cases of "maltreatment," the questionnaire asked: "By whom? (perhaps by colored soldiers?)."[70] Over the years, stock phrases of purple prose emerged for describing the deportations. A colonialist man recalled in 1931 the experiences of Ada Schnee, wife of the German East African governor, Heinrich Schnee, during the Belgian occupation of the town of Tabora: "The Belgians swept in with wild hordes from the Congo. The occupation of Tabora was indescribable . . . perhaps never before in the world had white women been subjected to such persecution. In the middle of the night the women suddenly found savages in their bedrooms; with shaggy hair, protruding lips and red eyes they stood there with knife in hand before a delicate European woman and demanded everything."[71] The author of this passage had not been present at these events, or even in Tabora; he was imagining them. In this case we can compare his statement directly with Ada Schnee's own. In her memoir, which by no means sought to minimize the violence and injustice of the Belgian occupation, Schnee described the situation in comparatively sober terms: "Many women found themselves suddenly facing a guard of *askaris*, with arms at the ready, in their bedrooms."[72] Ada Schnee did mention elsewhere instances of rape during the occupation of Tabora—but the rape victims were African, not German, women.[73]

Ada Schnee and Elly Proempeler, the deported widow of the district officer of Tabora killed in the war, did repeatedly mention sexual fear. But they made a point of differentiating between "German" Africans and other Africans. As Proempeler noted, Germans in Germany did not differentiate: "I have been asked here at home so often, 'Did not the blacks act very shamelessly toward us women as soon as we were alone?' "[74] Proempeler made a point of contradicting metropolitan Germans' assumptions, devoting an entire chapter to recording the aid rendered her by Africans and Afro-Arabs who had been under German rule. Here Proempeler was mobilizing the revisionist insistence on mutual affection between colonizer and colonized against a metropolitan racist sexual paranoia. Proempeler and Schnee reserved their language of sexual paranoia for the Congolese and other African soldiers under Entente rule. Even so, none of the memoirs by women deportees records any rape or lesser sexual molestation of a German woman by an African man.[75] Likewise, the deportees' responses to the government interviewers showed that German colonists suffered many serious hardships, such as being forced to march long distances while ill and underfed, arbitrary measures at the hands of local officials, and even stonings by hostile European colonists in French and Belgian colonies. They also indicated outrage and fear at being placed under the guard of African soldiers.[76] But none of the women among the interview respondents was able to confirm any instance of sexual violence.

Women deportees intended their published diaries to document Entente outrages, and they interpreted the shame of military defeat in terms of women's sexual vulnerability. Yet what these memoirs mainly conveyed to German readers was a record of German women's patriotic fortitude and ability to protect themselves, even in the absence of their husbands. Schnee, for example, referred repeatedly to how she faced down British and Belgian officials by simply refusing to follow their orders. Such instances of female bravery recalled the heroism of the *Farmersfrau*. They were victims, but without the stigma of sexual defeat.

Depictions of the second episode of rape scares about colonial soldiers, the "black shame on the Rhine" (*schwarze Schmach am Rhein*), stand in marked contrast to the expulsion of German settlers from the colonies. Between 1919 and 1925, France occupied the Rhineland with a military force that included soldiers from French colonies in Africa and Indochina. The occupation elicited outrage from German men and women of all political persuasions.[77] In letters, petitions, and assemblies they expressed their fury at African and other non-European soldiers' exercise of military authority over Germans and at purported occasions of violence toward civilians, especially women. None of these claims of assaults were substantiated in full; most were utter invention.[78] The campaign against the "black shame on the Rhine" was fed by imagination—an often pornographic imagination, as agitation materials from the campaign show—rather than facts.[79] Both women and men participated. In her pamphlet *Men Unarmed, Women Unprotected*, Luise Paasche asserted that women had to take up the struggle against the war guilt lie and the "black shame on the Rhine" because male political leaders had failed them.[80] Rape symbolized not only defeat at the hands of the uncivilized, but also the weakness of German men, especially those in charge of the new Weimar Republic. Black people's presence in Germany was associated with defeat, humiliation, and powerlessness. Interracial desire, which colonialists had admitted and sometimes even praised before the First World War, was now denied and reinterpreted as rape. The six to eight hundred children born to colonial soldiers and German women were stigmatized as "Rhineland bastards" and subjected to sterilization in 1937.[81]

Both episodes show that racial and sexual fears could overwhelm empirical facts in narratives of the end of German colonial rule. But while a reworking of reality into a symbolic narration took place in both the campaign against the "black shame on the Rhine" and in accounts of the colonial deportations, the stakes for German women were not the same in both. Sexual victimhood inside Germany was additional evidence of the injustice of the Versailles Treaty; indeed, the more extreme the sexual predation, the sounder the case revisionists could launch. Sexual victimhood in the former German colonies had another meaning that was difficult for colonialist women to express. White women's sexual vulnerability was one of the oldest arguments for excluding them from the African colonies — but colonialist women during and after the First World War wanted to forge ahead with colonial projects even in the absence of formal colonies. They had no intention of disqualifying themselves from active roles in the former colonies.

MOTHERS OF GERMANDOM IN GERMANY AND ABROAD

The Women's League posed as an organization that stood above politics. With the loss of formal empire, this depoliticized notion of female colonialist activism took on even more importance. It was achieved primarily through images of maternal solicitude. Adda von Liliencron, the first chairwoman of the Women's League, played the role of mother for "sons" (colonial soldiers); Hedwig Heyl did the same for "daughters" (women entering professionalized housework and other new or reformed women's careers), and Hedwig von Bredow, chairwoman between 1920 and 1932, presented herself as a mother to both sexes and all ages. Bredow was the first Women's League chairwoman to see a German colony firsthand (she traveled to Southwest Africa in 1927–1928 when she was seventy-five years old, and to Tanganyika and Southwest Africa in 1931), and she gained the nickname "Mother of the Germans in Africa" (Mutter der Afrikaner).[82] The Women's League represented itself as a caring and providing mother of colonial Germans: it offered loans to colonists' family members who happened to be visiting Germany in summer 1914 and were stranded there, it placed colonists' children with families in Germany as "colonial godchildren" (Kolonialpatenschaften), and it welcomed the deportees back to Germany with food and clothing.[83]

The mothers of Germans abroad continued their pre–First World War efforts to maintain German culture in communities abroad. They focused especially on youth and on schools, as institutions both close to home and ostensibly beyond politics,[84] and were quick to complain that the mandate administrations were neglecting the needs of German communities. Now other Europeans or whites, not "natives," were the greatest threat to German culture. Meanwhile, the Women's League saw African youth not as the object of German colonizing efforts but as rivals for the resources of the mandate administration.[85] Frobenius's successor as general secretary of the Women's League, Nora von Steinmeister, complained in 1933: "For negro children in today's Southwest and East Africa, the best has been provided, the mandate government and the missions have built beautiful schools for them. Even high schools are available for negro children — but *German* parents for the most part *lack the means* to provide even only a primary school education for their children."[86] The league demanded accommodation for white German students in the colonies.

The mandate administrations at first rejected German colonists' requests for special German schools or for German programs within existing white children's schools. Southwest Africa was the first to yield on the issue, and in late 1922 the Women's League began to reconstruct and expand German kindergartens, pupils' dormitories, and schools in Lüderitzbucht, Gibeon, Keetmanshoop, Karibib, and Swakopmund.[87] In 1932 the Women's League established a dormitory, the Hedwig von Bredow House, for German children from all over the mandate who were attending school in the capital, Windhoek. In April 1933 the Women's League opened the Hedwig Heyl Housekeeping School (Hedwig-Heyl-Haushaltungsschule) in Windhoek. The Women's League also shipped books and periodicals, as long as they were not "too modern," for the edification of youth and families in the mandate.[88]

After 1925, when Germans were allowed to reenter Tanganyika, as many as two thousand Germans settled there, most as coffee planters.[89] In contrast to Southwest Africa, German East Africa had offered hardly any schools for white German pupils before the war. The Women's League created new schools during the 1920s in Lupembe, Sunga, and Oldeani.[90] The league also sent governesses to isolated farmsteads in Tanganyika, Southwest Africa, and Angola, where Portugal allowed a number of German colonists to relocate. The Women's League also made an effort to complete children's sentimental education as Germans by bringing them to Germany for apprenticeships or university education.[91] It gave scholarships and operated dormitories for them in Bad Harzburg (1936), and in Wuppertal and Blankenburg (1939). Meanwhile, to sustain the interest of Germany-born youth in the former colonies, the Women's League carried out procolonial agitation in the schools, helped organize "colonial youth groups" (which had to join the

Hitler Youth in 1933), and contributed to a colonialist periodical for youth created in 1924, *Jambo*.

The Women's Red Cross Association concentrated on that other primary task of German mothers, nursing, declaring that "there can be no more beautiful task for the German woman than to see to it that Germans abroad do not have to do without German nursing care in case of need or illness."[92] The association managed to retain one hospital in the former colonies during the war, the Princess Rupprecht Convalescent Home in Swakopmund, Southwest Africa; all others were seized. But it was permitted to resume activities in Tanganyika in 1925 and in Cameroon in 1927, and it regained or founded anew several hospitals and clinics during the Weimar Republic.[93] It also continued its prewar efforts to sustain kindergartens. The association took on one new project: to "promote the image of Germandom in Turkey" by training "young Turkish women from good families" as nurses.[94] Like the Women's League, the Women's Red Cross Association sought to provide for the cultural needs of German youth, forming its own youth groups in Germany in 1926.[95]

In 1926 the Women's League resumed what had been its main prewar effort: the sponsorship of unmarried women's emigration. The first women emigrants to be sponsored after the war went to Southwest Africa and Tanganyika; in 1929 the Women's League began to send women to South Africa, Angola, Mozambique, Kenya, South America, and Mexico as well.[96] The numbers of women sponsored soon surpassed those of the prewar years.[97] Colonialist women and men still argued about what sort of women to sponsor.[98] The Women's League's continuing interest in women with certification led to the founding of a third colonial housekeeping school in Germany in 1926. A cooperative venture of the Women's League, the Holstein town of Rendsburg, and the Reich Ministry of Education (the Women's Red Cross Association had dropped out after showing early interest), its first students enrolled in 1927.[99] Unlike the earlier schools at Bad Weilbach and Witzenhausen, the school in Rendsburg was a resounding success. Enrolled at full capacity from 1930 onward, it grew in size continuously and remained in operation far longer — until 1945 — than its predecessors had during the era of actual colonial empire.[100] Also unlike the earlier women's schools, the Rendsburg school was intended not only to train "girls and women" (between seventeen and thirty-four years of age) from Germany for Africa, but also to train colonists' daughters in the ways of metropolitan German-ness. Its first pupils included young women from the Southwest African mandate.[101] The school's curriculum taught skills such as housecleaning, cooking, butchering, cheese making, woodworking, and livestock care, as well as basic medical skills and "colonial sciences," especially foreign languages, politics, and, beginning in 1930, genetics (*Vererbungslehre*).[102]

Agnes von Boemcken believed that domestic tasks such as cooking, sewing, and nursing were not necessarily the most important knowledge the school offered: "The deeper, more beautiful part of this school is this: that all who were united in a joyful year of youth should enter into life with the consciousness: We are German women, called upon to contribute in the smallest daily realms of life to keeping German that which is German. . . . We women, we German women want to prove that it is not governments and peoples who can take or give colonies as they see fit, but rather that they are built up and preserved through quiet, unobtrusive work; that the German wife and mother will be victorious in spite of all treaties and international agreements."[103] In Boemcken's rendition of Hedwig Heyl's decade-old motto, women were inherently revisionist because, as mothers, they lived and worked in a realm that superseded and was more powerful than politics.

The tensions over culture and education that pervaded the Weimar Republic also made themselves felt in the Women's League school projects. Echoes of the old radical nationalist quest for the "better" Germany, as well as fears of the "New Woman," were audible in the worries of Margarete von Zastrow, who led Women's League education efforts, and her husband, Berengar von Zastrow. Both were concerned that colonial girls were not becoming the right sort of German woman.[104] Berengar von Zastrow wrote that "the double life that they lead, on the one hand as the boss over against natives, on the other hand as helper of their mothers, is not easy for young girls to bring into harmony. The girls have no notion of what really strenuous work means. They lead a life on the farms that is much too free and unbound for them to be able to learn that."[105] Colonial racial privilege seemed to be spoiling young German women in the mandate (although the Zastrows did not question that privilege). But what if sending girls and young women to republican Germany infected them with modern ways? Former governor of German Southwest Africa Theodor Seitz warned that many colonists would not care for "the methods and results of raising children in today's Germany."[106] He had heard of several "drastic cases"; for example, "one of the girls soaked in our modern German civilization declared shortly after her return [to Southwest Africa] that she could no longer maintain social contact with her father, that he was too much of a philistine."[107] Even when the Nazis' seizure of power restored what many colonialists saw as proper family values, colonialists living in Germany still considered a stay in the mandates to be a necessary experience for young women. The male author of a Nazi-era colonialist propaganda book proclaimed the value of sending girls from Germany to a former German colony: "That which is not expressed in wage or salary is the real gain for our brave girls, to get out of the narrowness and constant control of some parental homes, to be able to delve into work and to be productive in the wide-open spaces and freedom, but also to ripen in the hardness of colonial life into a strong and proud German woman!"[108] This author attempted to drive home his point about hard work by asserting that African women never worked for German women in Southwest Africa; rather, German women did all household labor themselves. A photograph placed near this passage, showing African women doing laundry while young German women look on, belies his assertion.[109] It was not easy to reconcile the contradiction between colonial racial privilege and the enactment of German identity through hard, independent work in an insularly German domestic space.[110]

The Women's League's educational vision for German youth in the mandates was not much altered by the legal equality of men and women in the Weimar Republic. For boys, the league anticipated a technical apprenticeship or university education; it encouraged girls to take a course at the Rendsburg school and pursue nursing, bookkeeping, dressmaking, physical education, physical therapy, or photography.[111] The old pronatalism remained: Margarete von Zastrow noted that above all, girls needed to prepare for their future role as mothers who would "raise their sons to be men."[112] Yet the interwar years also saw new forms of feminine independence that had not been as readily available to earlier colonialist women such as Frieda von Bülow.

During and after the First World War, *comradeship* (*Kameradschaft*), became a ubiquitous term for both sexual and nonsexual relationships between women and men.[113] Men emerged from the war more vulnerable than before while women experienced new powers. Gender relations no longer presumed to the same extent women's dependency on men. Instead, women represented themselves working alongside men or even supplanting them. Yet while the prewar legal and social subordination of women changed in the 1920s and 1930s, equality did not take its place. The interwar period was a time of men's ambivalence about women and of women's ambivalence about emancipation.[114]

Across Europe, the "reconstruction of gender" and reordering of women's lives, appearances, and aspirations in the wake of the First World War was fundamental to the reconstruction of national identity.[115] At a time when masculine identity was extremely vulnerable, women emerged as symbols of a coherent culture and society, helping to limit, or at the very least provide a framework for, political change. Germans vented their fascination and irritation with the new possibilities of women through the image of the "New Woman." The dream of some and nightmare of others, the New Woman was politically enfranchised and economically and sexually independent. Free of family responsibilities, she embraced consumerism and entertainment and lived for herself. Both contemporaries and historians have been skeptical of the image of the New Woman, seeing it as a mask obscuring women's actual circumstances of continued low pay and family burdens. Indeed, the New Woman was more image than reality, given that few women really possessed their own economic security and autonomy from family responsibilities. Even if women did enjoy new freedoms, those freedoms were linked to new expectations: to be a cheerful, sexy, and tireless rationalized worker at home and in the workplace.[116]

Although the right and far right excoriated the New Woman, some women holding those political views evinced a New Woman–like independence. One was the anti-Semitic publicist Lenore Kühn, who was twice divorced, received a doctorate in philosophy in 1908, and joined many far right causes during Weimar, including the neopagan and anti-Semitic German Faith Movement (Deutsche Glaubensbewegung). She edited a women's supplement to the DNVP's official journal and briefly published her own monthly, *Woman and Nation (Frau und Nation)*, in the mid-1920s. She also penned a sex manual, *Diotima: The School of Love*, at the suggestion of Eugen Diederichs, a noted publisher close to the youth movement. She intended *Diotima* to be a "natural history of love" that avoided the "usual conflations of the social-ethical and the purely erotic."[117] After 1933 Kühn was close to Nazism without ever joining the party. Other, similarly independent-minded far right women did become active in the NSDAP, such as Lydia Gottschewski and Elsbeth Zander.[118] Some colonialist women displayed a New Woman–like independence as well. Else Frobenius, for example, twice-divorced and childless, was continuously immersed in her career as journalist, book author, and expert on political matters affecting borderlands Germans and Germans abroad from before the First World War through the end of the Second World War.

Some interwar colonialist women undertook journeys alone to the former colonies for purposes quite apart from marriage and motherhood. While such journeys were not unprecedented, their completely positive and serious reception in the colonialist movement was. Suspicion or sarcasm no longer inevitably greeted single women who were not intent on marriage, as it had before the war.[119] In 1928 the naturalist Gulla Pfeffer became the first German woman to carry out a research expedition in Africa "*without aid or accompaniment* by other Europeans."[120] Several women produced travelogues based on their journeys around the former colonies by automobile and airplane in which they visited scattered German settlers and reported on political and economic conditions. In the late 1930s Ilse Steinhoff toured Southwest Africa, South Africa, and Tanganyika by herself, dismissing the notion that her trip required any special bravery, and published a book of her photographs.[121] Another photojournalist, Eva MacLean, published an account of a trip she undertook alone to Cameroon.[122] Women like Steinhoff and MacLean needed no husband or family to take them to the colonies. They presented themselves as independent advocates of revisionism who were fully capable of judging Germans' political future and Africans' attitudes, much as Paul Rohrbach and Wilhelm Külz had done before the war. Indeed, in an echo of the prewar *Farmersfrau* literature, with which they were undoubtedly familiar, they claimed to be able to do everything men did, and some things—such as adhering to rules of hygiene while on safari—better.[123]

Interwar colonialist women's writings often depicted a comradeship with German men that permitted independence for women without feminist critique of existing social relations. A 1937 colonialist novel by Christine Holstein, for example, portrays a wife whose husband's physical frailty serves as a plot device for her guilt-free emancipation.[124] The two are struggling farmers, in part because of the lasting effects of her husband's injuries sustained in the First World War. After her husband's death she becomes a skillful farmer who proudly surveys her fields, "with sharp eyes sweeping across the wide open spaces, satisfied with her herds, her cornfields, her bank account."[125] Even though Southwest Africa was so far from Germany, and not even officially German any longer, it remained a colonial setting where women could weave together feminine independence, German nationalism and Nazism, deference to a (dead) husband, and economic success. The old image of the *Farmersfrau*, the woman who produced economic and cultural value apart from industrial capitalism, class conflict, and competition with men, retained its power. In fact, the *Farmersfrau* was to be the last role that colonialist women filled, and the Colonial School for Women in Rendsburg continued to train them right up until April 1945.[126]

THE END OF COLONIALIST ACTIVISM

Between the German victory over France in the summer of 1940 and the German defeat in North Africa in the spring of 1943, bureaucrats in the Colonial Policy Office of the NSDAP (Kolonialpolitisches Amt der NSDAP), the Ministry of the Interior, the Ministry of Justice, and the Reich Colonial League planned for renewed colonial empire in Africa. The anticipated territory, called as in the First World War Mittelafrika, was to include not only the former German colonies but also the British colonies of Nigeria, the Gold Coast, Uganda, Kenya, and Northern Rhodesia; the French colonies of Dahomey and French Equatorial Africa; and the Belgian Congo. (After the conclusion of the Tripartite Pact, colonialists ceased calling for restoration of Germany's Pacific colonies.)[127] The planners sketched out in some detail a projected colonial administration, a basic law for the colonial empire, and a colonial version of the Nuremberg racial laws called the Colonial Law for the Protection of Blood (Kolonialblutschutzgesetz). This intensive planning, as well as all colonialist agitation, was halted in early 1943 when Germany mobilized for total war.[128] Epp's Reich Colonial League, including Division IV (the former Women's League), was completely dismantled. Historians have therefore dated the final end of German procolonial activity to 1943.

Yet one institution remained: the Colonial School for Women at Rendsburg, which aimed to prepare "girls and women" for "all domestic and agricultural women's careers" with an eye to "settlement purposes both at home and abroad."[129] Its students were to serve as "loyal comrades to our fellow Germans far away."[130] The school almost failed financially in 1929 but survived with the aid of the federal government, which took over 90 percent of its founding capital; the Women's League and the city of Rendsburg each held only 5 percent thereafter.[131] That high level of state control may have contributed to the rapid Nazification of the school in 1933. In that year, a new contract among the shareholders gave sweeping powers to Reich agencies and explicitly Nazi language appeared in the school's publications. A "flawlessly National Socialist attitude" was expected of students, who were to be drawn from the "most racially sound" (*erbtüchtigsten*) German girls and women.[132] "National political instruction," genetics, eugenics (*Erbgesundheitslehre*), race science (*Rassenkunde*), Germandom abroad, "colonial questions," and, after 1940, "Eastern questions" appeared in the curriculum.[133] Nursing instruction was added in 1928 and augmented in 1941; in 1942 professors from Hamburg's Institute for Maritime and Tropical Diseases, including the noted eugenicist Ernst Rodenwaldt, came to Rendsburg to lecture.[134]

By 1936 the school had attracted the interest of Heinrich Himmler's Blackshirts (Schutzstaffel, SS). Two SS officers from the Colonial Policy Office of the NSDAP joined the school board.[135] In the same year, Himmler became head of police in the Ministry of the Interior (Chef der Deutschen Polizei im Ministerium des Innern) and commissioner for strengthening Germandom (Kommissar für die Festigung des deutschen Volkstums) as well as Reichsführer-SS, the title he had held since 1929. Himmler had discussed the racial importance of including women in the SS as wives and co-workers since 1929, and he arranged ties with several women's schools that trained women as members of the ss.[136] He was involved in the planning for a renewed African empire because, as head of police, he insisted on heading up the projected colonial police as well, even though this conflicted with the Colonial Policy Office's wish to maintain centralized control over all things colonial.[137] Soon the Rendsburg school was drawn into the competition among state agencies typical of the Third Reich.

The renewed colonial planning led to higher enrollments at Rendsburg. The school's newsletter noted in 1940 that "with the victorious end of the war . . . many female workers for the reconquered colonies will probably be needed"; the school's director, Karl Körner, put the number at 800–1,000 women.[138] Between 1938 and 1941 the number of students enrolled increased from 58 to 122, then to 199 in 1943. By 1944 a total of 1,082 women had enrolled in the school; 797 had graduated.[139] Before the war about a third took positions abroad: in the Southwest African mandate, Tanganyika, Turkey, Paraguay, Angola, Mexico, and the Canary Islands; and in Hungary, Switzerland, and Upper Silesia in Poland.[140] A graduate was permitted to take a posting abroad only if she were sponsored by the Women's League (after 1936, Division IV of the Reich Colonial League), which supplied return fare in case of unemployment.[141]

After 1939, war prevented the school's graduates from working overseas. While training for Africa remained part of the curriculum, Körner wanted graduates to be able to work meanwhile in Carinthia, Romania, and the occupied Eastern territories.[142] In 1943 he added Russian to the curriculum.[143] Graduates took part in "service in the East" (*Osteinsatz*) as early as 1939, though it is not clear where they went and what posts they filled. A school history produced by two women close to its alumnae mentions only that graduates filled "guest" positions on Norwegian farms in early 1944 that were arranged by the Reich Nutrition Estate (Reichsnährstand) and Reich Youth Leadership (Reichsjugendführung).[144] Yet archival records mention that Rendsburg graduates were employed in, for instance, Potok Złoty, a small town southeast of the city of Częstochowa in the General Government, Hans Frank's domain in occupied Poland.[145] In March and April 1944 Körner visited the General Government himself (his brother was in Frank's administration), and also received at Rendsburg a delegation of Himmler's personal staff and the Women's Leadership of the Warthegau (Frauen-führung des Warthegaus). The Warthegau, another part of occupied Poland, was to be settled by ethnic Germans after the expulsion of its Jewish and Christian Polish inhabitants.[146] Apparently Rendsburg graduates already worked for the ss by this time, because one of Himmler's personal staff conveyed Himmler's approval of the "achievements of the Rendsburg girls in service in the East as well as Dr. Körner's administration of the school."[147] Another ss representative who visited the school in April 1944 likewise told Körner that Himmler took a personal interest in the school and that "the most favorable experiences" had been had with Rendsburg graduates on the estates administered by the Economic and Administrative Main Office of the ss (Wirtschafts- und Verwaltungshauptamt ss) in the East.[148] The most obvious possibility was that Rendsburg graduates worked as settlement advisers to the ethnic Germans relocated to confiscated lands. However, given their multifaceted, if superficial, training, they could have been employed in a wide range of positions. Körner and the other men and women who ran the school emphasized that the uniqueness of the school lay in its independent, open-ended approach to qualifications. They wanted the school's curriculum to enable women "to find their way in life anywhere, whether overseas or at home."[149] A school board member insisted in 1935 that "the Colonial School for Women must be differentiated from other women's schools in that it trains its pupils much more strongly in independence."[150] The school even tried to make a virtue of its limited pedagogical resources, claiming that "the sometimes abbreviated introduction to various skills is to serve as encouragement to learn to help oneself in unexpected situations everywhere, so that later in extreme situations on farms, plantations or isolated settlements one will react in the exact same way."[151] The school was to act as a "sieve" that would find those women who were best suited to work under "primitive conditions."[152] Certainly there was demand in the occupied Eastern territories, for German officials there complained constantly of a shortage of staff.[153]

While Himmler strategized from his position near the apex of power in the Nazi state, the women who studied and taught at the school pursued their own ambitions. They evinced strong loyalty and enthusiasm for their school and were proud of the independence they learned there. The school's historians have concluded that "the power of attraction that this training without a doubt had on many girls surely lay not least in the fact that the form and content of instruction greatly widened one's horizons. For many girls, this time at school meant a first step into independence, in a new self-confidence, which certainly also often culminated in a quest for yet more education."[154]

With the Rendsburg school, colonialist women's activism had fully entered the deep contradictions of Nazi policy toward women, and of certain Nazi women's experiences of emancipation in the *völkisch* state. In a profoundly woman-hating state, these racially selected and specially trained women found a space of freedom in which to enact, or at least imagine, their own domination of colonial space and colonial others. The women pupils at Rendsburg continued to see in agriculture a feminine economic and cultural role that was consonant both with Nazism and their fantasies of independence. Between 1919 and 1945 colonialist women had positioned themselves first as victims, then as mothers and culture-bearers. The final setting for their dreams of freedom as independent colonizers was in the service of the most racist and murderous order in Europe.

Sixty years of colonialist women's activism did not inevitably culminate in the Rendsburg school's cooperation with the ss. But neither was the relationship coincidental. Colonialist women's organizations and official goals showed almost continuous intensification of racism and nationalism between 1885 and 1933. They engaged in ever more activities that presumed and relied on racial and national distinctions, and ever less in activities that could be at least theoretically separated from a raison d'être of racism. Among the many political currents and cultural norms that Nazism exploited, from bourgeois respectability to the glorification of work, colonialist women's ideas of race purity, of women's special duty and ability to preserve Germanness, and of the superiority of German culture and colonization were relatively obvious matches with Nazi thinking.

But it would be ahistorical to allow Nazism to define everything that came before it. The ss was only the last in a long line of groups, from radical nationalists to radical feminists, to see promise in colonialism for German women and men. Claiming membership in a colonizing nation and seeing the condition of women as an index of civilization led to no sharp divide between feminist and nonfeminist women in Germany. These women, whatever their own politics, faced a common exclusion from colonial settlement and planning. They seized on their unusual discursive position as both symbols of a high level of civilization — as the maxim about measuring civilization by the treatment of women held — and agents of civilization, members of a newly colonizing nation. They were able to oscillate between the statuses of symbol and agent when arguing that colonies that lacked women's full participation in public life could not advance and adequately represent German cultural prowess. The colonies were a fantasyland for both German men and German women. At times these fantasies were irreconcilable, as in the case of the colonial sex scandals; at other times they were complementary, as in the case of liberal national masculinity and its partnership with white German women. In either case, however, gender relations between Germans were mediated through race. Colonial racism, in all its intentions, manifestations, and effects, was a project implemented by German women and German men in interaction with each other.

The category "women" continues to be meaningful in measuring political participation, wealth, violence, and many other phenomena in the world today. But as the present story about gender, race, and empire suggests, the reasons for invoking a group of humans called "women" have been far from universal, transcultural, or transhistorical. Actual women have invoked that category from their specific, interested positions, and their interests have conflicted with the interests of women in other social or geographical positions. The thick layers of ideology covering the sweeping designation "women" are revealed in past and current applications of Mill's old maxim. "Is multiculturalism bad for women?" asks a recent collection of essays, reiterating the centuries-old counterposing of women's well-being with cultural difference.[1] What has been and can be a contestation within and across cultures is cast all too often as a contestation between cultures, in which one culture is proposed as an improvement or as a danger to another. German colonialist women's activism ended with the defeat of Nazism in 1945, but the entanglement of gender difference, feminism, and hierarchical cultural comparison did not.

Colonialist and Women's Organizations

The organizations that figure in this book have confusingly similar names. This appendix offers brief descriptions of each, using the shortened version of the name that appears most frequently in the text.

German Colonial Society. This organization was created in 1887 out of the merger of two older colonialist organizations: the German Colonial Association (Deutscher Kolonialverein), founded 1882, and Carl Peters's Society for German Colonization (Gesellschaft für deutsche Kolonisation), founded 1884. Several other colonialist organizations that focused on topics such as commerce, geography, and emigration also existed. These organizations had an overwhelmingly male membership and an exclusively male leadership.

Patriotic Women's Leagues. This federation of conservative nationalist women's charities formed the largest aggregation of women's groups in Imperial Germany. The Women's Association for Nursing became an auxiliary (*Hilfsverein*) of the Patriotic Women's Leagues in 1888.

Women's Association for Nursing. This organization for colonial nursing began in 1886 as the German-National Women's League, founded by Martha von Pfeil and Frieda von Bülow. After Bülow's departure it was renamed the German Women's Association for Nursing in the Colonies. In 1908, when it gained a closer affiliation with the Red Cross, its name was changed to German Women's Red Cross Association for Nursing in the Colonies. In 1922 its name changed once more, to German Women's Red Cross Association for Germans Overseas. It was "coordinated" into the Nazified Red Cross in 1936, falling under the Main Division — Overseas. After the Second World War it was refounded within the German Red Cross (Deutsches Rotes Kreuz) as DRK-Schwesternschaft "Übersee" e. V.

Women's League. This organization for German women's settlement in the colonies began in 1907 as the German-Colonial Women's League, founded by a committee of women including Luise Weitzenberg and Maria Kuhn; its first chairwoman was Adda von Liliencron. In 1908 it became the Women's League of the German Colonial Society, reflecting a formalized partnership with the older, male-run German Colonial Society. Hedwig Heyl was its chairwoman from 1910 until 1920 and Hedwig von Bredow from 1920 until 1932. In 1936 it was "coordinated" into the Nazified colonialist movement as Division IV of the Reich Colonial League, but it retained the same chairwoman, Agnes von Boemcken from 1932 until 1943.

Women's Welfare Association. This organization led by the radical bourgeois feminists Minna Cauer and Anna Pappritz sought to become involved in German women's settlement in the late 1890s and in 1907. Although the men of the German Colonial Society and Colonial Department rebuffed them, some of their ideas came to fruition in the Women's League under Hedwig Heyl.

Unless otherwise noted, all translations from the German are the author's.

INTRODUCTION

1   John Stuart Mill, *On Liberty, with The Subjection of Women and Chapters on Socialism,* ed. Stefan Collini (Cambridge: Cambridge University Press, 1989), 138.

2   Charles Fourier, *The Theory of the Four Movements,* ed. Gareth Stedman Jones and Ian Patterson (Cambridge: Cambridge University Press, 1996), 130; Friedrich Engels, "Socialism: Utopian and Scientific," in *The Marx-Engels Reader,* ed. Robert C. Tucker (New York: W. W. Norton, 1978), 690; and Karl Marx, *Early Writings,* trans. Rodney Livingstone and Gregor Benton, intro. Lucio Colletti (London: Penguin, 1974), 346–347.

3   Leila Ahmed, *Women and Gender in Islam: Historical Roots of a Modern Debate* (New Haven: Yale University Press, 1992), 153, see also 151–155. On imperialist language in feminist writings, see Clare Midgley, "Antislavery and the Roots of 'Imperial Feminism,'" in *Gender and Imperialism,* ed. Midgley (Manchester: Manchester University Press, 1998), 161–179. I found analogous material in German feminists' writings and presented it in an unpublished paper, "Feminism and Empire," at the Program for the Study of Women and Gender, Rice University, on 24 March 1998.

4   Hartmut Pogge von Strandmann, "Domestic Origins of Germany's Colonial Expansion under Bismarck," *Past and Present* 42 (February 1969): 140–159. The locations and timing of annexations depended on more than merely domestic factors, however.

5   Today, these lands comprise the following states: Namibia (German Southwest Africa), the Republic of Cameroon and part of Nigeria (German Cameroon), the Republic of Togo and part of Ghana (German Togo), and mainland Tanzania, Rwanda, and Burundi (German East Africa). German New Guinea is now the northeastern mainland of Papua New Guinea, its northern islands (Bismarck Archipelago, Bougainville, and Buka), and the Republic of the Marshall Islands.

6   The leased Chinese region of what Germans called Kiautschou (Kiao-Chow) is today called Jiaozhou. The islands gained in 1888, 1899, and 1900 are today, respectively, the Republic of Nauru; the Northern Mariana Islands, Palau, and part of the Federated State of Micronesia; and Western Samoa.

7   For population statistics and ranking of empires' sizes, see Wolfgang J. Mommsen, *Imperialismus: Seine geistigen, politischen und wirtschaftlichen*

Grundlagen. Ein Quellen- und Arbeitsbuch (Hamburg: Hoffmann und Campe, 1977), 37–38. On the constitutional and administrative organization of the colonial empire, see Ernst Rudolf Huber, *Deutsche Verfassungsgeschichte seit 1789,* vol. 4 (Stuttgart: W. Kohlhammer, 1969), 604–634.

8   In this book, I use *colonialist* to refer to persons who engaged in political activity in support of empire, either in Germany or in the colonies. *Colonists* were an overlapping group of persons who lived in the colonies and may or may not have been politically active.

9   Doris Kaufmann, *Frauen zwischen Aufbruch und Reaktion: Protestantische Frauenbewegung in der ersten Hälfte des 20. Jahrhunderts* (Munich: Piper, 1988), 124–189; and Mary Taylor Huber and Nancy C. Lutkehaus, eds., *Gendered Missions: Women and Men in Missionary Discourse and Practice* (Ann Arbor: University of Michigan Press, 1999), and references cited therein.

10 On "civilized" gender relations, especially the "cultured marriage" (*Kulturehe*), see Marianne Weber, *Ehefrau und Mutter in der Rechtsentwicklung* (Tübingen: J. C. B. Mohr [Paul Siebeck], 1907); Weber, "Beruf und Ehe," in *Beruf und Ehe: Die Beteiligung der Frau an der Wissenschaft. Zwei Vorträge* (Berlin: Schöneberg: Buchverlag der "Hilfe," 1906), 3–18; and Hans Sveistrup and Agnes von Zahn-Harnack, eds., *Die Frauenfrage in Deutschland: Strömungen und Gegenströmungen 1790–1930* (Burg b.M.: August Hopfer, 1934), 257–317.

11 Irene Stoehr, "Organisierte Mütterlichkeit," in *Frauen suchen ihre Geschichte,* ed. Karin Hausen, 2d, rev. ed. (Munich: C. H. Beck, 1987), 225–253.

12 Bärbel Clemens, *"Menschenrechte haben kein Geschlecht!" Zum Politikverständnis der bürgerlichen Frauenbewegung* (Pfaffenweiler: Centaurus, 1988), 79–89.

13 Leonore Niessen-Deiters, *Die deutsche Frau im Auslande und in den Schutzgebieten* (Berlin: Egon Fleischel, 1913), 7.

14 On the "surplus of women," see Elisabeth Gnauck-Kühne, *Die deutsche Frau um die Jahrhundertwende: Statistische Studie zur Frauenfrage* 2d, rev. ed. (Berlin: Otto Liebmann, 1907), 35–69; and Nancy Reagin, *A German Women's Movement: Class and Gender in Hanover, 1880–1933* (Chapel Hill: University of North Carolina Press, 1995), 99–122.

15 Except for Kiao-Chow and except for missionary work, German women did little charity, social, and educational work with colonial subjects, unlike, for example, British women in India. See, for example, Kumari Jayawardena, *The White Woman's Other Burden: Western Women and South Asia during British Rule* (New York: Routledge, 1995); and Antoinette Burton, *Burdens of History: British Feminists, Indian Women, and Imperial Culture* (Chapel Hill: University of North Carolina Press, 1994). On Jiaozhou, see *Musterkolonie Kiautschou: Die Expansion des Deutschen Reiches in China. Deutsch-Chinesische Beziehungen 1897 bis 1914. Eine Quellensammlung,* ed. Mechthild Leutner (Berlin: Akademie Verlag, 1997), 429–439, especially 429 and 433;

and Paul Rohrbach, *Deutschland in China voran!* (Berlin: Protestantischer Schriftenvertrieb, 1912).

16 Members of the urban and rural working classes were rare in colonialist organizations, but that may reflect those organizations' snobbery rather than working-class Germans' preferences. On Social Democrats' interest in empire, see Roger Fletcher, *Revisionism and Empire: Socialist Imperialism in Germany 1897–1914* (London: George Allen & Unwin, 1984), and references cited therein.

17 See, for example, Ann Laura Stoler and Frederick Cooper, "Between Metropole and Colony: Rethinking a Research Agenda," in *Tensions of Empire: Colonial Cultures in a Bourgeois World,* ed. Stoler and Cooper (Berkeley: University of California Press, 1997), 1–56, and the references to Stoler's work cited therein; Alice L. Conklin, *A Mission to Civilize: The Republican Idea of Empire in France and West Africa, 1895–1930* (Stanford: Stanford University Press, 1997); Nancy Rose Hunt, *A Colonial Lexicon of Birth Ritual, Medicalization, and Mobility in the Congo* (Durham: Duke University Press, 1999); Christopher Schmidt-Nowara, *Empire and Anti-slavery: Spain, Cuba, and Puerto Rico, 1833–1874* (Pittsburgh: University of Pittsburgh Press, 1999); and Susan Thorne, *Congregational Missions and the Making of an Imperial Culture in Nineteenth-Century England* (Stanford: Stanford University Press, 1999).

18 Lora Wildenthal, "The Places of Colonialism in the Writing and Teaching of German History," *European Studies Journal* 16 (1999): 9–23.

19 The first critical study of German colonialist women falls into the former category: Martha Mamozai, *Herrenmenschen: Frauen im deutschen Kolonialismus* (Reinbek bei Hamburg: Rowohlt, 1982). This pathbreaking book brings together a wide range of sources to argue that supporting the subordination of entire other peoples to German men helped colonialist women internalize their own subordination to men (20). While Mamozai works backward from the present-day gender politics of international inequalities, the present book works forward from historical sources. I take colonialist women seriously as people who made conscious choices from a range of existing possibilities — and whose choices are therefore to be scrutinized all the more critically. At the same time, I focus on their goals and usage of concepts such as "women" or "culture," in preference to repeating Mamozai's work of documenting how far short of humane practice they fell. See also Bodo von Borries, "'Hochmut,' 'Reue' oder 'Weltbürgersinn'? Zur Kolonialepoche in historischen Überblicksdarstellungen und allgemeinem Geschichtsbewusstsein," in *Afrika und der deutsche Kolonialismus: Zivilisierung zwischen Schnapshandel und Bibelstunde,* ed. Renate Nestvogel and Rainer Tetzlaff (Berlin: Dietrich Reimer, 1987), 153–181.

20 The two best efforts at documenting with historical detail connections between colonialism and Nazism as political movements are Woodruff Smith,

The Ideological Origins of Nazi Imperialism (New York: Oxford University Press, 1986); and Klaus Hildebrand, Vom Reich zum Weltreich: Hitler, NSDAP und koloniale Frage, 1919–1945 (Munich: W. Fink, 1969). Neither discusses the Holocaust, however. Hannah Arendt argues for much stronger connections than do Smith and especially Hildebrand, but lacks their differentiated detail, in The Origins of Totalitarianism, new ed. with added prefaces (New York: Harcourt Brace Jovanovich, 1973), especially "Imperialism."

21 See, for example, Susanne Zantop, Colonial Fantasies: Conquest, Family, and Nation in Precolonial Germany, 1770–1870 (Durham: Duke University Press, 1997); Sara Friedrichsmeyer, Sara Lennox, and Susanne Zantop, eds., The Imperialist Imagination: German Colonialism and Its Legacy (Ann Arbor: University of Michigan Press, 1999); Russell Berman, Enlightenment or Empire: Colonial Discourse in German Culture (Lincoln: University of Nebraska Press, 1998); and Nina Berman, Orientalismus, Kolonialismus und Moderne: Zum Bild des Orients in der deutschsprachigen Kultur um 1900 (Stuttgart: M & P, 1997).

22 See, for example, "The Concept of Race," in W. E. B. DuBois, Dusk of Dawn: An Essay toward an Autobiography of a Race Concept (reprint, New Brunswick: Transaction Publishers, 1984), 97–133; and, on Germany, Tina Campt, "'Afro-German': The Convergence of Race, Sexuality and Gender in the Formation of a German Ethnic Identity, 1919–1960" (Ph.D. diss., Cornell University, 1996); and May Opitz, Katharina Oguntoye, and Dagmar Schultz, eds., Showing Our Colors: Afro-German Women Speak Out, trans. Anne V. Adams (Amherst: University of Massachusetts Press, 1992). On the racialization of Jews in Germany, see Peter Pulzer, Jews and the German State: The Political History of a Minority, 1848–1933 (Oxford: Blackwell, 1992), 28–43.

23 Sylvia Walby, "Woman and Nation," in Mapping the Nation, ed. Gopal Balakrishnan (London: Verso, 1996), 235–254; Kumari Jayawardena, Feminism and Nationalism in the Third World (London: Zed Books, 1986), 1–24; and Selma Sevenhuijsen, "Mothers as Citizens: Feminism, Evolutionary Theory and the Reform of Dutch Family Law 1870–1910," in Regulating Womanhood: Historical Essays on Marriage, Motherhood and Sexuality, ed. Carol Smart (London: Routledge, 1992), 166–186. On nationalism, see Richard Handler, Nationalism and the Politics of Culture in Quebec (Madison: University of Wisconsin Press, 1988); and Daniel A. Segal and Richard Handler, "National Culture" and "Nationalism," in Encyclopedia of Cultural Anthropology (New York: Henry Holt, 1996), 840–848.

24 Ika Freudenberg, Die Frau und die Kultur des öffentlichen Lebens (Leipzig: C. F. Amelang, 1911), 56.

1. COLONIAL NURSING AS THE FIRST REALM OF COLONIALIST WOMEN'S ACTIVISM, 1885–1907

1   Claudia Prestel, "Erschliessung neuer Erwerbszweige für die jüdische Frau. Das Beispiel der Krankenschwester: Apologetik oder effektive Massnahme?" *Metis. Zeitschrift für historische Frauenforschung und feministische Praxis* 1 (1992): 41–62; and Marion A. Kaplan, *The Making of the Jewish Middle Class: Women, Family, and Identity in Imperial Germany* (New York: Oxford University Press, 1991), 196, 284 n. 27, and 288 n. 100.

2   Claudia Bischoff, *Frauen in der Krankenpflege: Zur Entwicklung von Frauenrolle und Frauenberufstätigkeit im 19. und 20. Jahrhundert*, 2d ed. (Frankfurt: Campus, 1992); and Eva Brinkschulte and Beate Vogt, "'Nicht um des Lohnes willen, sondern aus Liebe zum Herrn': Die Diakonissinnen des Elisabeth-Krankenhauses — Zur Entwicklung des 'typisch weiblichen' Berufs der Krankenschwester (1833–1865)," in *Ich bin meine eigene Frauenbewegung: Frauen-Ansichten aus einer Grossstadt*, ed. Bezirksamt Schöneberg/Kunstamt Schöneberg (Berlin: Edition Hentrich, 1991), 155–164. My discussion here also draws on histories of nursing in other states: Anne Summers, *Angels and Citizens: British Women as Military Nurses 1854– 1918* (London: Routledge & Kegan Paul, 1988); Martha Vicinus, "Reformed Hospital Nursing: Discipline and Cleanliness," in Vicinus, *Independent Women* (Chicago: University of Chicago Press, 1985), 85–120; Katrin Schultheiss, "'La Véritable Médecine des femmes': Anna Hamilton and the Politics of Nursing Reform in Bordeaux, 1900–1914," *French Historical Studies* 19 (1995): 183–214; Shula Marks, *Divided Sisterhood: Race, Class, and Gender in the South African Nursing Profession* (New York: St. Martin's Press, 1994); Susan Reverby, *Ordered to Care: The Dilemma of American Nursing, 1850–1945* (New York: Cambridge University Press, 1987); and Darlene Clark Hine, *Black Women in White: Racial Conflict and Cooperation in the Nursing Profession, 1890–1945* (Bloomington: Indiana University Press, 1989).

3   On the Red Cross, see Herbert Grundhewer, "Die Kriegskrankenpflege und das Bild der Krankenschwester im 19. und frühen 20. Jahrhundert," in *Medizin und Krieg: Vom Dilemma der Heilberufe 1865 bis 1985*, ed. Johanna Bleker and Heinz-Peter Schmiedebach (Frankfurt a.M.: Fischer, 1987), 140. On embourgeoisification, Bischoff, *Frauen in der Krankenpflege*, 140, and Grundhewer, "Die Kriegskrankenpflege," 138. On feminization, Hans-Peter Schaper, *Krankenwartung und Krankenpflege: Tendenzen der Verberuflichung in der ersten Hälfte des 19. Jahrhunderts* (Opladen: Leske Verlag & Budrich, 1987), 33–43, 47–50, 87–91, 117–118; and Johanna Bleker, "To Benefit the Poor and Advance Medical Science: Hospitals and Hospital Care in Germany, 1820–1870," in *Medicine and Modernity: Public Health and Medical Care in Nineteenth- and Twentieth-Century Germany*, ed. Manfred Berg and Geoffrey Cocks (Washington, D.C.: German Historical Institute; New York: Cambridge University Press, 1997), 17–33.

4 Bischoff, *Frauen in der Krankenpflege*, 81–92, 103–104.

5 *Unter dem rothen Kreuz* 4 (1893): 22. See also the goals of reconciling the social classes and of preventing intraclass gender conflict by diverting prospective female doctors into nursing in, respectively, J. Lob., "Über den Werth der Krankenpflege," *Unter dem rothen Kreuz* 2 (1891): 73; and F. Buttersack, "Die Frauen in der Heilkunde," *Unter dem rothen Kreuz* 4 (1893): 14.

6 Carl Peters, "Die Usagara Expedition," in *Gesammelte Schriften*, ed. Walter Frank (Munich: C. H. Beck, 1943), 1:285–318; Fritz Ferdinand Müller, *Deutschland — Zanzibar — Ostafrika: Geschichte einer deutschen Kolonialeroberung 1884–1890* (Berlin: Rütten & Loening, 1959), 115–133; and Harald Sippel, "Aspects of Colonial Land Law in German East Africa: German East African Company, Crown Land Ordinance, European Plantation and Reserved Areas for Africans," in *Land Law and Land Ownership in Africa: Case Studies from Colonial and Contemporary Cameroon and Tanzania*, ed. Robert Debusmann and Stefan Arnold (Bayreuth: Eckhard Breitinger, 1996), 3–38.

7 Suzanne Miers, "Slavery and the Slave Trade as International Issues 1890–1939," in *Slavery and Colonial Rule in Africa*, ed. Miers and Martin Klein (London: Frank Cass, 1999), 16–37; and Adam Hochschild, *King Leopold's Ghost: A Story of Greed, Terror, and Heroism in Colonial Africa* (Boston: Houghton Mifflin, 1998).

8 Jonathon Glassman, *Feasts and Riot: Revelry, Rebellion, and Popular Consciousness on the Swahili Coast, 1856–1888* (Portsmouth, N.H.: Heinemann, 1995), and references cited therein.

9 Eva von Pfeil und Klein-Ellguth, *Ein reiches Leben: Lebenserinnerungen und meine Arbeit für das Rote Kreuz in den Kolonien* (Dessau: Eduard H. de Rot [D. Schwalbe], 1914), 30–32, 38–43, 51, 53–58, 67–68, 76–77.

10 Pfeil, *Ein reiches Leben*, 46, 50.

11 Müller, *Deutschland — Zanzibar — Ostafrika*, 116–117; Carl Peters, "Die Gründung von Deutsch-Ostafrika: Kolonialpolitische Erinnerungen und Betrachtungen," in *Gesammelte Schriften*, 1:164–165; and Joachim von Pfeil, *Die Erwerbung von Deutsch-Ostafrika: Ein Beitrag zur Kolonial-Geschichte*, new ed. (Berlin: Karl Curtius, n.d. [1907]). The Pfeil sisters mentioned that Joachim von Pfeil was their cousin, but his name never arose in the context of their agitation (Pfeil, *Ein reiches Leben*, 68).

12 *Kolonialpolitische Korrespondenz* 1, no. 4 (1 July 1885): 4.

13 Pfeil, *Ein reiches Leben*, 68, 78. Diestelkamp had a long colonialist career and was later on the board of the German Colonial Society. Frieda von Bülow (see below) based the character Pastor Kistelhut on him in her novel *Margarete und Ludwig* (Stuttgart: J. Engelhorn, 1894), 132.

14 VEM M 2, Bl. 1 (minutes of the board, 26 October 1885).

15 VEM M 2, Bl. 1 (minutes of the board, 25 March 1886).

16 Joachim von Pfeil, *Die Erwerbung*, 44–45; VEM, M 352, Bl. 6 (Rentsch to

Büttner, 30 July 1887); and Hermann Krätschell, "Carl Peters 1856–1918: Ein Beitrag zur Publizistik des imperialistischen Nationalismus in Deutschland" (Ph.D. diss., Free University of Berlin, 1959), 27. Possibly Peters had noticed the usefulness of women supporters while teaching at a women's continuing education institute. At a time when independent financial activity was rare for middle-class German women, seventeen of the two hundred early shareholders in the company, or about 8 percent, were women. See *Kolonialpolitische Korrespondenz* 1, no. 6 (16 July 1885): 2–3.

17   Friedrich Lange, *Reines Deutschtum: Grundzüge einer nationalen Weltanschauung*, 3d ed. (Berlin: Alexander Duncker, 1904), 264, 268, 272–274, 279–281; Carl Peters, "Die Gründung," 206; and Henry Martin Bair Jr., "Carl Peters and German Colonialism: A Study in the Ideas and Actions of Imperialism" (Ph.D. diss., Stanford University, 1968), 128–129.

18   Among the contemporaries, see Veit Valentin, *Kolonialgeschichte der Neuzeit: Ein Abriss* (Tübingen: J. C. B. Mohr [Paul Siebeck], 1915), 203; Heinrich Schnee, "Carl Peters," in *Deutsches Biographisches Jahrbuch,* vol. 2: *1917–1920* (Stuttgart: Deutsche Verlagsanstalt, 1928), 285–298 (especially 297, where he noted Peters's "brutal recklessness" toward women); and GStA, Heinrich Schnee papers, Folder 22a, Bl. 72–77. Among historians, see Müller, *Deutschland — Zanzibar — Ostafrika,* 97–98; and Hans-Ulrich Wehler, *Bismarck und der deutsche Imperialismus* (reprint, Frankfurt a.M.: Suhrkamp, 1984), 337–338. Peters's only biographer is less critical, but also less persuasive in his effort to depict a more or less normal person; see Bair, "Carl Peters," especially 254–259. Peters reported his own cruelties in, for example, Peters, "Die Usagara-Expedition," 307–308, 309; and RKA 755, Bl. 95–96 (Peters to Gouvernement in Dar es Salaam, 5 September 1892).

19   Klaus J. Bade, *Friedrich Fabri und der Imperialismus in der Bismarckzeit: Revolution — Depression — Expansion* (Freiburg i.B.: Atlantis, 1975), 296–297.

20   VEM M 2, Bl. 1 (minutes of the board, 25 March 1886). See August Leue, *Dar es Salaam: Bilder aus dem Kolonialleben* (Berlin: W. Süsserott, 1903); and Fritz Bley, *Die Weltstellung des Deutschthums* (Munich: J. F. Lehmann, 1897).

21   On Bülow's family, see the entries (mostly written by Bülow herself) in *Bülowsches Familienbuch,* ed. Adolf von Bülow, vol. 2 (Schwerin: Eduard Herberger, 1914), 417–422; and the hagiographic but detailed Sophie Hoechstetter, *Frieda Freiin von Bülow. Ein Lebensbild* (Dresden: Carl Reissner, 1910), 21–31, 65. Thankmar von Münchhausen's wife was Anna von Münchhausen, née Keudell. Anna's younger sister Else von Keudell was one of the first women in Germany to pass the examination to be a secondary school teacher (*pro facultate docendi*) and later became head of a nursing motherhouse. See James Albisetti, "Women and the Professions in Imperial Germany," in *German Women in the Eighteenth and Nineteenth Centu-*

ries: *A Social and Literary History,* ed. Ruth-Ellen B. Joeres and Mary Jo Maynes (Bloomington: Indiana University Press, 1986), 105. Thankmar von Münchhausen was an ally of Count Paul Hoensbroech in the Antiultramontaner Reichsverband, an association that sought to perpetuate the *Kulturkampf* against the Catholic Center Party. See Herbert Gottwald, "Antiultramontaner Reichsverband," in *Lexikon zur Parteiengeschichte: Die bürgerlichen und kleinbürgerlichen Parteien und Verbände in Deutschland (1789–1945),* ed. Dieter Fricke (Cologne: Pahl-Rugenstein, 1983), 1:89–93.

22 Founded in 1836 by Theodor Fliedner and his first wife, Friederike Fliedner, the Kaiserswerth establishment promoted female nursing and sent its deaconesses to nurse and teach in Jerusalem, Istanbul, Smyrna, and Alexandria. See Theodor Fliedner, *Reisen in das heilige Land nach Smyrna, Beirut, Constantinopel, Alexandria und Cairo, in den Jahren 1861, 1856 und 1857* (Düsseldorf: H. Voss, 1858), v; and Catherine M. Prelinger, "The Nineteenth-Century Deaconessate in Germany: The Efficacy of a Family Model," in *German Women in the Eighteenth and Nineteenth Centuries,* ed. Joeres and Maynes, 215–229.

23 G. Burckhardt, *Die Brüdergemeine* (Gnadau: Unitäts-Buchhandlung, 1905); Horst Gründer, *Christliche Mission und deutscher Imperialismus 1884–1914* (Paderborn: Schöningh, 1982), 38–40; and Marcia Wright, *German Missions in Tanganyika 1891–1941: Lutherans and Moravians in the Southern Highlands* (Oxford: Clarendon, 1971), 9–13.

24 Bülow, *Die Schwestern: Geschichte einer Mädchenjugend,* 3d ed. (Dresden: Carl Reissner, 1909), 52. This novel was based on her childhood with her sister Margarete (Hoechstetter, *Frieda,* 35–36).

25 Sabina Streiter, "Frieda von Bülow und Ricarda Huch. Briefe aus dem Jahr 1895," *Jahrbuch der Deutschen Schillergesellschaft* 32 (1988): 63; and Hoechstetter, *Frieda,* 46–47.

26 Hoechstetter, *Frieda,* 59, 61; and Streiter, "Frieda von Bülow," 62. On the Crain Institute, see Gertrud Bäumer, *Helene Lange: Zu ihrem 70. Geburtstage,* 2d ed. (Berlin: W. Moeser, 1918), 13–14.

27 Hoechstetter, *Frieda,* 73–75.

28 Undated diary entry [between 9 April and 9 May 1884], cited in Hoechstetter, *Frieda,* 102.

29 Hoechstetter, *Frieda,* 114–115.

30 Friedrich Lange, "Frieda Freiin von Bülow," *Deutsche Zeitung,* 14 March 1909, reprinted in *Bülowsches Familienbuch,* 2:418.

31 Hoechstetter, *Frieda,* 117, 123.

32 A third woman, Baroness von Zelewska, was also briefly on the board; she was probably the sister of Lieutenant Emil von Zelewski, a company agent who played a key role in the coastal war's outbreak. See VEM M 2, Bl. 3 (minutes of the general assembly, 14 May 1886). Thankmar von Münchhausen was also on the board.

33 Gustav Warneck, "Nachschrift," *Beiblatt zur Allgemeinen Missions-Zeitschrift* 13, no. 3 (April 1886): 226–227.

34 RKA 5673, Bl. 22 (Pfeil to Johanna von Bismarck, 21 May 1887). Details of the goals varied according to the speaker, reflecting competing opinions within the organization. See RKA 5673, Bl. 6–7 (Bülow to Johanna von Bismarck, 9 October 1886); VEM M 167, Bl. 23–24 (Bülow to Büttner, 6 March 1887); *Nachrichten aus der ostafrikanischen Mission* 1, no. 1 (January 1887): 15, and vol. 1, no. 2 (February 1887): 20; and RKA 847, Bl. 2 ("Koloniales," *Norddeutsche Allgemeine Zeitung,* 12 January 1887), and Bl. 6 (*Kölnische Zeitung,* 14 April 1887).

35 VEM M 2, Bl. 8 (minutes of the board, 29 July 1886). See also Gerhard Jasper, *Das Werden der Bethel-Mission* (Bethel bei Bielefeld: Verlagshandlung, 1936), 9. Missionaries' and other colonialists' self-serving conflation of Christian virtue with Africans' hard labor for Europeans was common, though controversial. See Wright, *German Missions,* 16–20, especially 20. Peters, the son of a Protestant pastor, was willing to cultivate ties with Catholic and Protestant mission societies alike as long as they helped him to produce colonialist agitation material and promote labor discipline and cash trade for goods among Africans. He supported Father Amrhein's St. Benedict Missionary Association (St. Benediktus-Missions-Genossenschaft, founded in 1884 in Reichenbach in the Oberpfalz) and Pastor Ittameier's Evangelical-Lutheran Missionary Society (Gesellschaft für evangelisch-lutherische Mission in Ostafrika, founded in 1886 in Bavaria). Like Pfeil's group, these were enthusiastic nationalistic responses to the new German colonial empire. See Hans-Joachim Niesel, "Kolonialverwaltung und Missionen in Deutsch Ostafrika 1890–1914" (Ph.D. diss., Free University of Berlin, 1971), 43–45, 83–85; Heinrich Loth, "Die Gründung von Deutsch-Ostafrika und die christliche Mission," *Wissenschaftliche Zeitschrift der Karl-Marx-Universität Leipzig, Gesellschafts- und Sprachwissenschaftliche Reihe* 8, no. 2 (1958–1959): 339–347; and Gründer, *Christliche Mission,* 33–36.

36 Warneck, "Nachschrift," 228–229; E. Reichel, "Was haben wir zu thun, damit die deutsche Kolonialpolitik nicht zur Schädigung, sondern zur Förderung der Mission ausschläge?" *Allgemeine Missions-Zeitschrift* 13 (1886): 39–55; A. W. Schreiber, "Besetzung deutscher Kolonien mit deutschen Missionaren," *Allgemeine Missions-Zeitschrift* 13 (1886): 56–62; VEM M 2, Bl. 1 (minutes of the board, 12 April 1886); *Nachrichten aus der ostafrikanischen Mission* 1, no. 5 (May 1887): 66; Niesel, "Kolonialverwaltung," 40, 43; and Wright, *German Missions,* 1–8.

37 RKA 5673, Bl. 24 (bequest of J. W. J. Clever, 14 August 1886). Clever died in 1900, and his estate, Georgshof, near Mülheim am Rhein, became a convalescent home for colonial nurses. See *Unter dem rothen Kreuz* 12 (1901): 54–55.

38 VEM M 2, Bl. 5 (minutes of the board, 21 June 1886). Some contempo-

raries and historians have believed that Bülow was the sole founder of the German-National Women's League and colonial nursing generally. See, for example, Hoechstetter, *Frieda*, 118; and Krätschell, *Carl Peters*, 38. Bülow herself stated that she and Pfeil together founded the Evangelical Missionary Society (which was a slight exaggeration of her own role) and the German-National Women's League (*Bülowsches Familienbuch*, 2:419).

39   Hoechstetter, *Frieda*, 123.

40   Ibid., 118. The brochure was *Die höhere Mädchenschule und ihre Bestimmung*, reprinted in Helene Lange, *Kampfzeiten: Aufsätze und Reden aus vier Jahrzehnten*, vol. 1 (Berlin: F. A. Herbig, 1928), 7–58. See James Albisetti, "Could Separate Be Equal? Helene Lange and Women's Education in Imperial Germany," *History of Education Quarterly* 22 (1982): 301–317; and Ute Gerhard, *Unerhört: Die Geschichte der deutschen Frauenbewegung* (Reinbek bei Hamburg: Rowohlt, 1991), 140–148. Two other women attended the meetings, Baroness von Senfft-Pilsach and Baroness von Wangenheim, but little is known about them except for their husbands' conservative and anti-Semitic political activism. See Müller, *Deutschland—Zanzibar—Ostafrika*, 56; and James N. Retallack, *Notables of the Right: The Conservative Party and Political Mobilization in Germany, 1876–1918* (Boston: Unwin Hyman, 1988), 108, 214–216.

41   Lange, *Reines Deutschtum*, 105 (quote), 104–105, 193, 246–247, 373. On Lange, see Uwe Lohalm, *Völkischer Radikalismus: Die Geschichte des Deutschvölkischen Schutz- und Trutz-Bundes 1919–1923* (Hamburg: Leibniz, 1970), 33–35; Geoff Eley, *Reshaping the German Right: Radical Nationalism and Political Change after Bismarck* (reprint, Ann Arbor: University of Michigan Press, 1991), 186–187, 246–247; Roger Chickering, *We Men Who Feel Most German: A Cultural Study of the Pan-German League, 1886–1914* (Boston: Allen & Unwin, 1984), 234–236; and Müller, *Deutschland—Zanzibar—Ostafrika*, 99–100. On political anti-Semitism, which peaked as a party movement in the early 1890s and between 1910 and the First World War, see Peter Pulzer, *The Rise of Political Anti-Semitism in Germany and Austria*, rev. ed. (Cambridge: Harvard University Press, 1988); and Hans-Jürgen Puhle, *Agrarische Interessenpolitik und preussischer Konservatismus im wilhelminischen Reich (1893–1914): Ein Beitrag zur Analyse des Nationalismus in Deutschland am Beispiel des Bundes der Landwirte und der Deutsch-Konservativen Partei*, 2d ed. (Bonn: Neue Gesellschaft, 1975), 298–302.

42   Lohalm, *Völkischer Radikalismus*, 33; Lange, *Reines Deutschtum*, 41–44, 161–168, 382n.; and Dieter Fricke, "Der 'Deutschbund,'" in *Handbuch zur 'völkischen Bewegung' 1871–1918*, ed. Uwe Puschner et al. (Munich: K. G. Saur, 1996), 328–340.

43   Hahn was best known for his later post of director of the Agrarian League (Bund der Landwirte), a far-right, anti-Semitic lobbying group. He is thought to have served as the model for Diederich Hessling, the main char-

acter of Heinrich Mann's 1918 satirical novel of Imperial German society, *Der Untertan*, or *The Loyal Subject*, ed. Helmut Peitsch (New York: Continuum, 1998). See Puhle, *Agrarische Interessenpolitik*, 296; and George Vascik, "Agrarian Conservatism in Wilhelmine Germany: Diederich Hahn and the Agrarian League," in *Between Reform, Reaction, and Resistance: Studies in the History of German Conservatism from 1789 to 1945*, ed. Larry Eugene Jones and James Retallack (Providence: Berg, 1993), 229–260. Wendland became editor of the *Kreuzzeitung*, Germany's most important conservative newspaper.

44 At the time, Mauthner was the theater critic of the *Berliner Tageblatt*. See Theodor Kappstein, *Fritz Mauthner: Der Mann und sein Werk* (Berlin: Gebrüder Paetel, 1926), 14. Fritz Mauthner's major works are *Beiträge zu einer Kritik der Sprache*, 3 vols. (Leipzig: Felix Meiner, 1923), and *Der Atheismus und seine Geschichte im Abendlande*, 4 vols. (reprint, Frankfurt a.M.: Eichborn, 1989).

45 Streiter, "Frieda von Bülow," 59 n. 39; Hoechstetter, *Frieda*, 105. See also LBI, Mauthner papers, correspondence with Bülow, 1884–1900[?]; and LASA, Bülow to Andreas-Salomé, 2 February 1892 and 10 April 1894. Scattered remarks in this latter correspondence indicate tensions between Bülow and Mauthner, but key passages have been crossed out. One of Margarete von Bülow's short stories, "Herr im Hause," is reprinted in *Herr im Hause: Prosa von Frauen zwischen Gründerzeit und erstem Weltkrieg*, ed. Eva Kaufmann (Berlin: Verlag der Nation, 1989), 79–114.

46 Gershon Weiler, "Fritz Mauthner: A Study in Jewish Self Rejection," *Yearbook of the Leo Baeck Institute* 8 (1963): 136–148, especially 138, 143. Bülow probably drew on Mauthner's antiassimilationist opinions in sketching the only Jewish character in her fiction whom she depicted in a positive light: Prof. Dr. Mayer, in *Im Hexenring. Eine Sommergeschichte vom Lande* (Stuttgart: J. Engelhorn, 1901), see especially 147–148.

47 Clotilde von Bülow's diary, cited in Hoechstetter, *Frieda*, 123.

48 RKA 5673, Bl. 4 (*Deutsches Tageblatt*, 22 September 1886), and Bl. 9 (*Kreuzzeitung*, n.d.). On Grimm, see Müller, *Deutschland — Zanzibar — Ostafrika*, 146–147, 153, 178, 463; and Bade, *Friedrich Fabri*, 331.

49 Several of the women on the board, including Baroness Gertrud von Maltzahn, Frau Admiral Livonius, Frau Admiral Lucas, Frau Admiral von Knorr, and Peters's sister Elly Peters, were connected to colonial annexations and right-wing politics through male relatives. Almost half of the board members were unmarried women. See RKA 5673, Bl. 22 (Martha von Pfeil to Johanna von Bismarck, 21 May 1887).

50 *Kolonialpolitische Korrespondenz* 3, no. 8 (26 February 1887): 35–36 (quote is on 36); Krätschell, *Carl Peters*, 27, 38–39; and Müller, *Deutschland — Zanzibar — Ostafrika*, 179. On nationalists' idea of women as political conduits to the family, see Pieter M. Judson, "The Gendered Politics of German

Nationalism in Austria, 1880–1900," in *Austrian Women in the Nineteenth and Twentieth Centuries: Cross-Disciplinary Perspectives,* ed. David F. Good, Margarete Grandner, and Mary Jo Maynes (Providence: Berghahn, 1996), 1–17.

51 *Kolonialpolitische Korrespondenz* 3, no. 8 (26 February 1887): 36.

52 Ibid.

53 Pfeil, *Ein reiches Leben,* 68.

54 VEM M 2, Bl. 13 (minutes of the board, 25 November 1886).

55 RKA 5673, Bl. 21 (Martha von Pfeil to Johanna von Bismarck, 21 May 1887), and VEM M 167, Bl. 15 (Pastor Hänel to Büttner, 11 May 1887). The Women's League did not offer parity to Catholic donors. It did not dispatch a Catholic nurse until 1893, and did so then only at the insistence of its Cologne chapter. Rhenish Catholic business circles' interest centered on West Africa; see Ulrich S. Soénius, *Koloniale Begeisterung im Rheinland während des Kaiserreichs* (Cologne: Rheinisch-Westfälisches Wirtschaftsarchiv zu Köln, 1992), 106. The nurse was Marianne Bohler, who was hired for Togo. Because of hospital construction delays Bohler ended up working in German Southwest Africa. See *Unter dem rothen Kreuz* 4 (1893): 73.

56 François Renault, *Lavigerie, l'esclavage Africain, et l'Europe,* 2 vols. (Paris: Editions E. de Boccard, 1971), especially 2:144–156.

57 Klaus J. Bade, "Antisklavereibewegung in Deutschland und Kolonialkrieg in Deutsch-Ostfrika," *Geschichte und Gesellschaft* 3 (1977): 42–43. Some of the men in the Evangelical Missionary Society defended Pfeil's nonconfessional agitation: VEM M 167, Bl. 7 (Pastor Hänel to Büttner, 16 March 1887), Bl. 15 (Pastor Hänel to Büttner, 11 May 1887), and Bl. 29–30 (Livonius to Büttner, 24 April 1887).

58 Horst Gründer, "'Gott will es': Eine Kreuzzungsbewegung am Ende des 19. Jahrhunderts," *Geschichte in Wissenschaft und Unterricht* 28 (1977): 210–224; and Bade, "Antisklavereibewegung," 31–58.

59 On female leadership in nonconfessional religious charity, see Catherine M. Prelinger, *Charity, Challenge, and Change: Religious Dimensions of the Mid-Nineteenth-Century Women's Movement in Germany* (Westport, Conn.: Greenwood Press, 1987), especially 1–28.

60 RKA 5673, Bl. 22 (Martha von Pfeil to Johanna von Bismarck, 21 May 1887).

61 VEM M 167, Bl. 4 ("Rundschreiben des Deutschen Frauenbundes"). On fears about emigration and assimilation, see Mack Walker, *Germany and the Emigration 1816–1885* (Cambridge: Harvard University Press, 1964); and Woodruff D. Smith, *The Ideological Origins of Nazi Imperialism* (New York: Oxford University Press, 1986), 21–30.

62 VEM M 167, Bl. 4 ("Rundschreiben des Deutschen Frauenbundes").

63 Ibid.

64 VEM M 2, Bl. 10 (minutes of the board, 17 September 1886); Bade, *Friedrich*

Fabri, 15; and Gustav Menzel, *C. G. Büttner: Missionar, Sprachforscher und Politiker in der deutschen Kolonialbewegung* (Wuppertal: Verlag der Vereinten Evangelischen Mission, 1992), especially 140–162.

65 The main confrontation took place at the Bremen Mission Conference in October 1885. See Bade, *Friedrich Fabri*, 108, 264–265, 269.

66 *Nachrichten aus der ostafrikanischen Mission*, 1, no. 1 (January 1887): 8–9; VEM M 167, Bl. 28 (Bülow to Büttner, 22 March 1887), and Bl. 25 (Büttner to Bülow, 23 March 1887).

67 *Nachrichten der ostafrikanischen Mission* 2, no. 1 (January 1888): 5.

68 VEM M 167, Bl. 13–14 (Büttner to Pastor Hänel, 27 April 1887); *Nachrichten der ostafrikanischen Mission* 1, no. 3 (March 1887): 34, and vol. 2, no. 1 (January 1888): 8–9; and Menzel, *C. G. Büttner*, 191.

69 VEM M 167, Bl. 26 (Büttner to Bülow, 23 March 1887).

70 VEM, M 2, Bl. 17 (minutes of the board, 11 February 1887); *Nachrichten aus der ostafrikanischen Mission* 2, no. 1 (January 1888): 5; VEM M 167, Bl. 31 (Büttner to Martha von Pfeil, 16 July 1887).

71 *Nachrichten der ostafrikanischen Mission* 2, no. 1 (January 1888): 5.

72 RKA 5673, Bl. 10 (Diestelkamp, "Ein Krankenhaus in Dunda in Ostafrika"), and Bl. 49 (Consul Michahelles to Bismarck, 21 October 1887).

73 *Nachrichten aus der ostafrikanischen Mission* 2, no. 2 (February 1888): 26.

74 RKA 5673, Bl. 6–7 (Bülow to Johanna von Bismarck, 9 October 1886).

75 Bülow, "Weibliche Einjährige," *Die Zukunft* 32 (1900): 30–35, especially 32; *Bülowsches Familienbuch*, 2:419. The liberal-leaning Empress Frederick founded the Victoria Sisters in 1881 in response to Rudolf Virchow's call for secular nursing. See Lavinia L. Dock, *A History of Nursing*, vol. 4 (New York: G. P. Putnam, 1912), 2–3.

76 Hoechstetter, *Frieda*, 124; and Bülow, *Reisescizzen und Tagebuchblätter aus Deutsch-Ostafrika* (Berlin: Walther & Apolant, 1889), 169.

77 Andreas Blunck (Deutsche Fortschrittliche Partei) in *Stenographische Berichte über die Verhandlungen des Reichstages*, 20 March 1912, 868–869; and Charlotte Reichel, *Der Dienstvertrag der Krankenpflegerinnen unter Berücksichtigung der sozialen Lage* (Jena: Fischer, 1910).

78 Bülow and Pfeil came close to having Rentsch fired once and for all, but some of the pastors managed to keep her on. See VEM M 2, Bl. 14–15 (minutes of the board, 28 December 1886); and VEM M 167, Bl. 17 (Büttner to [?], 10 April 1887).

79 Frieda von Bülow, *Der Konsul: Vaterländischer Roman aus unseren Tagen* (Dresden: Carl Reissner, 1891), 151. See the almost identical statement in Lange, *Reines Deutschtum*, 127.

80 RKA 5673, Bl. 20 (Martha von Pfeil to Johanna von Bismarck, 21 May 1887).

81 VEM M 2, Bl. 19 (minutes of the board, 22 April 1887).

82 RKA 847, Bl. 27–28 (Evangelical Missionary Society for German East Africa

flier, December 1887); and *Nachrichten aus der ostafrikanischen Mission* 2, no. 1 (January 1888): 11.

83 Pfeil, *Ein reiches Leben,* 69.

84 Bülow, *Reisescizzen,* 10–11.

85 Ibid., 13.

86 Ibid., 49, 69. The standard political history of the German intervention in Zanzibar during 1887–1890 is Müller, *Deutschland—Zanzibar—Ostafrika;* an overview in English is in Norman R. Bennett, *A History of the Arab State of Zanzibar* (London: Methuen, 1978), 124–164. Glassman, *Feasts and Riot,* gives insight into the African context.

87 As Peters later recalled, she provided a "stylish representation vis-à-vis foreigners," and the British consul, Holmwood, was particularly attracted to her. (Peters, "Die Gründung," 217, 218 [quote]). A Holmwood-like character, the British consul Darnley, appears in Bülow's novel *Am andern Ende der Welt* (Berlin: Janke, 1890).

88 Bülow, *Reisescizzen,* 30, 56.

89 Ibid., 162; and Frederick Cooper, *Plantation Slavery on the East Coast of Africa* (New Haven: Yale University Press, 1977). "Arab" denoted social status more than literal ancestry (Glassman, *Feasts and Riot,* 33).

90 Susanne Zantop, *Colonial Fantasies: Conquest, Family, and Nation in Precolonial Germany, 1770–1870* (Durham: Duke University Press, 1997), 216–217 n. 3.

91 Bülow, *Reisescizzen,* 146.

92 Ibid., 7, 11, 26, 38, 39, 44, 45, 55, 78, 107–108, 117, 150, 157.

93 Ibid., 42 (quote); and LASA, Bülow to Lou Andreas-Salomé, 30 November 1908.

94 Bülow, *Reisescizzen,* 60–62.

95 Sayyida Salme/Emily Ruete, *An Arabian Princess between Two Worlds: Memoirs, Letters Home, Sequels to the Memoirs, Syrian Customs and Usages,* ed. E. Van Donzel (Leiden: E. J. Brill, 1993).

96 Bülow, *Reisescizzen,* 82–83. On the Ottoman reality of the harem, see Leslie P. Peirce, *The Imperial Harem: Women and Sovereignty in the Ottoman Empire* (New York: Oxford University Press, 1993), 3–12. On Europeans' myths of it, see Malek Alloula, *The Colonial Harem,* trans. Myrna Godzich and Wlad Godzich (Minneapolis: University of Minnesota Press, 1986).

97 Frieda von Bülow, "Eine unblutige Eroberungsfahrt an der ostafrikanischen Küste," and "In der Station," both in *Daheim* 24 (1888): 22–24, 38–40 and 135–139; and *Kolonialpolitische Korrespondenz* 3 (1887): 174, 197, 243–244, 259–260, 276–277, 341.

98 VEM M 167, Bl. 106 (Dr. A. P., in an unidentified newspaper clipping from 1887), and Bl. 61 (Büttner to ?, 18 January 1889).

99 Bülow, *Reisescizzen,* 37–38, 41, 50–53, 65, 111, 123–124, 132–133, 157.

100 Ibid., 28–29.

101 Ibid., 70–79.
102 Ibid., 27–28, 81; RKA 5673, Bl. 22 (Martha von Pfeil to Johanna von Bismarck, 21 May 1887); Jan-Georg Deutsch, "Inventing an East African Empire: The Zanzibar Delimitation Commission of 1885/1886," in *Studien zur Geschichte des deutschen Kolonialismus in Afrika,* ed. Peter Heine and Ulrich van der Heyden (Pfaffenweiler: Centaurus, 1995), 210–219.
103 Bülow, *Reisescizzen,* 168.
104 Niesel, "Kolonialverwaltung," 45; Loth, "Die Gründung"; VEM M 2, Bl. 2 (minutes of the board, 13 May 1886), and Bl. 10 (minutes of the board, 17 September 1886).
105 Bair, "Carl Peters," 158, 165–167.
106 Ibid., 152, 160–161.
107 Krätschell, "Carl Peters," 26.
108 RKA 5673, Bl. 48–49 (Consul Michahelles to Bismarck, 21 October 1887).
109 RKA 5673, Bl. 54 (Foreign Office to Consul Michahelles, 28 November 1887), and Bl. 56–57 (German East African Company to Bismarck, 28 November 1887).
110 Bülow, *Reisescizzen,* 170–172.
111 Pfeil, *Ein reiches Leben,* 69.
112 VEM M 352, Bl. 37 (Rentsch to Büttner, 4 January 1888), Bl. 38 (Greiner to Rentsch, 12 January 1888), and Bl. 40 (Rentsch to Büttner, 17 January 1888).
113 RKA 5673, Bl. 45–46 (Consul Michahelles to Bismarck, 21 October 1887); and VEM M 352, Bl. 22 (Rentsch to Büttner, 20 October 1887).
114 VEM M 352, Bl. 9, 10 (quote, Rentsch to Büttner, 30 July 1887).
115 VEM M 352, Bl. 8 (Rentsch to Büttner, 30 July 1887).
116 Ibid.
117 VEM M 352, Bl. 37 (Rentsch to Büttner, 4 January 1888). Incidentally, Joachim von Pfeil was a member of the hospital committee and got along well with Rentsch.
118 RKA 5673, Bl. 43–44 (Bourjau and Lucas to Bismarck), 16 November 1887), Bl. 47, 49 (Consul Michahelles to Bismarck, 21 October 1887), Bl. 52–53 (Foreign Office to German East African Company, 26 November 1887), Bl. 54 (Foreign Office to Consul Michahelles, 28 November 1887), and Bl. 56–57 (German East African Company to Bismarck, 28 November 1887).
119 RKA 5673, Bl. 47 (Consul Michahelles to Bismarck, 21 October 1887).
120 VEM M 352, Bl. 22 (Rentsch to Büttner, 20 October 1887).
121 Müller, *Deutschland — Zanzibar — Ostafrika,* 242–244; and RKA 4815, Bl. 15 (report from prison director, 13 January 1900).
122 RKA 5673, Bl. 60–61 (Consul Michahelles to Bismarck, 17 December 1887).
123 Niesel, "Kolonialverwaltung," 85.
124 Bülow did not explain the hospital struggle in *Travel Sketches* but did mention bursting into tears of frustration a couple of days before the first meet-

ing, and feeling in low spirits the day after the second one (Bülow, *Reisesciz-zen,* 147, 176).

125   VEM M 352, Bl. 7, 9 (Rentsch to Büttner, 30 July 1887), Bl. 20 (Rentsch to Büttner, 31 August 1887), and Bl. 36 (Rentsch to Büttner, 4 January 1888).

126   VEM M 352, Bl. 21 (Rentsch to Büttner, 20 October 1887).

127   Ibid.

128   VEM M 352, Bl. 43 (Rentsch to Büttner, 15 February 1888), and Bl. 40 (Rentsch to Büttner, 17 January 1888).

129   VEM M 352, Bl. 21 (Rentsch to Büttner, 20 October 1887).

130   Ibid.

131   VEM M 167, Bl. 47 (Diestelkamp to Büttner, 23 December 1887).

132   BAB, Carl Peters papers, Folder 91, Bl. 30–31 (Bülow to Elly Peters, 30 October 1890). To judge by Peters's own reputation and by Bülow's novelistic dramatization of her first stay in East Africa, specifically the passages in which the heroine Maleen Dietlas is wracked with jealousy over Krome's affair with Maria Beta, a young German-Abyssinian woman, Peters's sexual infidelity was probably the cause. See Bülow, *Im Lande der Verheissung,* 6th ed. (Dresden: Carl Reissner, 1914), 150–152, 158, 178; and Hoechstetter, *Frieda,* 157–158. However, in the absence of Bülow's private papers, it is impossible to know.

133   Bülow, *Reisescizzen,* 157–158, 194–195; see also VEM M 352, Bl. 39 (Rentsch to Büttner, 11 January 1888).

134   Pfeil, *Ein reiches Leben,* 69.

135   Streiter, "Frieda von Bülow," 63. The Foreign Office had never looked favorably on her plans. See RKA 5673, Bl. 11 (Foreign Office to Bülow, 13 October 1886), Bl. 13–14 (Consul Arendt to Bismarck, 18 December 1886), Bl. 15 (Kayser to Diestelkamp, 22 January 1887), Bl. 26 (Foreign Office internal memo, 23 May 1887, and Bl. 34 (Foreign Office to Evangelical Missionary Society board, 2 September 1887, marginalia).

136   See, for example, VEM M 167, Bl. 34 (Büttner to Pantenius, 27 November 1887). However, a pastor in the Evangelical Missionary Society who was sympathetic to Pfeil named her as founder. See VEM M 167, Bl. 110 (Ferdinand Hänel, "Die Kolonisation und Mission in Ostafrika," *Evangelisches Gemeindeblatt für Rheinland und Westfalen* 3, no. 20 [15 May 1887]: 156). The conflicts I have documented here have given rise to conflicting accounts by historians. Mission historians such as Jasper and Menzel have retained details of the women's involvement. See, for example, Gustav Menzel, *Die Bethel-Mission: Aus 100 Jahren Missionsgeschichte* (Neukirchen-Vluyn: Neukirchener Verlag des Erziehungsvereins, 1986), 14–15. Secular historians missed the struggle between women and men in the first years of the mission. Horst Gründer mentions no women in *Christliche Mission,* 37; nor does Niesel in "Kolonialverwaltung," 43. Wolfgang U. Eckart and Fritz Ferdinand Müller discuss Pfeil and Bülow, but not their relationship to the

Evangelical Missionary Society, in Eckart, *Medizin und Kolonialimperialis-mus: Deutschland 1884–1945* (Paderborn: Schöningh, 1997), 41–50; and Müller, *Deutschland — Zanzibar — Ostafrika*, 178–179.

137 Jasper, *Das Werden*, 14–15; and Menzel, *Die Bethel-Mission*, 44–45, 71.

138 *Unter dem rothen Kreuz* 1 (1889): 2; and Ludwiga Lehr, "Der Deutsche Frauenverein vom Roten Kreuz für die Kolonien," *Koloniale Rundschau* (1913): 674. No official history of the organization mentioned Bülow until 1928, when a brief account on the occasion of its fortieth anniversary noted that "the well-known Frieda von Bülow" was one of its founders: *Der Kolonialdeutsche* 8, no. 9 (1 May 1928): 147.

139 *Unter dem rothen Kreuz* 1 (1890): 66.

140 On Monts, née von Ingersleben, see *Biographisches Jahrbuch und Deutscher Nekrolog*, ed. Anton Bettelheim (Berlin: Georg Reimer, 1905), 79.

141 The association's affiliation with the Patriotic Women's Leagues was as an "auxiliary" (*Hilfsverein*), probably because its duties outside Germany devi-ated too far from the Patriotic Women's Leagues statutes' domestic focus. In 1871 Empress Augusta (wife of Emperor Wilhelm I) united the regional leagues in the federation usually called the Patriotic Women's Leagues (Vaterländische Frauenvereine) but after 1878 formally named the Federa-tion of the German Women's Aid and Nursing Associations under the Red Cross (Verband der Deutschen Frauen-Hilfs- und Pflegevereine unter dem Roten Kreuz). The member leagues were the (north German) Vaterländ-ischer Frauen-Verein, Bayerischer Frauenverein vom Roten Kreuz, Sächs-ischer Albert-Verein, Württembergischer Wohltätigkeits-Verein, Badischer Frauenverein, Hessischer Alice-Frauen-Verein, and Patriotisches Institut der Frauenvereine für das Grossherzogtum Sachsen. There is no com-prehensive history of the Patriotic Women's Leagues, but see Ute Daniel, "Die Vaterländischen Frauenvereine in Westfalen," *Westfälische Forschungen* 39 (1989): 158–179; Ilka Reimann, "Die Rolle der Frauenvereine in der Sozialpolitik: Vaterländischer Frauenverein und gemässigter Flügel der Frauenbewegung zwischen 1865 und 1918," in *Die armen Frauen: Frauen und Sozialpolitik*, ed. Ilona Kickbusch and Barbara Riedmüller (Frankfurt: Suhrkamp, 1984), 201–224; Gilla Dölle, *Die (un)heimliche Macht des Geldes: Finanzierungsstrategien der bürgerlichen Frauenbewegung in Deutschland zwischen 1865 und 1933* (Frankfurt a.M.: dipa-Verlag, 1997), 130–138; Carl Misch, *Geschichte des Vaterländischen Frauen-Vereins 1866–1916* (Berlin: Carl Heymann, 1917); and most recently, Jean H. Quataert, *Staging Philan-thropy: Patriotic Women and the National Imagination in Dynastic Germany, 1813–1916* (Ann Arbor: University of Michigan Press, 2001).

142 Ludwig Kimmle, ed., *Das Deutsche Rote Kreuz: Entstehung, Entwicklung und Leistungen der Vereinsorganisationen seit Abschluss der Genfer Convention i. J. 1864* (Berlin: Boll & Pickardt, 1910), 2:1–2. On the nationalist mythology of Queen Luise, see Wulf Wülfing, "Königin Luise von Preussen," in *Historische*

Mythologie der Deutschen 1798–1918, by Wülfing, Karin Bruns, and Rolf Parr (Munich: Wilhelm Fink, 1991), 59–111.

143 To do so the leagues had to place themselves under the Central Committee of German Associations of the Red Cross (Centralkomitee der Deutschen Vereine vom Roten Kreuz). The women insisted on a loose affiliation so as not to subordinate their greater numbers and success to the exclusively male Central Committee. See Grundhewer, "Die Kriegskrankenpflege," 140; Felix Grüneisen, *Das Deutsche Rote Kreuz in Vergangenheit und Gegenwart* (Potsdam-Babelsberg: Deutsches Rotes Kreuz, 1939), 76; and Kimmle, ed., *Das Deutsche Rote Kreuz,* 6. The German Red Cross became a unified statewide organization in 1921 (Grüneisen, *Das Deutsche Rote Kreuz,* 157–161). See also John F. Hutchinson, *Champions of Charity: War and the Rise of the Red Cross* (Boulder: Westview Press, 1996), especially 57–149; and Herbert Grundhewer, "Von der freiwilligen Kriegskrankenpflege bis zur Einbindung des Roten Kreuzes in das Heeressanitätswesen," in *Medizin und Krieg: Vom Dilemma der Heilberufe 1865 bis 1985,* ed. Johanna Bleker and Heinz-Peter Schmiedebach (Frankfurt a.M.: Fischer, 1987), 29–44.

144 In 1873, only two years after the Patriotic Women's Leagues were founded, they claimed 30,000 members. By 1914 they had a phenomenal 800,000 members, as well as fifty-two Red Cross motherhouses employing more than six thousand nurses (Grüneisen, *Das Deutsche Rote Kreuz,* 139). The next largest federation, the Federation of German Women's Associations (Bund Deutscher Frauenvereine), claimed 500,000 members. Richard J. Evans points out the repeat counting of members with multiple affiliations in that federation and gives a revised figure of no more than 250,000 in *The Feminist Movement in Germany 1894–1933* (London: Sage, 1976), 193–194. The Patriotic Women's Leagues figure is probably similarly inflated, but Evans (22) and the more recent account of Ute Gerhard (*Unerhört,* 91) agree that the leagues were collectively the largest women's organization in Germany.

145 Historians of German colonialism have assumed that the Women's Association was a purely unpolitical organization. See Richard V. Pierard, "The German Colonial Society, 1882–1914" (Ph.D. diss., State University of Iowa, 1964), 90; and Müller, *Deutschland — Zanzibar — Ostafrika,* 179. Yet medical practices have never existed outside specific political and cultural contexts, nor have they been determined solely by practicality; see, for example, Eckart, *Medizin und Kolonialimperialismus,* 145–161, 201–208. On medical care in the colonial tropics, see Philip D. Curtin, *Death by Migration: Europe's Encounter with the Tropical World in the Nineteenth Century* (New York: Cambridge University Press, 1989); and Curtin, *Disease and Empire: The Health of European Troops in the Conquest of Africa* (New York: Cambridge University Press, 1998).

146 Louise Otto-Peters, *Frauenleben im Deutschen Reich: Erinnerungen aus*

der Vergangenheit mit Hinweis auf Gegenwart und Zukunft (reprint, Paderborn: Hüttemann, 1988), 163–166; and Lina Morgenstern, *Frauenarbeit in Deutschland, I.* Teil: *Geschichte der deutschen Frauenbewegung und Statistik der Frauenarbeit auf allen ihr zugänglichen Gebieten* (Berlin: Verlag der Deutschen Hausfrauen-Zeitung, 1893), 12–14.

147 Morgenstern, *Frauenarbeit in Deutschland;* Gerhard, *Unerhört,* 93–94; Irmgard Maya Fassmann, *Jüdinnen in der deutschen Frauenbewegung 1865–1919* (Hildesheim: Georg Olms, 1996), 179–216; and Heinz Knobloch, *Die Suppenlina: Wiederbelebung einer Menschenfreundin* (Berlin: Edition Hentrich, 1997).

148 "Die Juden und die deutschen Kolonien," *Im deutschen Reich. Zeitschrift des Centralvereins deutschen Staatsbürger jüdischen Glaubens* 16, no. 11 (November 1910): 724.

149 John Hutchinson (*Champions of Charity,* 352) refers to the effective subsidy to states by the Red Cross as "voluntary taxation."

150 Wolfgang U. Eckart, "Der ärztliche Dienst in den ehemaligen deutschen Kolonien: Die Einrichtungen der Krankenversorgung am Beispiel Kameruns," *Arzt und Krankenhaus* 10 (1981): 426.

151 Bade, *Friedrich Fabri,* 330.

152 *Unter dem rothen Kreuz* 2 (1891): 42.

153 Eduard Hüsgen, *Ludwig Windthorst: Sein Leben, sein Wirken* (Cologne: J. P. Bachem, 1911), 296. David Blackbourn kindly pointed out this reference to me.

154 See, in general, Jan-Georg Deutsch, "The 'Freeing' of the Slaves in German East Africa: The Statistical Record, 1890–1914," in *Slavery and Colonial Rule in Africa,* ed. Miers and Klein, 109–132.

155 Wright, *German Missions,* 50–51.

156 Lehr, "Der Deutsche Frauenverein," 6/9. In 1913 there were six of these *Landesverbände:* Anhalt, Württemberg, Bavaria, Baden, Hessia, and Sachsen-Weimar-Eisenach. Each was headed by a *Landesfürstin* (princess of the realm) or her representative.

157 The Women's Association's official records have been destroyed. See Bernhard Naarmann, "Koloniale Arbeit unter dem Roten Kreuz: Der Deutsche Frauenverein vom Roten Kreuz für die Kolonien zwischen 1888–1917" (Ph.D. diss., University of Münster, 1986), 77. While membership statistics appeared periodically in official histories, the social analysis of membership here is based on announcements of new members in *Unter dem rothen Kreuz,* because these announcements include the women's names, marital status, and often an indication of the husband's occupation. The announcements are not comprehensive but are probably representative. These calculations are based on the sample years 1889–1890, 1891, 1895, 1899, and 1907. The percentage of nobility increased steeply within Berlin and on boards of local chapters; more than half of the Berlin chapter board in 1892 was aristocratic,

for example. For a social history of noblewomen, see Christa Diemel, *Adelige Frauen im bürgerlichen Jahrhundert: Hofdamen, Stiftsdamen, Salondamen 1800–1870* (Frankfurt a.M.: Fischer, 1998).

158 Eight Women's Association nurses came from the Provinzial-Krankenpflegerinnenanstalt Clementinenhaus. On its origins, see Grüneisen, *Das Deutsche Rote Kreuz*, 106; and Schaper, *Krankenwartung*, 137–145.

159 RKA 5654, Bl. 27 ("Bestimmungen für die Aufnahme von Krankenpflegerinnen in den Schwesternverband des Clementinenhauses").

160 See, for example, P. Chuchul, *Das Rote Kreuz: Ein die Geschichte, Organisation und Bedeutung der Bestrebungen unter dem Roten Kreuz behandelnder Vortrag,* 3d ed. (Cassel: Gebrüder Gotthelft, 1905), 23–24.

161 *Unter dem rothen Kreuz* 3 (1892): 64–65.

162 The association hired only nurses who held a state certificate in nursing. Several of its nurses also held a state certificate in midwifery and an extra certificate from a university clinic stating that they were capable of overseeing difficult births without the presence of a doctor (a special colonial provision generally forbidden to midwives in Germany). Association nurses were also trained to run apothecaries and laboratories. After 1898, nurses were trained in microscope work in order to monitor the blood level of quinine for the new method of malaria prevention that Robert Koch developed that year in German East Africa. See Lehr, "Der Deutsche Frauenverein," 675. Starting in 1900, when the Institute for Seafaring and Tropical Hygiene (Institut für Schiffs- und Tropenhygiene) was created in Hamburg, the association sent its nurses there for training.

163 Frieda von Bülow's brother Albrecht became engaged, then discovered that as a colonial army officer he would be refused permission to marry unless he promised in writing to leave his wife in Germany. See BAB, Carl Peters papers, Folder 91, Bl. 45 (Bülow to Elly Peters, 6 February 1892).

164 *Unter dem rothen Kreuz* 3 (1892): 18.

165 *Unter dem rothen Kreuz* 4 (1893): 9–10.

166 *Unter dem rothen Kreuz* 4 (1893): 66–67.

167 RKA 5654, Bl. 6 (Count Ludwig Pückler-Limpurg to Bismarck, 27 June 1889).

168 Ibid.

169 RKA 5654, Bl. 13 (Rudolf von Bennigsen to Count Pückler-Limpurg, 3 July 1889).

170 *Unter dem rothen Kreuz* 8 (1897): 3. She returned to Germany permanently in 1897.

171 Cameroon had the worst record for nurses' illness. See *Unter dem rothen Kreuz* 4 (1893): 43.

172 Lehr, "Der Deutsche Frauenverein," 676.

173 *Unter dem rothen Kreuz* 1 (1890): 89.

174 *Unter dem rothen Kreuz* 4 (1893): 69.

175 *Unter dem rothen Kreuz* 3 (1892): 70.

176 *Unter dem rothen Kreuz* 3 (1892): 88.

177 VEM M 356, Bl. 1 (Borcke to C. G. Büttner, 18 June 1889). Although Borcke was actually employed by the Evangelical Missionary Society, she worked directly with several association nurses and had many comparable work experiences.

178 *Unter dem rothen Kreuz* 4 (1893): 4–5. See also Johanna Wittum, *Unterm Roten Kreuz in Kamerun und Togo* (Heidelberg: Evangelischer Verlag, 1899); and Helene von Borcke, *Ostafrikanische Erinnerungen einer freiwilligen Krankenpflegerin* (Berlin: Buchhandlung der Deutschen Lehrer-Zeitung [Fr. Zillessen], 1891), 27.

179 *Unter dem rothen Kreuz* (1893): 12. Antislavery enthusiasm was characteristic of nurses from the Clementinenhaus, the first motherhouse from which the association hired nurses. Unfortunately, there is no scholarly literature on German women and antislavery comparable to Clare Midgley's *Women against Slavery: The British Campaigns, 1780–1870* (London: Routledge, 1992).

180 *Unter dem rothen Kreuz* 4 (1893): 4.

181 VEM M 356, Bl. 1 (Borcke to C. G. Büttner, 18 June 1889).

182 Ibid.

183 Borcke, *Ostafrikanische Erinnerungen,* 26–27, 36–37, 59–60.

184 Ibid., 34.

185 See, for example, nurse Anna Bässler's remarks about Cameroonians in *Unter dem rothen Kreuz* 4 (1893): 21.

186 Adolf Rüger, "Der Aufstand der Polizeisoldaten (Dezember 1893)," in *Kamerun unter deutscher Kolonialherrschaft: Studien,* ed. Helmuth Stoecker (Berlin: Rütten & Loening, 1960), 1:97–147; for a historian's dismissal of sexual abuse of Cameroonian women as a matter of German men's "instinct," see Harry R. Rudin, *Germans in the Cameroons 1884–1914: A Case Study in Modern Imperialism* (London: Jonathan Cape, 1938), 210–212.

187 *Unter dem rothen Kreuz* 4 (1893): 28, 43, 70.

188 Heinrich Leist, "Der Fall Leist," *Die Zukunft* 16 (1896): 267–268.

189 Ibid., 268.

190 *Unter dem rothen Kreuz* 6 (1895): 11.

191 Ibid., 12.

192 Ibid.

193 *Unter dem rothen Kreuz* 5 (1894): 47.

194 Ibid., 62.

195 Helmut Bley, *Namibia under German Rule* (reprint, Hamburg: Lit, 1996), 214, cited in Smidt, "Germania," 158.

196 *Nachrichten aus der ostafrikanischen Mission* 1, no. 11 (November 1887): 161.

197 Borcke, *Ostafrikanische Erinnerungen,* 67–70; and VEM M 356, Bl. 7 (Borcke to C. G. Büttner, 28 December 1889).

198 *Medizinal-Berichte über die deutschen Schutzgebiete für das Jahr 1903/04* (Berlin: E. S. Mittler, 1905), 180. She was described as a "former nurse" and no superior overseeing her work was mentioned.

199 *Unter dem rothen Kreuz* 1 (1890): 45, vol. 3 (1892): 26; and Bülow, *Reisescizzen,* 183.

200 In the nineteenth and early twentieth centuries, a tension between "lady nurses," dominating administration and education, and working nurses pervaded nursing. See Schaper, *Krankenwartung,* 127; Brinkschulte and Vogt, "Nicht um des Lohnes willen," 159; and Anna Davin, "Imperialism and Motherhood," *History Workshop Journal* 5 (1978): 9–65.

201 See, for example, *Unter dem rothen Kreuz* 2 (1891): 53–55.

202 *Unter dem rothen Kreuz* 3 (1892): 3.

203 *Unter dem rothen Kreuz* 2 (1891): 82–83, and 4 (1893): 80.

204 *Unter dem rothen Kreuz* 4 (1893): 22–23. Clara Schröder-Poggelow was married to Schröder's brother, the pan-German politician Wilhelm Schröder-Poggelow.

205 *Unter dem rothen Kreuz* 4 (1893): 23.

206 Marie Baum, *Rückblick auf mein Leben* (Heidelberg: F. H. Kerle, 1950), 70–71. Baum earned a doctorate in chemistry in Zurich in 1899 and taught social policy at the University of Heidelberg. She became one of Germany's first female factory inspectors.

207 Baum, *Rückblick,* 71.

208 *Unter dem rothen Kreuz* 4 (1893): 31. Stuhlmann had also "bought into freedom" (*freigekauft*) a male "pygmy" or "dwarf," but that man died before leaving Zanzibar for Germany. Stuhlmann preserved his skeleton "for research."

209 *Unter dem rothen Kreuz* 4 (1893): 26. The director of the Museum of Ethnology (Museum für Völkerkunde), Adolf Bastian, arranged for that museum to be the venue.

210 Sierra Ann Bruckner, "The Tingle-Tangle of Modernity: Popular Anthropology and the Cultural Politics of Identity in Imperial Germany" (Ph.D. diss., University of Iowa, 1999); *Unter dem rothen Kreuz* 4 (1893): 26.

211 *Unter dem rothen Kreuz* 4 (1893): 28.

212 Ibid., 54.

213 Ibid., 70.

214 Ibid., 28.

215 Ibid.

216 Ibid.

217 Ibid.

218 Ibid.

219 Ibid., 54.

220 Ibid., 53.
221 Ibid., 70.
222 Ibid., 82–83, and 5 (1894): 28.

2. THE FEMININE RADICAL NATIONALISM
OF FRIEDA VON BÜLOW

1 Those scholars who have discussed Bülow's fiction have drawn on only a few
   of her many titles. The best of these analyses is Marcia Klotz, "White
   Women and the Dark Continent: Gender and Sexuality in German Colonial
   Discourse from the Sentimental Novel to the Fascist Film" (Ph.D. diss.,
   Stanford University, 1995), ch. 1. Also useful are Barbara Shumannfang,
   "Envisioning Empire: Jewishness, Blackness and Gender in German Colonial Discourse from Frieda von Bülow to the Nazi *Kolonie und Heimat*"
   (Ph.D. diss., Duke University, 1998), chs. 1–3; Russell A. Berman, *Enlight-
   enment or Empire: Colonial Discourse in German Culture* (Lincoln: University
   of Nebraska Press, 1998), 172–202; Friederike Eigler, "Engendering Ger-
   man Nationalism: Gender and Race in Frieda von Bülow's Colonial Writings," in *The Imperialist Imagination: German Colonialism and Its Legacy*, ed.
   Sara Friedrichsmeyer, Sara Lennox, and Susanne Zantop (Ann Arbor: University of Michigan Press, 1999), 69–85; and Lora Wildenthal, "'When
   Men Are Weak': The Imperial Feminism of Frieda von Bülow," *Gender and
   History* 10 (1998): 53–77. Additional information can be found in Joachim
   Warmbold, "Germania in Afrika: Frieda Freiin von Bülow, 'Schöpferin des
   deutschen Kolonialromans,'" *Jahrbuch des Instituts für deutsche Geschichte* 15
   (1986): 309–336; Warmbold, *Germania in Africa: Germany's Colonial Liter-
   ature* (New York: Peter Lang, 1989), 49–65; Sabina Streiter, "Frieda von
   Bülow und Ricarda Huch. Briefe aus dem Jahr 1895," *Jahrbuch der Deutschen
   Schillergesellschaft* 32 (1988): 51–73; Streiter, "Nachwort," in *Das Haus:
   Familiengeschichte vom Ende vorigen Jahrhunderts*, by Lou Andreas-Salomé
   (Frankfurt: Ullstein, 1987), 239–252; and Streiter, "Nachwort," in *Die
   schönsten Novellen der Frieda von Bülow über Lou Andreas-Salomé und andere
   Frauen*, by Frieda von Bülow (Frankfurt a.M.: Ullstein, 1991), 236–252.
   Streiter mostly ignores colonialism and racism, and does not always provide
   references to her sources.

2 Sophie Hoechstetter, *Frieda Freiin von Bülow. Ein Lebensbild* (Dresden: Carl
   Reissner, 1910), 182 (quote), 205; and Streiter, "Frieda von Bülow und
   Ricarda Huch," 61. Lou Andreas-Salomé concluded that Bülow conflated
   "art" with "reportage" in "Ketzereien gegen die moderne Frau," *Die Zukunft*
   26 (1899): 237.

3 LBI, Mauthner papers, correspondence with Frieda von Bülow (Bülow to
   Mauthner, 9 November 1895); and Warmbold, *Germania in Africa*, 236
   n. 109.

4 Rainer Maria Rilke, *Briefe aus den Jahren 1907 bis 1914*, ed. Ruth Sieber-Rilke

and Carl Sieber (Leipzig: Insel, 1933), 68 (Rilke to Hoechstetter, 18 July 1909).

5 Bülow, "Lear-Patriotismus," *Die Zukunft* 30 (1900): 570. See also the character Fabricius in Bülow, *Tropenkoller: Episode aus dem Kolonialleben* (Berlin: F. Fontane, 1896), especially 105–107.

6 She presented nobles both as victims of forces beyond their control and as willfully oblivious to necessary change. See, for example, Bülow, *Ludwig von Rosen: Eine Erzählung aus zwei Welten* (Berlin: F. Fontane, 1892), 116; Bülow, *Wenn Männer schwach sind. Roman* (Berlin: Alfred Schall, 1908); and Bülow, "Die stilisierte Frau," in *Die schönsten Novellen,* ed. Streiter, 145–202. Her novels *Hüter der Schwelle,* 2d ed. (Dresden: Carl Reissner, 1907) and *Die Schwestern: Geschichte einer Mädchenjugend,* 3d ed. (Dresden: Carl Reissner, 1909) deal with young noblewomen in traditional families who are hard-pressed for respectable sources of income. On feminists' selfishness, see, for example, Bülow, *Die Töchter* (Dresden: Carl Reissner, 1906), 367. On Bülow's dislike of the untitled wealthy, see Hoechstetter, *Frieda,* 187–188.

7 See, for example, Eigler, "Engendering German Nationalism," 75.

8 Not all radical nationalists favored overseas colonialism, and not all colonialists were radical nationalists. See Hartmut Pogge von Strandmann, "Nationale Verbände zwischen Weltpolitik und Kontinentalpolitik," in *Marine und Marinepolitik im kaiserlichen Deutschland 1871–1914,* ed. Herbert Schottelius and Wilhelm Deist (Düsseldorf: Droste, 1972), 296–317.

9 Bülow's nephew Thankmar von Münchhausen (whose father of the same name was close to Bülow) altered her novel *In the Promised Land* by removing scenes of sexual encounters between the characters Maria Beta, an Abyssinian-European woman, and Rainer Waltron and Ralf Krome (Maleen Dietlas's brother and lover, respectively). The new edition appeared in 1937 and went through three editions by 1943. See Bülow, *Im Lande der Verheissung,* ed. Thankmar von Münchhausen, 3d ed. (Berlin: Oswald Arnold, 1943). On the changes, see Shumannfang, "Envisioning Empire," 205–216.

10 On the Emin Pasha expedition, see Ralph A. Austen, *Northwest Tanzania under German and British Rule: Colonial Policy and Tribal Politics, 1889–1939* (New Haven: Yale University Press, 1968), 24–30.

11 BAB, Carl Peters papers, Folder 91, Bl. 26 (Bülow to Elly Peters, 24 June 1890).

12 BAB, Carl Peters papers, Folder 91, Bl. 24, 26 (Bülow to Elly Peters, 24 June 1890). On Yorck and Blücher, see Gordon A. Craig, *The Politics of the Prussian Army 1640–1945* (New York: Oxford University Press, 1955), 57–60.

13 Fritz Stern, *The Politics of Cultural Despair: A Study in the Rise of the Germanic Ideology* (New York: Anchor, 1961), especially 197–227.

14 BAB, Carl Peters papers, Folder 91, Bl. 50–51 (Bülow to Elly Peters, 21 Jan-

uary 1893). Count Bülow von Dennewitz (1755–1816), to whom she referred, was the Prussian general who defeated Napoleonic France in the Netherlands and was the brother of her great-grandfather.

15 BAB, Carl Peters papers, Folder 4, Bl. 12 (Bülow to Carl Peters, 10 March 1902).

16 See the characters Rosenstiel in *Am andern Ende der Welt. Roman* (Berlin: Janke, 1890); Löwenthal in *Ludwig von Rosen;* Hüter in *Margarete und Ludwig. Roman* (Stuttgart: J. Engelhorn, 1894); Lindenlaub in *Der Konsul: Vaterländischer Roman aus unseren Tagen* (Dresden: Carl Reissner, 1891); Susi/Ilka in *Im Hexenring: Eine Sommergeschichte vom Lande* (Stuttgart: J. Engelhorn, 1901) (a non-Jewish Polish character until exposed late in the narrative as a Jew); Dr. Mohrenthal in *Hüter der Schwelle;* and Kohnheim in *Frauentreue. Roman* (Dresden: Carl Reissner, 1910). The only Jewish character whom Bülow depicted in a positive light, Dr. Mayer in *Im Hexenring,* is given startlingly anti-Jewish lines to speak (Bülow, *Im Hexenring,* 147–148). On Bülow's anti-Semitism, see Hoechstetter, *Frieda,* 21, 181–182, 220–221; Wildenthal, "When Men Are Weak," 61–64; and LASA, F000005 and F000014 (Bülow to Lou Andreas-Salomé, n.d.).

17 Eigler, "Engendering German Nationalism," 83.

18 Slav characters in her fiction include Rakosky in "Die stilisierte Frau," Susi/Ilka in *Im Hexenring,* and Josefa in *Der Konsul.* It is interesting to note that Bülow's fiction contains no fulminations against socialists, another classic foe of radical nationalists.

19 On utopian escape from social relations in colonial space, see, for example, J. M. Coetzee, *White Writing: On the Culture of Letters in South Africa* (New Haven: Yale University Press, 1988), 1–35.

20 Her colonial novels and novellas include *Am andern Ende der Welt, Der Konsul, Deutsch-Ostafrikanische Novellen* (Dresden: Carl Reissner, 1892), *Ludwig von Rosen, Tropenkoller,* and *Im Lande der Verheissung. Margarete und Ludwig* is in part a novel about the colonialist movement in Germany. The German colonial novels that remain most widely known today use the theme of men's nationalist renewal in the colonies that she first developed; see Gustav Frenssen, *Peter Moors Fahrt nach Südwest: Ein Feldzugsbericht* (Berlin: G. Grote, 1906); and Hans Grimm, *Volk ohne Raum* (Munich: A. Langen, 1926). On the latter, see Woodruff D. Smith, "The Colonial Novel as Political Propaganda: Hans Grimm's *Volk ohne Raum,*" *German Studies Review* 6 (1983): 215–235.

21 On men and love, see the discussion of *Deutsch-Ostafrikanische Novellen* in Berman, *Enlightenment,* 182–184.

22 Klotz, "White Women," 49. Klotz further argues that German women's real value for Bülow was as arbiters of male heroism (62–63).

23 Rosen appears in *Ludwig von Rosen, Tropenkoller,* and *Im Lande der Verheissung.* A plot summary and interpretation of *Ludwig von Rosen* are in

Berman, *Enlightenment*, 174–179 (however, the female character is Eva, not Sophie, Biron). See also the characters Reginald Witmann in "Der Heilige von Kialmasi," Gerhard Rüdiger in "Mlinga Goni," and Derendorff in "Das Kind," all in *Deutsch-Ostafrikanische Novellen*; Karl von Uglar in *Im Hexenring*; and Walter Gerald/Otrida (whose education took place in the American West) in *Margarete and Ludwig*.

24 Bülow, *Ludwig von Rosen*, 27.

25 Ibid., 173.

26 I therefore disagree with Berman's argument (in *Enlightenment*, 177) that Bülow depicted a progression "from patriarchy to parity" between the (German) sexes in the colonies.

27 On *Tropenkoller*, see Klotz, "White Women," 36–48. In a third novel, *Im Hexenring*, two secondary characters enjoy a happy ending after the primary hero has undergone moral purification in the Boer War.

28 Bülow, *Am andern Ende der Welt*, 41–42, 97 (quote).

29 Ibid., 191, 198 (quote).

30 For examples of the former, see Wildenthal, "When Men Are Weak," 66–68; and Bülow, *Im Hexenring*. An example of the latter is Bülow, "Die stilisierte Frau."

31 Bülow, *Kara. Roman in drei Büchern* (Stuttgart: J. G. Cotta, 1897).

32 See, for example, the characters Sophie Landolf in "Mlinga Goni," Wilhelma in *Frauentreue*, and Gunne in *Allein ich will. Roman* (Dresden: Carl Reissner, 1903).

33 Hoechstetter, *Frieda*, 156.

34 LBI, Mauthner papers, correspondence with Frieda von Bülow (Bülow to Mauthner, 18 November 1889).

35 Lou Andreas-Salomé, *Looking Back. Memoirs*, ed. Ernst Pfeiffer, trans. Breon Mitchell (New York: Paragon, 1991); and Biddy Martin, *Woman and Modernity: The (Life)Styles of Lou Andreas-Salomé* (Ithaca: Cornell University Press, 1991), and references cited therein.

36 Streiter, "Nachwort," in Lou Andreas-Salomé, *Das Haus: Familiengeschichte vom Ende vorigen Jahrhunderts* (Frankfurt: Ullstein, 1987), 246–248; Streiter, "Nachwort," in Bülow, *Die schönsten Novellen*, 239–242; and Hoechstetter, *Frieda*, 163.

37 Hoechstetter, *Frieda*, 191; and Andreas-Salomé, *Looking Back*, 67.

38 Bülow, "Zwei Menschen" (1898), reprinted in Bülow, *Die schönsten Novellen*, 7–67; and Andreas-Salomé, *Das Haus*. Certainly Bülow did not agree with Andreas-Salomé's "egotism" (i.e., falling in love or leaving a lover when one pleases). This was a theme in Bülow's "Zwei Menschen" and *Freie Liebe* (Dresden: Carl Reissner, 1909). See Streiter, "Nachwort," in Bülow, *Die schönsten Novellen*, 239.

39 Bülow, "Männerurtheil über Frauendichtung," *Die Zukunft* 26 (1899): 26–

29; Andreas-Salomé, "Ketzereien," *Die Zukunft* 26 (1899): 237–240; and Martin, *Woman and Modernity*, 169–171.

40 Streiter, "Nachwort," in Andreas-Salomé, *Das Haus*, 247–248.

41 Martin, *Woman and Modernity*, 41; and Streiter, "Nachwort," in Bülow, *Die schönsten Novellen*, 245. Streiter supplies no source.

42 A nickname for Bülow between the two women was "your brown boy." See LASA, Bülow to Andreas-Salomé, 15 July 1893, 10 August 1893, and 7 January 1894; see also Andreas-Salomé, *Looking Back*, 66.

43 Hoechstetter, *Frieda*, 208 (quote); *Bülowsches Familienbuch*, ed. Adolf von Bülow (Schwerin: Eduard Herberger, 1914), 2:422; and BAB, Carl Peters papers, Folder 91, Bl. 53 (Bülow to Elly Peters, 19 February 1893), Bl. 54 (Bülow to Elly Peters, 20 March 1893), and Bl. 56 (Bülow to Elly Peters, 3 May 1893). The plantation's location can be seen on a map facing plate 37 in *Kolonialgeschichte im Familienalbum: Frühe Fotos aus der Kolonie Deutsch-Ostafrika*, ed. Norbert Aas and Werena Rosenke (Münster: Unrast, 1992). On Scharlach's 1892 venture, see Horst Drechsler, *Südwestafrika unter deutscher Kolonialherrschaft*, Bd. 2: *Die grossen Land- und Minengesellschaften (1885–1914)* (Stuttgart: Franz Steiner, 1996), 81–114.

44 Hoechstetter, *Frieda*, 167.

45 BAB, Carl Peters papers, Folder 91, Bl. 60 (Bülow to Elly Peters, 22 February 1894).

46 Baron von Gravenreuth was dead; Walter von St. Paul Illaire and Justus Strandes and his wife ignored her at first. See Hoechstetter, *Frieda*, 167–168; and BAB, Carl Peters papers, Folder 91, Bl. 60 (Bülow to Elly Peters, 22 February 1894).

47 LASA, Bülow to Andreas-Salomé, 10 August 1893, Bülow to Andreas-Salomé, 7 January 1894; and Hoechstetter, *Frieda*, 168.

48 BAB, Carl Peters papers, Folder 91, Bl. 58, 59 (quote), 61 (Bülow to Elly Peters, 22 February 1894). On Bülow's image of farming, see Hoechstetter, *Frieda*, 185–186; and Bülow, *Die Schwestern*, 82.

49 LASA, Bülow to Andreas-Salomé, 15 July 1893.

50 Bülow, "Allerhand Alltägliches aus Deutsch-Ostafrika," *Die Frau* 2, no. 1 (October 1894): 25–30, and vol. 2, no. 2 (November 1894): 93–98; and Bülow, "Ein Werkeltag in Deutsch-Ostafrika," *Die Frau* 3, no. 12 (September 1896): 740–745. She briefly described her servant Hamisi to Andreas-Salomé as faithful but stupid (LASA, Bülow to Andreas-Salomé, 15 July 1893).

51 Hoechstetter, *Frieda*, 169. See paragraph 17 of "Verordnung, betreffend Rechtsverhältnisse in Deutsch-Ostafrika. Vom 1. Januar 1891," *Deutsches Kolonialblatt* 2, no. 2 (15 January 1891): 26; and Harald Sippel, "Aspects of Colonial Land Law in German East Africa: German East African Company, Crown Land Ordinance, European Plantation and Reserved Areas for Afri-

cans," in *Land Law and Land Ownership in Africa: Case Studies from Colonial and Contemporary Cameroon and Tanzania,* ed. Robert Debusmann and Stefan Arnold (Bayreuth: Eckhard Breitinger, 1996), 18.

52 While Bülow and Lange remained good friends, Bülow apparently had little affection for Scharlach. She referred to Scharlach as "her personal Jew [*Leibjude*]" in LASA, Bülow to Andreas-Salomé, 16 February 1895; and to having "disinfected" herself after talking to him in LASA F000012 (Bülow to Andreas-Salomé, n.d. [1896]).

53 *Bülowsches Familienbuch,* 2:419. The next year, in 1895, she briefly attempted another kind of agrarian idyll: she and Andreas-Salomé tried to establish a writer's colony in the Lower Silesian town of Brieg (today, Brzeg, Poland), but that too failed.

54 Hoechstetter, *Frieda,* 167, see also 169–170. Hoechstetter was active as a feminist and in defending the rights of homosexual men and women through the Wissenschaftlich-humanitäres Komitee. She was the lover of writer and translator Toni Schwabe, a close friend of Bülow's. See Brian Keith-Smith, ed., *An Encyclopedia of German Women Writers 1900–1933. Biographies and Bibliographies with Exemplary Readings,* vol. 4 (Lewiston, N.Y.: Edwin Mellen, 1997), 189.

55 Ralph Freedman, *Life of a Poet: Rainer Maria Rilke* (New York: Farrar, Straus and Giroux, 1996), 63. Some of Bülow's correspondence with Rilke appears in Rainer Maria Rilke, *Briefe und Tagebücher aus der Frühzeit 1899 bis 1902,* ed. Ruth Sieber-Rilke and Carl Sieber (Leipzig: Insel, 1931), 7–8, 9–11, 15–18, 19–21, 61–63, 420; Rilke, *Briefe aus den Jahren 1892 bis 1904,* ed. Ruth Sieber-Rilke and Carl Sieber (Leipzig: Insel, 1939), 44–47, 68–70, 72–75, 116–118; and *Letters of Rainer Maria Rilke 1892–1910,* trans. Jane Bannard Greene and M. D. Herter Norton (New York: Norton, 1945), 31–33, 49–50. Rilke had a wide circle of correspondents, some of whom also knew Bülow, such as Karl and Elisabeth von der Heydt (investors in both German East Africa and modern art), the playwrights Carl and Gerhart Hauptmann, Fritz Mauthner, and Bülow's nephew Thankmar von Münchhausen. On modernism and primitivism, see Elazar Barkan and Ronald Bush, eds., *Prehistories of the Future: The Primitivist Project and the Culture of Modernism* (Stanford: Stanford University Press, 1995).

56 Freedman, *Life of a Poet,* 67 (quote), 64; and Streiter, "Nachwort," in Andreas-Salomé, *Das Haus,* 247.

57 Rudolf Herz and Brigitte Bruns, eds., *Hof-Atelier Elvira 1887–1928: Ästheten, Emanzen, Aristokraten* (Munich: Münchner Stadtmuseum, 1985).

58 Other women had held such licenses, but only as wives or widows; that is, through their husbands. See Heinz Gebhardt, *Königliche bayerische Photographie 1838–1918* (Munich: Laterna magica, 1978), 79.

59 Gertrud Bäumer, "Ika Freudenberg," in *Studien über Frauen,* 3d, exp. ed.

(Berlin: F. A. Herbig, 1924), 135–152, especially 139. Bülow apparently did not have much to do with Goudstikker's former lover, Anita Augspurg, who had left Munich in 1893 to study law in Zurich and became the first female lawyer in Germany in 1897. See Lida Gustava Heymann and Anita Augspurg, *Erlebtes — Erschautes: Deutsche Frauen kämpfen für Freiheit, Recht und Frieden 1850–1940,* ed. Margrit Twellmann (Meisenheim am Glan: Anton Hain, 1972).

60 Bülow, "Das Weib in seiner Geschlechtsindividualität," *Die Zukunft* 18 (27 March 1897): 596–601; Bülow, "Weibliche Einjährige," *Die Zukunft* 32 (1900): 30–35.

61 Bülow, "Männerurtheil über Frauendichtung."

62 Bülow, "Die stilisierte Frau"; and Bülow, *Einsame Frauen* (Dresden: Carl Reissner, 1897). On the former, see Livia Wittmann, "Zwischen 'femme fatale' and 'femme fragile' — die Neue Frau? Kritische Bemerkungen zum Frauenbild des literarischen Jugendstils," *Jahrbuch für internationale Germanistik* 17 (1985): 87–94.

63 Hoechstetter, *Frieda,* 6; LBI, Mauthner papers, correspondence with Frieda von Bülow (Bülow to Mauthner, 27 June 1886, 13 February 1889, 9 June 1895, and 24 August 1897).

64 Marie Stritt, "Einsame Frauen," *Die Frauenbewegung* 3, no. 11 (1 June 1897): 114.

65 Gertrud Bäumer, "Frieda von Bülow," *Die Frau* 16, no. 7 (April 1909): 408, see also 407. See also Anna Brunnemann, "Frieda Freiin von Bülow," *Das litterarische Echo. Halbmonatsschrift für Litteraturfreunde* 5, no. 9 (1902–1903): 598–599; and LASA, Bülow to Lou Andreas-Salomé, 27 November 1902 (where Bülow mentioned that the feminist and sex reformer Helene Stöcker had asked her to write an essay, probably for the *Die Frauen-Rundschau,* then edited by Stöcker).

66 Hoechstetter, *Frieda,* 119.

67 Ibid., 200. See the character Renate in Andreas-Salomé, *Das Haus,* especially 67. According to Streiter, Andreas-Salomé based the character on Bülow (Streiter, "Nachwort," in Andreas-Salomé, *Das Haus,* 247). On feminists and Nietzsche, see Heide Schlüpmann, "Radikalisierung der Philosophie: Die Nietzsche-Rezeption und die sexualpolitische Publizistik Helene Stöckers," *Feministische Studien* 3 (1984): 10–34.

68 LASA, Bülow to Andreas-Salomé, 10 February 1897.

69 See, for example, her critical remarks about Helene Stöcker in LASA, Bülow to Andreas-Salomé, 27 November 1902.

70 On Bülow's sense of duty, see Rilke, cited in Hoechstetter, *Frieda,* 214; on feminism as a part of a larger nationalism, see Bülow, "Weibliche Einjährige."

71 Hoechstetter, *Frieda,* 179.

72 LASA, Bülow to Andreas-Salomé, 24 September 1908. Peters married Thea Herbers in February 1909. See also LASA, Bülow to Andreas-Salomé, 16 September 1907, 20 October 1907; Bülow and Peters met on the latter date.

73 See the characters Susi/Ilka in *Im Hexenring;* Mrs. Whig in *Am andern Ende der Welt,* especially 72–76; and Marion in *Wenn Männer schwach sind.* On the latter, see Wildenthal, "When Men Are Weak," 66–68.

74 BAB, Carl Peters Papers, Folder 91, Bl. 70 (Bülow to Elly Peters, n.d. [1891]). *Danai* is a Latin word for the Greeks; the reference is to Virgil's *Aeneid,* 2:49. On men and freedom, see Frieda von Bülow, "Mann über Bord," 21 *Die Zukunft* (1897): 554.

75 Bülow, *Freie Liebe,* 100; and Andreas-Salomé, *Das Haus.*

76 Bülow, "Das Weib in seiner Geschlechtsindividualität," 601. The article is a review of Max Runge, *Das Weib in seiner Geschlechtsindividualität* (Berlin: J. Springer, 1896).

77 RKA 4815, Bl. 15 (report from prison director, 13 January 1900).

78 VEM M 352, Bl. 22 (Rentsch to Büttner, 20 October 1887); and Fritz Ferdinand Müller, *Deutschland — Zanzibar — Ostafrika: Geschichte einer deutschen Kolonialeroberung 1884–1890* (Berlin: Rütten & Loening, 1959), 242–244.

79 Anna Pappritz, ed., *Einführung in das Studium der Prostitutionsfrage* (Leipzig: J. A. Barth, 1919); and Elisabeth Meyer-Renschhausen, *Weibliche Kultur und soziale Arbeit: Eine Geschichte der Frauenbewegung am Beispiel Bremens 1810–1927* (Cologne: Böhlau, 1989), 271–319.

80 Adolf Rüger, "Die Duala und die Kolonialmacht 1884–1914: Eine Studie über die Ursprünge des afrikanischen Antikolonialismus," in *Kamerun unter deutscher Kolonialherrschaft. Studien,* ed. Helmuth Stoecker (Berlin: Verlag der Wissenschaften, 1968), 206, 212–215; and Harry R. Rudin, *Germans in the Cameroons 1884–1914: A Case Study in Modern Imperialism* (London: Jonathan Cape, 1938), 148.

81 See "The Saint from Kialmasi" (e.g., 37), "Mlinga Goni," and "Das Kind" (e.g., 279), all in the volume *Deutsch-Ostafrikanische Novellen; Margarete und Ludwig* (e.g., 27–28); *Tropenkoller;* and *Im Lande der Verheissung.* One novel set in Germany portrays a German man whipping a German woman: *Wenn Männer schwach sind,* 272–274.

82 Henry Martin Bair Jr., "Carl Peters and German Colonialism: A Study in the Ideas and Actions of Imperialism" (Ph.D. diss., Stanford University, 1968), 158–159; and Carl Peters, "Die Gründung von Deutsch-Ostafrika: Kolonialpolitische Erinnerungen und Betrachtungen," in *Gesammelte Schriften,* ed. Walter Frank, (Munich: C. H. Beck, 1943), 1:248. On Germans' rapes of local women in this early period, see Norman R. Bennett, ed., *The Zanzibar Letters of Edward D. Ropes, Jr. 1882–1892* (Boston: Boston University African Studies Center, 1973), 60–61, 101–103. See also August Leue, *Dar-es-Salaam: Bilder aus dem Kolonialleben* (Berlin: Wilhelm Süsserott, 1903), 5;

and Norman R. Bennett, *A History of the Arab State of Zanzibar* (London: Methuen, 1978), 135.

83 Suzanne Miers, "The Brussels Conference of 1889–1890: The Place of the Slave Trade in the Policies of Great Britain and Germany," in *Britain and Germany in Africa: Imperial Rivalry and Colonial Rule,* ed. Prosser Gifford and W. Roger Louis (New Haven: Yale University Press, 1967), 97–98.

84 Streiter, "Frieda von Bülow und Ricarda Huch," 63.

85 *Kolonialpolitische Korrespondenz* 1, no. 22 (12 December 1885): 2 (quote); Müller, *Deutschland — Zanzibar — Ostafrika,* 240; and Joachim von Pfeil, *Die Erwerbung von Deutsch-Ostafrika: Ein Beitrag zur Kolonial-Geschichte,* new ed. (Berlin: Karl Curtius, n.d. [1907]), 160–162. A group of Africans from Dunda, the German East African Company station that Albrecht founded, traveled to Zanzibar to protest that no treaty in fact permitted the station to be built. See Bennett, *A History of the Arab State of Zanzibar,* 133.

86 *Kolonialpolitische Korrespondenz* 1, no. 22 (12 December 1885): 3. Because the word *kraal* could refer to either an enclosure containing dwellings and livestock or to livestock pens alone, it is not clear whether Albrecht von Bülow was saying that he shot at the villagers' homes or at their livestock.

87 RKA 694, Bl. 152 (Deinhard to [?], 3 December 1888); and Bennett, *A History of the Arab State of Zanzibar,* 142–143.

88 BAB, Carl Peters papers, Folder 91, Bl. 38–39 (Bülow to Elly Peters, 30 October 1891).

89 Even Joachim von Pfeil criticized Peters's rough behavior, although he denied that Peters engaged in "cruelty" (*Grausamkeit*) in 1884 (Pfeil, *Die Erwerbung,* 71).

90 Heinrich Leist, "Der Fall Leist," *Die Zukunft* 16 (8 August 1896): 259. The editor of *Die Zukunft,* Maximilian Harden, defended Leist. See Maximilian Harden, "Leist," *Die Zukunft* 9 (10 November 1894): 286–288.

91 On the Peters case, see Martin Reuss, "The Disgrace and Fall of Carl Peters: Morality, Politics and *Staatsräson* in the Time of Wilhelm II," *Central European History* 14 (1981): 110–141; Heinrich Schnee, "Carl Peters," *Deutsches Biographisches Jahrbuch,* vol. 2: *1917–1920* (Stuttgart: Deutsche Verlagsanstalt, 1928), 293–296; Wildenthal, "When Men Are Weak," 60; and Franz Giesebrecht, *Ein deutscher Kolonialheld: Der Fall "Peters" in psychologischer Beleuchtung* (Zurich: Caesar Schmidt, 1897).

92 Reuss, "Disgrace and Fall," 129.

93 BAB, Carl Peters papers, Folder 54, Bl. 14 (quote); Folders 51 and 52 contain press references to the remark; also see Reuss, "Disgrace and Fall," 122, 125.

94 August Bebel (SPD), in *Stenographische Berichte über die Verhandlungen des Reichstages* (13 March 1896): 1434.

95 BAB, Carl Peters papers, Folder 91, Bl. 63–65 (Bülow to Elly Peters,

19 March 1896); LASA, Bülow to Andreas-Salomé, 6 December 1897; Bülow, "Mann über Bord," especially 552.

96 BAB, Carl Peters papers, Folder 4, Bl. 16 (Bülow to Carl Peters, 17 November 1897).

97 Marcia Klotz argues convincingly that Bülow used race to divide "a female fantasy of masochistic pleasure from that of voyeuristic enjoyment of the hero's sadistic brutality . . . the sadistic male hero, if he is in fact a hero, will never turn his violence against a white victim" (Klotz, "White Women," 46, 50–51, 53 [quote]).

98 For an example of ambivalence, see the scene in Bülow, *Kara,* in which Joachim von Bruckring drives his carriage full speed at workers who had mocked him and Kara, running one over (308–309). By contrast, the depiction of Ludwig von Rosen's particular brand of violence in *Tropical Rage* is outright admiring.

99 GStA, Heinrich Schnee papers, Folder 22a, unpublished memoirs, Bl. 75, 77; and Bair, "Carl Peters," 158.

100 LASA, Bülow to Andreas-Salomé, 9 December 1902.

101 BAB, Carl Peters papers, Folder 91, Bl. 51 (Bülow to Elly Peters, 21 January 1893).

102 Andreas-Salomé, *Das Haus,* 57, 147.

103 Hoechstetter, *Frieda,* 206, 209.

104 An exception is a novel by Hanna Christaller, *Alfreds Frauen* (Stuttgart: Francksche Verlagshandlung, 1916). See Adjaï Oloukpona-Yinnon, "Mut gegen Tabu. Hanna Christaller: Die Bahnbrecherin der deutschen Kolonialbelletristik über Togo," *Etudes Germano-Africaines,* no. 10 (1992): 85–91.

105 See, for example, Orla Holm, *Pioniere: Ein Kolonialdrama aus Deutsch-Südwest-Afrika* (Berlin: F. Fontane, 1906); and Holm, *Ovita: Episode aus dem Hererolande* (Dresden: Carl Reissner, 1909).

3. A NEW COLONIAL MASCULINITY: THE MEN'S DEBATE OVER "RACE MIXING" IN THE COLONIES

1 This idea is discussed in Margaret Strobel, *European Women and the Second British Empire* (Bloomington: Indiana University Press, 1991), 1–15; and Kumari Jayawardena, *The White Woman's Other Burden: Western Women and South Asia during British Rule* (New York: Routledge, 1995).

2 I use the term *race mixing* because that is how the persons in my sources referred to the phenomenon of sexual relations and marriage between "races." Such terms express not merely facts, but also how human affairs are imagined through metaphors; therefore, they are not interchangeable across historical and cultural contexts. The term *miscegenation* has a distinctly United States context and history. See Sidney Kaplan, "The Miscegenation Issue in the Election of 1864," *Journal of Negro History* 34 (1949): 274–343.

3 For other studies of race via legal family relations, see Jean Elisabeth Ped-

ersen, "'Special Customs': Paternity Suits and Citizenship in France and the Colonies, 1870–1912," in *Domesticating the Empire: Race, Gender and Family Life in French and Dutch Colonialism,* ed. Julia Clancy-Smith and Frances Gouda (Charlottesville: University Press of Virginia, 1998), 43–64; Virginia Domínguez, *White by Definition: Social Classification in Creole Louisiana* (New Brunswick: Rutgers University Press, 1986); Peggy Pascoe, "Miscegenation Law, Court Cases, and Ideologies of 'Race' in Twentieth-Century America," *Journal of American History* 83 (1996): 44–69; and Verena Martinez-Alier, *Marriage, Class and Colour in Nineteenth-Century Cuba: A Study of Racial Attitudes and Sexual Values in a Slave Society* (reprint, Ann Arbor: University of Michigan Press, 1989).

4 For example, the colonial administration listed only forty-two in the year 1903 in German Southwest Africa. See Theodor Leutwein, *Elf Jahre Gouverneur in Deutsch-Südwestafrika* (Berlin: E. S. Mittler, 1906), 232.

5 The colonial administration counted 240 such children and 254 male European colonial residents (including forty-two missionaries). See RKA 5421, Bl. 33 (Schreiber to Colonial Office, 16 July 1913).

6 There is no historical study of these transfers of wealth in the German colonies. For Samoa, a point of departure is R. W. Robson, *Queen Emma: The Samoan-American Girl Who Founded an Empire in Nineteenth-Century New Guinea* (Sydney: Pacific Publications, 1979). See also RKA 5421, Bl. 4 (*Deutsche Warte,* 20 April 1906), Bl. 18 (*Deutschostafrikanische Zeitung,* 20 April 1907); and DKG 155, Bl. 114 (Women's League of the German Colonial Society flier, ca. 1909).

7 On patriarchy in Europe, see Ute Gerhard, "Die Rechtsstellung der Frau in der bürgerlichen Gesellschaft des 19. Jahrhunderts," in *Bürgertum im 19. Jahrhundert: Deutschland im europäischen Vergleich,* ed. Jürgen Kocka (Munich: Deutscher Taschenbuch Verlag, 1988), 1:439–468; and Gerhard, *Verhältnisse und Verhinderungen: Frauenarbeit, Familie und Rechte der Frauen im 19. Jahrhundert* (Frankfurt a.M.: Suhrkamp, 1978).

8 Max Buchner, *Kamerun: Skizzen und Betrachtungen* (Leipzig: Duncker & Humblot, 1887), 191.

9 Ibid., 154–155. The later governor of Cameroon, Jesco von Puttkamer, likewise recommended concubinage. See Harry R. Rudin, *Germans in the Cameroons 1884–1914: A Case Study in Modern Imperialism* (London: Jonathan Cape, 1938), 304–305.

10 Albert Plehn, "Die Akklimatisationsaussichten der Germanen im tropischen Afrika," in *Verhandlungen des Deutschen Kolonialkongresses 1910* (Berlin: Dietrich Reimer, 1910), 892.

11 Karl Dove, *Südwest-Afrika: Kriegs- und Friedensbilder aus der ersten deutschen Kolonie* (Berlin: Allgemeiner Verein für deutsche Litteratur, 1896), 268 (quotes), 335. On the same tendency in French colonialism, see Penny Edwards, "Womanizing Indochina: Fiction, Nation, and Cohabitation in

Colonial Cambodia, 1890–1930," in *Domesticating the Empire*, ed. Clancy-Smith and Gouda, 108–130.

12 Dove, *Südwest-Afrika*, 124 and facing photograph, and 129. The Rehobother, Grootfonteiner, and Rietfonteiner Basters had migrated from the Northern Cape to Namibia by the 1870s. By contrast, Dove was unimpressed with the nurses who arrived under the auspices of the Women's Association for Nursing in 1893 (308).

13 One kind of evidence for that was African men's protests. See, for example, Horst Drechsler, *"Let Us Die Fighting"*: *The Struggle of the Herero and Nama against German Imperialism (1884–1915)* (London: Zed Press, 1980), 133–135, 167–168 n. 6; and Helmut Bley, *Namibia under German Rule* (reprint, Hamburg: Lit, 1996), 42, 89–90, 90 n. 48.

14 On racialized sexuality as a public marker in colonial societies, see Ann Stoler, "Sexual Affronts and Racial Frontiers: European Identities and the Cultural Politics of Exclusion in Colonial Southeast Asia," *Comparative Studies in Society and History* 34 (1992): 514–551; Stoler, "Carnal Knowledge and Imperial Power: Gender, Race, and Morality in Colonial Asia," in *Gender at the Crossroads of Knowledge: Feminist Anthropology in the Postmodern Era*, ed. Micaela di Leonardo (Berkeley: University of California Press, 1991), 51–101; and Stoler, *Race and the Education of Desire: Foucault's History of Sexuality and the Colonial Order of Things* (Durham: Duke University Press, 1995), 95–136.

15 Most Germans were citizens of their own state (e.g., Bavaria, Baden, or Prussia) and Reich citizens only by virtue of that citizenship. Direct citizenship in the Reich was possible only after the citizenship law of 1913. See Franz Massfeller, *Deutsches Staatsangehörigkeitsrecht von 1870 bis zur Gegenwart* (Frankfurt a.M.: Verlag für Standesamtswesen, 1953), 13–14.

16 James J. Sheehan, "What Is German History? Reflections on the Role of the *Nation* in German History and Historiography," *Journal of Modern History* 53 (1981): 1–23; and Jonathan Sperber, *The European Revolutions, 1848–1851* (New York: Cambridge University Press, 1994), 64–71, 87–101.

17 On left-liberals' influence at the municipal level (where property qualifications gave them an advantage, unlike in Reichstag elections), see Dieter Langewiesche, "Liberalism in the Second Empire, 1871–1914," in *In Search of a Liberal Germany: Studies in the History of German Liberalism from 1789 to the Present*, ed. Konrad H. Jarausch and Larry Eugene Jones (New York: Berg, 1990), 230, 232; and James J. Sheehan, "Liberalism and the City in Nineteenth-Century Germany," *Past and Present* 51 (May 1971): 116–137.

18 Cornelia Essner, "Der Kampf um das Kolonialgericht oder Kolonialgesetzgebung als Verfassungsproblem," *Historische Mitteilungen* 5 (1992): 79.

19 Paul Fischer, "Das Verordnungsrecht in den Kolonien," in *Verhandlungen des Deutschen Kolonialkongresses 1905* (Berlin: Dietrich Reimer [Ernst Vohsen],

1906), 369–370, 373–374, 378 (comments by Matthias Erzberger). More generally, see Ernst Rudolf Huber, *Deutsche Verfassungsgeschichte seit 1789*, Bd. 4: *Struktur und Krisen des Kaiserreichs* (Stuttgart: W. Kohlhammer, 1969), 628–629.

20 Essner, "Der Kampf um das Kolonialgericht," 87.

21 Uday Mehta, "Strategies of Liberal Exclusion," in *Tensions of Empire: Colonial Cultures in a Bourgeois World*, ed. Frederick Cooper and Ann L. Stoler (Berkeley: University of California Press, 1997), 59–86; and Eric Stokes, *The English Utilitarians and India* (Oxford: Clarendon, 1959).

22 Lora Wildenthal, "Race, Gender and Citizenship in the German Colonial Empire," in *Tensions of Empire*, ed. Cooper and Stoler, 263–283, and references cited therein; Cornelia Essner, "'Wo Rauch ist, da ist auch Feuer': Zu den Ansätzen eines Rassenrechts für die deutschen Kolonien," in *Rassendiskriminierung, Kolonialpolitik und ethnisch-nationale Identität*, ed. Winfried Wagner et al. (Münster: Lit, 1992), 145–160b; Essner, "Zwischen Vernunft und Gefühl: Die Reichstagsdebatten von 1912 um koloniale 'Rassenmischehe' und 'Sexualität,'" *Zeitschrift für Geschichtswissenschaft* 45 (1997): 503–519; and Pascal Grosse, *Kolonialismus, Eugenik und bürgerliche Gesellschaft in Deutschland, 1850–1918* (Frankfurt a.M.: Campus, 2000), 145–192.

23 See RKA 5420, passim.

24 See, for example, Alice L. Conklin, "Redefining 'Frenchness': Citizenship, Race Regeneration, and Imperial Motherhood in France and West Africa, 1914–40," in *Domesticating the Empire*, ed. Clancy-Smith and Gouda, 65–83; Ann L. Stoler, "Making Empire Respectable: The Politics of Race and Sexual Morality in Twentieth-Century Colonial Cultures," *American Ethnologist* 16 (1989): 634–660; Stoler, "Sexual Affronts," and Ronald Hyam, *Empire and Sexuality: The British Experience* (Manchester: Manchester University Press, 1990).

25 Max Fleischmann, "Die Mischehen in den deutschen Schutzgebieten vom Rechtsstandpunkte," in *Verhandlungen des Deutschen Kolonialkongresses 1910* (Berlin: Dietrich Reimer, 1910), 561.

26 RKA 5423, Bl. 5–12 (Denkschrift betr. die Schliessung von Ehen zw. Weissen und Farbigen, quote on Bl. 8); see also Bl. 2 (Büttner to Kayser, 8 June 1887), and Bl. 3–4 (Büttner, Kersten, and Weger to Bismarck, 7 May 1887). On other advocates of intermarriage, see Maximilian Bayer, *The Rehoboth Baster Nation of Namibia*, trans. and intro. Peter Carstens (reprint, Basel: Basler Afrika Bibliographien, 1984), 33; RKA 5421, Bl. 4 (*Deutsche Warte*, 20 April 1906); and RKA 5423, Bl. 20 (Schreiber to Kayser, 10 March 1896).

27 RKA 5423, Bl. 6–9 (quote on 6) (Denkschrift betr. die Schliessung von Ehen zw. Weissen und Farbigen).

28 RKA 5423, Bl. 10 (quotes) (Denkschrift betr. die Schliessung von Ehen zw. Weissen und Farbigen); and John J. Grotpeter, *Historical Dictionary of*

Namibia (Metuchen, N.J.: Scarecrow Press, 1994), 453. The Schmelen name appears in some sources as "Schmehl."

29   RKA 5423, Bl. 11 (Denkschrift betr. die Schliessung von Ehen zw. Weissen und Farbigen).

30   These missionaries were the Germans Baumann and Hegner and the Finns Björklund and Rautanen. It was typical of the 1890s that two German observers praised the Rautanens and Hegner without any mention, much less criticism, of the wives' African descent. See Dove, *Südwest-Afrika*, 2–3, 19; and Ludwig von Estorff, *Wanderungen und Kämpfe in Südwestafrika, Ostafrika und Südafrika 1894–1910,* ed. Christoph-Friedrich Kutscher (Wiesbaden: privately published, 1968), 46.

31   RKA 5423, Bl. 11 (Denkschrift betr. die Schliessung von Ehen zw. Weissen und Farbigen).

32   RKA 5423, Bl. 5 (Denkschrift betr. die Schliessung von Ehen zw. Weissen und Farbigen).

33   RKA 5423, Bl. 5–6 (Denkschrift betr. die Schliessung von Ehen zw. Weissen und Farbigen).

34   RKA 5423, Bl. 6 (Denkschrift betr. die Schliessung von Ehen zw. Weissen und Farbigen).

35   RKA 5423, Bl. 12 (Denkschrift betr. die Schliessung von Ehen zw. Weissen und Farbigen).

36   The state gave full recognition only to civil marriage since its introduction in Germany in 1875. See RKA 5423, Bl. 14–15 (Foreign Office to Goering, 23 June 1887).

37   RKA 5423, Bl. 132–134 (Leinhos case).

38   On Ludwig Baumann, see Wildenthal, "Race, Gender and Citizenship," 273–275; on Mathilde Kleinschmidt, see Essner, "Wo Rauch ist, da ist auch Feuer," 158. An argument of Steven Aschheim is apposite for these cases: that the concept of race became more prominent in the "Jewish question" not as an expression of existing difference, but rather in a period when differences between Christian Germans and assimilated German Jews were less marked than ever. See Steven E. Aschheim, *Brothers and Strangers: The East European Jews in German and German Jewish Consciousness, 1800–1923* (Madison: University of Wisconsin Press, 1982), 76.

39   RKA 5423, Bl. 21 (internal memo, 12 March 1896).

40   Estorff, *Wanderungen und Kämpfe,* 49.

41   Paul Rohrbach, *Deutsch-Südwest-Afrika ein Ansiedlungs-Gebiet?* 2d, rev. ed. (Berlin-Schöneberg: Buchverlag der "Hilfe," 1910), 27. Curt von François and his brother Hugo, another officer, both lived with their wives in the colony in the 1890s; Estorff never married.

42   RKA 5423, Bl. 21 (internal memo, 12 March 1896).

43   Dove, *Südwest-Afrika,* 82; see also RKA 2084, Bl. 75 (anonymous letter from

Keetmanshoop, German Southwest Africa, to Foreign Office of Baden, 17 November 1904).

44   Dove, *Südwest-Afrika*, 82.

45   RKA 5423, Bl. 19 (Schreiber to Kayser, 10 March 1896).

46   RKA 5423, Bl. 24 (Leutwein to Hohenlohe, 21 June 1896); see also Bl. 19 (Schreiber to Kayser, 10 March 1896), Bl. 21 (internal memo, 12 March 1896), and Bl. 34 (Leutwein to Colonial Department, 23 August 1898).

47   For example, he concluded treaties with the Witbois, Rehobothers, and other African groups that provided for military training and conscription into the German colonial army. See Bley, *Namibia under German Rule*, 37, 84; Leutwein, *Elf Jahre*, 216–217; and RKA 5423, Bl. 26 (Colonial Department to Leutwein, 17 August 1897). RKA 5423, Bl. 34–35 (Leutwein to Colonial Department, 23 August 1898). For Germans' differentiated perceptions of Africans in the colony during the 1890s, see Bley, *Namibia under German Rule*, 73–145.

48   Leutwein, *Elf Jahre*, 232–235.

49   Wilhelm Külz, *Deutsch-Südafrika im 25. Jahre Deutscher Schutzherrschaft: Skizzen und Beiträge zur Geschichte Deutsch-Südafrikas* (Berlin: Wilhelm Süsserott, 1909), 177; and Leutwein, *Elf Jahre*, 216.

50   Gentz, "Die rechtliche Stellung der Bastards in Deutsch-Südwestafrika," *Beiträge zur Kolonialpolitik und Kolonialwirtschaft* 4 (1902–1903): 90–92. Burgsdorff, like the François brothers, lived with his wife in the colony. Leutwein, *Elf Jahre*, 460.

51   RKA 5423, Bl. 28 (internal memo, 13 February 1898).

52   The relevant laws are the "Gesetz vom 4. Mai 1870 betreffend die Eheschliessung und die Beurkundung des Personenstandes von Bundesangehörigen im Auslande," "Gesetz vom 1. Juni 1870 über die Erwerbung und Verlust der Bundes- und Staatsangehörigkeit," "Gesetz vom 6. Februar 1875 über die Beurkundung des Personenstandes und die Eheschliessung," and the later modifications in the "Gesetz vom 22. Juni 1913," paragraphs 6, 17. Since these were basic civil law for all of Germany, they are widely available; one source is O. Riebow et al., eds., *Die deutsche Kolonialgesetzgebung: Sammlung der auf die deutschen Schutzgebiete bezüglichen Gesetze, Verordnungen, Erlasse und internationalen Vereinbarungen*, 13 vols. (Berlin: E. S. Mittler, 1893–1910).

53   RKA 5423, Bl. 26 (Colonial Department to Leutwein, 17 August 1897), and Bl. 28 (internal memo, 13 February 1898).

54   Some Germans saw Boers as models of rough rural virtue and counted them as cousins to the Germans. On European pro-Boer sentiment, see Ulrich Kröll, *Die internationale Buren-Agitation 1899–1902* (Münster: Regensberg, 1973). Other Germans looked with distaste on Boers' undercapitalized farms and "broken" Dutch, and saw the Boers themselves as not quite white

or European. On images of the Boers, see J. M. Coetzee, *White Writing: On the Culture of Letters in South Africa* (New Haven: Yale University Press, 1988), 28–35. Opinion about the desirability of Boer women as wives for German colonists often divided along the same lines as opinion about Rehobother women: both were either lauded as hard-working, useful wives or maligned as bad influences on German men. In either case, much the same language appeared. See, for example, Estorff, *Wanderungen und Kämpfe*, 52–53, 101; RKA 5423, Bl. 35 (Leutwein to Colonial Department, 23 August 1898); Leutwein, *Elf Jahre*, 413–417; Paul Rohrbach, *Aus Südwest-Afrikas schweren Tagen: Blätter von Arbeit und Abschied* (Berlin: Wilhelm Weicher, 1909), 30–31; RKA 5421, Bl. 4 (*Deutsche Warte*, 20 April 1906); and DKG 153, Bl. 12 (Women's League flier, ca. 1908).

55 RKA 5423, Bl. 28 (internal memo, 13 February 1898), and Bl. 35 (Leutwein to Colonial Department, 23 August 1898).

56 RKA 5423, Bl. 49 (Colonial Department to Leutwein, 3 August 1899). Family law clauses 1303–1315, in *Bürgerliches Gesetzbuch für das Deutsche Reich* (Reutlingen: Ensslin & Laiblin, n.d.), 214–215.

57 RKA 5423, Bl. 31, 34, 38–40, 41, 42–43, 46–48, 49; Georg Braun, *Zur Frage der Rechtsgültigkeit der Mischehen in den deutschen Schutzgebieten* (Greifswald: Julius Abel, 1912); Karl Stengel, "Zur Frage der Mischehen in den deutschen Schutzgebieten," *Zeitschrift für Kolonialpolitik, Kolonialrecht und Kolonialwirtschaft* 14 (1912): 738–780; Wilhelm Pfläging, *Zum kolonialrechtlichen Problem der Mischbeziehungen zwischen deutschen Reichsangehörigen und Eingeborenen der deutschen Schutzgebiete, unter besonderer Berücksichtigung des Unterhaltsanspruches der unehelichen Mischlinge* (Berlin: Gustave Schade [Otto Francke], 1913); and Kurt Hedrich, *Der Rassegedanke im deutschen Kolonialrecht: Die rechtliche Regelung der ehelichen und ausserehelichen Beziehungen zwischen Weissen und Farbigen* (Schramberg: Gatzer & Hahn, 1941).

58 Ludwig Othenberg, *Die Zuständigkeit in privatrechtlichen Mischprozessen nach deutschem Kolonialrecht* (Hanover: Gustav Jacob, 1914).

59 RKA 5423, Bl. 32 (internal memo, 18 February 1898), and Bl. 48 (Richter to Leutwein, 10 June 1899). See also RKA 5421, Bl. 14 (Haber to Colonial Department, 9 May 1906); Huber, *Deutsche Verfassungsgeschichte seit 1789*, B. 4, 625–630, 633–634; and Essner, "Wo Rauch ist, da ist auch Feuer," 147–148.

60 A decision on the legality of mixed marriage was put off repeatedly: until the Schutzgebietsgesetz of 1900 (RKA 5423, Bl. 40 [internal memo, 31 July 1899]), then until the proposed new citizenship law, planned in 1903 but not promulgated until 1913 (RKA 5423, Bl. 57 [internal memo, 5 October 1903]). In 1906 Colonial Director Prince Ernst zu Hohenlohe-Langenburg upheld the legality of performing mixed marriages (RKA 5424, Bl. 15 [Colonial Department to *Justizamt* Lüneburg, 9 May 1906]). As late as 1911 the Colonial Office under Colonial Secretary Friedrich von Lindequist stated

that the Colonial Office was not "in a position" to produce regulations on mixed marriage (RKA 5432, Bl. 73–74 [Colonial Office to Solf, August 1911]). On internal divisions, which lasted through 1914, see RKA 5423, Bl. 32 (internal memo, 18 February 1898); RKA 5432, Bl. 79 (Colonial Secretary Solf to Grevel, 17 January 1912); RKA 5424, Bl. 31–32 (Hoesch to Colonial Office, 25–29 April 1913, marginalia); RKA 5430, Bl. 8 (Imperial German Consulate for the South Sea Islands, Apia, to Imperial Chancellor Hohenlohe-Schillingsfürst, 16 October 1897), and Bl. 16–17 (Colonial Department to Jaluit Company, 4 February 1898).

61 *Deutsche Kolonialzeitung* 9 (neue Folge), no. 25 (20 June 1896): 197. For a more detailed account of this meeting, see Karen Smidt, "'Germania führt die deutsche Frau nach Südwest': Auswanderung, Leben und soziale Konflikte deutscher Frauen in der ehemaligen Kolonie Deutsch-Südwestafrika 1884–1920. Eine sozial- und frauengeschichtliche Studie" (Ph.D. diss., University of Magdeburg, 1995), 26.

62 Erich Prager, *Die Deutsche Kolonialgesellschaft 1882–1907: Im Auftrage des Ausschusses der Deutschen Kolonialgesellschaft dargestellt* (Berlin: Dietrich Reimer [Ernst Vohsen], 1908), 79–80.

63 Winkler, "Zur kolonialen Frauenfrage," *Deutsche Kolonialzeitung* 29, no. 16 (20 April 1912): 258.

64 RKA 5423, Bl. 19 (Schreiber to Kayser, 10 March 1896), Bl. 24 (Leutwein to Hohenlohe, 21 June 1896), Bl. 60 (Richter to Colonial Department, 20 February 1904), and Bl. 62 (*Tägliche Rundschau*, 25 March 1904); RKA 5432, Bl. 33 (Solf to Dernburg, 15 September 1907); Leutwein, *Elf Jahre*, 232, 234; Prager, *Die Deutsche Kolonialgesellschaft 1882–1907*, 111; and Oskar Hintrager, *Südwestafrika in der deutschen Zeit* (Munich: R. Oldenbourg, 1955), 77.

65 In 1902 there were fewer than 1,034 German women in the entire colonial empire. In 1913, when German settlement and development were at their height, there were still fewer than 4,817. I specify "fewer" because each figure refers to the number of "white women," not specifically to women with German citizenship. See "Bevölkerung der Schutzgebiete," in *Deutsches Kolonial-Lexikon,* ed. Heinrich Schnee (Leipzig: Quelle & Meyer, 1920), 1:196. The greatest single concentration of those women was in German Southwest Africa. In that colony in 1912, for example, there were 2,277 adult German women and 7,696 men. See "Südwestafrika 1912. Die weisse Bevölkerung in staatsbürgerlicher Hinsicht," in *Die deutschen Schutzgebiete: Amtliche Jahresberichte in Afrika und der Südsee. 1911/12,* ed. Reichskolonialamt (Berlin: E. S. Mittler, 1913), 20–21, 24–25.

66 Similar "dual marriage systems" were typical of colonial, slave, and post-emancipation societies. See Raymond T. Smith, "Hierarchy and the Dual Marriage System in West Indian Society," in Smith, *The Matrifocal Family: Power, Pluralism, and Politics* (New York: Routledge, 1996), 59–80. On

sexual choices in racially organized societies, see Martinez-Alier, *Marriage, Class and Colour in Nineteenth-Century Cuba;* and Martha Hodes, *White Women, Black Men: Illicit Sex in the Nineteenth Century South* (New Haven: Yale University Press, 1997), 147–208.

67 Moritz J. Bonn, *Wandering Scholar* (New York: John Day, 1948), 145.

68 RKA 5423, Bl. 44 (Panzlaff's petition for a civil marriage, 6 June 1899), and Bl. 60–61 (Richter to Colonial Department, 20 February 1904).

69 RKA 5423, Bl. 35 (Leutwein to Colonial Department, 23 August 1898), and Bl. 45–46 (Richter to Leutwein, 10 June 1899).

70 RKA 5423, Bl. 43 (Leutwein to Colonial Department, 20 June 1899). On Johr, see Dove, *Südwest-Afrika*, 193, 251–253.

71 RKA 5423, Bl. 44 (Panzlaff's petition for a civil marriage, 6 June 1899), Bl. 42 (Leutwein to Colonial Department, 20 June 1899), Bl. 45 (Richter to Leutwein, 10 June 1899), and Bl. 49 (Colonial Department to Leutwein, 3 August 1899).

72 RKA 5423, Bl. 61 (Richter to Colonial Department, 20 February 1904). *Windhuk* was the German spelling; the city's name is now once again spelled *Windhoek.*

73 For a similar case, concerning the farmer Carl Becker, see Bley, *Namibia under German Rule,* 216–218; and Wildenthal, "Race, Gender and Citizenship," 268–271.

74 RKA 5423, Bl. 242 (Vietsch to Seitz, 11 July 1912). Becker also worked his way up from humble beginnings as a trader. See Rohrbach, *Aus Südwest-Afrikas schweren Tagen,* 58.

75 RKA 5418, Bl. 271 (Colonial Office to Witkowski, 2 December 1913).

76 RKA 5423, Bl. 56 (Tecklenburg, internal memo, 24 September 1903).

77 RKA 5423, Bl. 56 (quote) and 57 (Tecklenburg, internal memo, 24 September 1903).

78 RKA 5423, Bl. 54 (Tecklenburg, internal memo, 24 September 1903).

79 *Nonnative (Nichteingeborene/r)* was a term intended to include non-German white people and others in the colony whose status was equal to whites, or at least higher than that of colonial subjects. See RKA 5423, Bl. 55 (Tecklenburg, internal memo, 24 September 1903).

80 RKA 5423, Bl. 45–48 (Richter to Leutwein, 10 June 1899). Judge Richter claimed that no one minded the Panzlaff children's presence at the German school, and that in upbringing and appearance they were "hardly distinguishable" from the other white children (RKA 5423, Bl. 61 [Richter to Colonial Department, 20 February 1904]).

81 On the war, see Drechsler, *"Let Us Die Fighting"*; and Jon M. Bridgman, *The Revolt of the Hereros* (Berkeley: University of California Press, 1981). The war's nature and effects remain controversial; see Tilman Dedering, "The German-Herero War of 1904: Revision of Genocide or Imaginary Histori-

ography," *Journal of Southern African Studies* 19 (March 1993): 80–88; Henning Melber, "Kontinuitäten totaler Herrschaft: Völkermord und Apartheid in 'Deutsch-Südwestafrika.' Zur kolonialen Herrschaftspraxis im Deutschen Kaiserreich," *Jahrbuch für Antisemitismusforschung 1* (Frankfurt a.M.: Campus, 1992), 91–116; Gunter Spraul, "Der 'Völkermord' an den Herero: Untersuchungen zu einer neuen Kontinuitätsthese," *Geschichte in Wissenschaft und Unterricht* 39 (1988): 713–739; and Neville Alexander, "The Namibian War of Anti-colonial Resistance, 1904–7," in *Namibia 1884–1984,* ed. Brian Wood (London: Namibia Support Committee; Lusaka: U.N. Institute for Namibia, 1988), 193–203. About 80 percent of the original Herero population and 50 percent of the Nama were killed or died of hunger and thirst during the war and its violent aftermath. See Drechsler, *"Let Us Die Fighting,"* 214; and Bridgman, *The Revolt of the Hereros,* 131. The percentages are imprecise because prewar population data are flawed, but both critics and supporters of the war at the time described German policy as "destruction" or "extermination" (*Vernichtung*) of the Herero. See, for example, Ludwig von Estorff, *Wanderungen und Kämpfe,* 134. About twenty thousand German soldiers were dispatched for the war. The German side suffered about two thousand casualties, of which about one hundred were civilian farmers and traders (Bridgman, *The Revolt of the Hereros,* 112, 164). These were far fewer than the African losses, but far greater than Germans expected. The war ultimately cost as much as 600 million marks, which also far exceeded expectations (Külz, *Deutsch-Südafrika,* 173).

82 Drechsler, *"Let Us Die Fighting,"* 156–167; and Bley, *Namibia under German Rule,* 163–169.

83 Woodruff D. Smith, *The German Colonial Empire* (Chapel Hill: University of North Carolina Press, 1978), 211–212; and Hintrager, *Sudwestafrika in der deutschen Zeit,* especially 75, 233.

84 RKA 5423, Bl. 71 (Tecklenburg to Colonial Department, 23 October 1905).

85 RKA 5423, Bl. 80 (Lindequist to Colonial Department, 12 August 1906).

86 Hintrager, *Südwestafrika in der deutschen Zeit,* 75.

87 The First World War interrupted plans for the creation of a colonial supreme court in Hamburg; one of the first issues to be put before it was to have been the legality of banning intermarriage. See RKA 5418, Bl. 329 (internal memo, ca. March 1914); and Essner, "Der Kampf um das Kolonialgericht."

88 RKA 5423, Bl. 68 (Tecklenburg to Colonial Department, 23 October 1905). Tecklenburg and Hintrager apparently drew up the ban and this letter together. See Hintrager, *Südwestafrika in der deutschen Zeit,* 76.

89 RKA 5423, Bl. 68 (Tecklenburg to Colonial Department, 23 October 1905).

90 RKA 5423, Bl. 69 (Tecklenburg to Colonial Department, 23 October 1905).

91 Drechsler, *"Let Us Die Fighting,"* 161. The German army's chief of general staff, Count Alfred von Schlieffen (originator of the "Schlieffen Plan" of the First World War) also used the phrase (ibid., 163).

92 Gustav Menzel, *Die Rheinische Mission* (Wuppertal: Verlag der Vereinten Evangelischen Mission, 1978), 242–243.

93 Drechsler, *"Let Us Die Fighting,"* 156, 159; and Bridgman, *The Revolt of the Hereros*, 138.

94 Hans Tecklenburg drafted these regulations in mid-1905. See Drechsler, *"Let Us Die Fighting,"* 214–216; and Bley, *Namibia under German Rule*, 170–173, 226–248. The Rehobothers and Ovambos were excepted from the Native Regulations.

95 Külz, *Deutsch-Südafrika*, 59–60, 63.

96 See, for example, *Windhuker Nachrichten*, 15 July 1908, 3, in which the writer argued for self-administration on the grounds that a genuine German society including all classes and callings had developed in German Southwest Africa; and Bley, *Namibia under German Rule*, 190. On social differentiation as part of nation formation, see Miroslav Hroch, "From National Movement to the Fully-Formed Nation: The Nation-Building Process in Europe," reprinted in *Becoming National. A Reader*, ed. Geoff Eley and Ronald Grigor Suny (New York: Oxford University Press, 1996), 60–77; and Gary B. Cohen, *The Politics of Ethnic Survival: Germans in Prague, 1861–1914* (Princeton: Princeton University Press, 1981). On the ethnic identity formation of the colonists after the period of German rule, see Brigitta Schmidt-Lauber, *Die abhängigen Herren: Deutsche Identität in Namibia* (Hamburg: Lit, 1993). While Schmidt-Lauber dates the origins of a German Namibian ethnic identity to the First World War, her discussion could fruitfully be extended back to the war of 1904–1907.

97 Külz, *Deutsch-Südafrika*, 177.

98 Bley, *Namibia under German Rule*, 79–81, 83–85, 184–196; Külz, *Deutsch-Südafrika*, 200; and Rohrbach, *Aus Südwest-Afrikas schweren Tagen*, 168.

99 Klaus Epstein, "Erzberger and the German Colonial Scandals, 1905–1910," *English Historical Review* 74 (1959): 637–663.

100 Some on the right wing of the Social Democratic Party, such as Gustav Noske, began to develop a socialist colonial program in the periodical *Sozialistische Monatshefte*. See Hans-Christoph Schröder, *Gustav Noske und die Kolonialpolitik des Deutschen Kaiserreiches* (Bonn: Dietz, 1979).

101 Bernhard Dernburg, *Koloniale Lehrjahre* (Stuttgart: Union Deutsche Verlagsgesellschaft, 1907); and Franz-Josef Schulte-Althoff, "Koloniale Krise und Reformprojekte: Zur Diskussion über eine Kurskorrektur in der deutschen Kolonialpolitik nach der Jahrhundertwende," in *Weltpolitik, Europagedanke, Regionalismus: Festschrift für Heinz Gollwitzer zum 65. Geburtstag am 30. Januar 1982*, ed. Heinz Dollinger, Horst Gründer, and Alwin Hanschmidt (Münster: Aschendorff, 1982), 407–425.

102 Werner Schiefel, *Bernhard Dernburg 1865–1937: Kolonialpolitiker und Bankier im wilhelminischen Deutschland* (Zurich: Atlantis, 1974), 119–120, 134, 141.

103 See, for example, Robert Gordon, *The Bushman Myth: The Making of a Namibian Underclass* (Boulder: Westview Press, 1992), 53–75.

104 Schiefel, *Dernburg*, 129. Two years before becoming colonial secretary, Dernburg had belonged to the Progressive Union (Freisinnige Vereinigung).

105 *Windhuker Nachrichten*, 15 August 1908, 1; see also 21 October 1908, 1–2; Schiefel, *Dernburg*, 86, 88; and Arthur J. Knoll, "Decision-Making for the German Colonies," in *Germans in the Tropics*, ed. Arthur J. Knoll and Lewis H. Gann (Westport, Conn.: Greenwood Press, 1987), 138–144.

106 *Windhuker Nachrichten*, 15 July 1908, 3 (quote), and 11 November 1908, 1. See also 15 August 1908, 1, 2, and 27 February 1909, 1, of the *Zweites Blatt* supplement; and Külz, *Deutsch-Südafrika*, 201. On Dernburg's and the colonists' divergent ideas of self-administration, see Smith, *The German Colonial Empire*, 165–166.

107 Bley, *Namibia under German Rule*, 76; and Drechsler, *"Let Us Die Fighting,"* 154. The Colonial Council (Kolonialrat), an advisory body, discussed the white proletariat as a problem already in 1899; see *Deutsches Kolonialblatt* 10, no. 22 (15 November 1899): 758. On social groups and class conflicts in the colony, see Bley, *Namibia under German Rule*, 174–181, 186, 189, 196–201, 212–219; and Rohrbach, *Deutsch-Südwest-Afrika ein Ansiedlungs-Gebiet?* 2d ed., 27–28.

108 *Windhuker Nachrichten*, 12 August 1908, 3; see also the 15 August 1908 issue, 1, of its *Zweites Blatt*.

109 Bley, *Namibia under German Rule*, 196–199.

110 Ibid., 219; and "Dernburg über seine Politik," *Koloniale Zeitschrift* 13, no. 37 (13 September 1912): 601–602.

111 RKA 5421, Bl. 19–20 (Dernburg to Rechenberg, 31 August 1907), and Bl. 19 (Conze to Rechenberg, 31 August 1907).

112 Hintrager, *Südwestafrika in der deutschen Zeit*, 77, 91–92; and RKA 2174, Bl. 6, 78 (minutes of Government Council).

113 RKA 5421, Bl. 13 (Paul Warncke, "Die Rassenfrage in unseren Schutzgebieten," *Deutsche Tageszeitung*, 19 May 1906).

114 RKA 5423, Bl. 76 (internal memo); RKA 5423, Bl. 77 ("Der Aufstand in Deutsch-Südwestafrika," *Leipziger Neueste Nachrichten*, 8 March 1906); and Bley, *Namibia under German Rule*, 213.

115 Schulte-Althoff, "Rassenmischung," 61.

116 RKA 5423, Bl. 132–134 (Leinhos case), especially Bl. 133.

117 Prefect Apostolic von Krolikowski married a German bricklayer named Polster to the Rehobother Katharina Diergaard in 1912, which unleashed a furor. RKA 5418, Bl. 221 (*Preussische Kreuzzeitung*, 23 August 1913), Bl. 222–236, 282–285, 287; RKA 5424, Bl. 34 (*Hamburger Nachrichten*, 30 May 1913, 34, 74–75; and *Keetmanshooper Zeitung*, 13 April 1912, 3, 22 May 1912, 3 [which mentions that the couple had cohabited for years and had chil-

dren], and 25 May 1912, 2). Krolikowski was sentenced for violating the ban, but the case was dropped the next year; Polster was ordered to divorce Diergaard or be deported from the colony. On general Catholic disapproval of the ban, see RKA 5421, Bl. 7 (*Germania*, 21 April 1906), and Bl. 9 (*Kölnische Volkszeitung*, 30 April 1906). Prefect Apostolic Klaegle of northern Southwest Africa sent the Colonial Office a memo explaining that Catholic canonical law did permit bans on marriage (RKA 5418, Bl. 3–7 [Klaegle to Solf, 26 August 1912]). Protestant Rhenish missionaries in the colony agreed at a 1913 conference in Karibib to support the ban, although that directly opposed the position of the Rhenish Missionary Society in Germany (RKA 5424, Bl. 62 [Pastor Hans Hasenkamp to Solf, 21 July 1913]); and Bley, *Namibia under German Rule*, 215.

118 RKA 5423, Bl. 57 (Tecklenburg, internal memo, 24 September 1903); RKA 5421, Bl. 18 (*Deutschostafrikanische Zeitung*, 20 April 1907), and Bl. 23 (*Hamburger Nachrichten*, 10 April 1912). By contrast, in 1887 Büttner had cited Spanish America and the Cape Colony as models for German Southwest Africa regarding the use of intermarriage as a tool of colonization (RKA 5423, Bl. 8–9 [Denkschrift betr. die Schliessung von Ehen zw. Weissen und Farbigen]).

119 *Windhuker Nachrichten*, 21 October 1908, 2.

120 Walter Mogk, *Paul Rohrbach und das "Grössere Deutschland": Ethischer Imperialismus im wilhelminischen Zeitalter. Ein Beitrag zur Geschichte des Kulturprotestantismus* (Munich: Wilhelm Goldmann, 1972). See also Henry Cord Meyer, *Mitteleuropa in German Thought and Action, 1815–1945* (The Hague: Martinus Nijhoff, 1955), especially 95–99; and Woodruff D. Smith, *The Ideological Origins of Nazi Imperialism* (New York: Oxford University Press, 1986), 160–164.

121 Bley, *Namibia under German Rule*, 200–201.

122 Ibid., 190 (quote); Smith, *Ideological Origins*, 21–40, 162–163; and Rohrbach, *Deutsch-Südwest-Afrika ein Ansiedlungs-Gebiet?* 2d ed., 32, see also 31.

123 Cited in Bley, *Namibia under German Rule*, 200.

124 On the relationship between liberal and radical nationalist ideas, see Woodruff D. Smith, "Colonialism and Colonial Empire," in *Imperial Germany: A Historiographical Companion*, ed. Roger Chickering (Westport, Conn.: Greenwood Press, 1996), 438–440.

125 The most thorough biography is Armin Behrendt, *Wilhelm Külz: Aus dem Leben eines Suchenden* (Berlin: Der Morgen, 1968). After his colonial sojourn Külz embarked on a political career and gravitated to the left over the course of his life. An unsuccessful National Liberal candidate for the Reichstag in 1912, he served as delegate of the German Democratic Party (Deutsche Demokratische Partei, DDP) to the National Assembly in 1919. He was a Reichstag member between 1920 and 1932 and minister of the interior in 1926–1927. In 1931 he became mayor of a third city, Dresden, but

was forced to go on "leave" in 1933. He was imprisoned in 1934, then worked as a private consultant between 1938 and 1944.

126 Wilhelm Külz, *Die Feststellung der Friedenspräsenzstärke des Deutschen Heeres, rechtswissenschaftlich dargestellt* (Leipzig-Reudnitz: August Hoffmann, 1900); Külz, *Die Fürsorgeerziehung im Königreich Sachsen und ihre Mängel* (Leipzig-Reudnitz: August Hoffmann, 1904).

127 Bley, *Namibia under German Rule*, 188.

128 Ibid., 191 (quote); *Windhuker Nachrichten*, 5 September 1908, 1–2, 16 September 1908, 1–2, and 21 October 1908, 2; Külz, *Deutsch-Südafrika*, 215.

129 *Windhuker Nachrichten*, 18 July 1908, 1, 5 September 1908, 2, and 21 October 1908, 1.

130 Bley, *Namibia under German Rule*, 247.

131 *Windhuker Nachrichten*, 21 October 1908, 2; see also *Windhuker Nachrichten*, 18 July 1908, 1, and 21 October 1908, 1.

132 BAK, Külz papers, unpublished memoirs, N / 1042, Nr. 11, Bl. 121.

133 Rohrbach, *Deutsch-Südwest-Afrika ein Ansiedlungs-Gebiet?* 2d ed., 32.

134 BAK, Külz papers, unpublished memoirs, N / 1042, Nr. 11, Bl. 17.

135 Paul Rohrbach, *Aus Südwest-Afrikas schweren Tagen*, 29, see also 54, 59.

136 BAK, Külz papers, unpublished memoirs, N / 1042, Nr. 11, Bl. 117.

137 Rohrbach, *Deutsch-Südwest-Afrika ein Ansiedlungs-Gebiet?* 2d ed., 21.

138 BAK, Külz papers, unpublished memoirs, N / 1042, Nr. 11, Bl. 125.

139 Rohrbach, *Deutsch-Südwest-Afrika ein Ansiedlungs-Gebiet?* 2d ed., 18.

140 Rohrbach, *Aus Südwest-Afrikas schweren Tagen*, 26; and Külz, *Deutsch-Südafrika*, 369–370.

141 Rohrbach, *Deutsch-Südwest-Afrika ein Ansiedlungs-Gebiet?* 2d ed., 12–13.

142 Ibid., 28–30. He reiterated the importance of a white German wife in the introduction and conclusion of both editions of this advice pamphlet; see 6, 30; and Rohrbach, *Deutsch-Sudwest-Afrika ein Ansiedlungs-Gebiet?* 1st ed. (Berlin-Schöneberg: Buchverlag "Die Hilfe," 1905), 8, 29–33.

143 Rohrbach, *Aus Südwest-Afrikas schweren Tagen*, 18.

144 *Koloniale Zeitschrift* 13, no. 40 (4 October 1912): 667; and Paul Rohrbach, "Der koloniale Frauenbund," *Das grössere Deutschland* 1, no. 12 (27 June 1914): 341–345.

145 *Koloniale Zeitschrift* 13, no. 25 (21 June 1912): 392.

146 Rohrbach, *Deutsch-Südwest-Afrika ein Ansiedlungs-Gebiet?* 2d ed., 29. See the similar harangue in Rohrbach, *Aus Südwest-Afrikas schweren Tagen*, 65.

147 Rohrbach, *Deutsch-Südwest-Afrika ein Ansiedlungs-Gebiet?* 2d ed., 29. Rohrbach admitted on rare occasions that not all intermarried couples were poor and demoralized, but he insisted that in those cases all the credit belonged to the man.

148 Rohrbach, *Aus Südwest-Afrikas schweren Tagen*, 13–14, 158. World travel together was a way of life for the Rohrbachs, who were married the day before departing on a major study trip to Anatolia. The 1904 outbreak of

war interfered with the Rohrbachs' plans to reunite in the colony. He arrived in September 1903, and Clara Rohrbach and their children finally followed in October 1904; another child was born there, in 1905. See Rohrbach, *Aus Südwest-Afrikas schweren Tagen*, 231.

149 Rohrbach, *Aus Südwest-Afrikas schweren Tagen*, 166–167, 179, 181–182, 187, 190, 198, 230; and BAK, Rohrbach papers, Folder 67 (Rohrbach to his parents, 22 September 1903).

150 BAK, Külz papers, unpublished memoirs, N / 1042, Nr. 11, Bl. 118, 124.

151 Elisabeth Gottheiner, "Das kommunale und kirchliche Wahlrecht der Frau," in *Der internationale Frauen-Kongress in Berlin 1904* (Berlin: Carl Habel, 1905), 497; see also E[lse] L[üders], "Eine Propagandareise für das Frauenstimmrecht in Süd-Afrika," *Zeitschrift für Frauenstimmrecht* 6, no. 4 (1 May 1912): 3; and Lüders, "Rassen- und Rechtsfragen in den Kolonien: Auch ein Kulturproblem," *Zeitschrift für Frauenstimmrecht* 6, no. 7 (1 August 1912): 2–3.

152 Wilhelm Külz, "Frauenstimmrecht in den Kolonien?" *Deutsche Kolonialzeitung* 26, no. 43 (1909): 707.

153 *Windhuker Nachrichten*, 24 October 1908, 1. Passive suffrage required one to be at least thirty years old. The colonial newspaper *Windhuker Nachrichten* mocked universal, equal manhood suffrage as a harbinger of racial equality: "Here no one wants any universal and equal suffrage that might even be given to negroes, Hottentots, and Bushmen" (*Windhuker Nachrichten*, 24 October 1908, 1).

154 Paragraph 17f was the specific clause of the charter excluding those in mixed sexual relationships. Other grounds for exclusion were prison or detention on remand, civic degradation (i.e., loss of *bürgerliche Ehrenrechte*), and being in arrears with municipal duties. See Fischer, "Selbstverwaltung," in *Deutsches Koloniallexikon*, ed. Heinrich Schnee (Leipzig: Quelle & Meyer, 1920), 3:345.

155 Bley, *Namibia under German Rule*, 194; and Smidt, "Germania führt die deutsche Frau nach Südwest," 430. The municipality (*Gemeindeverband*) was the basic unit of Southwest Africa's self-administration; the municipal council represented it (Fischer, "Selbstverwaltung").

156 The cases concerned the Leinhos and Denk families (RKA 5424, Bl. 15 [Colonial Department to *Justizamt* Lüneburg, 9 May 1906]).

157 RKA 5421, Bl. 18 (*Deutschostafrikanische Zeitung*, 20 April 1907).

158 "Verordnung des Gouverneurs von Deutsch-Südwestafrika über die Mischlingsbevölkerung vom 23. Mai 1912," in *Deutsches Kolonialblatt* 23, no. 16 (15 August 1912): 752.

159 Smidt, "Germania führt die deutsche Frau nach Südwest," 158; Bley, *Namibia under German Rule*, 214.

160 Judith R. Walkowitz, *Prostitution and Victorian Society: Women, Class, and the State* (New York: Cambridge University Press, 1980); and Judy Whitehead,

"Bodies Clean and Unclean: Prostitution, Sanitary Legislation, and Respectable Femininity in Colonial North India," *Gender and History* 7 (1995): 41–63.

161 RKA 5423, Bl. 128 (*Windhuker Nachrichten*, 27 April 1910), Bl. 129; and Essner, "Zwischen Vernunft und Gefühl," 510–511.

162 RKA 5423, Bl. 129 (*Deutsch-Südwestafrikanische Zeitung*, 7 May 1910); and RKA 5423, Bl. 149 (Governor Seitz to Colonial Office, 24 February 1911), which specified cash penalties for white men who had had sexual relations with a woman who later bore a mixed-descent child. In Cameroon, the Catholic bishop wanted to ban all interracial concubinage; a tropical doctor who worked there, Hans Ziemann, suggested establishing brothels instead. See Rudin, *Germans in the Cameroons*, 305. On praise for the United States's criminalization of interracial sex, see RKA 5421, Bl. 5 (Richard Nordhausen, "Rassenschmach," *Der Tag*, 26 April 1906), and Bl. 30 (*Deutsche Tageszeitung*, 11 April 1913).

163 Hedrich, *Der Rassegedanke im deutschen Kolonialrecht*, 30. Missionaries sometimes called for German fathers of illegitimate mixed-descent children to be compelled to pay child support. See, for example, RKA 5421, Bl. 33 (A. W. Schreiber [of the Norddeutsche Missionsgesellschaft] to Colonial Office, 16 July 1913).

164 RKA 5421, Bl. 5 (Richard Nordhausen, "Rassenschmach," *Der Tag*, 26 April 1906), Bl. 18 (*Deutschostafrikanische Zeitung*, 20 April 1907), and Bl. 24–25 (Colonial Office to all governors, 29 July 1912).

165 Smidt, "Germania führt die deutsche Frau nach Südwest," 160.

166 RKA 5421, Bl. 24 (Colonial Office to Governor Schnee, 29 July 1912).

167 RKA 5421, Bl. 24–25 (Colonial Office to Governor Schnee, 29 July 1912). A similar version is in RKA 5426, Bl. 6–7; see also Fischer, "Selbstverwaltung," 345.

168 RKA 5423, Bl. 242 (Vietsch to Seitz, 11 July 1912).

169 RKA 5424, Bl. 51 (judgment of Ludwig Baumann).

170 RKA 5424, Bl. 52 (internal memo, 18 September 1913). Colonial Secretary Solf apparently learned about the Baumann judgment from reading the newspaper in Berlin (the *Berliner Tageblatt* of 8 April 1913). The Colonial Office merely remonstrated with Governor Seitz, tried to avoid publicity about the case, and took refuge in its usual delaying tactics. See RKA 5424, Bl. 26 (Solf to Seitz, 23 April 1913); see also RKA 5424, Bl. 24 (internal memo, April 1913).

171 RKA 5424, Bl. 48 (Seitz to Solf, 23 June 1913).

172 RKA 5421, Bl. 13 (Paul Warncke, "Die Rassenfrage in unseren Kolonien," *Deutsche Tageszeitung*, 19 May 1906).

173 See, for example, Magdalene von Prince, *Eine deutsche Frau im Innern Deutsch-Ostafrikas: Elf Jahre nach Tagebuchblättern erzählt*, 3d ed. (Berlin: E. S. Mittler, 1908), vii.

174 There were 180 European planters in 1905, 315 in 1906, 750 in 1912, and 882 in 1913. The 1905 and 1913 figures are from Horst Gründer, *Geschichte der deutschen Kolonien*, 3d, rev. ed. (Paderborn: Schöningh, 1995), 166; the 1906 and 1912 figures and the comparison with British East Africa are from L. H. Gann and Peter Duignan, *The Rulers of German Africa 1884–1914* (Stanford: Stanford University Press, 1977), 140.

175 Fischer, "Selbstverwaltung," 341–343. Juhani Koponen discusses the recasting of settler society in German East Africa in *Development for Exploitation: German Colonial Policies in Mainland Tanzania, 1884–1914* (Hamburg: Lit, 1995), especially 220–221, 242–258, 272–277, and 287–290.

176 Detlef Bald, *Deutsch-Ostafrika 1900–1914. Eine Studie über Verwaltung, Interessengruppen und wirtschaftliche Erschliessung* (Munich: Weltforum, 1970), 35–74.

177 John Iliffe, *Tanganyika under German Rule* (London: Cambridge University Press, 1969), 49–81, 118–141. Rechenberg was not a democrat, *contra* Bald, *Deutsch-Ostafrika*, 93.

178 Bald, *Deutsch-Ostafrika*, 91–92.

179 Heinrich Schnee, "Die europäische Besiedlung Deutsch-Ostafrikas," *Koloniale Zeitschrift* 13, no. 32 (9 August 1912): 505–506.

180 RKA 5421, Bl. 26 (*Hamburger Nachrichten*, 19 September 1912).

181 RKA 5421, Bl. 22 (marginalia); *Medizinal-Berichte über die Deutschen Schutzgebiete für das Jahr 1903/04* (Berlin: E. S. Mittler, 1905), 72; *Medizinal-Berichte . . . für das Jahr 1905/06* (Berlin: E. S. Mittler, 1907), 80; *Medizinal-Berichte . . . für das Jahr 1907/08* (Berlin: E. S. Mittler, 1909), 15.

182 Jürgen Becher, *Dar es Salaam, Tanga und Tabora: Stadtentwicklung in Tansania unter deutscher Kolonialherrschaft (1885–1914)* (Stuttgart: Franz Steiner, 1997), 141–142.

183 The only example in my sources besides the ones discussed in the present text is a brief mention that "many years ago" a member of the colonial army asked permission to marry an African woman, was refused, and was sent back to Germany (RKA 5421, Bl. 3 [*Berliner Neueste Nachrichten*, 17 April 1906]).

184 Sayyida Salme / Emily Ruete, *An Arabian Princess between Two Worlds: Memoirs, Letters Home, Sequels to the Memoirs, Syrian Customs and Usages*, ed. and intro. E. van Donzel (Leiden: E. J. Brill, 1993), 63–81.

185 John Gray, "Memoirs of an Arabian Princess," *Tanganyika Notes and Records* 37 (July 1954): 49–70.

186 On her memoirs' reception, see Sayyida Salme / Ruete, *An Arabian Princess*, 6–7.

187 Ibid., 422 (quote), 421, 469–471.

188 Ibid., 87.

189 Malek Alloula, *The Colonial Harem* (Minneapolis: University of Minnesota Press, 1986).

190 Eugen Brandeis was governor of the Marshall Islands until 1906, when he was removed from office for cruelty (flogging) and the Marshall Islands were joined to German New Guinea. On Eugen Brandeis, see Dirk H. R. Spennemann, *An Officer, Yes, but a Gentleman? A Biographical Sketch of Eugen Brandeis, Military Adviser, Imperial Judge and Administrator in the German Colonial Service in the South Pacific* (Sydney: Centre for South Pacific Studies, University of New South Wales, 1998). The couple had a daughter, Gretchen, there. See the following by Antonie Brandeis: *Ethnographische Beobachtungen über die Marshall Insulaner* (n.d.); *Südsee-Bilder* (Berlin: Verlag der Kolonialen Zeitschrift, 1902); "Die deutsche Hausfrau in den Kolonien," *Kolonie und Heimat* 1, no. 4 (10 November 1907): 13; and *Kochbuch für die Tropen: Nach langjähriger Erfahrung zusammengestellt* (Berlin: D. Reimer, 1907). She was an early member of the Women's League of the German Colonial Society. In the early 1920s she separated from her husband and lived in Hamburg. Emily Said-Ruete's other daughter, Rosalie, married a man named Troemer. Her third child, a son named Rudolph, married a Jewish-German woman, lived in Egypt for several years, and became an advocate of Arab-Jewish understanding and antiracism. He wrote a biography of his grandfather: Rudolph Said-Ruete, *Said bin Sultan (1791–1856): Ruler of Oman and Zanzibar. His Place in the History of Arabia and East Africa* (London: Alexander-Ouseley, 1929).

191 May Opitz, Katharina Oguntoye, and Dagmar Schultz, eds., *Showing Our Colors: Afro-German Women Speak Out,* trans. Anne V. Adams (Amherst: University of Massachusetts Press, 1992), 56–76; and Katharina Oguntoye, *Eine afro-deutsche Geschichte: Zur Lebenssituation von Afrikanern und Afro-Deutschen in Deutschland von 1884 bis 1950* (Berlin: Hoho Verlag Christine Hoffmann, 1997).

192 RKA 5421, Bl. 13 (Paul Warncke, "Die Rassenfrage in unseren Schutzgebieten," *Deutsche Tageszeitung,* 19 May 1906), Bl. 26 (*Hamburger Nachrichten,* 19 September 1912), Bl. 30 (*Deutsche Tageszeitung,* 11 April 1913); Freiherr Oswald von Richtofen (National Liberal Party), *Stenographische Berichte über die Verhandlungen des Reichstages,* 7 May 1912, 1729.

193 Mtoro bin Mwinyi Bakari, *The Customs of the Swahili People: The Desturi za Waswahili of Mtoro bin Mwinyi Bakari and Other Swahili Persons,* ed. and trans. J. W. T. Allen (Berkeley: University of California Press, 1981), ix.

194 Carl Velten, ed., *Sitten und Gebräuche der Suaheli: Nebst einem Anhang über Rechtsgewohnheiten der Suaheli* (Göttingen: Vandenhoeck & Ruprecht, 1903). The book was published simultaneously in Swahili under the title *Desturi za wasuaheli na khabari za desturi za sheri'a za wasuaheli.*

195 RKA 5422, Bl. 11 (Sachau to Colonial Department, 28 October 1905), and Bl. 61 (Director of Seminar for Oriental Languages to Ministry for Science, Art, and Education, 31 July 1922). On the Oriental Seminar, see Eduard Sachau, "Das Seminar für Orientalische Sprachen," *Geschichte der König-*

lichen Friedrich-Wilhelm-Universität zu Berlin, vol. 3, ed. Max Lenz (Halle: Buchhandlung des Waisenhauses, 1910), 239–247.

196 RKA 5422, Bl. 53 (Gluer to Rechenberg via Colonial Office, 10 December 1907).

197 RKA 5422, Bl. 11 (Sachau to Colonial Department, 28 October 1905).

198 RKA 5422, Bl. 3 (internal memo, 15 June 1904), Bl. 4 (Colonial Department to Sachau, 23 June 1904), Bl. 4–5 (Colonial Department to Götzen, 23 June 1904), Bl. 6 (Götzen to Colonial Department, 2 September 1904), and Bl. 7 (Colonial Department to Mtoro Bakari, 30 September 1904). There is no evidence (such as marginalia) of any official's indignation or even surprise at the marriage plans.

199 Idi Marijani, a Swahili from Bagamoyo, told a different story: friends and pupils suggested that he remain in Germany and start a school of his own, but the German colonial administration required him to return to German East Africa, and he only then decided to go with his wife to take up "duty" there. See Mtoro bin Mwinyi Bakari, *The Customs of the Swahili People,* ix. The Colonial Office records do not indicate that the colonial administration officially assigned him to any position in German East Africa, although in later years he did refer to being invited to become mayor of Bagamoyo (RKA 5422, Bl. 57 [Mtoro Bakari to Ministry for Art, Science, and Education, May 1922]). Sachau and others at the Oriental Seminar and the Colonial Office probably made a number of promises as well as threats.

200 RKA 5422, Bl. 13 (internal memo, 19 November 1915). In fact, Governor von Götzen needed a bureaucratic reason to expel the couple, specifically in order to be able to charge their return passage to some public account, so he declared them to be indigent, the only indisputable way to prevent a German (or other person) from entering the colony. Expulsion on grounds of political discretion probably could have been appealed. See RKA 5422, Bl. 29 (Haber to Colonial Department, 5 July 1906).

201 Idi Marijani, cited in Mtoro bin Mwinyi Bakari, *The Customs of the Swahili People,* ix.

202 RKA 5422, Bl. 24 (Mtoro Bakari to King [of Prussia] Wilhelm, 8 January 1906), and Bl. 37 (Mtoro Bakari to Colonial Director Bernhard Dernburg, 21 December 1906).

203 RKA 5422, Bl. 10 (Hermann Wilder, "Auch etwas zur Eingebornenpolitik," *Usambara Post,* 16 October 1905).

204 For other such inventions, see RKA 5421, Bl. 12–13 (Paul Warncke, "Die Rassenfrage in unseren Schutzgebieten," *Deutsche Tageszeitung,* 19 May 1906).

205 RKA 5422, Bl. 10 (Hermann Wilder, "Auch etwas zur Eingebornenpolitik," *Usambara Post,* 16 October 1905).

206 RKA 5422, Bl. 8 (internal memo, 12 October 1905). Apparently the personnel of that division of the Colonial Office had turned over almost completely

between 1904 and late 1905 (the colonial director changed, too, but not until November 1905). Only three sets of initials are common to both periods; one of these persons protested his innocence and the others offered no written explanation of their actions at that time.

207 RKA 5421, Bl. 18 (*Deutschostafrikanische Zeitung*, 20 April 1907).

208 RKA 5422, Bl. 9 (Colonial Department to Sachau, 21 October 1905), and Bl. 12 (internal memo).

209 RKA 5422, Bl. 12 (Schmidt-Dargitz, 23 November 1905).

210 RKA 5422, Bl. 13 (internal memo, 19 November 1905).

211 RKA 5422, Bl. 14, 15, 18, 19 (internal memos, 1905).

212 RKA 5422, Bl. 36 (marginalia); see also Bl. 24, 28, 39, 45, 49, 51.

213 RKA 5422, Bl. 41 (Lindequist to Police President of Charlottenburg, 10 June 1907).

214 RKA 5422, Bl. 25 (Mtoro Bakari to Wilhelm II, 1 August 1906).

215 RKA 5422, Bl. 57–58 (Mtoro Bakari to the "Government of the German Reich," May 1922).

216 RKA 5422, Bl. 52 (Gluer to Rechenberg, 10 December 1907), and Bl. 27 (CVJM to Colonial Department, 19 June 1906).

217 RKA 5422, Bl. 24 (Mtoro Bakari to William II, 8 January 1906).

218 RKA 5422, Bl. 37 (Mtoro Bakari to Bernhard Dernburg, 21 December 1906).

219 RKA 5421, Bl. 15 (Thiel to Götzen, 22 February 1906).

220 RKA 5421, Bl. 16 (Götzen to Thiel, 17 March 1906).

221 RKA 5421, Bl. 16–17 (Götzen to district officials in Dar es Salaam, Wilhelmstal, Langenburg, Moshi).

222 However, Götzen's assistant, Haber, did cite a legal argument against the permissibility of intermarriage in correspondence with the Colonial Department (RKA 5421, Bl. 14 [Haber to Colonial Department, 12 June 1906]).

223 RKA 5421, Bl. 8 (Hohenlohe to Götzen, 9 May 1906), and Bl. 14 (Haber to Colonial Department, 12 June 1906).

224 RKA 5421, Bl. 6 (*Tägliche Rundschau*, 27 April 1906), and Bl. 28–29 (minutes of the Government Council, 20 and 22 June 1912). Mission Superintendent Martin Klamroth voted in favor of a resolution against intermarriage and mixed sexual relations generally after asking for assurance that African mothers who complained to the district courts would obtain child support for their illegitimate children by white fathers.

225 RKA 5421, Bl. 13 (Paul Warncke, "Die Rassenfrage in unseren Kolonien," *Deutsche Tageszeitung*, 19 May 1906).

226 RKA 5421, Bl. 19 (Conze to Rechenberg, 31 August 1907).

227 RKA 5421, Bl. 22 (Winterfeld to Dernburg, 26 December 1907). The Colonial Office's marginalia contain a worried comment that some of these children did look white.

228 RKA 5421, Bl. 22 (Winterfeld to Dernburg, 26 December 1907).

229 RKA 5421, Bl. 26 (*Hamburger Nachrichten,* 19 September 1912). The Hamburg paper was citing a statement by the board of directors of the Economic Union of the Northern Districts (Wirtschaftlicher Verband der Nordbezirke), an association of planters. The planters had metropolitan allies in the colonialist movement, such as the German-National Colonial Association (Deutschnationaler Kolonialverein). See "Deutschnationaler Kolonialverein," in *Deutsches Kolonial-Lexikon,* ed. Heinrich Schnee (Leipzig: Quelle & Meyer, 1920), 1:315.

230 RKA 5421, Bl. 26 (*Hamburger Nachrichten,* 19 September 1912).

231 *Stenographische Berichte über die Verhandlungen des Reichstages,* no. 380, in *Anlagen* 2 (1912): 325.

232 RKA 5421, Bl. 26 (*Hamburger Nachrichten,* 19 September 1912).

233 RKA 5421, Bl. 35 (Schnee to district offices, 6 September 1913).

234 Karl Oetker, cited in *Kolonialgeschichte im Familienalbum: Frühe Fotos aus der Kolonie Deutsch-Ostafrika,* ed. Norbert Aas and Werena Rosenke (Münster: Unrast, 1992), 81.

235 RKA 5421, Bl. 23 (*Usambara Post,* 16 March 1912, cited in *Hamburger Nachrichten,* 10 April 1912). A socialist deputy to the Reichstag used the image of the policeman's nightstick rather than a pitchfork to make the same point about the inevitability of male sexual desire. Georg Ledebour (SPD), *Stenographische Berichte über die Verhandlungen des Reichstages,* 17 February 1912, 98.

236 RKA 5421, Bl. 26 (*Hamburger Nachrichten,* 19 September 1912).

237 RKA 5421, Bl. 30 (*Deutsche Tageszeitung,* 11 April 1913).

238 The numbers of German men and women were calculated from the census of 1 January 1913, cited in *Deutsches Kolonial-Lexikon,* 3:231. The statistic on mixed couples is taken from *Keetmanshooper Zeitung,* 7 May 1914, 2; whether the men in these marriages were German citizens only or "white" is not clear.

239 Margaret Mead, "Weaver of the Border," in *In the Company of Man. Twenty Portraits by Anthropologists,* ed. Joseph B. Casagrande (New York: Harper & Bros., 1960), 200, 202.

240 See, for example, GStA, Schnee papers, Folder 22a, Bl. 39.

241 RKA 5432, Bl. 82 (Solf to Schultz-Ewerth, 17 January 1912).

242 RKA 5432, Bl. 47–48 (Judge Schultz to Governor Solf, 27 September 1910); and GStA, Schnee papers, Folder 22a (unpublished memoirs), Bl. 127.

243 Smith, *The German Colonial Empire,* 217; and Eberhard von Vietsch, *Wilhelm Solf: Botschafter zwischen den Zeiten* (Tübingen: Rainer Wunderlich Verlag Hermann Leins, 1961), 23, 61–75, 339.

244 Richard Deeken, *Maniua Samoa! Samoanische Reiseskizzen und Beobachtungen* (Oldenburg: Gerhard Stalling, 1901).

245 Vietsch, *Wilhelm Solf,* 68; and Gründer, *Geschichte,* 184–185.

246 RKA 2320, Bl. 132 (judgment of Richard Deeken, 16 June 1904); Vietsch, *Wilhelm Solf,* and RKA 3131, passim.

247 Vietsch, *Wilhelm Solf,* 59, 66.

248 RKA 5432, Bl. 33 (Solf to Dernburg, 15 September 1907); Vietsch, *Wilhelm Solf,* 69, 89–90, 107–108, 116–117. Solf opposed small-scale settlers in any of the colonies and mocked Friedrich von Lindequist, who favored small farmers as governor of German Southwest Africa and colonial secretary, for pursuing "radish politics" (Vietsch, *Wilhelm Solf,* 99).

249 RKA 5432, Bl. 60 (*Rheinisch-Westfälische Zeitung,* 1 August 1911); Franz Kolbe, "Nochmals 'Mischlingssorgen in Samoa,'" *Koloniale Zeitschrift* 13, no. 37 (13 September 1912): 600.

250 RKA 5421, Bl. 18 (*Deutschostafrikanische Zeitung,* 20 April 1907); and RKA 5432, Bl. 22–23 (*Rheinisch-Westfälische Zeitung,* 16 August 1906). On rules that prevented lower-ranking members of the colonial civil service from marrying or from bringing wives with them from Germany to the colonies, see, for example, RKA 5421, Bl. 33 (Schreiber to Colonial Office, 16 July 1913).

251 Klaus Epstein, "Erzberger and the German Colonial Scandals," *English Historical Review* 74 (1959): 663; and Vietsch, *Wilhelm Solf,* 90, 96–97.

252 GStA, Schnee papers, Folder 22a (unpublished memoirs), Bl. 126.

253 RKA 5432, Bl. 8–10, 15–16.

254 Robson, *Queen Emma;* and GStA, Schnee papers, Folder 22a (unpublished memoirs), Bl. 28–29.

255 GStA, Schnee papers, Folder 22a (unpublished memoirs), Bl. 38–39.

256 RKA 5432, Bl. 23 (Solf to Colonial Department, 18 August 1906).

257 RKA 5432, Bl. 25–33 (Solf to Colonial Secretary Dernburg, 15 September 1907), and Bl. 75 (Solf to Colonial Secretary von Lindequist, 3 October 1911); see also Bl. 76.

258 Solf was apparently proud of his analysis, for he repeated it several years later in the Reichstag. The abolition of slavery in the United States was "misguided humaneness" and a "warning sign [*Menetekel*]" for all colonizing nations" (Solf, *Stenographische Berichte über die Verhandlungen des Reichstages,* 2 May 1912, 1648). Solf's use of *menetekel* was a reference to the Bible (Daniel 5:25–28).

259 RKA 5432, Bl. 31 (Solf to Dernburg, 15 September 1907).

260 RKA 5432, Bl. 32 (Solf to Dernburg, 15 September 1907). In August 1908 Solf likewise advocated a ban on intermarriage for Samoa while visiting the Colonial Office in Berlin (RKA 5432, Bl. 34 [internal memo]).

261 RKA 5432, Bl. 43–44 (draft of a decree by Governor Solf, 7 October 1909), Bl. 54 (District Judge Schlettwein to Governor Solf, 19 June 1910), and Bl. 197 (draft of a letter from Colonial Office to von Valentini, March 1914). Franz Kolbe, the editor of *Koloniale Zeitschrift* and an advocate of small-scale

settlers, credited Schlettwein alone with the responsibility for the shift to a more racially conscious policy (Kolbe, "Nochmals 'Mischlingssorgen in Samoa,'" 597). On the two couples, see RKA 5432, Bl. 55–56 (District Judge Schlettwein to Governor Solf, 19 June 1910).

262 RKA 5432, Bl. 52 (District Judge Schlettwein to Governor Solf, 19 June 1910).

263 RKA 5432, Bl. 76 (Solf to Lindequist, 3 October 1911). On the Grevel case, see RKA 5432, Bl. 63–81, 107, 176–179, 183–184, 190–191, 215.

264 RKA 5432, Bl. 79 (Solf to Grevel, 17 January 1912).

265 Solf modeled this provision on British practice, which he admired. See RKA 5421, Bl. 20 (British High Commissioner in Fiji, "Definition [Native] Regulation 1907").

266 RKA 5432, Bl. 108–109 (Solf to all governors, 29 July 1912), and Bl. 170 (Governor Solf to Governor Schultz-Ewerth, 31 March 1913).

267 GStA, Schnee papers, Folder 22a (unpublished memoirs), Bl. 126–127 (quote on 127); and RKA 5432, Bl. 25 and 79.

268 Matthias Erzberger (Catholic Center Party), in *Stenographische Berichte über die Verhandlungen des Reichstages,* 8 May 1912, 1741.

269 Solf, in *Stenographische Berichte über die Verhandlungen des Reichstages,* 2 May 1912, 1648. See also Georg Ledebour (SPD), 2 May 1912, 1650; and Adolf Gröber (Catholic Center Party), 7 May 1912, 1727.

270 *Stenographische Berichte über die Verhandlungen des Reichstages,* 8 May 1912, 1747.

271 Essner, "Zwischen Vernunft und Gefühl," 507–508, 517; and Essner, "Der Kampf um das Kolonialgericht," 78–95, especially 94–95.

272 *Stenographische Berichte über die Verhandlungen des Reichstages,* 5 December 1911, 8365. Colonial Secretary Lindequist resigned in protest against Kiderlen-Wächter's action (Smith, *The German Colonial Empire,* 212–214).

273 "Zur Genese des Mischehenbeschlusses," *Koloniale Korrespondenz,* cited in *Keetmanshooper Zeitung,* 10 July 1912, 4. In fact, the Reichstag had already passed a resolution to restrict the power of decree and increase its own influence over colonial affairs in March 1906, the same month of Governor von Götzen's ban in German East Africa. See *Stenographische Berichte über die Verhandlungen des Reichstages,* 20 March 1906, 2180.

274 "Zur Genese des Mischehenbeschlusses," *Koloniale Korrespondenz,* cited in *Keetmanshooper Zeitung,* 10 July 1912, 4.

275 See, for example, Georg Ledebour (SPD), *Stenographische Berichte über die Verhandlungen des Reichstages,* 7 May 1912, 1736. For an analysis of the racist consensus in the Reichstag debates over intermarriage, see Helmut Walser Smith, "The Talk of Genocide, the Rhetoric of Miscegenation: Notes on Debates in the German Reichstag concerning Southwest Africa, 1904–14," in *The Imperialist Imagination: German Colonialism and Its Legacy,* ed. Sara

Friedrichsmeyer, Sara Lennox, and Susanne Zantop (Ann Arbor: University of Michigan Press, 1998), 107–123.

276 RKA 5421, Bl. 24 (quote), 25 (Colonial Office to Governor Schnee, 29 July 1912).

277 RKA 5421, Bl. 31 (Solf to Governor Schnee, 12 July 1913).

278 See, for example, RKA 5421, Bl. 13 (Paul Warncke, "Die Rassenfrage in unseren Schutzgebieten," *Deutsche Tageszeitung*, 19 May 1906).

4. A NEW COLONIAL FEMININITY: FEMINISM, RACE PURITY, AND DOMESTICITY, 1898–1914

1 Jonathan Steinberg, *Yesterday's Deterrent: Tirpitz and the Birth of the German Battle Fleet* (New York: Macmillan, 1965), 163–193; and Geoff Eley, *Reshaping the German Right: Radical Nationalism and Political Change after Bismarck* (reprint, Ann Arbor: University of Michigan Press, 1991).

2 Mack Walker, *Germany and the Emigration, 1816–1885* (Cambridge: Harvard University Press, 1964).

3 Klaus J. Bade, "From Emigration to Immigration: The German Experience in the Nineteenth and Twentieth Centuries," in *Migration Past, Migration Future: Germany and the United States*, ed. Klaus J. Bade and Myron Wiener (Providence: Berghahn, 1997), 1–37; and Ulrich Herbert, *A History of Foreign Labor in Germany, 1880 1980: Seasonal Workers, Forced Laborers, Guest Workers*, trans. William Templer (Ann Arbor: University of Michigan Press, 1990).

4 Wolfe Schmokel, "The Myth of the White Farmer: Commercial Agriculture in Namibia, 1900–1983," *International Journal of African Historical Studies* 18, no. 1 (1985): 93–108.

5 Woodruff D. Smith, *The Ideological Origins of Nazi Imperialism* (New York: Oxford University Press, 1986), 83–111.

6 On Verein "Frauenwohl," see Ute Gerhard, *Unerhört: Die Geschichte der deutschen Frauenbewegung* (Reinbek bei Hamburg: Rowohlt, 1991), 164, 217–220; and Lida Gustava Heymann and Anita Augspurg, *Erlebtes— Erschautes: Deutsche Frauen kämpfen für Freiheit, Recht und Frieden 1850–1940*, ed. Margrit Twellmann (Meisenheim am Glan: Anton Hain, 1972), 88.

7 [Minna Cauer], "Vor den Wahlen," *Die Frauenbewegung* 4, no. 6 (15 March 1898): 61–62.

8 Else Lüders, *Minna Cauer: Leben und Werk. Dargestellt an Hand ihrer Tagebücher und nachgelassenen Schriften* (Gotha: Leopold Klotz, 1925), 104.

9 C. L., "Eingesandt: Warnung," *Die Frauenbewegung* 4, no. 2 (15 January 1898): 21.

10 A. von Rheinsberg, "Ueber die Sendung deutscher Frauen nach dem Schutzgebiete," *Die Frauenbewegung* 4, no. 11 (1 June 1898): 124–125.

11 Gertrud Bülow von Dennewitz, "Noch einmal über die Frauenauswan-

derung nach Südwest-Afrika," *Die Frauenbewegung* 4, no. 14 (15 July 1898): 153. On Bülow von Dennewitz, see Gerhard, *Unerhört*, 270.

12   Bülow von Dennewitz, "Noch einmal über die Frauenauswanderung," 153.

13   On "domesticating colonialism," see Susanne Zantop, *Colonial Fantasies: Conquest, Family, and Nation in Precolonial Germany, 1770–1870* (Durham: Duke University Press, 1997), 121–140.

14   [Minna Cauer], "Zur Frauen-Kolonisationsfrage," *Die Frauenbewegung* 4, no. 7 (1 April 1898): 78.

15   Ibid.

16   [Cauer], "Zur Frauen-Kolonisationsfrage," 77.

17   Theodor Leutwein, "Offener Brief an die Herausgeberin," *Die Frauenbewegung* 4, no. 9 (1 May 1898): 99–100.

18   While Leutwein refused to meet with Cauer, eventually Friedrich von Lindequist did. See RKA 6693, Bl. 3–4 (Cauer to Dernburg, 18 January 1907). Lindequist, then a member of the Colonial Department and later governor of Southwest Africa (1905–1907) and colonial secretary (1910–1911), was a radical nationalist and advocate of small-scale family settlement and race purity. Their meeting was inconclusive, but the fact that he was willing to meet with her at all was another indication that male advocates of race purity were the most likely to take seriously the participation of women.

19   *Stenographische Berichte über die Verhandlungen des Reichstages,* 11 March 1899, 1471–1477. For more detail, see Karen Smidt, "'Germania führt die deutsche Frau nach Südwest': Auswanderung, Leben und soziale Konflikte deutscher Frauen in der ehemaligen Kolonie Deutsch-Südwestafrika 1884–1920. Eine sozial- und frauengeschichtliche Studie" (Ph.D. diss., University of Magdeburg, 1995), 45–50; and Krista O'Donnell, "The Colonial Woman Question: Gender, National Identity, and Empire in the German Colonial Society Female Emigration Program, 1896–1914" (Ph.D. diss., Binghamton University, 1996), 59–65, 67. A second men's organization with considerable overlap with the German Colonial Society's membership, the Evangelical Association for Africa (Evangelischer Afrikaverein), also helped establish the settlement scheme.

20   RKA 6693, Bl. 5 ("Vorschläge für die Übersiedelung von Mädchen nach den deutschen Kolonien"). This pamphlet was reprinted in *Die Frauenbewegung, Beilage,* no. 8 (15 June 1899): 29–30.

21   Ibid.

22   Ibid. *Gebildet* also carries the meanings "cultured" and "refined." On the United British Women's Emigration Society, see A. James Hammerton, *Emigrant Gentlewomen: Genteel Poverty and Female Emigration, 1830–1914* (London: Croom Helm, 1979).

23   Minna Cauer, "Falscher Weg," *Die Frauenbewegung* 5, no. 7 (1 April 1899): 61–63; see also Minna Cauer, "Die Uebersiedlung deutscher Frauen nach den Kolonien," *Die Frauenbewegung* 5, no. 15 (1 August 1899): 129–130.

24 Lüders, *Minna Cauer*, 138–139.

25 [Minna Cauer], "Weckrufe," *Die Frauenbewegung* 12, no. 24 (15 December 1906): 186.

26 Kolonialpolitisches Aktionskomitee, ed., *Schmoller, Dernburg, Delbrück, Schäfer, Sering, Schillings, Brunner, Jastrow, Penck, Kahl über Reichstagsauflösung und Kolonialpolitik. Offizieller stenographischer Bericht über die Versammlung in der Berliner Hochschule für Musik am 8. Januar 1907* (Berlin: Dr. Wedekind, 1907).

27 On the Prussian Law of Association, see Gerhard, *Unerhört*, 73–74.

28 RKA 6693, Bl. 7 (mimeographed flier). See Rohrbach, *Deutsche Kolonialwirtschaft* (Berlin-Schöneberg: Buchverlag der "Hilfe," 1907), 393, in which he advocated the settlement of German couples over single German men.

29 RKA 6693, Bl. 3 (Cauer to Dernburg, 18 January 1907).

30 RKA 6693, Bl. 9 (Dernburg to Cauer, 19 January 1907).

31 Lüders, *Minna Cauer*, 139.

32 Ibid.

33 *Kolonie und Heimat* 1, no. 19 (6 June 1908): 10.

34 Gertrud von Richtofen-Damsdorf, "Der Frauenbund der Deutschen Kolonialgesellschaft," in *Hedwig Heyl: Ein Gedenkblatt zu ihrem 70. Geburtstage dem 5. Mai 1920 von ihren Mitarbeitern und Freunden*, ed. Elise von Hopffgarten (Berlin: Dietrich Reimer [Ernst Vohsen], 1920), 119. A private letter from Philalethes Kuhn to Ludwig Sander mentions that during a hiatus after the transports of 1898 and 1899, Sander had suggested handing over the program to women and founding a "colonial women's organization" (DKG 154, Bl. 124–125 [Kuhn to Sander, 28 January 1910]). See also DKG 153, Bl. 14 (Sander to Weitzenberg, 2 May 1907), and Bl. 15 (Mecklenburg to Liliencron, 17 May 1907).

35 See, for example, *Stenographische Berichte über die Verhandlungen des Reichstages*, 29 April 1912, 1518–1519, 7 May 1912, 1730, and 20 March 1914, 8146.

36 Adda von Liliencron, *Krieg und Frieden: Erinnerungen aus dem Leben einer Offiziersfrau* (Berlin: R. Eisenschmidt, 1912), 299.

37 Liliencron, *Krieg*, 3–4, 13.

38 Ibid., 40, 42; see also 47.

39 Ibid., 110, 125, 140 (quote). Her group of volunteers was presumably a local chapter of the Patriotic Women's Leagues.

40 Ibid., 141, 147–148, 191–198, 239, 240, 249, 260.

41 Ibid., 263–265, 276 (quote).

42 Adda von Liliencron, *Getreu bis zuletzt* (Berlin 1912).

43 Liliencron, *Krieg*, 262.

44 Ibid., 111, 125, 186, 259–260, 298, 303–306, 309, 310.

45 *Wer ist's* (Leipzig: H. A. Ludwig Degener, 1906), 706.

46 Liliencron, *Krieg*, 268.

47 Ibid., 268–269.

48 Ibid., 272; see also 269–270.

49 Ibid., 272; see also 273.

50 Ibid., 273–275.

51 Adda von Liliencron, *Kriegsklänge der kaiserlichen Schutztruppe in Deutsch-Südwestafrika* (1905); and Liliencron, *Reiterbriefe aus Südwest: Briefe und Gedichte aus dem Feldzuge in Südwest-Afrika in den Jahren 1904–1906* (Oldenburg: Gerhard Stalling, 1907).

52 Liliencron, *Krieg*, 280–281.

53 DKG 153, Bl. 101 (*Vossische Zeitung*, 7 November 1907).

54 Liliencron, *Krieg*, 281. German colonists who dealt with German Southwest Africa were fond of using Afrikaans words such as *orlog*.

55 Ibid.

56 DKG 153, Bl. 12 (Women's League flier, 1908). The flier cited the census of 1907, which counted 1,179 German women and 4,899 German men in that colony.

57 DKG 153, Bl. 12–13 (Women's League flier, 1908).

58 DKG 154, Bl. 22 ("Aufruf zur Sammlung für ein Mädchen-Heim in Keetmanshoop").

59 DKG 153, Bl. 12 (Women's League flier, 1908).

60 LAB, Vereinsregister, Frauenbund der Deutschen Kolonialgesellschaft, A/a/3, aa. Nr. 6, Bl. 1 (*Satzung des Frauenbundes der Deutschen Kolonialgesellschaft*); and DKG 153, Bl. 8 (*Deutschkolonialer Frauenbund. Satzungen*, Berlin, 1907).

61 DKG 153, Bl. 164–165 (Sander to Beck, 6 June 1908).

62 Liliencron, *Krieg*, 301; see also Roger Chickering, "'Casting Their Gaze More Broadly': Women's Patriotic Activism in Imperial Germany," *Past and Present* 118 (February 1988): 176, 182–183.

63 See, for example, Uwe Timm, *Deutsche Kolonien* (Munich: AutorenEdition, 1981), 38–39; Marie Lorbeer and Beate Wild, eds., *Menschenfresser, Negerküsse: Das Bild vom Fremden im deutschen Alltag* (Berlin: Elefanten-Press, 1993), 48; and the film *Wir hatten eine Dora in Südwest,* dir. Tink Diaz (Germany, 1991).

64 RKA 5147, Bl. 208–209, 220, 227–229 (correspondence among German consulate in Vienna, Foreign Office, and Reichsminister für Wiederaufbau [colonial administration], 1921–1922). Anna Teho Ramsay, who lived in Vienna, was seeking regularization of her name and German citizenship; this was refused her.

65 On these groups, see Richard V. Pierard, "The German Colonial Society, 1882–1914," in *Germans in the Tropics,* ed. Arthur J. Knoll and Lewis H. Gann (Westport, Conn.: Greenwood Press, 1987), 287–288. The German-Populist Colonial Association praised the Women's League and criticized the German Colonial Society in its periodical, *Koloniale Zeitschrift.*

66 DKG 153, Bl. 45 (*Kolonie und Heimat in Wort und Bild,* Probenummer, 15 July 1907, 2).

67 Ibid.

68 Ibid. At a cost to the general public of two marks and sixty pfennigs a year, it was much cheaper than the publications of the German Colonial Society (eight marks) and Women's Association for Nursing (six marks).

69 DKG 153, Bl. 40–41 (Liliencron to Mecklenburg, 5 August 1907).

70 Ibid. (quotes); and DKG 153, Bl. 58 (memo by Richard Volkmann). On Liliencron's efforts to keep dues low, see DKG 153, Bl. 123–124 (Liliencron to Mecklenburg, 12 December 1907), Bl. 126 (German Colonial Society to Liliencron, 20 December 1907), Bl. 127 (German Colonial Society to Ludwig Sander, 23 December 1907), Bl. 127a (Liliencron to Sander, n.d.), Bl. 128–129 (Sander to Liliencron, 31 December 1907), and Bl. 218 (Liliencron to Mecklenburg, 29 August 1908). Dues for the Women's League were always at least a mark cheaper than those for the Women's Association for Nursing. See LAB, Vereinsregister, Frauenbund der Deutschen Kolonialgesellschaft, Bd. 1, Bl. 107, 118 (Women's League statutes).

71 DKG 153, Bl. 42 (letter from Dernburg, 8 May 1907), and Bl. 43 (letter from Bülow, 15 May 1907).

72 DKG 153, Bl. 128–129 (Sander to Liliencron, 31 December 1907).

73 See, for example, DKG 153, Bl. 180 (minutes of German Colonial Society annual convention, 12 June 1908), and Bl. 272 (Volkmann to *Deutsche Kolonialzeitung,* 27 March 1909).

74 See, for example, DKG 153, Bl. 122 (Sander to Liliencron, n.d. [ca. November 1907]); DKG 154, Bl. 26 (Winkler to Women's League, 26 July 1909), Bl. 28 (Richtofen to DKG, 27 July 1909), Bl. 54 (Sander to Women's League, 22 October 1909), Bl. 57 (Ramsay to German Colonial Society, 28 October 1909), Bl. 85–86 (Richtofen to DKG, 3 December 1909), and Bl. 233 (Winkler to Women's League, 22 August 1910); and DKG 155, Bl. 1–3 (memos by Winkler), Bl. 17 (German Colonial Society to Frl. von Wedell, 14 November 1911), and Bl. 62 (Winkler to Women's League, 30 October 1911). See also Winkler, "Aussendung von Frauen und Mädchen nach Südwest," *Deutsche Kolonialzeitung* 27 (1910): 551–552; Winkler, "Aussendung von Frauen und Mädchen nach Deutsch-Südwestafrika," *Deutsche Kolonialzeitung* 28 (1911): 652–653; and Winkler, "Zur kolonialen Frauenfrage," *Deutsche Kolonialzeitung* 29 (1912): 258.

75 Else Frobenius, *10 Jahre Frauenbund der Deutschen Kolonialgesellschaft* (Berlin: "Kolonie und Heimat" Verlagsgesellschaft, 1918), 41–82.

76 Paul Rohrbach, "Der koloniale Frauenbund," *Das grössere Deutschland,* 1, no. 12 (27 June 1914): 341–345; DKG 154, Bl. 18 (Irmgard von Richtofen to DKG, 13 July 1909), and Bl. 75 (Ramsay to *Zeitschrift für Kolonialpolitik, Kolonialrecht und Kolonialwirtschaft,* 18 November 1909); and *Deutsches Kolonialblatt* 20, no. 23 (1 December 1909): 113.

77 On both Kuhns, see their son Roland Kuhn's biography: *Lebensbild von Maria Kuhn geb. Ritter und Philalethes Kuhn* (Bonn: privately published, 1964); and Richard Volkmann, "Generaloberarzt Professor Dr. Kuhn," *Die Frau und die Kolonien*, no. 9 (September 1937): 132–134.

78 Paul Rohrbach, *Aus Südwest-Afrikas schweren Tagen: Blätter von Arbeit und Abschied* (Berlin: Wilhelm Weicher, 1909), 40.

79 Wolfgang Eckart, "Malaria-Prävention und Rassentrennung: Die ärztliche Vorbereitung und Rechtfertigung der Duala-Enteignung 1912–1914," *History and Philosophy of the Life Sciences* 10 (1988): 363–378.

80 On the relationship between colonialism and the natural sciences in the Kaiserreich, see Pascal Grosse, *Kolonialismus, Eugenik und bürgerliche Gesellschaft in Deutschland, 1850–1918* (Frankfurt: Campus, 2000).

81 DKG 155, Bl. 12 (Thiessen to Women's League, 5 December 1911); see also DKG 153, Bl. 161, 163 (Liliencron to Beck, 27 May 1908), Bl. 179–180 (motion of Berlin chapter of German Colonial Society), Bl. 183–184 (Liliencron to Mecklenburg, 7 July 1908), Bl. 290 (motion of Berlin chapter of German Colonial Society), Bl. 285 (minutes of German Colonial Society executive committee, 14 May 1909); and DKG 155, Bl. 19–48 (memo by Schulte im Hof and documents related to Kuhn's dispute over the Women's League Berlin chapters).

82 Ludwig Külz, *Blätter und Briefe eines Arztes aus dem tropischen Deutschafrika* (Berlin: Wilhelm Süsserott, 1906); reprinted in 1910 and 1943.

83 Hans Ziemann, *Wie erobert man Afrika für die weisse und farbige Rasse?* (Leipzig: Johann Ambrosius, 1907), 27.

84 Han Ziemann, *Über das Bevölkerungs- und Rassenproblem in den Kolonien: Vortrag gehalten am 31. Oktober 1912 in der Deutschen Kolonial-Gesellschaft, Abteilung Westliche Vororte* (Berlin: Wilhelm Süsserott, 1912), 9. See also Richard Hindorf's comments in *Unter dem rothen Kreuz* 4, no. 3 (March 1893): 23; Karl Daeubler, "Die Möglichkeit der Kolonisation und Anpassung der Europäer an die Tropen," *Deutsche Kolonialzeitung* 7, no. 7 (23 June 1894): 93–95; and Albert Plehn, "Die Akklimatisationsaussichten der Germanen im tropischen Africa," in *Verhandlungen des Deutschen Kolonialkongresses 1910* (Berlin: Dietrich Reimer [Ernst Vohsen], 1910), 888–906, especially 898, 903. In 1911 the Association for Social Policy took up the issue of European family settlement in the Tropics (RKA 6281, passim; see also RKA 6279). In general, boosters of family settlement and white supremacy such as Philalethes Kuhn and Hans Ziemann tended to downplay the dangers of the tropics for women, while their opponents who favored large-scale business or indirect rule usually argued that white women could not remain healthy there, especially as mothers. Pascal Grosse documents how politics drove innovation in medical opinion about acclimatization in his *Kolonialismus, Eugenik und bürgerliche Gesellschaft*, 53–95. See also

the discussion of liberalism and acclimatization in Ann L. Stoler, "Sexual Affronts and Racial Frontiers: European Identities and the Cultural Politics of Exclusion in Colonial Southeast Asia," *Comparative Studies in Society and History* 34 (1992): 514–551.

85 According to Nancy Rose Hunt, white women's settlement and maternity in the Belgian Congo was thought feasible by some as early as 1910, but was generally accepted only in the 1940s. See Nancy Rose Hunt, "'Le bébé en brousse': European Women, African Birth Spacing, and Colonial Intervention in Breast Feeding in the Belgian Congo," in *Tensions of Empire: Colonial Cultures in a Bourgeois World,* ed. Frederick Cooper and Ann L. Stoler (Berkeley: University of California Press, 1997), 287–321, especially 293–297. Ann Stoler notes that white women's emigration from the Netherlands to the Dutch East Indies increased sharply only in the 1920s ("Sexual Affronts," 544). Alice Conklin indicates a similar chronology for France, placing the shift in opinion toward the viability of white women as mothers in French West Africa in the 1920s, in *A Mission to Civilize: The Republican Idea of Empire in France and West Africa, 1895–1930* (Stanford: Stanford University Press, 1997), 168–171; and Conklin, "Redefining 'Frenchness': Citizenship, Race Regeneration, and Imperial Motherhood in France and West Africa, 1914–40," in *Domesticating the Empire: Race, Gender and Family Life in French and Dutch Colonialism,* ed. Julia Clancy-Smith and Frances Gouda (Charlottesville: University Press of Virginia, 1998), 65–83.

86 The names of three nobles — Frieda von Bülow, Frau Major von Wolff, and Intendantur-Rat (a lower colonial army officer's position) Edmund von Lagiewski — appeared in May 1907 in the Women's League's first public appeal. However, correspondence from the first months of the Women's League makes no mention of Bülow or Wolff, which suggests that their names were summoned for public display. Lagiewski served as treasurer but was soon replaced by the nonnoble Richard Volkmann. When Liliencron accepted the invitation to become chairwoman, that added a fourth noble name; finally, Duchess Elisabeth of Mecklenburg (wife of the chairman of the German Colonial Society) was the first "protectress" of the league. However, she was much more closely involved in the Women's Association for Nursing.

87 DKG 153, Bl. 218 (Liliencron to Mecklenburg, 29 August 1908).

88 DKG 153, Bl. 242 (Liliencron to Mecklenburg, n.d., received 21 October 1908) (quote). See also Bl. 246 (Sander to Women's League, 28 October 1909), and Bl. 249 (Sander to Women's League, 13 November 1908); and DKG 155, Bl. 101 (Oechelhäuser to DKG, 25 May 1911), and Bl. 5 (Strauch to Thiessen, 23 December 1911).

89 DKG 153, Bl. 218 (Liliencron to Mecklenburg, 28 August 1908). On the veterans' associations of the "little people" — urban and rural workers, peas-

ants, and artisans—see Thomas Rohkrämer, *Der Militarismus der "kleinen Leute": Die Kriegervereine im Deutschen Kaiserreich 1871–1914* (Munich: R. Oldenbourg, 1990), especially 35.

90 For 1909 (3,954 women and 463 men), see Frobenius, *10 Jahre*, 8. For 1910, see Chickering, "Casting Their Gaze," 177 n. 50.

91 For example, the sex reform organization led by the important radical feminist Helene Stöcker, the League for the Protection of Mothers (Bund für Mutterschutz), had a 35 percent male membership (2,424 women and 1,302 men). See Kaiserliches Statistisches Amt, ed., *Statistik der Frauenorganisationen im Deutschen Reiche* (Berlin: Carl Heymann, 1909), 18; and Richard J. Evans, *The Feminist Movement in Germany 1894–1933* (London: Sage, 1976), 129. Even the Federation for Woman Suffrage (Verband für Frauenstimmrecht) had 216 men along with 2,242 women (ibid., 94).

92 DKG 153, Bl. 9 (1907 statutes).

93 DKG 155, Bl. 2–3 (Winkler to Stein, 29 December 1911); and Hedwig Heyl, *Aus meinem Leben* (Berlin: C. A. Schwetschke, 1925), 87.

94 DKG 155, Bl. 2–3 (Winkler to Stein, 29 December 1911).

95 DKG 155, Bl. 9 (Kirchner to German Colonial Society, 29 November 1911).

96 DKG 155, Bl. 2 (Winkler to Stein, 29 December 1911), Bl. 4 (Strauch [?] to Women's League, 27 December 1911), Bl. 5 (Strauch [?] to Thiessen, 23 December 1911), and Bl. 11 (Thiessen to Henoch, 30 November 1911).

97 DKG 154, Bl. 265 (Heyl to Mecklenburg, 6 December 1910) (quote); DKG 155, Bl. 9 (Kirchner to German Colonial Society, 29 November 1911), Bl. 117 (Holleben to Heyl, 28 February 1911), and Bl. 112 (Heyl to Holleben, 2 March 1911).

98 On Clara Brockmann's and Maria Karow's agitation for the Women's League, see DKG 153, Bl. 232 (Liliencron to Mecklenburg, 30 September 1908); and Frobenius, *10 Jahre*, 41, 43, 62, 77, 80.

99 On the internal workings of some of these texts as opposed to their propaganda function, see Marcia Klotz, "Memoirs from a German Colony: What Do White Women Want?" in *Eroticism and Containment: Notes from the Flood Plain*, ed. Carol Siegel and Ann Kibbey (New York: New York University Press, 1994), 154–187 (on Margarethe von Eckenbrecher, Ada Cramer, and Brockmann); and Lora Wildenthal, "'She Is the Victor': Bourgeois Women, Nationalist Identities, and the Ideal of the Independent Woman Farmer in German Southwest Africa," in *Society, Culture, and the State in Germany, 1870–1930*, ed. Geoff Eley (Ann Arbor: University of Michigan Press, 1997), 371–395 (on Brockmann).

100 On radical nationalist men's interest in agrarian utopia, see Smith, *The Ideological Origins of Nazi Imperialism*, 83–111, and references cited therein. On feminists' interest in the farm and overcoming the division between home and workplace, see Lily Braun, *Die Frauenfrage: Ihre geschichtliche Entwicklung und wirtschaftliche Seite* (Leipzig: Hirzel, 1901); and Elisabeth

Gnauck-Kühne, *Die soziale Lage der Frau* (Berlin: Liebmann, 1895). Agriculture was the leading employment sector for women in Germany until the First World War. See Volker Berghahn, *Imperial Germany* (Providence: Berghahn Books, 1994), 309.

101 A guide to this literature may be found in *Die Frauenfrage in Deutschland: Strömungen und Gegenströmungen 1790–1930,* ed. Hans Sveistrup and Agnes von Zahn-Harnack (Burg b.M.: August Hopfer, 1934), 479–503.

102 Magdalene von Prince, *Eine deutsche Frau im Innern Deutsch-Ostafrikas: Elf Jahre nach Tagebuchblättern erzählt,* 3d ed. (Berlin: E. S. Mittler, 1908).

103 Anonymous, *Aus Südwestafrika: Blätter aus dem Tagebuch einer deutschen Frau 1902–1904* (Leipzig: Veit, 1905); Anonymous [Julia Jobst], *Musste es sein?* (Munich: Friedrich Rothbarth, 1904); Else Sonnenberg, *Wie es am Waterberg zuging: Ein Beitrag zur Geschichte des Hereroaufstandes* (Berlin: Wilhelm Süsserott, 1905); and Helene von Falkenhausen, *Ansiedlerschicksale: Elf Jahre in Deutsch-Südwestafrika 1893–1904* (Berlin: Dietrich Reimer [Ernst Vohsen], 1905). See also the shorter sketches in *Deutsch-Südwestafrika: Kriegs- und Friedensbilder. Selbsterlebnisse,* ed. Margarethe von Eckenbrecher, Helene von Falkenhausen, Philalethes Kuhn, and Stuhlmann (Leipzig: Wilhelm Weicher, 1907).

104 O'Donnell, "The Colonial Woman Question," 210–216; and Mechthild Rommel and Hulda Rautenberg, *Die kolonialen Frauenschulen von 1908–1945* (Witzenhausen: Gesamthochschule Kassel — Fachbereich Internationale Agrarwirtschaft in Witzenhausen et al., 1983), 11–20.

105 DKG 154, Bl. 169 (minutes of Women's League executive committee, 14 March 1910).

106 Margarethe von Eckenbrecher, *Was Afrika mir gab und nahm: Erlebnisse einer deutschen Ansiedlerfrau in Südwestafrika* (Berlin: E. S. Mittler, 1907). Eckenbrecher also wrote a book about her experiences in German East Africa and urged women not to be deterred by the climate there: Margarete von Eckenbrecher, *Im dichten Pori: Reise- und Jagdbilder aus Deutsch-Ostafrika* (Berlin: E. S. Mittler, 1912), especially vii–viii.

107 DKG 153, Bl. 241 (Winkler to Liliencron, 19 October 1908); and Frobenius, *10 Jahre,* 65, 68–69, 72, 81.

108 Margarethe von Eckenbrecher, *Was Afrika mir gab und nahm: Erlebnisse einer deutschen Frau in Südwestafrika 1902–1936,* 7th ed. (Berlin: E. S. Mittler, 1937), 156.

109 Maria Karow, *Wo sonst der Fuss des Kriegers trat: Farmerleben in Südwest nach dem Kriege* (Berlin: E. S. Mittler, 1909); Clara Brockmann, *Die deutsche Frau in Südwestafrika: Ein Beitrag zur Frauenfrage in unseren Kolonien* (Berlin: E. S. Mittler, 1910); and Brockmann, *Briefe eines deutschen Mädchens aus Südwest* (Berlin: E. S. Mittler, 1912).

110 This gender-linked pattern of opinion was not confined to German colonialists. For an analogous situation in the case of U.S. colonialism in the Philip-

pines, see Warwick Anderson, "The Trespass Speaks: White Masculinity and Colonial Breakdown," *American Historical Review* 102 (1997): 1354.

111 Frieda Zieschank, *Ein Jahrzehnt auf Samoa (1906–1916)* (Leipzig: E. Haberland, 1918), 13.

112 Grete Ziemann, *Mola Koko! Grüsse aus Kamerun. Tagebuchblätter* (Berlin: Wilhelm Süsserott, 1907), 177.

113 Ibid.

114 Ibid., 178.

115 Liliencron had been forced to leave office for family and health reasons; Baroness Irmgard von Richtofen, the wife of prominent geographer and China specialist Ferdinand von Richtofen, was already ill when she took office in 1909; she died in 1910.

116 Frobenius, *10 Jahre,* 8, 11.

117 See membership lists in *Kolonie und Heimat* 1 (1907–1908); and DKG 153, Bl. 248 (Winkler to Women's League, 10 November 1908).

118 Heyl, *Aus meinem Leben,* 39–40.

119 They were Paula Mueller and Frl. von Carnap (Frobenius, *10 Jahre,* 40).

120 This is Richard J. Evans's argument in *The Feminist Movement.* Other historians of feminism have relativized and differentiated his interpretation, but this aspect of it remains valid.

121 Hedwig Heyl, "Hauswirtschaftliche Bildung und Volkskultur," in *Der deutsche Frauenkongress. Berlin, 27. Februar bis 2. März 1912. Sämtliche Vorträge herausgegeben im Auftrage des Vorstandes des Bundes Deutscher Frauenvereine,* ed. Gertrud Bäumer (Leipzig: Teubner, 1912), 5; see also Chickering, "Casting Their Gaze More Broadly," 178–179.

122 Although she affiliated herself with the National Liberals, she claimed a special admiration for the Progressives (Freisinnigen), including Ludwig Bamberger, Eugen Richter, and Karl Schrader. See *Wer ist's* (Leipzig: H. A. Ludwig Degener, 1914), 691; and Heyl, *Aus meinem Leben,* 21.

123 Heyl, *Aus meinem Leben,* 3.

124 Breymann married Karl Schrader in 1872 and moved to Berlin, where she founded the Verein für häusliche Gesundheitspflege, the Viktoriahaus für Krankenpflege (a secular nursing order that Frieda von Bülow's sister Sophie joined), the Pestalozzi-Fröbelhaus (which trained kindergarten teachers), and its supporting agency the Verein für Volkserziehung (of which Heyl was a cofounder). On Fröbel and Breymann, see Ann Taylor Allen, *Feminism and Motherhood in Germany 1800–1914* (New Brunswick: Rutgers University Press, 1991), 111–131.

125 Heyl, *Aus meinem Leben,* 33.

126 Ibid., 5.

127 Karl Schrader was director of railroads for various companies and for the Deutsche Bank; he also represented the Progressive Union (Freisinnige Vereinigung), a left-liberal splinter party, in the Reichstag; after 1910 he joined

the Progressive People's Party (Fortschrittliche Volkspartei). Schrader contributed to his wife's work for the Pestalozzi-Fröbelhaus and Verein für Volkserziehung.

128 Heyl, *Aus meinem Leben*, 12.

129 Ibid., 28–30, 33.

130 Anna von Gierke, "Entwicklung des Jugendheims," in *Hedwig Heyl*, 71–76; and Heyl, *Aus meinem Leben*, 33.

131 Heyl, *Aus meinem Leben*, 28, 160.

132 Marie von Bunsen, *Die Welt in der ich lebte: Erinnerungen aus glücklichen Jahren 1860–1912* (Leipzig: Koehler & Amelang, 1929), 195. Heyl turned the gardening school over to another protegée, Ida von Kortzfleisch, who established a series of so-called Reifenstein gardening schools and became a well-known proponent of gardening and landscape architecture as women's careers.

133 Marie Stritt, ed., *Der Internationale Frauen-Kongress in Berlin 1904* (Berlin: Carl Habel, 1905); and Deutscher Lyzeum-Club, ed., *Ausstellung Die Frau in Haus und Beruf Berlin 1912* (Berlin: Rudolf Mosse, 1912).

134 DKG 154, Bl. 209 (minutes of Women's League executive committee, 2 May 1910), and Bl. 241 (minutes of the Women's League executive committee, 3 October 1910).

135 DKG 154, Bl. 118–119 (minutes of Women's League executive committee, 3 January 1910), Bl. 162 (minutes of the Women's League executive committee, 31 January 1910), Bl. 170 (minutes of Women's League executive committee, 14 March 1910); DKG 154, Bl. 235 (minutes of the Women's League executive committee, 1 July 1910); and Gilla Dölle, *Die (un)heimliche Macht des Geldes: Finanzierungsstrategien der bürgerlichen Frauenbewegung in Deutschland zwischen 1865 und 1933* (Frankfurt a.M.: dipa-Verlag, 1997), 69–82.

136 See DKG 154, Bl. 94 (minutes of the Women's League executive committee, 24 November 1909); Heyl, *Aus meinem Leben*, 83; and Frobenius, *10 Jahre*, 15, 19, 22.

137 DKG 154, Bl. 99 (minutes of the Women's League executive committee, 6 December 1909).

138 DKG 154, Bl. 118 (minutes of the Women's League executive committee, 3 January 1910), Bl. 163 (minutes of the Women's League executive committee, 31 January 1910), and Bl. 247 (Burckhardt to German Colonial Society, n.d., received 19 November 1910).

139 Hedwig Heyl, *ABC der Küche*, 4th ed. (Berlin: Carl Habel, 1897). It was reprinted as late as 1938.

140 Else Frobenius, "Der goldene Schlüssel. Erinnerungen aus meinem Leben," 103. This is a typescript written in 1942–1944 and now held in a private family archive. See also Ute Daniel, *The War from Within: German Working-Class Women in the First World War* (New York: Berg, 1997), 73.

141 On Heyl's myriad activities, see Heidi Koschwitz-Newby, "Hedwig Heyl: Die beste Hausfrau Berlins," in *Unter allen Umständen: Frauengeschichte(n) in Berlin,* ed. Christiane Eifert and Susanne Rouette (Berlin: Rotation, 1986), 60–79 (unfortunately the author jumbles statistics and dates related to the Women's League); *Wer ist's* (Leipzig: H. A. Ludwig Degener, 1914), 691; Gerhard, *Unerhört,* 210–212, 374; and Rommel and Rautenberg, *Die kolonialen Frauenschulen,* 7–8. On feminists' views of Heyl, see Gertrud Bäumer, "Hedwig Heyl in der deutschen Frauenbewegung," in *Hedwig Heyl,* 142; and Koschwitz-Newby, "Hedwig Heyl," 73. See also the remarks of Hellmut von Gerlach, who found Heyl unbearably conservative, in Margrit Twellmann, ed., *Die deutsche Frauenbewegung: Ihre Anfänge und erste Entwicklung 1843–1889* (Meisenheim am Glan: Anton Hain, 1972), 273. The lengthiest recent treatment and contextualization of Heyl's work is in Allen, *Feminism and Motherhood,* 99, 111–131. Most briefer accounts ignore Heyl's role in colonialist agitation, although Heyl herself devoted a chapter of her memoirs to it. See, for example, Twellmann, ed., *Die deutsche Frauenbewegung,* 273; Gerhard, *Unerhört,* 210, 212, 374; and the local history by Arbeitsgruppe Historischer Stadtrundgang, *"O Charlottenburg, du frauenfreundlichste unter den Städten . . .": Wege zur Frauengeschichte Charlottenburgs 1850–1930* (Berlin: Frauenforschungs- bildungs- und informationszentrum, 1989), 5, 37.

142 Hedwig Heyl, cited in *Centralblatt des Bundes Deutscher Frauenvereine,* reprinted in *Kolonie und Heimat* 5, no. 18 (1911): 8.

143 Elise von Hopffgarten, "Lebensbild," in *Hedwig Heyl,* 14.

144 Bunsen, *Die Welt in der ich lebte,* 98.

145 Anna Davin, "Imperialism and Motherhood," *History Workshop Journal* 5 (1978): 9–65; and Nancy R. Reagin, *A German Women's Movement: Class and Gender in Hanover, 1880–1933* (Chapel Hill: University of North Carolina Press, 1995), especially 23–97.

146 Bunsen, *Die Welt in der ich lebte,* 97.

147 Heyl, *Aus meinem Leben,* 39–40.

148 The Women's League also forbade the women it sponsored from accepting jobs in bars because that was thought to lead to prostitution. See DKG 154, Bl. 242 (minutes of the Women's League executive committee, 3 October 1910); and DKG 155, Bl. 146 (Heyl to Mecklenburg, 16 January 1911).

149 Frobenius, *10 Jahre,* 18.

150 Ibid.

151 Ibid., 8.

152 On the experiences of the women sponsored by the program, see Krista O'Donnell, "The Colonial Woman Question," passim; Winkler, "Zur kolonialen Frauenfrage," 258; Richard Pierard, "The Transportation of White Women to German Southwest Africa, 1898–1914," *Race* 12 (1971): 317–322.

153 Frobenius, *10 Jahre*, 17.

154 See, for example, "Aus der Frauenbewegung," *Die Frauenbewegung* 4, no. 18 (15 September 1898): 196 (which notes that six to seven hundred women made inquiries with Leutwein during his tour of Germany in 1898); DKG 153, Bl. 34 (Mathilde Princzinski [?] to German Colonial Society, 9 July 1907), Bl. 20–24 (inquiries from a journalist and bookkeeper), Bl. 117, 125, and 201 (two teachers), Bl. 182, 186–187 (a woman medical doctor), and Bl. 248 (Winkler to Women's League, 10 November 1908).

155 DKG 153, Bl. 24 (German Colonial Society to Ringer, 27 June 1907), Bl. 25 ([?] to Liliencron, 27 June 1907), and Bl. 201–202 (Prager to Women's League, 1 August 1908).

156 See, for example, DKG 159, Bl. 561 (Hatten to German Colonial Society, 9 February 1911), and Bl. 562 (Winkler to Women's League, 6 February 1911).

157 DKG 153, Bl. 196 (Prager to Women's League n.d. [July 1908]; and *Keetmanshooper Zeitung*, 17 July 1912, 6.

158 LAB, Vereinsregister, Frauenbund der Deutschen Kolonialgesellschaft, Bd. 1, Bl. 61–62. Heyl tried to increase the Women's League's formal and informal power over the female emigration program. See DKG 154, Bl. 227–228 (Schulte im Hofe to [?], 24 July 1910); Bl. 234–235 (minutes of Women's League executive committee, 1 July 1910), and Bl. 241 (minutes of the Women's League executive committee, 3 October 1910).

159 DKG 155, Bl. 115 (Berlin chapter of Women's League flier, ca. 1909 [date of lecture 19 January 1909]).

160 DKG 154, Bl. 96 (minutes of Women's League executive committee, 6 December 1909), and Bl. 100 (minutes of Women's League executive committee, 6 December 1909).

161 Margarete Schnitzker, "Die Auswahl der Mädchen für Südwest," *Kolonie und Heimat* 5, no. 16 (1911): 8; see also DKG 154, Bl. 87 (Richtofen to Strauch, 7 December 1909).

162 Schnitzker, "Die Auswahl," 8.

163 Ibid.

164 Ibid., 9.

165 Frobenius, *10 Jahre*, 15–17.

166 DKG 154, Bl. 132–137, especially Bl. 133 ("Denkschrift über die Notwendigkeit des Heimatshauses in Keetmanshoop"), and Bl. 22 ("Aufruf zur Sammlung für ein Mädchenheim in Keetmanshoop"). See also Philalethes Kuhn and W. Harbers, "Die Auswanderung von Frauen und Kindern in die britischen Kolonien," in *Zeitschrift für Kolonialpolitik, Kolonialrecht und Kolonialwirtschaft* 12, no. 11 (November 1910): 833–858.

167 DKG 154, Bl. 259–260 (sample contract for Heimathaus).

168 DKG 154, Bl. 167 (minutes of the Women's League executive committee,

14 March 1910); Frobenius, *10 Jahre*, 14–18; and *Keetmanshooper Zeitung*, 20 November 1913, 3.

169 DKG 154, Bl. 199 (Zastrow to Women's League, 5 February 1910). In 1913 the Women's League raised Cauer's old suggestion of a salaried matron who would accompany the sponsored women on their passage to the colony and prevent unsuitable acquaintances. Only the protests of Women's League members in German Southwest Africa that such a position would be an extravagance induced the league's leadership to give up the idea; missionaries were asked to chaperone the women instead. See Frobenius, *10 Jahre*, 23.

170 DKG 154, Bl. 22–23 ("Aufruf zur Sammlung für ein Mädchenheim in Keetmanshoop").

171 Hedwig Heyl, "Die Kolonial-Frauenschule in Weilbach," *Kolonie und Heimat* 5, no. 41 (1912): 9.

172 Unlike the Women's Association for Nursing, the Women's League never discussed training African women as either domestic servants in European homes or as European-style housewives in their own homes. For an example of such training, see Jacklyn Cock, "Domestic Service and Education for Domesticity: The Incorporation of Xhosa Women into Colonial Society," in *Women and Gender in Southern Africa*, ed. Cherryl Walker (London: James Currey, 1990), 76–96.

173 Rommel and Rautenberg, *Die kolonialen Frauenschulen*, 18; and *Deutsche Kolonialzeitung* (1910): 459. Between the failure of Zech's school and the establishment of a new one, Heyl referred women to the gardening schools of her protegée Ida von Kortzfleisch. See DKG 154, Bl. 268 (minutes of Women's League executive committee, 5 December 1910).

174 Rommel and Rautenberg, *Die kolonialen Frauenschulen*, 7–8. It was modeled on Ida von Kortzfleisch's curriculum.

175 *Keetmanshooper Zeitung*, 31 July 1913, 2. In comparison, a domestic servant in German Southwest Africa earned at most 600 marks and a certified governess 1,800 marks. See Leonore Niessen-Deiters, *Die deutsche Frau im Auslande und in den Schutzgebieten* (Berlin: Egon Fleischel, 1913), 62.

176 Rommel and Rautenberg, *Die kolonialen Frauenschulen*, 25.

177 *Keetmanshooper Zeitung*, 31 July 1913, 2.

178 Heyl, "Die Kolonial-Frauenschule in Weilbach," 8.

179 *Keetmanshooper Zeitung*, 31 July 1913, 2.

180 DKG 155, Bl. 12 (Thiessen to DKG, 5 December 1911), and Bl. 36 (minutes of Women's League executive committee, 3 July 1911); and Frobenius, *10 Jahre*, 24.

181 Richtofen-Damsdorf, "Der Frauenbund," 119–120. See, more generally, Karen Tranberg Hansen, *Distant Companions: Servants and Employers in Zambia, 1900–1985* (Ithaca: Cornell University Press, 1989), 29–83.

182 Niessen-Deiters, *Die deutsche Frau im Auslande*, 7.

183 Frobenius, *10 Jahre*, 9–11, 18–19; DKG 153, Bl. 232–233 (Liliencron to

Mecklenburg, 30 September 1908); and *Keetmanshooper Zeitung,* 4 December 1913, 2, 16 April 1914, 1, 14 May 1914, 3, and 21 May 1914, 3. By 1914, forty of the sixty-six nurses dispatched by the Women's Association for Nursing were trained in midwifery. See Hildegard von Lekow, "50 Jahre Rotkreuzarbeit," in *Das Buch der deutschen Kolonien,* ed. Heinrich Schnee et al. (Leipzig: W. Goldmann, 1937), 287–288. In 1902 the Women's Association had opened a kindergarten in Windhuk that Theodor Leutwein greeted as a racial segregation measure. See Theodor Leutwein, *Elf Jahre Gouverneur in Deutsch-Südwestafrika* (Berlin: E. S. Mittler, 1906), 235.

184 E. Steudel, "Deutscher Frauenverein vom Roten Kreuz für die Kolonien," in *Deutsches Kolonial-Lexikon,* ed. Heinrich Schnee (Leipzig: Quelle & Meyer, 1920), 1:311; and Frobenius, *10 Jahre,* 11.

185 *Unter dem rothen Kreuz* 20, no. 5 (May 1909): 58.

186 On conflicts between the two groups over founding new chapters, see DKG 153, Bl. 224 (Buchmann to *Deutsche Kolonialzeitung,* 22 September 1908), Bl. 246 (Sander to Women's League, 28 October 1909), Bl. 249 (Sander to Women's League, 13 November 1908), and Bl. 279 (minutes of the German Colonial Society executive committee, 30 April 1909); *Unter dem rothen Kreuz* 24, no. 6 (June–July 1913): 78; and DKG 154, Bl. 250–251 (Kuhn to Mecklenburg, 19 November 1910, and Winkler to Kuhn, 21 November 1910).

187 DKG 153, Bl. 251 (motion of Bamberg chapter of the German Colonial Society, ca. November 1908); see also Bl. 255 (minutes of German Colonial Society executive committee, 27 November 1908), and Bl. 279 (minutes of the German Colonial Society executive committee, 20 April 1909); DKG 154, Bl. 168–169 (minutes of the Women's League executive committee, 14 March 1910); and the remarks of the Lieutenant-Colonel Schlagintweit in *Verhandlungen des Deutschen Kolonialkongresses 1910,* 965.

188 DKG 153, Bl. 264–265 (quote on Bl. 265) (Thiessen to Mecklenburg, 26 January 1909).

189 DKG 154, Bl. 168–169 (minutes of the Women's League executive committee, 14 March 1910).

190 Remarks of Nathalie von Rümelin, in *Verhandlungen des Deutschen Kolonialkongresses 1910,* 966.

191 DKG 153, Bl. 251 (motion of Bamberg chapter of the German Colonial Society).

192 At the previous German Colonial Congress in 1905 there were no women speakers at all. In 1910, Heyl requested half a day; Hans von Ramsay wanted every session to include a woman speaker, and a second male supporter of the League, A. Meyer-Gerhard, wanted a woman plenary speaker. See DKG 154, Bl. 112 (minutes of the Women's League executive committee, 3 January 1910), and Bl. 160–161 (minutes of the Women's League executive committee, 31 January 1910). The two speeches were Maria Kuhn, "Die

Stellung der Frau in den Kolonien," in *Verhandlungen des Deutschen Kolonial-kongresses 1910, 945–964*; and Ludwiga Lehr, "Über die Leistungen des Roten Kreuzes in den deutschen Kolonien," in the same volume, 932–945.

5. THE WOMAN CITIZEN AND THE LOST COLONIAL EMPIRE IN WEIMAR AND NAZI GERMANY

1   On education, see Ken Holston, "A Measure of the Nation: Colonial Enthusiasm, Education and Politics in Germany, 1890–1936" (Ph.D. diss., University of Pennsylvania, 1996); on "colonial sciences," see *Verhandlungen des Deutschen Kolonialkongresses 1924* (Berlin: Verlag Kolonialkriegerdank "Koloniale Rundschau," 1924); and Ernst Gerhard Jacob, *Deutsche Kolonial-kunde*, 2d, rev. ed. (Dresden: L. Ehlermann, 1940), 95–99. A few of the monuments are noted in *Der Kolonialdeutsche* 5, no. 9 (September 1925): 173 (Braunschweig), and vol. 6, no. 22 (1926): 365–366 (Frankfurt a.d. Oder); and Heinrich Schnee, *Als letzter Gouverneur in Deutsch-Ostafrika. Erinnerungen* (Heidelberg: Quelle & Meyer, 1964), 74 (memorial to Carl Peters).

2   See, for example, Lydia Höpker, *Um Scholle und Leben: Schicksale einer deutschen Farmerin in Südwest-Afrika* (Minden in Westfalen: Wilhelm Köhler, 1927), republished in 1936 as *Als Farmerin in Deutsch-Südwest: Was ich in Afrika erlebte;* and Charlotte Deppe and Ludwig Deppe, *Um Ostafrika. Erinnerungen* (Dresden: E. Beutelspacher, 1925).

3   Klaus Hildebrand, *Vom Reich zum Weltreich: Hitler, NSDAP und koloniale Frage, 1918–1945* (Munich: Wilhelm Fink, 1969), 89–95.

4   "Reply to the Allied and Associated Powers to the Observations of the German Delegation on the Conditions of Peace," 16 June 1919, in *Urkunden zum Friedensvertrage von Versailles vom 28. Juni 1919*, Erster Teil, ed. Herbert Kraus and Gustav Rödiger (Berlin: Franz Vahlen/Hans Robert Engelmann, 1920), 604.

5   Italy was otherwise compensated. France took over most of Togo and Cameroon, with small areas of each going to Britain; Britain took most of German East Africa, which became the Tanganyika Territory; the remainder, Rwanda and Burundi, went to Belgium, with a small area becoming part of Portuguese Mozambique. German Southwest Africa went to South Africa. Australia took over German New Guinea and the Bismarck Archipelago, and New Zealand took over German Samoa. Japan took over Jiaozhou (until 1923), as well as the Mariana, Caroline, Marshall, and Palau Islands that lay north of the equator. The formerly German Pacific islands south of the equator were divided among Australia, the United States, and Britain. See W. O. Henderson, *The German Colonial Empire, 1884–1919* (London: Frank Cass, 1993), 118–122, 124–126.

6   Ida Schuffenhauer, *Komm wieder Bwana: Ein deutsches Schicksal* (Berlin: W. Süsserott, 1940); and Senta Dinglreiter, *Wann kommen die Deutschen*

endlich wieder? Eine Reise durch unsere Kolonien in Afrika (Leipzig: Koehler & Amelang, 1935). On loyalists, see, for example, Johanna Rosenkranz, "Eine Hamburger Schule zeigt ihre Kolonialschau," *Die Frau und die Kolonien,* no. 12 (December 1937): 184; and "Brief eines Kamerun-Negers," *Übersee- und Kolonialzeitung* 8, no. 19 (1 October 1928): 327. Colonialists frequently invoked the colony Togo and the East African soldiers (*askaris*) who fought under General Paul von Lettow-Vorbeck in the First World War as collectively loyal. See, for example, the best-known colonial revision tract, Heinrich Schnee's *German Colonization Past and Future: The Truth about the German Colonies* (London: George Allen & Unwin, 1926), especially 167–168; and Adjaï Oloukpona-Yinnon, *Unter deutschen Palmen: Die "Musterkolonie" Togo im Spiegel deutscher Kolonialliteratur (1884–1914)* (Frankfurt a.M.: IKO Verlag für interkulturelle Kommunikation, 1998).

7   Oloukpona-Yinnon, *Unter deutschen Palmen,* 11–13, 33, 65–66.

8   Manfred Sell, "Die schwarze Völkerwanderung," in *Preussische Jahrbücher* 224, no. 2 (May 1931): 157–181; and Sell, *Die schwarze Völkerwanderung: Der Einbruch des Negers in die Kulturwelt* (Vienna: Wilhelm Frick, 1940).

9   Tina Campt, Pascal Grosse, and Yara-Colette Lemke-Muñiz de Faria, "Blacks, Germans, and the Politics of Imperial Imagination, 1920–60," in *The Imperialist Imagination: German Colonialism and Its Legacy,* ed. Sara Friedrichsmeyer, Sara Lennox, and Susanne Zantop (Ann Arbor: University of Michigan Press, 1999), 217–222 (quotes on 217); and Saul Friedländer, *Nazi Germany and the Jews,* vol. 1: *The Years of Persecution, 1933–1939* (New York: HarperCollins, 1997), 208.

10 See, for example, Kurt Hedrich, *Der Rassegedanke im deutschen Kolonialrecht: Die rechtliche Regelung der ehelichen und ausserehelichen Beziehungen zwischen Weissen und Farbigen* (Schramberg: Gatzer & Hahn, 1941), 2–3.

11 Klaus Theweleit, *Male Fantasies,* vol. 1: *Women, Floods, Bodies, History* (Minneapolis: University of Minnesota Press, 1987); and Regina Schulte, "The Sick Warrior's Sister: Nursing during the First World War," in *Gender Relations in German History: Power, Agency and Experience from the Sixteenth to the Twentieth Century* (London: UCL Press, 1996), 121–141.

12 On victimhood, gender relations, and national identity in the early Federal Republic, see Elizabeth Heineman, "The Hour of the Woman: Memories of Germany's 'Crisis Years' and West German National Identity," *American Historical Review* 101 (1996): 354–395; and Robert G. Moeller, "War Stories: The Search for a Usable Past in the Federal Republic of Germany," *American Historical Review* 101 (1996): 1008–1048.

13 On maternalist rhetoric after 1918, see Raffael Scheck, "Women against Versailles: Maternalism and Nationalism of Female Bourgeois Politicians in the Early Weimar Republic," *German Studies Review* 22 (1999): 21–42.

14 There had been 14,830 Germans in German Southwest Africa in 1914; colonialists counted about 12,000 in the mandate by 1930. In German East

Africa before the war, there had been 5,336 German colonists; by 1930 there were 2,000 in postwar Tanganyika. See Wilhelm Arning, "Die Stellung des Frauenbundes in der Kolonialpolitik von heute," in *Koloniale Frauenarbeit*, ed. Frauenbund der Deutschen Kolonialgesellschaft (Berlin: Zentrale des Frauenbundes der Deutschen Kolonialgesellschaft, 1930), 39.

15   Cited in Frobenius, *30 Jahre koloniale Frauenarbeit* (Berlin: Reichskolonialbund, 1936), 17.

16   Arning, "Die Stellung des Frauenbundes," 39.

17   Raffael Scheck, "German Conservatism and Female Political Activism in the Early Weimar Republic," *German History* 15 (1997): 34–55; and Ute Planert, *Antifeminismus im Kaiserreich: Diskurs, soziale Formation und politische Mentalität* (Göttingen: Vandenhoeck & Ruprecht, 1998), 241–245.

18   Renate Bridenthal, "Professional Housewives: Stepsisters of the Feminist Movement," in *When Biology Became Destiny: Women in Weimar and Nazi Germany*, ed. Atina Grossmann, Marion Kaplan, and Renate Bridenthal (New York: Monthly Review, 1984), 153–173.

19   Doris Kaufmann, *Frauen zwischen Aufbruch und Reaktion: Protestantische Frauenbewegung in der ersten Hälfte des 20. Jahrhunderts* (Munich: Piper, 1988); and Planert, *Antifeminismus im Kaiserreich*, esp. 130–151.

20   Sabine Hering, *Die Kriegsgewinnlerinnen: Praxis und Ideologie der deutschen Frauenbewegung im Ersten Weltkrieg* (Pfaffenweiler: Centaurus, 1990), 47–80.

21   Else Frobenius, "Der goldene Schlüssel. Erinnerungen aus meinem Leben," 132. This typescript, written in 1942–1944, is held in a private family archive.

22   Weimar-era women in the colonial sciences included the linguist Elise Kootz-Kretschmer, author of *Die Safwa, ein ostafrikanischer Volksstamm in seinem Leben und Denken* (Berlin: Dietrich Reimer [Ernst Vohsen], 1926–1929); and anthropologist Hilde Thurnwald, author of *Die schwarze Frau im Wandel Afrikas: Eine soziologische Studie unter ostafrikanischen Stämmen* (Stuttgart: Kohlhammer, 1935), and *Menschen der Südsee: Charaktere und Schicksale* (Stuttgart: F. Enke, 1937), among other works.

23   Heyl responded to the war with even greater determination to "promote and uplift the calling of the housewife and mother in all strata of the population" (Frobenius, "Der goldene Schlüssel," 103).

24   Kolonial-Wirtschaftliches Komitee, ed., *Die deutsche Hausfrau und die Kolonien* (Berlin: E. S. Mittler, n.d.), 9.

25   *Der Kolonialdeutsche* 5, no. 5 (1 May 1925): 99.

26   *Der Kolonialdeutsche* 5, no. 1 (31 December 1924): 15, and vol. 6, no. 17 (1 September 1926): 294–295; and *Die Brücke zur Heimat* (1928): 170, and (1929): 60.

27   *Der Kolonialdeutsche* 4, no. 11 (29 October 1924): 195.

28   Moritz J. Bonn, *Wandering Scholar* (New York: John Day, 1948), 149. An

anti-Nazi liberal democrat and a Jew, Bonn resigned as rector of the Berlin School of Commerce (Handelshochschule) in April 1933 and fled first to Austria, then to the United States.

29 Fritz Fischer, *Germany's Aims in the First World War* (New York: W. W. Norton, 1967), 102–103, 317–319, 359–360, 596.

30 Adolf Rüger, "Das Streben nach kolonialer Restitution in den ersten Nachkriegsjahren," in *Drang nach Afrika: Die deutsche koloniale Expansionpolitik und Herrschaft in Afrika von den Anfängen bis zum Verlust der Kolonien,* ed. Helmuth Stoecker, 2d, rev. ed. (Berlin: Akademie Verlag, 1991), 265; and Alfred Mansfeld, ed., *Sozialdemokratie und Kolonieen* (reprint, Münster: Lit Verlag, 1987).

31 Mary E. Townsend, *The Rise and Fall of Germany's Colonial Empire 1884–1918* (New York: Howard Fertig, 1966), 387.

32 DKG 158, Bl. 56–58 ("Nie wieder Kolonien!" flier). Augspurg and her companion, Lida Gustava Heymann, later wrote that while they rejected "hitherto existing methods of colonization," that did not mean that one had to be an "opponent of any colonization whatever." They seemed to argue here that colonialism had been historically cruel because men had controlled it; women might render colonialism, which they seemed to equate with economic development per se, more humane. Lida Gustava Heymann and Anita Augspurg, *Erlebtes — Erschautes: Deutsche Frauen kämpfen für Freiheit, Recht und Frieden 1850–1940* (Meisenheim am Glan: Anton Hain, 1972), 198.

33 *Der Kolonialdeutsche* 8, no. 5 (1 March 1928): 77, 78 (quote). On Hoppstock-Huth, see Ute Gerhard, *Unerhört: Die Geschichte der deutschen Frauenbewegung* (Reinbek bei Hamburg: Rowohlt, 1991), 352, 384.

34 Hans Zache, "Deutschland und der Kongress der 'unterdrückten Völker,'" *Koloniale Rundschau,* no. 4 (1927): 99.

35 Hans Paasche, *Die Forschungsreise des Afrikaners Lukanga Mukara ins innerste Deutschland,* ed. Franziskus Hähnel, afterword by Iring Fetscher (Munich: Goldmann, 1988), 117.

36 Frobenius, "Der goldene Schlüssel," 122, 125.

37 Woodruff D. Smith, *The Ideological Origins of Nazi Imperialism* (New York: Oxford University Press, 1986), 196–230; and Rüger, "Das Streben nach kolonialer Restitution."

38 Wilhelm Solf, *Afrika für Europa: Der koloniale Gedanke des XX. Jahrhunderts* (Neumünster i.H.: Theodor Dittmann Verlag, 1920). Later Solf and to a greater extent his wife, Hanna Solf, and daughter Countess Lagi Ballestrem-Solf became active in the resistance to Nazism. See Rudolf Pechel, *Deutscher Widerstand* (Erlenbach-Zurich: Eugen Rentsch, 1947), 88–93.

39 Adolf Rüger, "Richtlinien und Richtungen deutscher Kolonialpolitik 1923–1926," in *Studien zur Geschichte des deutschen Kolonialismus in Afrika: Festschrift zum 60. Geburtstag von Peter Sebald,* ed. Peter Heine and Ulrich van der

Heyden (Pfaffenweiler: Centaurus, 1995), 454, 461; and Franz Ansprenger, *The Dissolution of the Colonial Empires* (New York: Routledge, 1989), 125– 126. Schacht later served as president of the Reichsbank and minister of economics under Hitler.

40 Rüger, "Richtlinien," 461. Külz's position is also documented there.

41 Ibid., 460–461. Föllmer was the editor of the populist and race purity– oriented *Koloniale Zeitschrift* before the war.

42 Although British and Belgian forces had occupied most of German East Africa by late 1916, Lettow-Vorbeck's force did not surrender until after Germany itself did in November 1918. On Lettow-Vorbeck, see Theweleit, *Male Fantasies.*

43 "Kolonialpropaganda beim jüdischen Frontsoldatenbund," *Der Kolonial-deutsche* 7, no. 5 (1 March 1927): 75.

44 Friedländer, *Nazi Germany and the Jews,* 73–75.

45 Hildebrand, *Vom Reich zum Weltreich,* 89–100.

46 Hildebrand shows the tensions and distinctions between these two movements, although he divides them too neatly in terms of ideology. He implies, for example, that it was the Nazis who introduced concepts of race to the colonialist movement, and concludes without any discussion that colonial racism had no connection to fascism simply because such racism had also existed in the other modern colonial empires (Hildebrand, *Vom Reich zum Weltreich,* 100, 219, 437).

47 Ibid., 100–247, especially 185–187 on Schnee.

48 Gertrud Scholtz-Klink, *Die Frau im Dritten Reich. Eine Dokumentation* (Tübingen: Grabert, 1978), 267–268.

49 National Archives II (College Park, Md.), Berlin Document Center microform records, NSDAP membership card file, card for Else Frobenius. On Frobenius, see Lora Wildenthal, "Mass-Marketing Colonialism and Nationalism: The Career of Else Frobenius in Weimar and Nazi Germany," in *Nation, Politik und Geschlecht: Frauenbewegungen und Nationalismus in der Moderne,* ed. Ute Planert (Frankfurt: Campus, 2000), 328–345.

50 National Archives II (College Park, Md.), Berlin Document Center microform records, NSDAP membership card file, card for Agnes von Boemcken. Boemcken's husband, a colonial army officer, had been pro-Nazi since at least 1931 (Hildebrand, *Vom Reich zum Weltreich,* 175). Boemcken, who succeeded Hedwig von Bredow as chairwoman of the Women's League after the latter's death in 1932, had lived in German Southwest Africa and German East Africa for sixteen years; she had also visited Cameroon. During the First World War she nursed wounded soldiers in German East Africa and returned as part of General von Lettow-Vorbeck's triumphant procession to Germany.

51 Cited in Frobenius, "Der goldene Schlüssel," 105.

52 *Grüne Blätter* 9, no. 2 (March 1933).

53 Frobenius, *30 Jahre*, 27; and Steinmeister, "Jahresbericht . . . 1929/30," 7. Its rapid expansion in the latter half of the 1920s reawakened the old conflict with the German Colonial Society over men who joined the former but not the latter. See DKG 158, Bl. 18 (Steinmeister to DKG, 24 July 1929), Bl. 27 (DKG to Women's League, 10 June 1929), Bl. 191–192 (letter fragment), and the lists of men's names in Bl. 103–158 and 177–190, which included Dernburg, Kuhn, Lindequist, Meyer-Gerhard, and Ramsay (Bl. 108, 184).

54 *Der Kolonialdeutsche* 8, no. 9 (1 May 1928): 147; and Hildegard von Lekow, "50 Jahre Rotkreuzarbeit," in *Das Buch der deutschen Kolonien,* by Heinrich Schnee et al. (Leipzig: W. Goldmann, 1937), 290.

55 Hildebrand, *Vom Reich zum Weltreich,* 179, 348.

56 RKA 1168, Bl. 3 (Gunzert to *Reichsstelle für Devisenbewirtschaftung,* 6 December 1935), and Bl. 16 (memo, 24 March 1936). Frieda Wunderlich was a social work and economics expert who had fled Nazi Germany earlier and became the first woman professor on the faculty for the New School for Social Research. See Theresa Wobbe, "Frieda Wunderlich (1884–1965). Weimarer Sozialreform und die New Yorker Universität im Exil," in *Frauen in der Soziologie. Neun Portraits,* ed. Claudia Honegger and Theresa Wobbe (Munich: C. H. Beck, 1998), 203–225.

57 On the Weimar state's reluctance to naturalize Africans, see RKA 5149, Bl. 152–153 (Auswärtiges Amt to Fehn, 17 January 1930); and RKA 5147, Bl. 208–209, 220, 227–229 (case of Anna Teho Ramsay), and 250–253 (case of Alfreda Mtoro Maria Baptista).

58 RKA 5148, Bl. 131 (case of Fritz Tamé).

59 Friedländer, *Nazi Germany and the Jews,* 27.

60 RKA 5156, Bl. 60 (Reichsministerium des Innern to Schnee and Schultz-Ewerth, 7 December 1933). On arbitrariness as a tool of the Nazi racial state, see Friedländer, *Nazi Germany and the Jews,* 145, 148.

61 *Der Kolonialdeutsche* 6, no. 12 (15 June 1926): 213.

62 For general observations about women's organizations' treatment of their Jewish members after January 1933, see Marion Kaplan, "Sisterhood under Siege: Feminism and Anti-Semitism in Germany, 1904–1933," in *When Biology Became Destiny,* ed. Grossmann, Kaplan, and Bridenthal, 187, 189–190.

63 Antonie Brandeis-Ruete, "Koloniale Frauenschule in Rendsburg," *Der Kolonialdeutsche* 6, no. 15 (1 August 1926): 261; and Brandeis-Ruete, "Südsee-Bilder," in *Das deutsche Kolonialbuch,* ed. Hans Zache (Berlin: Wilhelm Andermann, 1925), 486–490. Her ex-husband, Eugen Brandeis, was Catholic.

64 There is a brief and vague mention of changes in the school board connected with the Nazi takeover in Mechthild Rommel and Hulda Rautenberg, *Die kolonialen Frauenschulen von 1908–1945* (Witzenhausen: Gesamthochschule Kassel — Fachbereich Internationale Agrarwirtschaft in Witzenhausen et al. 1983), 37.

65 The Reichskolonialbund published a new version of *Kolonie und Heimat*

between 1936 and 1943, parallel to the Women's League's organ *Die Frau und die Kolonien*. For an analysis of the former, see Barbara Shumannfang, "Envisioning Empire: Jewishness, Blackness and Gender in German Colonial Discourse from Frieda von Bülow to the Nazi *Kolonie und Heimat*" (Ph.D. diss., Duke University, 1998), 225–342.

66 Frobenius, *30 Jahre*, 31.

67 Pascal Grosse, *Kolonialismus, Eugenik und bürgerliche Gesellschaft in Deutschland, 1850–1918* (Frankfurt a.M.: Campus, 2000), 193–238; and Melvin E. Page, "Introduction: Black Men in a White Men's War," in *Africa and the First World War*, ed. Page (New York: St. Martin's Press, 1987), 2–3.

68 Margaret Strobel, *European Women and the Second British Empire* (Bloomington: Indiana University Press, 1991), 5–6.

69 Henderson, *The German Colonial Empire*, 125.

70 RKA 1895, Bl. 4 (questionnaire).

71 Hans Draeger, "Ada Schnee, die Gattin," in *Gouverneur Schnee: Ein Künder und Mehrer deutscher Geltung. Zu seinem 60. Geburtstag*, ed. Draeger (Berlin: Georg Stilke, 1931), 125–126.

72 Ada Schnee, *Meine Erlebnisse während der Kriegszeit in Deutsch-Ostafrika* (Leipzig: Quelle & Meyer, 1918), 110. Schnee became a celebrity because of her experiences. Minna Cauer arranged to meet her personally in March 1918, noted Schnee's revisionist arguments in her diary, and invited her to address the Women's Welfare Association on colonial issues. See Else Lüders, *Minna Cauer: Leben und Werk. Dargestellt an Hand ihrer Tagebücher und nachgelassenen Schriften* (Gotha: Leopold Klotz, 1925), 215–216.

73 Schnee, *Meine Erlebnisse*, 109.

74 Elly Proempeler, *Kriegsgefangen quer durch Afrika: Erlebnisse einer deutschen Frau im Weltkriege* (Berlin: Otto Elsner, 1918), 33.

75 These are Schnee, *Meine Erlebnisse;* Proempeler, *Kriegsgefangen quer durch Afrika;* Maria Roscher, *Zwei Jahre Kriegsgefangen in West- und Nord-Afrika: Erlebnisse einer deutschen Frau* (Zurich: Jean Frey, 1918); and Maria Matuschka, *Meine Erinnerungen aus Deutsch-Ostafrika von 1911–1919* (Leipzig: Xenien-Verlag, n.d. [1919]).

76 Reichskolonialamt, ed., *Die Kolonialdeutschen aus Kamerun und Togo in französischer Gefangenschaft* (Berlin: Reichsdruckerei, 1917); on African soldiers as guards, see 2, 160, and throughout the cited memoirs.

77 Some smaller number of Africans and other non-Europeans may have remained part of the occupation force until the end of the occupation in 1930. See Gisela Lebzelter, "Die 'schwarze Schmach': Vorurteile — Propaganda — Mythos," *Geschichte und Gesellschaft* 11 (1985): 37–58; Robert C. Reinders, "Racialism on the Left: E. D. Morel and the 'Black Horror on the Rhine,'" *International Review of Social History* 13 (1968): 1–28; and Campt et al., "Blacks, Germans, and the Politics of Imperial Imagination," 208–214.

78 Sally Marks, "Black Watch on the Rhine: A Study in Propaganda, Prejudice

and Prurience," *European Studies Review* 13 (1983): 297–334; and Reiner Pommerin, *Sterilisierung der Rheinlandbastarde: Das Schicksal einer farbigen deutschen Minderheit 1918–1937* (Düsseldorf: Droste, 1979), 23.

79   See the images reproduced in May Opitz, Katharina Oguntoye, and Dagmar Schultz, eds., *Showing Our Colors: Afro-German Women Speak Out*, trans. Anne V. Adams (Amherst: University of Massachusetts Press, 1992), 46–47; and Pommerin, *Sterilisierung der Rheinlandbastarde*, 14, 31.

80   Luise Paasche, *Männer wehrlos, Frauen schutzlos: Unsere Propagandareise gegen die Schuldlüge* (Neckargemünd: privately published, 1927), especially 17–18; see also 20–28.

81   Campt et al., "Blacks, Germans, and the Politics of Imperial Imagination," 208 (statistic); and Pommerin, *Sterilisierung der Rheinlandbastarde*.

82   Frobenius, *30 Jahre*, 18 (see also 27); and Frobenius, "'Und wenn sie gleich alt werden . . .' Dem Gedächtnis von Hedwig von Bredow," *Die Frau* 40 (1932–1933): 93.

83   Frobenius, *30 Jahre*, 13–14. Some twenty years later, when the first German deportees from Tanganyika began to arrive in Germany in 1940, the Women's League (then Division IV of the Reich Colonial League) repeated these tasks. See Agnes von Boemcken, "Deutsche Rückkehrer aus Ostafrika in der Heimat," *Die Frau und die Kolonien*, no. 3 (March 1940): 17–21.

84   While its statutes were not officially changed, the Women's League did publish a revised set of organizational goals that placed youth and education at the top. See, for example, endpapers of *Koloniale Frauenarbeit*; see also Gertrud Schröder, "Frauenaufgaben in Südwestafrika," *Der Kolonialdeutsche* 8, no. 1 (1 January 1928): 7.

85   Karl Körner, "Vom deutschen Schulwesen in Südwest," in *Koloniale Frauenarbeit*, 14.

86   Nora von Steinmeister, "Aus dem Leben der Kolonialdeutschen," in *Das Buch der deutschen Kolonien*, ed. Anton Mayer (Potsdam: Volk und Heimat, 1933), 304; see also RKA 995, Bl. 224 (flier, n.d.).

87   Körner, "Vom deutschen Schulwesen in Südwest," 13.

88   Anne Maag, "Einrichtung von Lesemappen und Büchereien in Südwestafrika," in *Koloniale Frauenarbeit*, 20–21.

89   The reentry dates for Germans in other former colonies varied according to each territory's administrative decision. Germans managed to repurchase expropriated plantations in Cameroon from 1925; in 1928, Germans were allowed to reenter New Guinea. See Frobenius, *30 Jahre*, 26.

90   Theodor Gunzert, "Deutsches Schulwesen in Ostafrika," in *Koloniale Frauenarbeit*, 9–10. See also RKA 995, passim; and Marcia Wright, *German Missions in Tanganyika 1891–1941: Lutherans and Moravians in the Southern Highlands* (Oxford: Clarendon, 1971), 162, 188.

91   Margarete von Zastrow, "Fortbildung afrikanischer Jugend in Deutschland," *Koloniale Frauenarbeit*, 31–34.

92 *Der Kolonialdeutsche* 8 (1928): 58.

93 Hildegard von Lekow, "Rotkreuzarbeit in den Kolonien," in *Das Buch der deutschen Kolonien,* ed. Anton Mayer (Potsdam: Volk und Heimat, 1933), 289–291; and Hintrager, "Unsere Frauenauswanderung," in *Koloniale Frauenarbeit,* 26–27.

94 *Der Kolonialdeutsche* 6, no. 12 (15 June 1926): 214, vol. 6, no. 15 (1 August 1926): 261, and vol. 7 (1927): 411 (quote).

95 *Der Kolonialdeutsche* 6, no. 4 (1 March 1926): 62, and no. 8 (15 April 1926): 134.

96 Nora von Steinmeister, "Jahresbericht des Frauenbundes der Deutschen Kolonialgesellschaft 1929/30," in *Koloniale Frauenarbeit,* 5. On Tanganyika, see RKA 72, passim.

97 In 1929–1930, for example, the Women's League dispatched eighty-eight women and girls to Southwest Africa and Tanganyika, including sixty-four unmarried women (Steinmeister, "Jahresbericht . . . 1929/30," 4).

98 Men still saw marriage and motherhood as the main goals. See Hintrager, "Unsere Frauenauswanderung," 30; and Paul Rohrbach, *Afrika: Beiträge zu einer praktischen Kolonialkunde* (Berlin: Verlagshaus Werner, 1943), 289. Hintrager, one of the authors of the German Southwest African ban on intermarriage, now directed the Reich Office for Emigration Affairs (Reichstelle für das Auswanderungswesen). See also RKA 72, Bl. 94 (Gunzert to Women's League, 20 August 1928), and Bl. 240 (Gunzert to Women's League, 28 March 1931). The new consensus that emerged is apparent in Steinmeister, "Jahresbericht . . . 1929/30," 5; and Hintrager, "Unsere Frauenauswanderung," 30; see also "Die Akademikerin ist die beste Kolonistin," *Die Frau und die Kolonien* 1, no. 11 (November 1932): 145. An article encouraging women to study at university appeared in the Women's League organ in 1937: Susi Teubner, "Mädel mit 'Kopf fürs Studium,'" *Die Frau und die Kolonien,* no. 12 (December 1937): 179–180.

99 Frobenius, *30 Jahre,* 24; and Rommel and Rautenberg, *Die kolonialen Frauenschulen,* especially 31, 33, 35.

100 Rommel and Rautenberg, *Die kolonialen Frauenschulen,* 87.

101 Frobenius, *30 Jahre,* 24; Rommel and Rautenberg, *Die kolonialen Frauenschulen,* 52; and RdI 27215, Bl. 3 (Körner, "Bericht," n.d. [1934]).

102 Rommel and Rautenberg, *Die kolonialen Frauenschulen,* 40, 67. Its curriculum, like that of the Bad Weilbach school, was based on the Reifenstein school run by Ida von Kortzfleisch.

103 Agnes von Boemcken, "Koloniale Frauenschule Rendsburg," in *Koloniale Frauenarbeit,* 18–19; see also 17.

104 Zastrow, "Südwestafrikanische Erziehungsfragen," 13.

105 DKG 158, Bl. 19 (Berengar von Zastrow to German Colonial Society, 22 July 1929).

106   DKG 158, Bl. 21 (Seitz, memo, 12 July 1929).

107   Ibid.

108   Paul H. Kuntze, *Das Volksbuch der deutschen Kolonien* (Leipzig: George Doll-heimer, 1938), 160.

109   Ibid., 156, and plate 49.

110   The problem of sustaining a German national character identified neither too closely with republican Germany nor with the mandated territories has persisted in changing forms until the present day among German Nami-bians. See Brigitte Schmidt-Lauber, *Die abhängigen Herren: Deutsche Identi-tät in Namibia* (Hamburg: Lit, 1993), 8–9, 86–92, 102, 152.

111   Zastrow, "Fortbildung afrikanischer Jugend," 32–33.

112   Zastrow, "Südwestafrikanische Erziehungsfragen," 12.

113   One of countless examples, in this case from the pen of a colonialist woman, may be found in Else Frobenius, "Eine Frauenfahrt an die Front," *Die Frau* 24 (1916–1917): 541. See Elisabeth Domansky, "Militarization and Repro-duction in World War I Germany," in *Society, Culture, and the State in Ger-many 1870–1930,* ed. Geoff Eley (Ann Arbor: University of Michigan Press, 1996), 461–462.

114   Renate Bridenthal, "Something Old, Something New: Women between the Two World Wars," in *Becoming Visible,* 2d ed., ed. Renate Bridenthal, Claudia Koonz, and Susan Stuard (Boston: Houghton Mifflin, 1987), 473–497.

115   Mary Louise Roberts, *Civilization without Sexes: Reconstructing Gender in Postwar France, 1917 1927* (Chicago: University of Chicago Press, 1994); Susan Kingsley Kent, *Making Peace: The Reconstruction of Gender in Interwar Britain* (Princeton: Princeton University Press, 1993); and Victoria de Grazia, *How Fascism Ruled Women: Italy 1922–1945* (Berkeley: University of California Press, 1992).

116   Else Hermann, Siegfried Kracauer, and Hilde Walter, as excerpted in *The Weimar Republic Sourcebook,* ed. Anton Kaes, Martin Jay, and Edward Dimendberg (Berkeley: University of California Press, 1994), 207–208, 216–218, 210–211; Friedrun Bastkowski, Christa Lindner, and Ulrike Pro-kop, eds., *Frauenalltag und Frauenbewegung im 20. Jahrhundert,* Bd. 2: *Frau-enbewegung und die "Neue Frau" 1800–1933* (Frankfurt a.M.: Historisches Museum, 1980); and Renate Bridenthal and Claudia Koonz, "Beyond *Kinder, Küche, Kirche:* Weimar Women in Politics and Work," in *When Biol-ogy Became Destiny,* ed. Grossmann, Kaplan, and Bridenthal, 33–65.

117   Detlev Kühn, "Lenore Kühn—eine nationale Mitstreiterin der Frauen-bewegung," *Nordost-Archiv,* nos. 61–62 (1981): 39–56, and nos. 63–64 (1981): 31–54 (quote on 32–33). See *Diotima: Die Schule der Liebe* (Jena: Eugen Diederichs, 1930), which was published anonymously and ran into several editions up to 1965.

118 On Gottschewski and Zander, see Claudia Koonz, "The Competition for a Women's *Lebensraum,* 1928–1934," in *When Biology Became Destiny,* ed. Grossmann, Kaplan, and Bridenthal, 199–236; and Koonz, *Mothers in the Fatherland: Women, the Family and Nazi Politics* (New York: St. Martin's Press, 1987).

119 Lene Haase satirized that prewar response to a German woman traveling alone for pleasure to German Southwest Africa in her book *Raggys Fahrt nach Südwest. Roman* (Berlin: Egon Fleischel, 1910); see also Clara Brockmann, *Die deutsche Frau in Südwestafrika: Ein Beitrag zur Frauenfrage in unseren Kolonien* (Berlin: E. S. Mittler & Sohn, 1910).

120 Gulla Pfeffer, "Meine Kamerun-Nigeria-Expedition," *Der Kolonialdeutsche* 8, no. 18 (15 September 1928): 304. See also Gulla Pfeffer, *Die weisse Mah: Allein bei Urvölkern und Menschenfressern* (Minden i.W.: Wilhelm Köhler, 1929).

121 Ilse Steinhoff, *Deutsche Heimat in Afrika: Ein Bildbuch aus unseren Kolonien* (Berlin: Reichskolonialbund, 1939), unpaginated. During the Second World War, Steinhoff worked as a reporter in Croatia. See her article "Ein neuer Staat entsteht," in the *Berliner Illustrierte Zeitung* of 15 May 1941, 550–551, reprinted in *Konkret* (January 1992): 36–37.

122 Eva MacLean, *Unser Kamerun von heute. Ein Fahrtenbuch,* 2d ed. (Munich: Fichte Verlag Paul Wustrow, 1940). An example of her short journalism is Eva MacLean, "Shopping in Sansibar," *Die Frau und die Kolonien* (1932): 139–143. See also Dinglreiter, *Wann kommen die Deutschen endlich wieder?;* and Louise Diel, *Die Kolonien warten! Afrika im Umbruch* (Leipzig: Paul List, 1939).

123 Inge Wild, "Der andere Blick: Reisende Frauen in Afrika," *Etudes Germano-Africaines,* no. 10 (1992): 125.

124 Christine Holstein, *Deutsche Frau in Südwest: Den Erlebnissen einer Farmersfrau im heutigen Afrika nacherzählt* (Leipzig: Koehler & Amelang, 1937). Holstein was the pseudonym of Margarete Jähne.

125 Ibid., 139.

126 Rommel and Rautenberg, *Die kolonialen Frauenschulen,* 77–78.

127 Alexandre Kum'a N'dumbe, *Was wollte Hitler in Afrika? NS-Planungen für eine faschistische Neugestaltung Afrikas* (Frankfurt a.M.: IKO Verlag für interkulturelle Kommunikation, 1993), 50–57, 68–80 (on 1940 plans), 81–157 (on Nazi-era colonial thinking generally), and 238–243 (on 1943); and Wolfe Schmokel, *Dream of Empire: German Colonialism 1919–1945* (New Haven: Yale University Press, 1964), 137–184, especially 141.

128 Hildebrand, *Vom Reich zum Weltreich,* 713–744, 941–942; and Kum'a N'dumbe, *Was wollte Hitler in Afrika?* 239–240.

129 RdI 27215, Bl. 33, 44 ("Gesellschaftsvertrag").

130 School prospectus (1926–1927), cited in Rommel and Rautenberg, *Die kolonialen Frauenschulen,* 40.

131 Ibid., 37, 80; and RdI 27215, Bl. 18 (Körner, "Bericht," n.d. [1934]).

132 RdI 27215, Bl. 7–8, 3–4 (Körner, "Bericht," n.d. [1934]).

133 Rommel and Rautenberg, *Die kolonialen Frauenschulen*, 42, 67.

134 Ibid., 44, 66.

135 Ibid., 37–38. They were SS-Standartenführer Dr. Jung and Oberstleutnant a.D. Bauszus.

136 Gudrun Schwarz, "Frauen in der SS: Sippenverband und Frauenkorps," in *Zwischen Karriere und Verfolgung: Handlungsspielräume von Frauen im nationalsozialistischen Deutschland*, ed. Kirsten Heinsohn, Barbara Vogel, and Ulrike Weckel (Frankfurt: Campus, 1997), 223, 231–236.

137 Schmokel, *Dream of Empire*, 156–158, 165.

138 *Mitteilungsblatt der Kolonialen Frauenschule Rendsburg*, June 1940, unpaginated; and RdI 27215, Bl. 118 (Körner). Körner was director since 1930. He had run *Oberrealschulen* in Adana, Turkey, during the First World War, and in Southwest Africa during the 1920s. See RdI 27215, Bl. 17–18 (Körner, "Bericht," n.d. [1934]). He was on the board of the Women's League (RdI 27215, Bl. 18).

139 Rommel and Rautenberg, *Die kolonialen Frauenschulen*, 87.

140 Ibid., 55.

141 Ibid., 74.

142 RdI 27215, Bl. 15 (Körner, "Bericht," n.d. [1934]), and Bl. 118, 120 (Körner, n.d.). See also Rommel and Rautenberg, *Die kolonialen Frauenschulen*, 67.

143 Rommel and Rautenberg, *Die kolonialen Frauenschulen*, 67.

144 Ibid., 74.

145 RdI 27215, Bl. 125 (Körner to RdI, 11 March 1944).

146 RdI 27215, Bl. 126 (Körner to RdI, 21 March 1944). On the Reichsfrauenführung's activities in occupied Poland, see Jill Stephenson, *The Nazi Organisation of Women* (London: Croom Helm, 1981), 225, 199.

147 RdI 27215, Bl. 122 (Körner, n.d.).

148 RdI 27215, Bl. 127 (RdI to Körner, 6 April 1944).

149 From a school prospectus from 1926–1927, cited in Rommel and Rautenberg, *Die kolonialen Frauenschulen*, 40.

150 RdI 27215, Bl. 88 (Friedrich Thilo to RdI, 26 February 1935), emphasis in original.

151 Rommel and Rautenberg, *Die kolonialen Frauenschulen*, 65–66.

152 Ibid., 73.

153 On German women's employment in the occupied territories, see Schwarz, "Frauen in der SS," 237; Stephenson, *The Nazi Organisation of Women*, 190–199; Elizabeth Harvey, "La Polonia sotto la Germania nazista: Il ruolo delle donne nell colonizzazione delle provincie annesse," *Italia Contemporanea* 200 (1995): 423–436; and Harvey, "'Die deutsche Frau im Osten': 'Rasse', Geschlecht und öffentlicher Raum im besetzten Polen 1940–1944," in *Archiv für Sozialgeschichte* 38 (1998): 191–214.

154 Rommel and Rautenberg, *Die kolonialen Frauenschulen,* 80. See also the documentary directed by Tink Diaz, *Wir hatten eine Dora in Südwest* (Germany, 1991). Young women's adventure fiction popularized the school among youth. See, for example, Else Steup, *Wiete will nach Afrika: Ein Jungmädchenbuch* (Berlin: Ullstein, 1936); and Steup, *Wiete erlebt Afrika: Ein junges Mädchen bei deutschen Farmern* (Berlin: Deutscher Verlag, 1938).

EPILOGUE

1 Susan Moller Okin et al., *Is Multiculturalism Bad for Women?* (Princeton: Princeton University Press, 1999).

ARCHIVAL MATERIALS

Bundesarchiv Berlin (BAB)

Bestand Deutsche Kolonialgesellschaft (DKG)

DKG 153. Frauenbund der Deutschen Kolonialgesellschaft. 1907–1909.

DKG 154. Frauenbund der Deutschen Kolonialgesellschaft. 1909–1910.

DKG 155. Frauenbund der Deutschen Kolonialgesellschaft. 1911.

DKG 158. Frauenbund der Deutschen Kolonialgesellschaft. 1927–1929.

DKG 159. Frauenbund der Deutschen Kolonialgesellschaft. 1911–1914.

Bestand Reichskolonialamt (RKA)

RKA 72. Auswanderung von Frauen nach Deutsch-Ostafrika. 1926–1931.

RKA 73. Auswanderung von Frauen nach Ost-Afrika. 1931–1936.

RKA 694. Politische Zustände in Deutsch-Ostafrika. 1888.

RKA 755. Entsendung des Dr. Peters als Kais. Kommissar nach Ostafrika. 1891–1894.

RKA 847. Evangelische Missionsgesellschaft für Deutsch-Ostafrika, jetzt: Bethel-Mission. 1887–1907.

RKA 995. Die Regierungs- und Kommunalschulen in Deutsch-Ostafrika. Schule in Lupembe. 1925–1929.

RKA 1168. Juden und Halbjuden in Südwestafrika. 1935–1939.

RKA 1895. Vernehmungen über die Erlebnisse in Deutsch-Südwestafrika und in englischer Gefangenschaft. 1916.

RKA 2174. Verhandlungen des Gouvernementrats in Windhuk. 1906.

RKA 2678. Ausweisungen — Neuguinea. 1901–1926.

RKA 3131. Zwistigkeiten des Gouverneurs Solf mit Pflanzer Deeken. 1907–1910.

RKA 4815. Rechtspflege in Deutsch-Ostafrika (Einzelne Urteile). 1900–1902.

RKA 5147. Reichsangehörigkeitsverhältnisse, Naturalisationen. Deutsch-Ostafrika. 1913–1924.

RKA 5148. Reichsangehörigkeitsverhältnisse. Naturalisationen. Deutsch-Ostafrika. 1924–1941.

RKA 5156. Reichsangehörigkeits-Verhältnisse, Naturalisationen. [Samoa].

RKA 5421. Mischehen und Mischlinge in rechtlicher Beziehung. Deutsch-Ostafrika. 1906–1913.

RKA 5422. Mischehen und Mischlinge. Deutsch-Ostafrika. 1904–1923.

RKA 5423. Mischehen und Mischlinge in rechtlicher Beziehung. Deutsch-Südwestafrika. 1887–1912.

RKA 5424. Mischehen und Mischlinge in rechtlicher Beziehung. Deutsch-Südwestafrika. 1913–1919.

RKA 5430. Mischehen und Mischlinge in rechtlicher Beziehung. Südsee (Marschallinseln, Karolinen). 1897–1913.

RKA 5433. Rechtsverhältnisse der Mischlinge in Samoa. 1933–1936.

RKA 5654. Arzt und das Hospital in Zanzibar. 1889.

RKA 5673. Krankenpflege der Missionen in Deutsch-Ostafrika. 1886–1909.

RKA 6032/13. Deutscher Frauenverein für Krankenpflege in den Colonien. 1907–1914.

RKA 6032/14. Deutscher Frauenverein für Krankenpflege in den Colonien. 1914–1920.

RKA 6032/15. Frauenverein vom Roten Kreuz für Deutsche über See. 1926–1939.

RKA 6040. Bekämpfung der Geschlechtskrankheiten in den Colonien. 1908–1918.

RKA 6279. Die Frage der Besiedelungsfähigkeit tropischer Kolonien. (Acclimatisationsfähigkeit der weissen Rasse). 1912.

RKA 6281. Enquete des Vereins für Sozialpolitik über die Tropenbesiedelung durch Weisse. 1910–1913.

RKA 6693. Frauenbund der Deutschen Kolonialgesellschaft. 1907–1930.

RKA 6694. Frauenbund der Deutschen Kolonialgesellschaft. 1930–1932.

RKA 6695. Frauenbund der Deutschen Kolonialgesellschaft. 1933–1936.

RKA 6696. Frauenbund der Deutschen Kolonialgesellschaft. 1936–1939.

RKA 6682/1. Verwaltung der Schutzgebiete — Allgemeines. 1885–1919.

RKA 7427. Bevölkerungsstatistik der deutschen Kolonien — Allgemeines. 1890–1939.

Bestand Reichsministerium des Innern

RdI 27215. Koloniale Frauenschule Rendsburg. 1940–1944.

Nachlass Carl Peters (90 Pe 1).

Bundesarchiv Koblenz (BAK)
Wilhelm Külz papers.
Paul Rohrbach papers.

Geheimes Staatsarchiv Preussischer Kulturbesitz, Berlin (GStA)
Heinrich Schnee papers.

Landesarchiv Berlin (LAB)
Vereinsregister. Frauenbund der Deutschen Kolonialgesellschaft.

Leo Baeck Institute, New York (LBI)
Fritz Mauthner papers. Correspondence with Frieda von Bülow.

Lou-Andreas-Salomé-Archiv, Göttingen (LASA)
Correspondence with Frieda von Bülow, 1892–1908.

Archiv der Vereinten Evangelischen Mission, Wuppertal (VEM) Bestand Bethel-Mission
M 2 (old number: M I 1.2). Bethel-Mission. Vorstandsprotokolle, 26.10.1885–
  21.2.1887.
M 167 (old number: M I 14.1). Deutscher Frauenverein für Krankenpflege in den
  Kolonien, 1886–1891.
M 168 (old number: M I 14.2). Deutscher Frauenverein für Krankenpflege in den
  Kolonien, 1888–1890.
M 352 (old number: M II 5.2). Personalakte Marie Rentsch, Missionschwester,
  1886–1889.
M 356 (old number: M II 5.7). Personalakte Helene von Borcke, 1889–1890.

Papers of Else Frobenius, privately held.

PERIODICALS

Ausland und Heimat
Die Brücke zur Heimat
Centralblatt des Bundes Deutscher Frauenvereine
Deutsche Kolonialzeitung
Der Deutsche Lyzeumklub
Deutsches Kolonialblatt
Die Frau
Die Frau und die Kolonien
Die Frauenbewegung
Keetmanshooper Zeitung
Der Kolonialdeutsche
Koloniale Rundschau
Koloniale Zeitschrift
Kolonialpolitische Korrespondenz
Kolonie und Heimat
Mitteilungen der Deutschen Kolonialgesellschaft
Mitteilungsblatt der Kolonialen Frauenschule Rendsburg
Nachrichten aus der ostafrikanischen Mission
Unter dem rothen Kreuz
Zeitschrift für Kolonialpolitik, Kolonialrecht und Kolonialwirtschaft

Aas, Norbert, and Werena Rosenke, eds. *Kolonialgeschichte im Familienalbum: Frühe Fotos aus der Kolonie Deutsch-Ostafrika.* Münster: Unrast, 1992.

Ahmed, Leila. *Women and Gender in Islam: Historical Roots of a Modern Debate.* New Haven: Yale University Press, 1992.

"Die Akademikerin ist die beste Kolonistin." *Die Frau und die Kolonien* 1, no. 11 (November 1932): 145.

Albisetti, James. "Could Separate Be Equal? Helene Lange and Women's Education in Imperial Germany." *History of Education Quarterly* 22, no. 3 (fall 1982): 301–317.

———. "Women and the Professions in Imperial Germany." In *German Women in the Eighteenth and Nineteenth Centuries,* ed. Ruth-Ellen B. Joeres and Mary Jo Maynes, 94–109. Bloomington: Indiana University Press, 1986.

Alexander, Neville. "The Namibian War of Anti-colonial Resistance, 1904–7." In *Namibia 1884–1984,* ed. Brian Wood, 193–203. London: Namibia Support Committee; Lusaka: U.N. Institute for Namibia, 1988.

Allen, Ann Taylor. *Feminism and Motherhood in Germany 1800–1914.* New Brunswick: Rutgers University Press, 1991.

Alloula, Malek. *The Colonial Harem.* Trans. Myrna Godzich and Wlad Godzich. Minneapolis: University of Minnesota Press, 1986.

Anderson, Warwick. "The Trespass Speaks: White Masculinity and Colonial Breakdown." *American Historical Review* 102 (1997): 1343–1370.

Andreas-Salomé, Lou. *Das Haus: Familiengeschichte vom Ende vorigen Jahrhunderts.* Reprint, Frankfurt: Ullstein, 1987. Afterword by Sabina Streiter.

———. "Ketzereien gegen die moderne Frau." *Die Zukunft* 26 (1899): 237–240.

———. *Looking Back. Memoirs.* Ed. Ernst Pfeiffer. Trans. Breon Mitchell. Reprint, New York: Paragon, 1991.

Ansprenger, Franz. *The Dissolution of the Colonial Empires.* New York: Routledge, 1989.

Arbeitsgruppe Historischer Stadtrundgang. *"O Charlottenburg, du frauenfreundlichste unter den Städten . . .": Wege zur Frauengeschichte Charlottenburgs 1850–1930.* Berlin: Frauenforschungs- bildungs- und informationszentrum (FFBIZ), 1989.

Arendt, Hannah. *The Origins of Totalitarianism.* New ed. with added prefaces. New York: Harcourt Brace Jovanovich, 1973.

Arning, Wilhelm. "Die Stellung des Frauenbundes in der Kolonialpolitik von heute." In *Koloniale Frauenarbeit,* ed. Frauenbund der Deutschen Kolonialgesellschaft, 35–43. Berlin: Zentrale des Frauenbundes der Deutschen Kolonialgesellschaft, 1930.

Aschheim, Steven E. *Brothers and Strangers: The East European Jew in German and German Jewish Consciousness, 1800–1923.* Madison: University of Wisconsin Press, 1982.

Aus Südwestafrika: Blätter aus dem Tagebuch einer deutschen Frau 1902–1904. Leipzig: Veit, 1905.

Austen, Ralph. *Northwest Tanzania under German and British Rule: Colonial Policy and Tribal Politics, 1889–1939.* New Haven: Yale University Press, 1968.

Bade, Klaus J. "Antisklavereibewegung in Deutschland und Kolonialkrieg in Deutsch-Afrika." *Geschichte und Gesellschaft* 3 (1977): 31–58.

———. *Friedrich Fabri und der Imperialismus in der Bismarckzeit: Revolution — Depression — Expansion.* Freiburg i.B.: Atlantis, 1975.

———. "From Emigration to Immigration: The German Experience in the Nineteenth and Twentieth Centuries." In *Migration Past, Migration Future: Germany and the United States,* ed. Klaus J. Bade and Myron Wiener, 1–37. Providence: Berghahn, 1997.

Bair, Henry Martin Jr. "Carl Peters and German Colonialism: A Study in the Ideas and Actions of Imperialism." Ph.D. diss., Stanford University, 1968.

Bald, Detlef. *Deutsch-Ostafrika 1900–1914: Eine Studie über Verwaltung, Interessengruppen und wirtschaftliche Erschliessung.* Munich: Weltforum, 1970.

Barkan, Elazar, and Ronald Bush, eds. *Prehistories of the Future: The Primitivist Project and the Culture of Modernism.* Stanford: Stanford University Press, 1995.

Bastkowski, Friedrun, Christa Lindner, and Ulrike Prokop, eds. *Frauenalltag und Frauenbewegung im 20. Jahrhundert. Bd. 2. Frauenbewegung und die "Neue Frau" 1890–1933.* Frankfurt a.M.: Historisches Museum, 1980.

Baum, Marie. *Rückblick auf mein Leben.* Heidelberg: F. H. Kerle, 1950.

Bäumer, Gertrud. "Frieda von Bülow." *Die Frau* 16, no. 7 (April 1909): 407–412.

———. "Hedwig Heyl in der deutschen Frauenbewegung." In *Hedwig Heyl: Ein Gedenkblatt zu ihrem 70. Geburtstage dem 5. Mai 1920 von ihren Mitarbeitern und Freunden,* ed. Elise von Hopffgarten. Berlin: Dietrich Reimer (Ernst Vohsen), 1920.

———. *Helene Lange: Zu ihrem 70. Geburtstage.* 2d ed. Berlin: W. Moeser, 1918.

———. "Ika Freudenberg." In *Studien über Frauen,* 3d, exp. ed., 135–152. Berlin: F. A. Herbig, 1924.

Bayer, Maximilian. *The Rehoboth Baster Nation of Namibia.* Trans. and intro. Peter Carstens. Basel: Basler Afrika Bibliographien, 1984.

Becher, Jürgen. *Dar es Salaam, Tanga und Tabora: Stadtentwicklung in Tansania unter deutscher Kolonialherrschaft (1885–1914).* Stuttgart: Franz Steiner, 1997.

Behrendt, Armin. *Wilhelm Külz: Aus dem Leben eines Suchenden.* Berlin: Der Morgen, 1968.

Bennett, Norman R. *A History of the Arab State of Zanzibar.* London: Methuen, 1978.

———, ed. *The Zanzibar Letters of Edward D. Ropes, Jr. 1882–1892.* Boston: Boston University African Studies Center, 1973.

Benninghoff-Lühl, Sibylle. *Deutsche Kolonialromane 1884–1914 in ihrem Entstehungs- und Wirkungszusammenhang.* Bremen: Übersee-Museum, 1983.

Berghahn, Volker. *Imperial Germany.* Providence: Berghahn Books, 1994.

Berman, Nina. *Orientalismus, Kolonialismus und Moderne: Zum Bild des Orients in der deutschsprachigen Kultur um 1900.* Stuttgart: M & P, 1997.

Berman, Russell. *Enlightenment or Empire: Colonial Discourse in German Culture.* Lincoln: University of Nebraska Press, 1998.

Bischoff, Claudia. *Frauen in der Krankenpflege: Zur Entwicklung von Frauenrolle und Frauenberufstätigkeit im 19. und 20. Jahrhundert.* 2d rev. ed. Frankfurt: Campus, 1992.

Bleker, Johanna. "To Benefit the Poor and Advance Medical Science: Hospitals and Hospital Care in Germany, 1820–1870." In *Medicine and Modernity: Public Health and Medical Care in Nineteenth- and Twentieth-Century Germany,* ed. Manfred Berg and Geoffrey Cocks, 17–33. Washington, D.C.: German Historical Institute, 1997.

Bley, Fritz. *Die Weltstellung des Deutschthums.* Munich: J. F. Lehmann, 1897.

Bley, Helmut. *Namibia under German Rule.* Reprint, Hamburg: Lit, 1996.

Boak, Helen L. "Women in Weimar Germany: The 'Frauenfrage' and the Female Vote." In *Social Change and Political Development in Weimar Germany,* ed. Richard Bessel and E. J. Feuchtwanger, 155–173. London: Croom Helm, 1981.

Boemcken, Agnes von. "Deutsche Rückkehrer aus Ostafrika in der Heimat." *Die Frau und die Kolonien* no. 3 (March 1940): 17–21.

———. "Koloniale Frauenschule Rendsburg." In *Koloniale Frauenarbeit,* ed. Frauenbund der Deutschen Kolonialgesellschaft, 17–19. Berlin: Zentrale des Frauenbundes der Deutschen Kolonialgesellschaft, 1930.

Bonn, Moritz J. *Wandering Scholar.* New York: John Day, 1948.

Borcke, Helene von. *Ostafrikanische Erinnerungen einer freiwilligen Krankenpflegerin.* Berlin: Buchhandlung der Deutschen Lehrer-Zeitung (Fr. Zillessen), 1891.

Borries, Bodo von. "'Hochmut,' 'Reue' oder 'Weltbürgersinn'? Zur Kolonialepoche in historischen Überblicksdarstellungen und allgemeinem Geschichtsbewusstsein." In *Afrika und der deutsche Kolonialismus: Zivilisierung zwischen Schnapshandel und Bibelstunde,* ed. Renate Nestvogel and Rainer Tetzlaff, 153–181. Berlin: Dietrich Reimer, 1987.

Brandeis-Ruete, Antonie. "Die deutsche Hausfrau in den Kolonien." *Kolonie und Heimat* 1, no. 4 (10 November 1907): 13.

———. *Ethnographische Beobachtungen über die Marshall Insulaner.* N.d., n.p.

———. *Kochbuch für die Tropen: Nach langjähriger Erfahrung zusammengestellt.* Berlin: D. Reimer, 1907.

———. "Koloniale Frauenschule in Rendsburg." *Der Kolonialdeutsche* 6, no. 15 (1 August 1926): 261.

———. *Südsee-Bilder.* Berlin: Verlag der Kolonialen Zeitschrift, 1902.

———. "Südsee-Bilder." In *Das deutsche Kolonialbuch,* ed. Hans Zache, 486–490. Berlin: Wilhelm Andermann, 1925.

Braun, Georg. *Zur Frage der Rechtsgültigkeit der Mischehen in den deutschen Schutz-gebieten.* Greifswald: Julius Abel, 1912.

Braun, Lily. *Die Frauenfrage: Ihre geschichtliche Entwicklung und wirtschaftliche Seite.* Leipzig: Hirzel, 1901.

Bredow, Hedwig von. "Zum Geleit." In *Koloniale Frauenarbeit,* ed. Frauenbund der Deutschen Kolonialgesellschaft, 3. Berlin: Zentrale des Frauenbundes der Deutschen Kolonialgesellschaft, 1930.

Bridenthal, Renate. "Professional Housewives: Stepsisters of the Feminist Movement." In *When Biology Became Destiny: Women in Weimar and Nazi Germany,* ed. Atina Grossmann, Marion Kaplan, and Renate Bridenthal, 153–173. New York: Monthly Review, 1984.

———. "Something Old, Something New: Women between the Two World Wars." In *Becoming Visible,* 2d ed., ed. Renate Bridenthal, Claudia Koonz, and Susan Stuard, 473–497. Boston: Houghton Mifflin, 1987.

Bridenthal, Renate, and Claudia Koonz. "Beyond *Kinder, Küche, Kirche:* Weimar Women in Politics and Work." In *When Biology Became Destiny: Women in Weimar and Nazi Germany,* ed. Atina Grossmann, Marion Kaplan, and Renate Bridenthal, 33–65. New York: Monthly Review, 1984.

Bridgman, Jon M. *The Revolt of the Hereros.* Berkeley. University of California Press, 1981.

"Brief eines Kamerun-Negers." *Übersee- und Kolonialzeitung* 8, no. 19 (1 October 1928): 327.

Brinker-Gabler, Gisela, Karola Ludwig, and Angela Woffen, eds. *Lexikon deutsch-sprachiger Schriftstellerinnen 1800–1945.* Munich: Deutscher Taschenbuch Verlag, 1986.

Brinkschulte, Eva, and Beate Vogt. "'Nicht um des Lohnes willen, sondern aus Liebe zum Herrn': Die Diakonissinnen des Elisabeth-Krankenhauses — Zur Entwicklung des 'typisch weiblichen' Berufs der Krankenschwester (1833–1865)." In *Ich bin meine eigene Frauenbewegung: Frauen-Ansichten aus einer Grosstadt,* ed. Bezirksamt Schöneberg/Kunstamt Schöneberg, 155–164. Berlin: Edition Hentrich, 1991.

Brockmann, Clara. *Briefe eines deutschen Mädchens aus Südwest.* Berlin: E. S. Mittler, 1912.

———. *Die deutsche Frau in Südwestafrika: Ein Beitrag zur Frauenfrage in unseren Kolonien.* Berlin: E. S. Mittler, 1910.

Brose, Maximilian, ed. *Die deutsche Kolonialliteratur.* Berlin: Wilhelm Süsserott, 1884–1908.

Bruckner, Sierra Ann. "The Tingle-Tangle of Modernity: Popular Anthropology and the Cultural Politics of Identity in Imperial Germany." Ph.D. diss., University of Iowa, 1999.

Brunnemann, Anna. "Frieda Freiin von Bülow." *Das litterarische Echo. Halbmonats-schrift für Litteraturfreunde* 5, no. 9 (1902–1903): 598–604.

Buchner, Max. *Kamerun: Skizzen und Betrachtungen.* Leipzig: Duncker & Humblot, 1887.

Bülow, Adolf von, ed. *Bülowsches Familienbuch: Im Auftrage des Bülowschen Familien-Verbandes.* 2 vols. Schwerin: Eduard Herberger, 1911–1914.

Bülow, Frieda von. *Allein ich will. Roman.* Dresden: Carl Reissner, 1903.

———. "Allerhand Alltägliches aus Deutsch-Ostafrika." *Die Frau* 2, no. 1 (October 1894): 25–30, and vol. 2, no. 2 (November 1894): 93–98.

———. *Am andern Ende der Welt. Roman.* Berlin: Janke, 1890.

———. *Anna Stern. Roman.* Dresden: Carl Reissner, 1898.

———. *Deutsch-Ostafrikanische Novellen.* Dresden: Carl Reissner, 1892.

———. *Einsame Frauen.* Dresden: Carl Reissner, 1897.

———. *Frauentreue. Roman.* Dresden: Carl Reissner, 1910.

———. *Freie Liebe. Novelle.* Dresden: Carl Reissner, 1909.

———. *Hüter der Schwelle.* 2d ed. Dresden: Carl Reissner, 1907.

———. *Im Hexenring: Eine Sommergeschichte vom Lande.* Stuttgart: J. Engelhorn, 1901.

———. *Im Lande der Verheissung.* 6th ed. Dresden: Carl Reissner, 1914.

———. *Im Lande der Verheissung.* Ed. Thankmar von Münchhausen. Berlin: Oswald Arnold, 1943.

———. *Im Zeichen der Ernte: Italienisches Landleben von heute.* Dresden: Carl Reissner, 1904.

———. "In der Station." *Daheim* 24 (1888): 135–139.

———. *Irdische Liebe. Eine Alltagsgeschichte.* Dresden: Carl Reissner, 1905.

———. *Kara. Roman in drei Büchern.* Stuttgart: J. G. Cotta, 1897.

———. *Der Konsul: Vaterländischer Roman aus unseren Tagen.* Dresden: Carl Reissner, 1891.

———. "Lear-Patriotismus." *Die Zukunft* 30 (1900): 569–572.

———. *Ludwig von Rosen: Eine Erzählung aus zwei Welten.* Berlin: F. Fontane, 1892.

———. "Mann über Bord." *Die Zukunft* 21 (1897): 551–554.

———. "Männerurtheil über Frauendichtung." *Die Zukunft* 26 (1899): 26–29.

———. *Margarete und Ludwig. Roman.* 2 vols. Stuttgart: J. Engelhorn, 1894.

———. *Reisescizzen und Tagebuchblätter aus Deutsch-Ostafrika.* Berlin: Walther & Apolant, 1889.

———. *Die schönsten Novellen der Frieda von Bülow über Lou Andreas-Salomé und andere Frauen.* Ed. and afterword Sabina Streiter. Frankfurt a.M.: Ullstein, 1990.

———. *Die Schwestern: Geschichte einer Mädchenjugend.* 3d ed. Dresden: Carl Reissner, 1909.

———. "Die stilisierte Frau." In *Die schönsten Novellen der Frieda von Bülow über Lou Andreas-Salomé und andere Frauen,* ed. Sabina Streiter, 145–202. Frankfurt a.M.: Ullstein, 1990.

———. *Die Tochter. Roman.* Dresden: Carl Reissner, 1906.

———. *Tropenkoller: Episode aus dem deutschen Kolonialleben.* Berlin: F. Fontane, 1896.

———. "Eine unblutige Eroberungsfahrt an der ostafrikanischen Küste." *Daheim* 24 (1888): 22–24, 38–40.

———. "Das Weib in seiner Geschlechtsindividualität." *Die Zukunft* 18 (27 March 1897): 596–601.

———. "Weibliche Einjährige." *Die Zukunft* 32 (1900): 30–35.

———. *Wenn Männer schwach sind. Roman.* Berlin: Alfred Schall, 1908.

———. "Ein Werkeltag in Deutsch-Ostafrika." *Die Frau* 3, no. 12 (September 1896): 740–745.

Bülow, Margarete von. "Herr im Hause." In *Herr im Hause: Prosa von Frauen zwischen Gründerzeit und erstem Weltkrieg,* ed. Eva Kaufmann, 79–114. Berlin: Verlag der Nation, 1989.

Bülow von Dennewitz, Gertrud. "Noch einmal über die Frauenauswanderung nach Südwest-Afrika." *Die Frauenbewegung* 4, no. 14 (15 July 1898): 152–153.

Bunsen, Marie von. *Die Welt in der ich lebte: Erinnerungen aus glücklichen Jahren 1860–1912.* Leipzig: Koehler & Amelang, 1929.

Burckhardt, G. *Die Brüdergemeine. Erster Teil. Entstehung und geschichtliche Entwicklung der Brüdergemeine mit besonderer Berücksichtigung des Deutschen Zweiges der Unität.* Gnadau: Unitäts-Buchhandlung, 1905.

Burda, Josefine Margarete. "Frieda Freiin von Bülow." *Frauen-Rundschau* 10, no. 7 (1909): 183–184.

Bürgerliches Gesetzbuch für das Deutsche Reich. Reutlingen: Ensslin & Laiblin, n.d.

Burton, Antoinette. *Burdens of History: British Feminists, Indian Women, and Imperial Culture.* Chapel Hill: University of North Carolina Press, 1994.

Buttersack, F. "Die Frauen in der Heilkunde." *Unter dem rothen Kreuz* 4, no. 2 (February 1893): 14, and vol. 4, no. 3 (March 1893): 22.

C. L., "Eingesandt. Warnung." *Die Frauenbewegung* 4, no. 2 (15 January 1898): 21.

Campt, Tina. "'Afro-German': The Convergence of Race, Sexuality and Gender in the Formation of a German Ethnic Identity, 1919–1960." Ph.D. diss., Cornell University, 1996.

Campt, Tina, and Pascal Grosse. "'Mischlingskinder' in Nachkriegsdeutschland: Zum Verhältnis von Psychologie, Anthropologie und Gesellschaftspolitik nach 1945." *Psychologie und Geschichte* 6, nos. 1–2 (September 1994): 48–78.

Campt, Tina, Pascal Grosse, and Yara-Colette Lemke-Muñiz de Faria. "Blacks, Germans, and the Politics of Imperial Imagination, 1920–60." In *The Imperialist Imagination: German Colonialism and Its Legacy,* ed. Sara Friedrichsmeyer, Sara Lennox, and Susanne Zantop, 205–229. Ann Arbor: University of Michigan Press, 1999.

Cannibal Tours. Dir. Dennis O'Rourke. Australia. 1988.

Carsten, Francis L. "'Volk ohne Raum': A Note on Hans Grimm." In *Literature and Politics in the Twentieth Century,* ed. Walter Laqueur and George L. Mosse, 213–219. New York: Harper & Row, 1967.

Cauer, Minna. "Falscher Weg." *Die Frauenbewegung* 5, no. 7 (1 April 1899): 61–63.

———. "Die Uebersiedlung deutscher Frauen nach den Kolonien." *Die Frauenbewegung* 5, no. 15 (1 August 1899): 129–130.

———. "Vor den Wahlen." *Die Frauenbewegung* 4, no. 6 (15 March 1898): 61–62.

———. "Weckrufe." *Die Frauenbewegung* 12, no. 24 (15 December 1906): 185–186.

———. "Zur Frauen-Kolonisationsfrage." *Die Frauenbewegung* 4, no. 7 (1 April 1898): 77–78.

[Cauer, Minna, and Anna Pappritz]. "Vorschläge für die Übersiedelung von Mädchen nach den deutschen Kolonien." *Die Frauenbewegung, Beilage,* no. 8 (15 June 1899): 29–30.

Chickering, Roger. "'Casting Their Gaze More Broadly': Women's Patriotic Activism in Imperial Germany." *Past and Present* 118 (February 1988): 156–185.

———. *We Men Who Feel Most German: A Cultural Study of the Pan-German League, 1886–1914.* Boston: Allen & Unwin, 1984.

Christaller, Hanna. *Alfreds Frauen.* Stuttgart: Franckselche Verlagshandlung, 1916.

Chuchul, P. *Das Rote Kreuz: Ein die Geschichte, Organisation und Bedeutung der Bestrebungen unter dem Roten Kreuz behandelnder Vortrag.* 3d ed. Cassel: Gebrüder Gotthelft, 1905.

Clemens, Bärbel. *"Menschenrechte haben kein Geschlecht!" Zum Politikverständnis der bürgerlichen Frauenbewegung.* Pfaffenweiler: Centaurus, 1988.

Cock, Jacklyn. "Domestic Service and Education for Domesticity: The Incorporation of Xhosa Women into Colonial Society." In *Women and Gender in Southern Africa,* ed. Cherryl Walker, 76–96. London: James Currey, 1990.

Coetzee, J. M. *White Writing: On the Culture of Letters in South Africa.* New Haven: Yale University Press, 1988.

Cohen, Gary B. *The Politics of Ethnic Survival: Germans in Prague, 1861–1914.* Princeton: Princeton University Press, 1981.

Conklin, Alice. *A Mission to Civilize: The Republican Idea of Empire in France and West Africa, 1895–1930.* Stanford: Stanford University Press, 1997.

———. "Redefining 'Frenchness': Citizenship, Race Regeneration, and Imperial Motherhood in France and West Africa, 1914–40." In *Domesticating the Empire: Race, Gender and Family Life in French and Dutch Colonialism,* ed. Julia Clancy-Smith and Frances Gouda, 65–83. Charlottesville: University Press of Virginia, 1998.

Cooper, Frederick. *Plantation Slavery on the East Coast of Africa.* New Haven: Yale University Press, 1977.

Correspondence Relating to the Wishes of the Natives of the German Colonies as to Their Future Government. London, 1918.

Craig, Gordon. *The Politics of the Prussian Army, 1640–1945.* New York: Oxford University Press, 1955.

Curtin, Philip D. *Death by Migration: Europe's Encounter with the Tropical World in the Nineteenth Century.* New York: Cambridge University Press, 1989.

————. *Disease and Empire: The Health of European Troops in the Conquest of Africa.* New York: Cambridge University Press, 1998.

Daeubler, Karl. "Die Möglichkeit der Kolonisation und Anpassung der Europäer an die Tropen." *Deutsche Kolonialzeitung* 7, no. 7 (23 June 1894): 93–95.

Daniel, Ute. "Die Vaterländischen Frauenvereine in Westfalen." *Westfälische Forschungen* 39 (1989): 158–179.

————. *The War from Within: German Working-Class Woman in the First World War.* New York: Berg, 1997.

Davin, Anna. "Imperialism and Motherhood." *History Workshop Journal* 5 (1978): 9–65.

Dedering, Tilman. "The German-Herero War of 1904: Revisionism of Genocide or Imaginary Historiography." *Journal of Southern African Studies* 19 (March 1993): 80–88.

Deeken, Richard. *Maniua Samoa! Samoanische Reiseskizzen und Beobachtungen.* Oldenburg: Gerhard Stalling, 1901.

Delius, Käthe. "Das ländliche hauswirtschaftliche Bildungswesen." In *Deutsches Frauenstreben: Die deutsche Frau und das Vaterland,* ed. Clara Mende, 254–263. Stuttgart: Deutsche Verlags-Anstalt, 1931.

Deppe, Charlotte, and Ludwig Deppe. *Um Ostafrika. Erinnerungen.* Dresden: E. Beutelspacher, 1925.

Dernburg, Bernhard. *Koloniale Lehrjahre: Vortrag gehalten in Stuttgart am 23. Januar 1907.* Stuttgart: Union Deutsche Verlagsgesellschaft, 1907.

Deutsch, Jan-Georg. "The 'Freeing' of the Slaves in German East Africa: The Statistical Record, 1890–1914." In *Slavery and Colonial Rule in Africa,* ed. Suzanne Miers and Martin Klein, 109–132. London: Frank Cass, 1999.

————. "Inventing an East African Empire: The Zanzibar Delimitation Commission of 1885/1886." In *Studien zur Geschichte des deutschen Kolonialismus in Afrika,* ed. Peter Heine and Ulrich van der Heyden, 210–219. Pfaffenweiler: Centaurus, 1995.

Deutscher Lyzeum-Club, ed. *Ausstellung Die Frau in Haus und Beruf Berlin 1912.* Berlin: Rudolf Mosse, 1912.

Diel, Louise. *Die Kolonien warten! Afrika im Umbruch.* Leipzig: Paul List, 1939.

Diemel, Christa. *Adelige Frauen im bürgerlichen Jahrhundert: Hofdamen, Stiftsdamen, Salondamen 1800–1870.* Frankfurt a.M.: Fischer, 1998.

Dinglreiter, Senta. *Wann kommen die Deutschen endlich wieder? Eine Reise durch unsere Kolonien in Afrika.* Leipzig: Koehler & Amelang, 1935.

Dock, Lavinia L. *A History of Nursing.* 4 vols. New York: G. P. Putnam, 1912.

Dölle, Gilla. *Die (un)heimliche Macht des Geldes: Finanzierungsstrategien der bürgerlichen Frauenbewegung in Deutschland zwischen 1865 und 1933.* Frankfurt a.M.: dipa-Verlag, 1997.

Domansky, Elisabeth. "Militarization and Reproduction in World War I Germany." In *Society, Culture, and the State in Germany 1870–1930,* ed. Geoff Eley, 427–463. Ann Arbor: University of Michigan Press, 1996.

Domínguez, Virginia. *White by Definition: Social Classification in Creole Louisiana.* New Brunswick: Rutgers University Press, 1986.

Dove, Karl. *Südwest-Afrika: Kriegs- und Friedensbilder aus der ersten deutschen Kolonie.* Berlin: Allgemeiner Verein für deutsche Litteratur, 1896.

Draeger, Hans. "Ada Schnee, die Gattin." In *Gouverneur Schnee: Ein Künder und Mehrer deutscher Geltung. Zu seinem 60. Geburtstag,* ed. Draeger, 115–136. Berlin: Georg Stilke, 1931.

Drechsler, Horst. *"Let Us Die Fighting." The Struggle of the Herero and Nama against German Imperialism (1884–1915).* London: Zed Press, 1980.

———. *Südwestafrika unter deutscher Kolonialherrschaft.* Bd. 2. *Die grossen Land- und Minengesellschaften (1885–1914).* Stuttgart: Franz Steiner, 1996.

DuBois, W. E. B. *Dusk of Dawn: An Essay toward an Autobiography of a Race Concept.* Reprint, New Brunswick: Transaction, 1989.

Eckart, Wolfgang U. "Der ärztliche Dienst in den ehemaligen deutschen Kolonien: Die Einrichtungen der Krankenversorgung am Beispiel Kameruns." *Arzt und Krankenhaus* 10 (1981): 422–426.

———. "Malaria-Prävention und Rassentrennung: Die ärztliche Vorbereitung und Rechtfertigung der Duala-Enteignung 1912–1914." *History and Philosophy of the Life Sciences* 10 (1988): 363–378.

———. *Medizin und Kolonialimperialismus: Deutschland 1884–1945.* Paderborn: Schöningh, 1997.

Eckenbrecher, Margarethe von. *Im dichten Pori: Reise- und Jagdbilder aus Deutsch-Ostafrika.* Berlin: E. S. Mittler, 1912.

———. *Was Afrika mir gab und nahm: Erlebnisse einer deutschen Ansiedlerfrau in Südwestafrika.* Berlin: E. S. Mittler, 1907.

———. *Was Afrika mir gab und nahm: Erlebnisse einer deutschen Frau in Südwestafrika 1902–1936.* 7th rev. and exp. ed. Berlin: E. S. Mittler, 1937.

Eckenbrecher, Margarethe von, Helene von Falkenhausen, Philalethes Kuhn, and Oberleutnant Stuhlmann, eds. *Deutsch-Südwestafrika: Kriegs- und Friedensbilder. Selbsterlebnisse.* Leipzig: Wilhelm Weicher, 1907.

Edwards, Penny. "Womanizing Indochina: Fiction, Nation, and Cohabitation in Colonial Cambodia, 1890–1930." In *Domesticating the Empire: Race, Gender, and Family Life in French and Dutch Colonialism,* ed. Julia Clancy-Smith and Frances Gouda, 108–130. Charlottesville: University Press of Virginia, 1998.

Eigler, Friederike. "Engendering German Nationalism: Gender and Race in Frieda von Bülow's Colonial Writings." In *The Imperialist Imagination: German Colonialism and Its Legacy,* ed. Sara Friedrichsmeyer, Sara Lennox, and Susanne Zantop, 69–85. Ann Arbor: University of Michigan Press, 1999.

Eley, Geoff. *Reshaping the German Right: Radical Nationalism and Political Change after Bismarck.* 1980. Reprint, Ann Arbor: University of Michigan Press, 1991.

Elster, Ruth. "Gründung und Entwicklung der Berufsorganisation der Krankenpflegerinnen Deutschlands. Der 11. Januar 1903 — ist er auch 1978 noch von Interesse und Bedeutung?" *Krankenpflege* 32, no. 1 (January 1978): 13–14, 27.

Engels, Friedrich. "Socialism: Utopian and Scientific." In *The Marx-Engels Reader*, ed. Robert C. Tucker, 683–717. New York: W. W. Norton, 1978.

Epstein, Klaus. "Erzberger and the German Colonial Scandals, 1905–1910." *English Historical Review* 74 (1959): 637–663.

Essner, Cornelia. "Der Kampf um das Kolonialgericht oder Kolonialgesetzgebung als Verfassungsproblem." *Historische Mitteilungen* 5, no. 1 (1992): 78–95.

———. " 'Wo Rauch ist, da ist auch Feuer': Zu den Ansätzen eines Rassenrechts für die deutschen Kolonien." In *Rassendiskriminierung, Kolonialpolitik und ethnisch-nationale Identität*, ed. Winfried Wagner et al., 145–160b. Münster: Lit, 1992.

———. "Zwischen Vernunft und Gefühl: Die Reichstagsdebatten von 1912 um koloniale 'Rassenmischehe' und 'Sexualität.'" *Zeitschrift für Geschichtswissenschaft* 45, no. 6 (1997): 503–519.

Estorff, Ludwig von. *Wanderungen und Kämpfe in Südwestafrika, Ostafrika und Südafrika 1894–1910*. Ed. Christoph-Friedrich Kutscher. Wiesbaden: privately published, 1968.

Evans, Richard J. *The Feminist Movement in Germany 1894–1933*. London: Sage, 1976.

Falkenhausen, Helene von. *Ansiedlerschicksale: Elf Jahre in Deutsch-Südwestafrika 1893–1904*. Berlin: Dietrich Reimer (Ernst Vohsen), 1905.

Fassmann, Irmgard Maya. *Jüdinnen in der deutschen Frauenbewegung 1865–1919.* Hildesheim: Georg Olms, 1996.

Fischer, Fritz. *Germany's Aims in the First World War*. New York: W. W. Norton, 1967.

Fischer, Paul. "Selbstverwaltung." In *Deutsches Kolonial-Lexikon*, ed. Heinrich Schnee, 344–345. Leipzig: Quelle & Meyer, 1920.

———. "Das Verordnungsrecht in den Kolonien." In *Verhandlungen des Deutschen Kolonialkongresses 1905*, 364–381. Berlin: Dietrich Reimer (Ernst Vohsen), 1906.

Fleischmann, Max. "Die Mischehen in den deutschen Schutzgebieten vom Rechts-standpunkte." In *Verhandlungen des Deutschen Kolonialkongresses 1910*, 561. Berlin: Dietrich Reimer, 1910.

Fletcher, Roger. *Revisionism and Empire: Socialist Imperialism in Germany 1897–1914*. London: George Allen & Unwin, 1984.

Fliedner, Theodor. *Reisen in das heilige Land nach Smyrna, Beirut, Constantinopel, Alexandrien und Cairo, in den Jahren 1851, 1856 und 1857*. Düsseldorf: H. Voss, 1858.

Freedman, Ralph. *Life of a Poet: Rainer Maria Rilke*. New York: Farrar, Straus and Giroux, 1996.

Frenssen, Gustav. *Peter Moors Fahrt nach Südwest. Ein Feldzugsbericht*. Berlin: G. Grote, 1906.

Freudenberg, Ika. *Die Frau und die Kultur des öffentlichen Lebens*. Leipzig: C. F. Amelang, 1911.

Fricke, Dieter. "Der 'Deutschbund.'" In *Handbuch zur "völkischen Bewegung" 1871–1918*, ed. Uwe Puschner et al., 328–340. Munich: K. G. Saur, 1996.

——, ed. *Lexikon zur Parteiengeschichte: Die bürgerlichen und kleinbürgerlichen Parteien und Verbände in Deutschland.* 4 vols. Cologne: Paul-Rugenstein, 1983.

Friedländer, Saul. *Nazi Germany and the Jews.* Vol. 1. *The Years of Persecution, 1933–1939.* New York: HarperCollins, 1997.

Friedrichs, Elisabeth, ed. *Die deutschsprachigen Schriftstellerinnen des 18. und 19. Jahrhunderts. Ein Lexikon.* Stuttgart: J. B. Metzler, 1981.

Friedrichsmeyer, Sara, Sara Lennox, and Susanne Zantop, eds. *The Imperialist Imagination: German Colonialism and Its Legacy.* Ann Arbor: University of Michigan Press, 1999.

Frobenius, Else. "Aus der Geschichte des Frauenbundes." In *Koloniale Frauen-Arbeit,* ed. Frauenbund der Deutschen Kolonialgesellschaft. Berlin: Frauenbund der Deutschen Kolonialgesellschaft, 1926.

——. "Die Arbeit des Frauenbundes der Deutschen Kolonial-Gesellschaft." *Koloniale Rundschau* (1921): 266–270.

——. *30 Jahre kolonialer Frauenarbeit.* Berlin: Reichskolonialbund, 1936.

——. "Eine Frauenfahrt an die Front." *Die Frau* 24 (1916–1917): 530–541.

——. *Das Heimathaus in Keetmanshoop und das Jugendheim in Lüderitzbucht, die "Adda v. Liliencron-Stiftung."* Berlin: Frauenbund der Deutschen Kolonialgesellschaft, 1914.

——. "Koloniale Frauenarbeit." *Die Frau* 25 (1917–1918): 295–298.

——. "'Und wenn sie gleich alt werden . . .?': Dem Gedächtnis von Hedwig von Bredow." *Die Frau* 40 (1932–1933): 92–93.

——. "Warum müssen die Frauenverbände Kolonialpropaganda treiben?" In *Koloniale Frauenarbeit,* ed. Frauenbund der Deutschen Kolonialgesellschaft, 44–48. Berlin: Zentrale des Frauenbundes der Deutschen Kolonialgesellschaft, 1930.

——. *10 Jahre Frauenbund der Deutschen Kolonialgesellschaft.* Ed. Ausschuss des Frauenbundes der Deutschen Kolonialgesellschaft. Berlin: "Kolonie und Heimat" Verlagsgesellschaft, 1918.

Gann, L. H. "German Governors: An Overview." In *African Proconsuls: European Governors in Africa,* ed. L. H. Gann and Peter Duignan, 467–472. New York: Free Press, 1978.

Gann, L. H., and Peter Duignan. *The Rulers of German Africa 1884–1914.* Stanford: Stanford University Press, 1977.

Gebhardt, Heinz. *Königliche bayerische Photographie 1838–1918.* Munich: Laterna magica, 1978.

Gentz. "Die rechtliche Stellung der Bastards in Deutsch-Südwestafrika." *Beiträge zur Kolonialpolitik und Kolonialwirtschaft* 4 (1902–1903): 90–92.

Gerhard, Ute. "Die Rechtsstellung der Frau in der bürgerlichen Gesellschaft des 19. Jahrhunderts." In *Bürgertum im 19. Jahrhundert: Deutschland im europäischen Vergleich,* ed. Jürgen Kocka, 1:439–468. Munich: Deutscher Taschenbuch Verlag, 1988.

———. *Unerhört: Die Geschichte der deutschen Frauenbewegung.* With Ulla Wischermann. Reinbek bei Hamburg: Rowohlt, 1991.

———. *Verhältnisse und Verhinderungen: Frauenarbeit, Familie und Rechte der Frauen im 19. Jahrhundert.* Frankfurt a.M.: Suhrkamp, 1978.

Germany. Reichstag. *Stenographische Berichte über die Verhandlungen des Deutschen Reichstages.* Berlin: Verlag der Buchdruckerei der "Norddeutschen Allgemeinen Zeitung," 1896–1914.

Gierke, Anna von. "Entwicklung des Jugendheims." In *Hedwig Heyl: Ein Gedenkblatt zu ihrem 70. Geburtstage dem 5. Mai 1920 von ihren Mitarbeitern und Freunden,* ed. Elise von Hopffgarten, 71–76. Berlin: Dietrich Reimer (Ernst Vohsen), 1920.

Giesebrecht, Franz. *Ein deutscher Kolonialheld: Der Fall "Peters" in psychologischer Beleuchtung.* 2d ed. Zurich: Caesar Schmidt, 1897.

Glassman, Jonathon. *Feasts and Riot: Revelry, Rebellion, and Popular Consciousness on the Swahili Coast, 1856–1888.* Portsmouth, N.H.: Heinemann, 1995.

Gnauck-Kühne, Elisabeth. *Die deutsche Frau um die Jahrhundertwende. Statistische Studie zur Frauenfrage.* 2d, rev. ed. Berlin: Otto Liebmann, 1907.

———. *Die soziale Lage der Frau.* Berlin: Liebmann, 1895.

Goodman, Kay. "Motherhood and Work: The Concept of the Misuse of Women's Energy, 1895–1905." In *German Women in the Eighteenth and Nineteenth Centuries: A Social and Literary History,* ed. Ruth-Ellen B. Joeres and Mary Jo Maynes, 110–127. Bloomington: Indiana University Press, 1986.

Gordon, Robert. *The Bushman Myth: The Making of a Namibian Underclass.* Boulder: Westview Press, 1992.

Gottheiner, Elisabeth. "Das kommunale und kirchliche Wahlrecht der Frau." In *Der internationale Frauen-Kongress in Berlin 1904,* ed. Marie Stritt, 492–497. Berlin: Carl Habel, 1905.

Gottwald, Herbert. "Antiultramontaner Reichsverband." In *Lexikon zur Parteiengeschichte: Die bürgerlichen und kleinbürgerlichen Parteien und Verbände in Deutschland,* ed. Dieter Fricke, 1:89–93. Cologne: Pahl-Rugenstein, 1983.

Gray, John, "Memoirs of an Arabian Princess." *Tanganyika Notes and Records* 37 (July 1954): 49–70.

Grazia, Victoria de. *How Fascism Ruled Women: Italy 1922–1945.* Berkeley: University of California Press, 1992.

Greven-Aschoff, Barbara. *Die bürgerliche Frauenbewegung in Deutschland, 1894–1933.* Göttingen: Vandenhoeck & Ruprecht, 1981.

Grimm, Hans. *Volk ohne Raum.* Munich: A. Langen, 1926.

Grosse, Pascal. "Eugenik und Kolonialismus: Zum Verhältnis von Wissenschaft und Gesellschaftspolitik im Kaiserreich, 1885–1914." Ph.D. diss., Free University of Berlin, 1997.

———. *Kolonialismus Eugenik und bürgerliche Gesellschaft in Deutschland, 1850–1918* (Frankfurt a.M.: Campus, 2000).

———. "Kolonialismus und Öffentlichkeit im späten Kaiserreich: Die Deutschen Kolonialkongresse 1902, 1905 und 1910." M.A. thesis, Free University of Berlin, 1993.

Grotpeter, John J. *Historical Dictionary of Namibia*. Metuchen, N.J.: Scarecrow Press, 1994.

Gründer, Horst. *Geschichte der deutschen Kolonien*. 3d, rev. ed. Paderborn: Schöningh/UTB, 1995.

———. "'Gott will es.' Eine Kreuzzungsbewegung am Ende des 19. Jahrhunderts." *Geschichte in Wissenschaft und Unterricht* 28, no. 4 (April 1977): 210–224.

Grundhewer, Herbert. "Die Kriegskrankenpflege und das Bild der Krankenschwester im 19. und frühen 20. Jahrhundert." In *Medizin und Krieg: Vom Dilemma der Heilberufe 1865 bis 1985*, ed. Johanna Bleker and Heinz-Peter Schmiedebach, 135–152. Frankfurt a.M.: Fischer, 1987.

———. "Von der freiwilligen Kriegskrankenpflege bis zur Einbindung des Roten Kreuzes in das Heeressanitätswesen." In *Medizin und Krieg: Vom Dilemma der Heilberufe 1865 bis 1985*, ed. Johanna Bleker and Heinz-Peter Schmiedebach, 29–44. Frankfurt a.M.: Fischer, 1987.

Grüneisen, Felix. *Das Deutsche Rote Kreuz in Vergangenheit und Gegenwart*. Potsdam-Babelsberg: Deutsches Rotes Kreuz, 1939.

Gunzert, Theodor. "Deutsches Schulwesen in Ostafrika." In *Koloniale Frauenarbeit*, ed. Frauenbund der Deutschen Kolonialgesellschaft, 9–12. Berlin: Zentrales des Frauenbundes der Deutschen Kolonialgesellschaft, 1930.

Haase, Lene. *Raggys Fahrt nach Südwest. Roman*. Berlin: Egon Fleischel, 1910.

Hagen, William W. *Germans, Poles, and Jews: The Nationality Conflict in the Prussian East, 1772–1914*. Chicago: University of Chicago Press, 1980.

Hammerton, A. James. *Emigrant Gentlewomen: Genteel Poverty and Female Emigration, 1830–1914*. London: Croom Helm, 1979.

Handler, Richard. *Nationalism and the Politics of Culture in Quebec*. Madison: University of Wisconsin Press, 1988.

Hansen, Karen Tranberg. *Distant Companions: Servants and Employers in Zambia, 1900–1985*. Ithaca: Cornell University Press, 1989.

Harden, Maximilian. "Leist." *Die Zukunft* 9 (10 November 1894): 286–288.

Harvey, Elizabeth. "'Die deutsche Frau im Osten': 'Rasse,' Geschlecht und öffentlicher Raum im besetzten Polen 1940-1944." *Archiv für Sozialgeschichte* 38 (1998): 191–214.

———. "The Failure of Feminism? Young Women and the Bourgeois Feminist Movement in Weimar Germany 1918–1933." *Central European History* 28 (1995): 1–28.

———. "La Polonia sotto la Germania nazista: Il ruolo delle donne nella colonizzazione delle provincie annesse." *Italia Contemporanea* 200 (1995): 423–436.

———. "'Serving the Volk, Saving the Nation': Women in the Youth Movement and the Public Sphere in Weimar Germany." In *Elections, Mass Politics, and*

Social Change, ed. Larry Eugene Jones and James Retallack, 201–221. New York: Cambridge University Press, 1992.

Hausen, Karin. *Deutsche Kolonialherrschaft in Afrika: Wirtschaftsinteressen und Kolonialverwaltung in Kamerun vor 1914.* Zurich: Atlantis, 1970.

Hedrich, Kurt. *Der Rassegedanke im deutschen Kolonialrecht: Die rechtliche Regelung der ehelichen und ausserehelichen Beziehungen zwischen Weissen und Farbigen.* Schramberg: Gatzer & Hahn, 1941.

Heffter, Heinrich. *Die deutsche Selbstverwaltung im 19. Jahrhundert.* 2d, rev. ed. Stuttgart: K. F. Koehler, 1969.

Heineman, Elizabeth. "The Hour of the Woman: Memories of Germany's 'Crisis Years' and West German National Identity." *American Historical Review* 101, no. 2 (April 1996): 354–395.

Henderson, W. O. *The German Colonial Empire, 1884–1919.* London: Frank Cass, 1993.

Herbert, Ulrich. *A History of Foreign Labor in Germany, 1880–1980: Seasonal Workers, Forced Laborers, Guest Workers.* Trans. William Templer. Ann Arbor: University of Michigan Press, 1990.

Hering, Sabine. *Die Kriegsgewinnlerinnen: Praxis und Ideologie der deutschen Frauenbewegung im Ersten Weltkrieg.* Pfaffenweiler: Centaurus, 1990.

Herrmann, Rudolf. "Statistik der fremden Bevölkerung in den deutschen Schutzgebieten." *Beiträge zur Kolonialpolitik und Kolonialwirtschaft* 2 (1900–1901): 86–94.

Herz, Rudolf, and Brigitte Bruns, eds. *Hof-Atelier Elvira 1887–1928: Ästheten, Emanzen, Aristokraten.* Munich: Münchner Stadtmuseum, 1985.

Heyl, Hedwig. *ABC der Küche.* 4th ed. Berlin: Carl Habel, 1897.

———. *Aus meinem Leben.* Berlin: C. A. Schwetschke, 1925.

———. "Hauswirtschaftliche Bildung und Volkskultur." In *Der deutsche Frauenkongress. Berlin, 27. Februar bis 2. März 1912,* ed. Gertrud Bäumer, 1 6. Leipzig: Teubner, 1912.

———. "Die Kolonial-Frauenschule in Weilbach." *Kolonie und Heimat* 5, no. 41 (1911–1912): 8–9.

Heymann, Lida Gustava, and Anita Augspurg. *Erlebtes — Erschautes: Deutsche Frauen kämpfen für Freiheit, Recht und Frieden 1850–1940.* Ed. Margrit Twellmann. Meisenheim am Glan: Anton Hain, 1972.

Hildebrand, Klaus. *Vom Reich zum Weltreich: Hitler, NSDAP und koloniale Frage, 1919–1945.* Munich: Wilhelm Fink, 1969.

Hine, Darlene Clark. *Black Women in White: Racial Conflict and Cooperation in the Nursing Profession, 1890–1945.* Bloomington: Indiana University Press, 1989.

Hintrager, Oskar. *Südwestafrika in der deutschen Zeit.* Munich: R. Oldenbourg, 1955.

———. "Unsere Frauenauswanderung." In *Koloniale Frauenarbeit,* ed. Frauenbund der Deutschen Kolonialgesellschaft, 23–30. Berlin: Zentrale des Frauenbundes der Deutschen Kolonialgesellschaft, 1930.

Hochschild, Adam. *King Leopold's Ghost: A Story of Greed, Terror, and Heroism in Colonial Africa*. Boston: Houghton Mifflin, 1998.

Hodes, Martha. *White Women, Black Men: Illicit Sex in the Nineteenth Century South*. New Haven: Yale University Press, 1997.

Hoechstetter, Sophie. "Dem Gedächtnis Friedas v. Bülow." *Tägliche Rundschau* (Unterhaltungsbeilage), no. 64 (17 March 1909): 254.

——. *Frieda Freiin von Bülow. Ein Lebensbild*. Dresden: Carl Reissner, 1910.

Holm, Orla. *Ovita: Episode aus dem Hererolande*. Dresden: Carl Reissner, 1909.

——. *Pioniere: Ein Kolonialdrama aus Deutsch-Südwest-Afrika*. Berlin: F. Fontane, 1906.

Holstein, Christine [Margarete Jähne]. *Deutsche Frau in Südwest: Den Erlebnissen einer Farmersfrau im heutigen Afrika nacherzählt*. Leipzig: Koehler & Amelang, 1937.

Holston, Ken. "A Measure of the Nation: Colonial Enthusiasm, Education and Politics in Germany, 1890–1936." Ph.D. diss., University of Pennsylvania, 1996.

Hopffgarten, Elise von. "Lebensbild." In *Hedwig Heyl: Ein Gedenkblatt zu ihrem 70. Geburtstage dem 5. Mai 1920 von ihren Mitarbeitern und Freunden*, ed. Hopffgarten, 11–63. Berlin: Dietrich Reimer (Ernst Vohsen), 1920.

Höpker, Lydia. *Um Scholle und Leben: Schicksale einer deutschen Farmerin in Südwest-Afrika*. Minden in Westfalen: Wilhelm Köhler, 1927.

Horn, Peter. "Die Versuchung durch die barbarische Schönheit. Zu Hans Grimms 'farbigen' Frauen." *Germanisch-Romanische Monatsschrift* 35, no. 3 (1985): 317–341.

Hroch, Miroslav. "From National Movement to the Fully-Formed Nation: The Nation-Building Process in Europe." Reprinted in *Becoming National. A Reader*, ed. Geoff Eley and Ronald Grigor Suny, 60–77. New York: Oxford University Press, 1996. Originally published in *New Left Review*, 1993.

Hubatsch, Walter, et al., eds. *Grundriss zur deutschen Verwaltungsgeschichte 1815–1945. Bd. 22. Bundes- und Reichsbehörden*. Marburg/Lahn: Johann-Gottfried-Herder-Institut, 1983.

Huber, Ernst Rudolf. *Deutsche Verfassungsgeschichte seit 1789. Bd. 4. Struktur und Krisen des Kaiserreichs*. Stuttgart: W. Kohlhammer, 1969.

Huber, Mary Taylor, and Nancy Lutkehaus, eds. *Gendered Missions: Women and Men in Missionary Discourse and Practice*. Ann Arbor: University of Michigan Press, 1999.

Hunt, Nancy Rose. *A Colonial Lexicon of Birth Ritual, Medicalization, and Mobility in the Congo*. Durham: Duke University Press, 1999.

——. " 'Le bébé en brousse': European Women, African Birth Spacing, and Colonial Intervention in Breast Feeding in the Belgian Congo." In *Tensions of Empire: Colonial Cultures in a Bourgeois World*, ed. Frederick Cooper and Ann L. Stoler, 287–321. Berkeley: University of California Press, 1997.

Hüsgen, Eduard. *Ludwig Windthorst: Sein Leben, sein Wirken.* Cologne: J. P. Bachem, 1911.

Hutchinson, John F. *Champions of Charity: War and the Rise of the Red Cross.* Boulder: Westview Press, 1996.

Hyam, Ronald. *Empire and Sexuality: The British Experience.* Manchester: Manchester University Press, 1990.

Iliffe, John. *Tanganyika under German Rule.* London: Cambridge University Press, 1969.

Jacob, Ernst Gerhard. *Deutsche Kolonialkunde.* 2d., rev. ed. Dresden: L. Ehlermann, 1940.

Jasper, Gerhard. *Das Werden der Bethel-Mission.* Bethel bei Bielefeld: Verlagshandlung der Anstalt Bethel, 1936.

Jayawardena, Kumari. *Feminism and Nationalism in the Third World.* London: Zed Books, 1986.

——. *The White Woman's Other Burden: Western Women and South Asia during British Rule.* New York: Routledge, 1995.

[Jobst, Julia.] *Musste es sein?* Munich: Friedrich Rothbarth, 1904.

"Die Juden und die deutschen Kolonien." *Im deutschen Reich. Zeitschrift des Centralvereins deutschen Staatsbürger jüdischen Glaubens* 16, no. 11 (November 1910): 723–725.

Judson, Pieter M. "The Gendered Politics of German Nationalism in Austria, 1880–1900." In *Austrian Women in the Nineteenth and Twentieth Centuries: Cross-Disciplinary Perspectives,* ed. David F. Good, Margarete Grandner, and Mary Jo Maynes, 1–17. Providence: Berghahn, 1996.

Jusatz, Helmut J. "Wandlungen der Tropenmedizin am Ende des 19. Jahrhunderts." In *Medizin, Naturwissenschaft, Technik und das Zweite Kaiserreich,* ed. Gunter Mann and Rolf Winau, 227–238. Göttingen: Vandenhoeck & Ruprecht, 1977.

Kaes, Anton Kaes, Martin Jay, and Edward Dimendberg, eds. *The Weimar Republic Sourcebook.* Berkeley: University of California Press, 1994.

Kaiserliches Statistisches Amt, ed. *Statistik der Frauenorganisationen im Deutschen Reiche.* Berlin: Carl Heymann, 1909.

Kaplan, Marion A. *The Making of the Jewish Middle Class: Women, Family, and Identity in Imperial Germany.* New York: Oxford University Press, 1991.

——. "Sisterhood under Siege: Feminism and Anti-Semitism in Germany, 1904–1933." In *When Biology Became Destiny: Women in Weimar and Nazi Germany,* ed. Atina Grossmann, Marion Kaplan, and Renate Bridenthal, 174–196. New York: Monthly Review, 1984.

Kaplan, Sidney. "The Miscegenation Issue in the Election of 1864." *Journal of Negro History* 34 (1949): 274–343.

Kappstein, Theodor. *Fritz Mauthner: Der Mann und sein Werk.* Berlin: Gebrüder Paetel, 1926.

Karow, Maria. *Wo sonst der Fuss des Kriegers trat: Farmerleben in Südwest nach dem Kriege.* Berlin: E. S. Mittler, 1909.

Kaufmann, Doris. *Frauen zwischen Aufbruch und Reaktion: Protestantische Frauenbewegung in der ersten Hälfte des 20. Jahrhunderts.* Munich: Piper, 1988.

Keith-Smith, Brian, ed. *An Encyclopedia of German Women Writers 1900–1933. Biographies and Bibliographies with Exemplary Readings.* Lewiston, N.Y.: Edwin Mellen, 1997.

Kent, Susan Kingsley. *Making Peace: The Reconstruction of Gender in Interwar Britain.* Princeton: Princeton University Press, 1993.

Kimmle, Ludwig, ed. *Das Deutsche Rote Kreuz: Entstehung, Entwicklung und Leistungen der Vereinsorganisationen seit Abschluss der Genfer Convention i. J. 1864.* Bd. 2. Berlin: Boll & Pickardt, 1910.

Klotz, Marcia. "Memoirs from a German Colony: What Do White Women Want?" In *Eroticism and Containment: Notes from the Flood Plain,* ed. Carol Siegel and Ann Kibbey, 154–187. New York: New York University Press, 1994.

———. "White Women and the Dark Continent: Gender and Sexuality in German Colonial Discourse from the Sentimental Novel to the Fascist Film." Ph.D. diss., Stanford University, 1995.

Knobloch, Heinz. *Die Suppenlina: Wiederbelebung einer Menschenfreundin.* Berlin: Edition Hentrich, 1997.

Knoll, Arthur J. "Decision-Making for the German Colonies." In *Germans in the Tropics,* ed. Arthur J. Knoll and Lewis H. Gann, 131–149. Westport, Conn.: Greenwood Press, 1987.

Kolbe, Franz. "Nochmals 'Mischlingssorgen in Samoa.'" *Koloniale Zeitschrift* 13, no. 37 (13 September 1912): 600.

Koloniale Frauen-Arbeit. Berlin: Frauenbund der Deutschen Kolonialgesellschaft, 1926.

Koloniale Frauenarbeit. Berlin: Frauenbund der Deutschen Kolonialgesellschaft, 1930.

Kolonialpolitisches Aktionskomite, ed. *Schmoller, Dernburg, Delbrück, Schäfer, Sering, Schillings, Brunner, Jastrow, Penck, Kahl über Reichstagsauflösung und Kolonialpolitik. Offizieller stenographischer Bericht über die Versammlung in der Berliner Hochschule für Musik am 8. Januar 1907.* Berlin: Dr. Wedekind, 1907.

Kolonialwirtschaftliches Komitee, ed. "Die deutsche Hausfrau und die Kolonien." Berlin: E. S. Mittler, n.d. [ca. 1915].

Koonz, Claudia. "The Competition for a Women's *Lebensraum,* 1928–1934." In *When Biology Became Destiny: Women in Weimar and Nazi Germany,* ed. Atina Grossmann, Marion Kaplan, and Renate Bridenthal, 199–236. New York: Monthly Review, 1984.

———. *Mothers in the Fatherland: Women, the Family and Nazi Politics.* New York: St. Martin's Press, 1987.

Kootz-Kretschmer, Elise. *Die Safwa, ein ostafrikanischer Volksstamm in seinem Leben und Denken.* Berlin: Dietrich Reimer (Ernst Vohsen), 1926–1929.

Koponen, Juhani. *Development for Exploitation: German Colonial Policies in Mainland Tanzania, 1884–1914.* Hamburg: Lit Verlag, 1994.

Körner, Karl. "Vom deutschen Schulwesen in Südwest." In *Koloniale Frauenarbeit,* ed. Frauenbund der Deutschen Kolonialgesellschaft, 13–16. Berlin: Zentrale des Frauenbundes der Deutschen Kolonialgesellschaft, 1930.

Koschwitz-Newby, Heidi. "Hedwig Heyl: Die beste Hausfrau Berlins." In *Unter allen Umständen: Frauengeschichte(n) in Berlin,* ed. Christiane Eifert and Susanne Rouette, 60–79. Berlin: Rotation, 1986.

Krätschell, Hermann. "Carl Peters 1856–1918: Ein Beitrag zur Publizistik des imperialistischen Nationalismus in Deutschland." Ph.D. diss., Free University of Berlin, 1959.

Kraus, Herbert, and Gustav Rödiger, eds. *Urkunden zum Friedensvertrage von Versailles vom 28. Juni 1919.* Erster Teil. Berlin: Franz Vahlen / Hans Robert Engelmann, 1920.

Kröll, Ulrich. *Die internationale Buren-Agitation 1899–1902.* Münster: Regensberg, 1973.

Kuhlenbeck, Ludwig. "Die politischen Ergebnisse der Rassenforschung." In *Zwanzig Jahre alldeutscher Arbeit und Kämpfe,* ed. Hauptleitung des Alldeutschen Verbandes, 272–275. Leipzig: Dieterich, 1910.

Kühn, Detlev. "Lenore Kühn — eine nationale Mitstreiterin der Frauenbewegung." *Nordost-Archiv,* nos. 61–62 (1981): 39–56; and nos. 63–64 (1981): 31–54.

Kuhn, Maria. "Die Stellung der Frau in den Kolonien." In *Verhandlungen des Deutschen Kolonialkongresses,* 945–964. Berlin: Dietrich Reimer (Ernst Vohsen), 1910.

Kuhn, Philalethes, and W. Harbers. "Die Auswanderung von Frauen und Kindern in die britischen Kolonien." *Zeitschrift für Kolonialpolitik, Kolonialrecht und Kolonialwirtschaft* 12, no. 11 (November 1910): 833–858.

Kuhn, Roland. *Lebensbild von Maria Kuhn geb. Ritter und Philalethes Kuhn.* Bonn: privately published, 1964.

Kühnhold, Grete. *In Friedens- und Kriegszeiten in Kamerun.* Berlin: August Scherl, 1917.

Külz, Ludwig. *Blätter und Briefe eines Arztes aus dem tropischen Deutschafrika.* Berlin: Wilhelm Süsserott, 1906. Reprinted in 1943 as *Tropenarzt im afrikanischen Busch.*

Külz, Wilhelm. *Deutsch-Südafrika im 25. Jahre deutscher Schutzherrschaft: Skizzen und Beiträge zur Geschichte Deutsch-Südafrikas.* Berlin: Wilhelm Süsserott, 1909.

——. *Die Feststellung der Friedenspräsenzstärke des Deutschen Heeres, rechtswissenschaftlich dargestellt.* Leipzig-Reudnitz: August Hoffmann, 1900.

——. "Frauenstimmrecht in den Kolonien?" *Deutsche Kolonialzeitung* 26, no. 43 (1909): 707–708.

——. *Die Fürsorgeerziehung im Königreich Sachsen und ihre Mängel.* Leipzig-Reudnitz: August Hoffmann, 1904.

Kum'a N'dumbe, Alexandre. *Was wollte Hitler in Afrika? NS-Planungen für eine faschistische Neugestaltung Afrikas.* Frankfurt a.M.: IKO Verlag für interkulturelle Kommunikation, 1993.

Kuntze, Paul H. *Das Volksbuch der deutschen Kolonien.* Leipzig: George Dollheimer, 1938.

Lange, Bernhard. "Die Begründerin des deutschen Kolonialromans. Zum 75. Geburtstage von Frieda Freiin v. Bülow." *Deutsche Kolonialzeitung* 44 (1932): 272–273.

Lange, Friedrich. *Reines Deutschtum: Grundzüge einer nationalen Weltanschauung.* 3d, exp. ed. Berlin: Alexander Duncker, 1904.

Lange, Helene. "Altes und Neues zur Frauenfrage." *Die Frau* 2, no. 9 (June 1895): 536–541.

———. *Kampfzeiten: Aufsätze und Reden aus vier Jahrzehnten.* 2 vols. Berlin: F. A. Herbig, 1928.

Langewiesche, Dieter. "Liberalism in the Second Empire, 1871–1914." In *In Search of a Liberal Germany: Studies in the History of German Liberalism from 1789 to the Present,* ed. Konrad H. Jarausch and Larry Eugene Jones, 217–236. New York: Berg, 1990.

Lebzelter, Gisela. "Die 'schwarze Schmach': Vorurteile — Propaganda — Mythos." *Geschichte und Gesellschaft* 11 (1985): 37–58.

Lehr, Ludwiga. "Der Deutsche Frauenverein vom Roten Kreuz für die Kolonien." *Koloniale Rundschau* (1913): 674–679.

———. "Über die Leistungen des Roten Kreuzes in den deutschen Kolonien." In *Verhandlungen des Deutschen Kolonialkongresses 1910,* 932–945. Berlin: Dietrich Reimer (Ernst Vohsen), 1910.

Leist, Heinrich. "Der Fall Leist." *Die Zukunft* 16 (8 August 1896): 259–271.

Lekow, Hildegard von. "50 Jahre Rotkreuzarbeit." In *Das Buch der deutschen Kolonien,* ed. Heinrich Schnee et al., 368–371. Leipzig: W. Goldmann, 1937.

———. "Rotkreuzarbeit in den Kolonien." In *Das Buch der deutschen Kolonien,* ed. Anton Mayer, 288–291. Potsdam: Volk und Heimat, 1933.

Leue, August. *Dar es Salaam: Bilder aus dem Kolonialleben.* Berlin: W. Süsserott, 1903.

Leutner, Mechthild, ed. *"Musterkolonie Kiautschou": Die Expansion des Deutschen Reiches in China. Deutsch-Chinesische Beziehungen 1897 bis 1914. Eine Quellensammlung.* Berlin: Akademie, 1997.

Leutwein, Theodor. *Elf Jahre Gouverneur in Deutsch-Südwestafrika.* 2d ed. Berlin: E. S. Mittler, 1907.

———. "Offener Brief an die Herausgeberin." *Die Frauenbewegung* 4, no. 9 (1 May 1898): 99–100.

Liliencron, Adda von. *Getreu bis zuletzt.* Berlin 1912.

———. *Krieg und Frieden: Erinnerungen aus dem Leben einer Offiziersfrau.* Berlin: R. Eisenschmidt, 1912.

———. *Kriegsklänge der Kaiserlichen Schutztruppe in Deutsch-Südwestafrika. Soldatenlieder.* 1905.

———. *Reiterbriefe aus Südwest: Briefe und Gedichte aus dem Feldzuge in Südwest-Afrika in den Jahren 1904–1906.* Oldenburg: Gerhard Stalling, 1907.

Lob., J. "Über den Werth der Krankenpflege." *Unter dem rothen Kreuz* 2 (1891): 73.

Lohalm, Uwe. *Völkischer Radikalismus: Die Geschichte des Deutschvölkischen Schutz- und Trutz-Bundes 1919–1923.* Hamburg: Leibniz, 1970.

Lorbeer, Marie, and Beate Wild, eds. *Menschenfresser, Negerküsse: Das Bild vom Fremden im deutschen Alltag.* Berlin: Elefanten-Press, 1993.

Loth, Heinrich. "Die Gründung von Deutsch-Ostafrika und die christliche Mission." *Wissenschaftliche Zeitschrift der Karl-Marx-Universität Leipzig, Gesellschafts- und Sprachwissenschaftliche Reihe* 8, no. 2 (1958–1959): 339–347.

Lüders, Else. *Minna Cauer: Leben und Werk. Dargestellt an Hand ihrer Tagebücher und nachgelassenen Schriften.* Gotha: Leopold Klotz, 1925.

———. "Eine Propagandareise für das Frauenstimmrecht in Süd-Afrika." *Zeitschrift für Frauenstimmrecht* 6, no. 4 (1 May 1912): 3.

———. "Rassen- und Rechtsfragen in den Kolonien: Auch ein Kulturproblem." *Zeitschrift für Frauenstimmrecht* 6, no. 7 (1 August 1912): 2–3.

Maag, Anne. "Einrichtung von Lesemappen und Büchereien in Südwestafrika." In *Koloniale Frauenarbeit,* ed. Frauenbund der Deutschen Kolonialgesellschaft, 20–21. Berlin: Zentrale des Frauenbundes der Deutschen Kolonialgesellschaft, 1930.

MacLean, Eva. "Frieda von Bülow: Eine Pionierin der kolonialen Frauenarbeit." *Die Frau und die Kolonien* 8 (1937): 122–123.

———. "Shopping in Sansibar." *Die Frau und die Kolonien,* no. 11 (November 1932): 139–143.

———. *Unser Kamerun von heute. Ein Fahrtenbuch.* 2d ed. Munich: Fichte Verlag Paul Wustrow, 1940.

Mamozai, Martha. *Herrenmenschen: Frauen im deutschen Kolonialismus.* Reinbek bei Hamburg: Rowohlt, 1982.

Mann, Heinrich. *The Loyal Subject.* Ed. Helmut Peitsch. New York: Continuum, 1998.

Mansfeld, Alfred, ed. *Sozialdemokratie und Kolonieen.* Reprint, Münster: Lit Verlag, 1987.

Marks, Sally. "Black Watch on the Rhine: A Study in Propaganda, Prejudice and Prurience." *European Studies Review* 13 (1983): 297–334.

Marks, Shula. *Divided Sisterhood: Race, Class, and Gender in the South African Nursing Profession.* New York: St. Martin's Press, 1994.

Martin, Biddy. *Woman and Modernity: The (Life)Styles of Lou Andreas-Salomé.* Ithaca: Cornell University Press, 1991.

Martin, Peter. *Schwarze Teufel, edle Mohren.* Hamburg: Junius, 1993.

Martinez-Alier, Verena. *Marriage, Class and Colour in Nineteenth-Century Cuba: A Study of Racial Attitudes and Sexual Values in a Slave Society.* Reprint, Ann Arbor: University of Michigan Press, 1989.

Marx, Karl. *Early Writings.* Trans. Rodney Livingstone and Gregor Benton. London: Penguin, 1974.

Massfeller, Franz. *Deutsches Staatsangehörigkeitsrecht von 1870 bis zur Gegenwart.* Frankfurt a.M.: Verlag für Standesamtswesen, 1953.

Matuschka, Maria. *Meine Erinnerungen aus Deutsch-Ostafrika von 1911–1919.* Leipzig: Xenien-Verlag, n.d. [1919].

Mauthner, Fritz. *Der Atheismus und seine Geschichte im Abendland.* 4 vols. Frankfurt a.M.: Eichborn, 1989.

———. *Beiträge zu einer Kritik der Sprache.* 3 vols. Leipzig: Felix Meiner, 1923.

Mead, Margaret. "Weaver of the Border." In *In the Company of Man. Twenty Portraits by Anthropologists,* ed. Joseph B. Casagrande, 175–210. New York: Harper & Bros., 1960.

Medizinal-Berichte über die deutschen Schutzgebiete für das Jahr 1903/04. Berlin: E. S. Mittler, 1905.

Medizinal-Berichte über die deutschen Schutzgebiete für das Jahr 1905/06. Berlin: E. S. Mittler, 1907.

Medizinal-Berichte über die deutschen Schutzgebiete für das Jahr 1907/08. Berlin: E. S. Mittler, 1909.

Mehta, Uday. "Strategies of Liberal Exclusion." In *Tensions of Empire: Colonial Cultures in a Bourgeois World,* ed. Frederick Cooper and Ann Laura Stoler, 59–86. Berkeley: University of California Press, 1997.

Melber, Henning. "Kontinuitäten totaler Herrschaft: Völkermord und Apartheid in 'Deutsch-Südwestafrika.' Zur kolonialen Herrschaftspraxis im Deutschen Kaiserreich." *Jahrbuch für Antisemitismusforschung* 1 (1992): 91–116.

Menzel, Gustav. *Die Bethel-Mission: Aus 100 Jahren Missionsgeschichte.* Neukirchen-Vluyn: Neukirchener Verlag des Erziehungsvereins, 1986.

———. *C. G. Büttner: Missionar, Sprachforscher und Politiker im der deutschen Kolonialbewegung.* Wuppertal: Verlag der Vereinten Evangelischen Mission, 1992.

———. *Die Rheinische Mission.* Wuppertal: Verlag der Vereinten Evangelischen Mission, 1978.

Meyer, Henry Cord. *Mitteleuropa in German Thought and Action, 1815–1945.* The Hague: Martinus Nijhoff, 1955.

Meyer-Renschhausen, Elisabeth. *Weibliche Kultur und soziale Arbeit: Eine Geschichte der Frauenbewegung am Beispiel Bremens 1810–1927.* Cologne: Böhlau, 1989.

Midgley, Clare. "Anti-slavery and the Roots of 'Imperial Feminism.'" In *Gender and Imperialism,* ed. Midgley, 161–179. Manchester: Manchester University Press, 1998.

———. *Women against Slavery: The British Campaigns 1780–1870.* London: Routledge, 1992.

Miers, Suzanne. "The Brussels Conference of 1889–1890: The Place of the Slave Trade in the Policies of Great Britain and Germany." In *Britain and Germany in Africa: Imperial Rivalry and Colonial Rule,* ed. Prosser Gifford and W. Roger Louis, 83–118. New Haven: Yale University Press, 1967.

———. "Slavery and the Slave Trade as International Issues 1890–1939." In *Slavery and Colonial Rule in Africa,* ed. Suzanne Miers and Martin Klein, 16–37. London: Frank Cass, 1999.

Miers, Suzanne, and Martin Klein, eds. *Slavery and Colonial Rule in Africa.* London: Frank Cass, 1999.

Mill, John Stuart. *On Liberty, with The Subjection of Women and Chapters on Socialism.* Ed. Stefan Collini. Cambridge: Cambridge University Press, 1989.

Misch, Carl. *Geschichte des Vaterländischen Frauen-Vereins 1866–1916: Im Auftrage des Hauptvorstandes des Vaterländischen Frauen-Vereins.* Berlin: Carl Heymann, 1917.

Moeller, Robert G. "War Stories: The Search for a Usable Past in the Federal Republic of Germany." *American Historical Review* 101, no. 4 (October 1996): 1008–1048.

Mogk, Walter. *Paul Rohrbach und das "Grössere Deutschland": Ethischer Imperialismus im wilhelminischen Zeitalter. Ein Beitrag zur Geschichte des Kulturprotestantismus.* Munich: Wilhelm Goldmann, 1972.

Mommsen, Wolfgang J. "Domestic Factors in German Foreign Policy before 1914." In *Imperial Germany,* ed. James Sheehan, 223–268. New York: New Viewpoints, 1976.

———. *Imperialismus: Seine geistigen, politischen und wirtschaftlichen Grundlagen. Ein Quellen- und Arbeitsbuch.* Hamburg: Hoffmann & Campe, 1977.

Morgenstern, Lina. *Frauenarbeit in Deutschland.* I. Teil. *Geschichte der deutschen Frauenbewegung und Statistik der Frauenarbeit auf allen ihr zugänglichen Gebieten.* II. Teil. *Adressbuch und Statistik.* Berlin: Verlag der Deutschen Hausfrauen-Zeitung, 1893.

Mosse, George L. *Nationalism and Sexuality: Middle-Class Morality and Sexual Norms in Modern Europe.* Madison: University of Wisconsin Press, 1985.

Mtoro bin Mwinyi Bakari. *The Customs of the Swahili People: The* Desturi za Waswahili *of Mtoro bin Mwinyi Bakari and Other Swahili Persons.* Ed. and trans. J. W. T. Allen. Berkeley: University of California Press, 1981.

Müller, Fritz Ferdinand. *Deutschland — Zanzibar — Ostafrika: Geschichte einer deutschen Kolonialeroberung 1884–1890.* Berlin: Rütten & Loening, 1959.

Naarmann, Bernhard. "Koloniale Arbeit unter dem Roten Kreuz: Der Deutsche Frauenverein vom Roten Kreuz für die Kolonien zwischen 1888–1917." Ph.D. diss., University of Münster, 1986.

Niesel, Hans-Joachim. "Kolonialverwaltung und Missionen in Deutsch Ostafrika 1890–1914." Ph.D. diss., Free University of Berlin, 1971.

Niessen-Deiters, Leonore. *Die deutsche Frau im Auslande und in den Schutzgebieten: Nach Originalberichten aus fünf Erdteilen.* Berlin: Egon Fleischel, 1913.

O'Donnell, Krista. "The Colonial Woman Question: Gender, National Identity, and Empire in the German Colonial Society Female Emigration Program, 1896–1914," Ph.D. diss., Binghamton University, 1996.

Oguntoye, Katharina. *Eine afro-deutsche Geschichte: Zur Lebensituation von Afrikanern und Afro-Deutschen in Deutschland von 1884 bis 1950.* Berlin: Hoho Verlag Christine Hoffmann, 1997.

Okin, Susan Moller, et al. *Is Multiculturalism Bad for Women?* Princeton: Princeton University Press, 1999.

Oloukpona-Yinnon, Adjaï. "Mut gegen Tabu. Hanna Christaller: Die Bahnbrecherin der deutschen Kolonialbelletristik über Togo." *Etudes Germano-Africaines,* no. 10 (1992): 85–91.

———. *Unter deutschen Palmen: Die "Musterkolonie" Togo im Spiegel deutscher Kolonialliteratur (1884–1944).* Frankfurt a.M.: IKO Verlag für interkulturelle Kommunikation, 1998.

Opitz, May, Katharina Oguntoye, and Dagmar Schultz, eds. *Showing Our Colors: Afro-German Women Speak Out.* Trans. Anne V. Adams. Amherst: University of Massachusetts Press, 1992.

Othenberg, Ludwig. *Die Zuständigkeit in privatrechtlichen Mischprozessen nach deutschem Kolonialrecht.* Hanover: Gustav Jacob, 1914.

Otto-Peters, Louise. *Frauenleben im Deutschen Reich: Erinnerungen aus der Vergangenheit mit Hinweis auf Gegenwart und Zukunft.* Leipzig: Moritz Schäfer, 1876. Reprint, Paderborn: M. Hüttemann, 1988.

Paasche, Hans. *Die Forschungsreise des Afrikaners Lukanga Mukara ins innerste Deutschland.* Ed. Franziskus Hähnel, afterword by Iring Fetscher. Munich: Goldmann, 1988.

Paasche, Luise. *Männer wehrlos, Frauen schutzlos: Unsere Propagandareise gegen die Schuldlüge.* Neckargemünd: privately published, 1927.

Page, Melvin E. "Introduction: Black Men in a White Men's War." In *Africa and the First World War,* ed. Page, 1–27. New York: St. Martin's Press, 1987.

Pappritz, Anna, ed. *Einführung in das Studium der Prostitutionsfrage.* Leipzig: J. A. Barth, 1919.

Pascoe, Peggy. "Miscegenation Law, Court Cases, and Ideologies of 'Race' in Twentieth-Century America." *Journal of American History* 83 (June 1996): 44–69.

Pataky, Sophie, ed. *Lexikon deutscher Frauen der Feder: Eine Zusammenstellung der seit dem Jahre 1840 erschienenen Werke weiblicher Autoren, nebst Biographieen der lebenden und einem Verzeichnis der Pseudonyme.* Reprint, Bern: H. Lang, 1971.

Pedersen, Jean Elisabeth. "'Special Customs': Paternity Suits and Citizenship in France and the Colonies, 1870–1912." In *Domesticating the Empire: Race, Gender and Family Life in French and Dutch Colonialism,* ed. Julia Clancy-Smith and Frances Gouda, 43–64. Charlottesville: University Press of Virginia, 1998.

Peirce, Leslie P. *The Imperial Harem: Women and Sovereignty in the Ottoman Empire.* New York: Oxford University Press, 1993.

Peters, Carl. *Gesammelte Schriften.* Ed. Walter Frank. 2 vols. Munich: C. H. Beck, 1943.

Petschull, Jürgen, and Thomas Höpker. *Der Wahn vom Weltreich: Die Geschichte der deutschen Kolonien.* Hamburg: Stern-Buch/Gruner & Jahr, 1984.

Pfeffer, Gulla. "Meine Kamerun-Nigeria-Expedition." *Der Kolonialdeutsche* 8 (1928): 304.

———. *Die weisse Mah: Allein bei Urvölkern und Menschenfressern.* Minden i.W.: Wilhelm Köhler, 1929.

Pfeiffer, Ernst, ed. *Rainer Maria Rilke. Lou Andreas-Salomé. Briefwechsel.* Frankfurt a.M.: Insel, 1975.

Pfeil, Joachim von. *Die Erwerbung von Deutsch-Ostafrika: Ein Beitrag zur Kolonial-Geschichte.* New ed. Berlin: Karl Curtius, n.d. [1907].

———. *Vorschläge zur praktischen Kolonisation in Ost-Afrika.* Berlin: Rosenbaum & Hart, 1888.

Pfeil und Klein-Ellguth, Eva von. *Ein reiches Leben: Lebenserinnerungen und meine Arbeit für das Rote Kreuz in den Kolonien.* Dessau: Eduard H. de Rot (D. Schwalbe), 1914.

Pfläging, Wilhelm. *Zum kolonialrechtlichen Problem der Mischbeziehungen zwischen deutschen Reichsangehörigen und Eingeborenen der deutschen Schutzgebiete, unter besonderer Berücksichtigung des Unterhaltsanspruches der unehelichen Mischlinge.* Berlin: Gustave Schade (Otto Francke), 1913.

Pierard, Richard V. "The German Colonial Society." In *Germans in the Tropics,* ed. Arthur J. Knoll and Lewis H. Gann, 19–37. Westport, Conn.: Greenwood Press, 1987.

———. "The German Colonial Society, 1882–1914." Ph.D. diss., State University of Iowa, 1964.

———. "The Transportation of White Women to German Southwest Africa, 1898–1914." *Race* 12 (1971): 317–322.

Planert, Ute. *Antifeminismus im Kaiserreich: Diskurs, soziale Formation und politische Mentalität.* Göttingen: Vandenhoeck & Ruprecht, 1998.

Plehn, Albert. "Die Akklimatisationsausssichten der Germanen im tropischen Afrika." In *Verhandlungen des Deutschen Kolonialkongresses 1910,* 888–906. Berlin: Dietrich Reimer (Ernst Vohsen), 1910.

Pogge von Strandmann, Hartmut. "Domestic Origins of Germany's Colonial Expansion under Bismarck." *Past and Present* 42 (February 1969): 140–159.

———. "Nationale Verbände zwischen Weltpolitik und Kontinentalpolitik." In *Marine und Marinepolitik im kaiserlichen Deutschland 1871–1914,* ed. Herbert Schottelius and Wilhelm Deist, 296–317. Düsseldorf: Droste, 1972.

Pommerin, Reiner. *Sterilisierung der Rheinlandbastarde: Das Schicksal einer farbigen deutschen Minderheit 1918–1937.* Düsseldorf: Droste, 1979.

Prager, Erich. *Die Deutsche Kolonialgesellschaft 1882–1907: Im Auftrage des Ausschusses der Deutschen Kolonialgesellschaft dargestellt.* Berlin: Dietrich Reimer (Ernst Vohsen), 1908.

Prelinger, Catherine M. *Charity, Challenge, and Change: Religious Dimensions of the Mid-Nineteenth-Century Women's Movement in Germany.* Westport, Conn.: Greenwood Press, 1987.

———. "The Nineteenth-Century Deaconessate in Germany: The Efficacy of a Family Model." In *German Women in the Eighteenth and Nineteenth Centuries: A Social and Literary History,* ed. Ruth-Ellen B. Joeres and Mary Jo Maynes, 215–229. Bloomington: Indiana University Press, 1986.

Prestel, Claudia. "Erschliessung neuer Erwerbszweige für die jüdische Frau. Das Beispiel der Krankenschwester: Apologetik oder effektive Massnahme?" *Metis. Zeitschrift für historische Frauenforschung und feministische Praxis* 1, no. 2 (1992): 41–62.

Prince, Magdalene von. *Eine deutsche Frau im Innern Deutsch-Ostafrikas: Elf Jahre nach Tagebuchblättern erzählt.* 3d ed. Berlin: E. S. Mittler, 1908.

Proempeler, Elly. *Kriegsgefangen quer durch Afrika: Erlebnisse einer deutschen Frau im Weltkriege.* Berlin: Otto Elsner, 1918.

Puhle, Hans-Jürgen. *Agrarische Interessenpolitik und preussischer Konservatismus im wilhelminischen Reich (1893–1914): Ein Beitrag zur Analyse des Nationalismus in Deutschland am Beispiel des Bundes der Landwirte und der Deutsch-Konservativen Partei.* 2d ed. Bonn: Neue Gesellschaft, 1975.

Pulzer, Peter. *Jews and the German State: The Political History of a Minority, 1848–1933.* Oxford: Blackwell, 1992.

———. *The Rise of Political Anti-Semitism in Germany and Austria.* Rev. ed. Cambridge: Harvard University Press, 1988.

Quataert, Jean H. *Staging Philanthropy: Patriotic Women and the National Imagination in Dynastic Germany, 1813–1916.* Ann Arbor: University of Michigan Press, 2001.

Reagin, Nancy R. *A German Women's Movement: Class and Gender in Hanover, 1880–1933.* Chapel Hill: University of North Carolina Press, 1995.

Reichel, Charlotte. *Der Dienstvertrag der Krankenpflegerinnen unter Berücksichtigung der sozialen Lage.* Jena: Fischer, 1910.

Reichel, E. "Was haben wir zu thun, damit die deutsche Kolonialpolitik nicht zur Schädigung, sondern zur Förderung der Mission ausschläge?" *Allgemeine Missions-Zeitschrift* 13 (1886): 39–55.

Reichskolonialamt, ed. *Die Kolonialdeutschen aus Kamerun und Togo in französischer Gefangenschaft.* Berlin: Reichsdruckerei, 1917.

———. "Südwestafrika 1912: Die weisse Bevölkerung." In *Die deutschen Schutzgebiete: Amtliche Jahresberichte in Afrika und der Südsee. 1911/12,* 20–27. Berlin: E. S. Mittler, 1913.

Reinders, Robert C. "Racialism on the Left: E. D. Morel and the 'Black Horror on the Rhine.'" *International Review of Social History* 13 (1968): 1–28.

Reismann-Grone, Theodor, and Eduard von Liebert. "Überseepolitik oder Festlandpolitik." *Flugschriften des Alldeutschen Verbandes,* no. 22. Munich: J. F. Lehmann, 1905.

Renault, François. *Lavigerie, l'esclavage Africain, et l'Europe*. 2 vols. Paris: Editions E. de Boccard, 1971.

Report on the Natives and Their Treatment by Germany. Ed. Administrator's Office, Windhuk, South-West Africa. London: HMSO, 1918.

Retallack, James N. *Notables of the Right: The Conservative Party and Political Mobilization in Germany, 1876–1918*. Boston: Unwin Hyman, 1988.

Reuss, Martin. "The Disgrace and Fall of Carl Peters: Morality, Politics and *Staatsräson* in the Time of Wilhelm II." *Central European History* 14 (1981): 110–141.

Reverby, Susan. *Ordered to Care: The Dilemma of American Nursing, 1850–1945*. New York: Cambridge University Press, 1987.

Rheinsberg, A. von. "Ueber die Sendung deutscher Frauen nach dem Schutzgebiete." *Die Frauenbewegung* 4, no. 11 (1 June 1898): 124–125.

Richtofen-Damsdorf, Gertrud von. "Der Frauenbund der Deutschen Kolonialgesellschaft." In *Hedwig Heyl: Ein Gedenkblatt zu ihrem 70. Geburtstage dem 5. Mai 1920 von ihren Mitarbeitern und Freunden*, ed. Elise von Hopffgarten, 116–120. Berlin: Dietrich Reimer (Ernst Vohsen), 1920.

Ridley, Hugh. *Images of Imperial Rule*. London: Croom Helm, 1983.

Riebow, O., et al., eds. *Die deutsche Kolonialgesetzgebung: Sammlung der auf die deutschen Schutzgebiete bezüglichen Gesetze, Verordnungen, Erlasse und internationalen Vereinbarungen*. 13 vols. Berlin: E. S. Mittler, 1893–1910.

Riemann, Ilka. "Die Rolle der Frauenvereine in der Sozialpolitik: Vaterländischer Frauenverein und gemässigter Flügel der Frauenbewegung zwischen 1865 und 1918." In *Die armen Frauen: Frauen und Sozialpolitik*, ed. Ilona Kickbusch and Barbara Riedmüller, 201–224. Frankfurt: Suhrkamp, 1984.

Rilke, Rainer Maria. *Briefe aus den Jahren 1892 bis 1904*. Ed. Ruth Sieber-Rilke and Carl Sieber. Leipzig: Insel, 1939.

———. *Briefe aus den Jahren 1907 bis 1914*. Ed. Ruth Sieber Rilke and Carl Sieber. Leipzig: Insel, 1933.

———. *Briefe und Tagebücher aus der Frühzeit 1899 bis 1902*. Ed. Ruth Sieber-Rilke and Carl Sieber. Leipzig: Insel, 1931.

———. *Letters of Rainer Maria Rilke 1892–1910*. Trans. Jane Bannard Greene and M. D. Herter Norton. New York: W. W. Norton, 1945.

Roberts, Mary Louise. *Civilization without Sexes: Reconstructing Gender in Postwar France, 1917–1927*. Chicago: University of Chicago Press, 1994.

Robson, R. W. *Queen Emma: The Samoan-American Girl Who Founded an Empire in Nineteenth Century New Guinea*. Sydney: Pacific Publications, 1979.

Rohkrämer, Thomas. *Der Militarismus der "kleinen Leute": Die Kriegervereine im Deutschen Kaiserreich 1871–1914*. Munich: R. Oldenbourg, 1990.

Rohrbach, Paul. *Afrika: Beiträge zu einer praktischen Kolonialkunde*. Berlin: Verlagshaus Werner, 1943.

———. *Aus Südwest-Afrikas schweren Tagen: Blätter von Arbeit und Abschied*. Berlin: Wilhelm Weicher, 1909.

———. *Deutschland in China voran!* Berlin: Protestantischer Schriftenvertrieb, 1912.

———. *Deutsch-Südwest-Afrika ein Ansiedlungs-Gebiet?* 2d, rev. and exp. ed. Berlin-Schöneberg: Buchverlag der "Hilfe," 1910.

———. *Deutsch Südwest-Afrika ein Ansiedlungs-Gebiet?* Berlin-Schöneberg: Buchverlag der "Hilfe," 1905.

———. *Deutsche Kolonialwirtschaft.* Berlin-Schöneberg: Buchverlag der "Hilfe," 1907.

———. "Der koloniale Frauenbund." *Das grössere Deutschland* 1, no. 12 (27 June 1914): 341–345.

Rommel, Mechthild, and Hulda Rautenberg. *Die kolonialen Frauenschulen von 1908–1945.* Witzenhausen: Gesamthochschule Kassel — Fachbereich Internationale Agrarwirtschaft in Witzenhausen et al., 1983.

Roscher, Maria. *Zwei Jahre kriegsgefangen in West- und Nord-Afrika: Erlebnisse einer deutschen Frau.* Zurich: Jean Frey, 1918.

Rosenkranz, Johanna. "Eine Hamburger Schule zeigt ihre Kolonialschau." *Die Frau und die Kolonien,* no. 12 (December 1937): 184.

Rotberg, Robert I. "Resistance and Rebellion in British Nyasaland and German East Africa, 1888–1915." In *Britain and Germany in Africa: Imperial Rivalry and Colonial Rule,* ed. Prosser Gifford and W. Roger Louis, 667–690. New Haven: Yale University Press, 1967.

Rudin, Harry R. *Germans in the Cameroons 1884–1914: A Case Study in Modern Imperialism.* London: Jonathan Cape, 1938.

Rüger, Adolf. "Der Aufstand der Polizeisoldaten (Dezember 1893)." In *Kamerun unter deutscher Kolonialherrschaft. Studien,* ed. Helmuth Stoecker, 1:97–147. Berlin: Rütten & Loening, 1960.

———. "Die Duala und die Kolonialmacht 1884–1914: Eine Studie über die historischen Ursprünge des afrikanischen Antikolonialismus." In *Kamerun unter deutscher Kolonialherrschaft. Studien,* ed. Helmuth Stoecker, 2:18–257. Berlin: Deutscher Verlag der Wissenschaften, 1968.

———. "Richtlinien und Richtungen deutscher Kolonialpolitik 1923–1926." In *Studien zur Geschichte des deutschen Kolonialismus in Afrika: Festschrift zum 60. Geburtstag von Peter Sebald,* ed. Peter Heine and Ulrich van der Heyden, 453–465. Pfaffenweiler: Centaurus, 1995.

———. "Das Streben nach kolonialer Restitution in den ersten Nachkriegsjahren." In *Drang nach Afrika: Die deutsche koloniale Expansionpolitik und Herrschaft in Afrika von den Anfängen bis zum Verlust der Kolonien,* 2d, rev. ed., ed. Helmuth Stoecker, 262–283. Berlin: Akademie Verlag, 1991.

Runge, Max. *Das Weib in seiner Geschlechtsindividualität.* Berlin: J. Springer, 1896.

S. "Else Frobenius." *Baltische Rundschau,* no. 9 (1952): 8.

Sachau, Eduard. "Das Seminar für Orientalische Sprachen." In *Geschichte der Königlichen Friedrich-Wilhelm-Universität zu Berlin,* ed. Max Lenz, 3:239–247. Halle: Buchhandlung des Waisenhauses, 1910.

Sadji, Amadou Booker. *Das Bild des Negro-Afrikaners in der deutschen Kolonial-literatur (1884–1945): Ein Beitrag zur literarischen Imagologie Schwarzafrikas.* Berlin: Dietrich Reimer, 1985.

Said-Ruete, Rudolph. *Said bin Sultan (1791–1856): Ruler of Oman and Zanzibar. His Place in the History of Arabia and East Africa.* London: Alexander-Ouseley, 1929.

Sayyida Salme/Emily Ruete. *An Arabian Princess between Two Worlds: Memoirs, Letters Home, Sequels to the Memoirs, Syrian Customs and Usages.* Ed. and intro. E. van Donzel. Leiden: E. J. Brill, 1993.

Schaper, Hans-Peter. *Krankenwartung und Krankenpflege: Tendenzen der Verberuf-lichung in der ersten Hälfte des 19. Jahrhunderts.* Opladen: Leske Verlag & Budrich, 1987.

Scheck, Raffael. "German Conservatism and Female Political Activism in the Early Weimar Republic." *German History* 15 (1997): 34–55.

———. "Women against Versailles: Maternalism and Nationalism of Female Bourgeois Politicians in the Early Weimar Republic." *German Studies Review* 22 (1999): 21–42.

Schiefel, Werner. *Bernhard Dernburg 1865–1937: Kolonialpolitiker und Bankier im wilelminischen Deutschland.* Zurich: Atlantis, 1974.

Schlüpmann, Heide. "Radikalisierung der Philosophie: Die Nietzsche-Rezeption und die sexualpolitische Publizistik Helene Stöckers." *Feministische Studien* 3 (1984): 10–34.

Schmidt-Lauber, Brigitte. *Die abhängigen Herren: Deutsche Identität in Namibia.* Hamburg: Lit, 1993.

Schmidt-Nowara, Christopher. *Empire and Anti-slavery: Spain, Cuba, and Puerto Rico, 1833–1874.* Pittsburgh: University of Pittsburgh Press, 1999.

Schmokel, Wolfe. *Dream of Empire: German Colonialism 1919–1945.* New Haven: Yale University Press, 1964.

———. "The Myth of the White Farmer: Commercial Agriculture in Namibia, 1900–1983." *International Journal of African Historical Studies* 18 (1985): 93–108.

Schnee, Ada. *Meine Erlebnisse während der Kriegszeit in Deutsch-Ostafrika.* Leipzig: Quelle & Meyer, 1918.

Schnee, Heinrich. *Als letzter Gouverneur in Deutsch-Ostafrika. Erinnerungen.* Heidelberg: Quelle & Meyer, 1964.

———. "Carl Peters." In *Deutsches Biographisches Jahrbuch.* Überleitungsband 2. *1917–1920,* 285–298. Stuttgart, Deutsche Verlagsanstalt, 1928.

———, ed. *Deutsches Kolonial-Lexikon.* 3 vols. Leipzig: Quelle & Meyer, 1920.

———. *German Colonization Past and Future: The Truth about the German Colonies.* London: George Allen & Unwin, 1926.

Schnitzker, Margarete. "Die Auswahl der Mädchen für Südwest." *Kolonie und Heimat* 5, no. 16 (1911): 8.

Scholtz-Klink, Gertrud. *Die Frau im Dritten Reich. Eine Dokumentation.* Tübingen: Grabert, 1978.

Schrecker, John E. *Imperialism and Chinese Nationalism: Germany in Shantung.* Cambridge: Harvard University Press, 1971.

Schrieber, A. W. "Besetzung deutscher Kolonien mit deutschen Missionaren." *Allgemeine Missions-Zeitschrift* 13 (1886): 56–62.

Schröder, Gertrud. "Frauenaufgaben in Südwestafrika." *Der Kolonialdeutsche* 8, no. 1 (1 January 1928): 6–8.

Schröder, Hans-Christoph. *Gustav Noske und die Kolonialpolitik des Deutschen Kaiserreiches.* Bonn: Dietz, 1979.

———. *Sozialismus und Imperialismus: Die Auseinandersetzung der deutschen Sozialdemokratie mit dem Imperialismusproblem und der "Weltpolitik" vor 1914.* 2d, rev. ed. Bonn: Neue Gesellschaft, 1975.

Schuffenhauer, Ida. *Komm wieder Bwana: Ein deutsches Schicksal.* Berlin: W. Süsserott, 1940.

Schulte, Regina. "The Sick Warrior's Sister: Nursing during the First World War." In *Gender Relations in German History: Power, Agency and Experience from the Sixteenth to the Twentieth Century,* 121–141. London: UCL Press, 1996.

Schulte-Althoff, Franz-Josef. "Koloniale Krise und Reformprojekte: Zur Diskussion über eine Kurskorrektur in der deutschen Kolonialpolitik nach der Jahrhundertwende." In *Weltpolitik, Europagedanke, Regionalismus: Festschrift für Heinz Gollwitzer zum 65. Geburtstag am 30. Januar 1982,* ed. Heinz Dollinger, Horst Gründer, and Alwin Hanschmidt, 407–425. Münster: Aschendorff, 1982.

———. "Rassenmischung im kolonialen System: Zur deutschen Kolonialpolitik im letzten Jahrzehnt vor dem Ersten Weltkrieg." *Historisches Jahrbuch* 105 (1985): 52–94.

Schultheiss, Katrin. "'La Véritable Médecine des femmes': Anna Hamilton and the Politics of Nursing Reform in Bordeaux, 1900–1914." *French Historical Studies* 19, no. 1 (spring 1995): 183–214.

Schwarz, Gudrun. "Frauen in der SS: Sippenverband und Frauenkorps." In *Zwischen Karriere und Verfolgung: Handlungsspielräume von Frauen im nationalsozialistischen Deutschland,* ed. Kirsten Heinsohn, Barbara Vogel, and Ulrike Weckel, 223–244. Frankfurt: Campus, 1997.

Segal, Daniel A., and Richard Handler. "National Culture." In *Encyclopedia of Cultural Anthropology,* 840–844. New York: Henry Holt, 1996.

———. "Nationalism." In *Encyclopedia of Cultural Anthropology,* 844–848. New York: Henry Holt, 1996.

Sell, Manfred. "Die schwarze Völkerwanderung." In *Preussische Jahrbücher* 224, no. 2 (May 1931): 157–181.

———. *Die schwarze Völkerwanderung: Der Einbruch des Negers in die Kulturwelt.* Vienna: Wilhelm Frick, 1940.

Sevenhuijsen, Selma. "Mothers as Citizens: Feminism, Evolutionary Theory and the Reform of Dutch Family Law 1870–1910." In *Regulating Womanhood: Historical Essays on Marriage, Motherhood and Sexuality,* ed. Carol Smart, 166–186. London: Routledge, 1992.

Sheehan, James J. "Liberalism and the City in Nineteenth-Century Germany." *Past and Present* 51 (May 1971): 116–137.

———. "What Is German History? Reflections on the Role of the *Nation* in German History and Historiography." *Journal of Modern History* 53 (March 1981): 1–23.

Shumannfang, Barbara. "Envisioning Empire: Jewishness, Blackness and Gender in German Colonial Discourse from Frieda von Bülow to the Nazi *Kolonie und Heimat.*" Ph.D. diss., Duke University, 1998.

Sippel, Harald. "Aspects of Colonial Land Law in German East Africa: German East African Company, Crown Law Ordinance, European Plantation and Reserved Areas for Africans." In *Land Law and Land Ownership in Africa: Case Studies from Colonial and Contemporary Cameroon and Tanzania,* ed. Robert Debusman and Stefan Arnold, 3–38. Bayreuth: Eckhard Breitinger, 1996.

———. "Recht und Herrschaft in kolonialer Frühzeit: Die Rechtsverhältnisse in den Schutzgebieten der Deutsch-Ostafrikanischen Gesellschaft (1885–1890)." In *Studien zur Geschichte des deutschen Kolonialismus: Festschrift zum 60. Geburtstag von Peter Sebald,* ed. Peter Heine and Ulrich van der Heyden, 466–494. Pfaffenweiler: Centaurus, 1995.

Smidt, Karen. "'Germania führt die deutsche Frau nach Südwest': Auswanderung, Leben und soziale Konflikte deutscher Frauen in der ehemaligen Kolonie Deutsch-Südwestafrika 1884–1920. Eine sozial- und frauengeschichtliche Studie." Ph.D. diss., University of Magdeburg, 1995.

Smith, Helmut Walser. "The Talk of Genocide, the Rhetoric of Miscegenation: Notes on Debates in the German Reichstag concerning Southwest Africa, 1904–14." In *The Imperialist Imagination: German Colonialism and Its Legacy,* ed. Sara Friedrichsmeyer, Sara Lennox, and Susanne Zantop, 107–123. Ann Arbor: University of Michigan Press, 1998.

Smith, Raymond T. "Hierarchy and the Dual Marriage System in West Indian Society." In *The Matrifocal Family: Power, Pluralism, and Politics,* ed. Smith, 59–80. New York: Routledge, 1996.

Smith, Woodruff D. "The Colonial Novel as Political Propaganda: Hans Grimm's *Volk ohne Raum.*" *German Studies Review* 6 (1983): 215–235.

———. "Colonialism and Colonial Empire." In *Imperial Germany: A Historiographical Companion,* ed. Roger Chickering, 430–453. Westport, Conn.: Greenwood Press, 1996.

———. *The German Colonial Empire.* Chapel Hill: University of North Carolina Press, 1978.

———. *The Ideological Origins of Nazi Imperialism.* New York: Oxford University Press, 1986.

Soénius, Ulrich S. *Koloniale Begeisterung im Rheinland während des Kaiserreichs.* Cologne: Rheinisch-Westfälisches Wirtschaftsarchiv zu Köln, 1992.

Solf, Wilhelm. *Afrika für Europa: Der koloniale Gedanke des XX. Jahrhunderts.* Neumünster i.H.: Theodor Dittmann Verlag, 1920.

Sonnenberg, Else. *Wie es am Waterberg zuging: Ein Beitrag zur Geschichte des Hereroaufstandes.* Berlin: Wilhelm Süsserott, 1905.

Spellmeyer, Hans. *Deutsche Kolonialpolitik im Reichstag.* Stuttgart: W. Kohlhammer, 1931.

Spennemann, Dirk H. R. *An Officer, Yes, but a Gentleman? A Biographical Sketch of Eugen Brandeis, Military Adviser, Imperial Judge and Administrator in the German Colonial Service in the South Pacific.* Sydney: Centre for South Pacific Studies, University of New South Wales, 1998.

Sperber, Jonathan. *The European Revolutions, 1848–1851.* New York: Cambridge University Press, 1994.

Spidle, Jake. "Colonial Studies in Imperial Germany." *History of Education Quarterly* 13 (1973): 231–247.

Spraul, Gunter. "Der 'Völkermord' an den Herero: Untersuchungen zu einer neuen Kontinuitätsthese." *Geschichte in Wissenschaft und Unterricht* 39 (1988): 713–739.

Steinberg, Joanthan. *Yesterday's Deterrent: Tirpitz and the Birth of the German Battle Fleet.* New York: Macmillan, 1965.

Steinhoff, Ilse. *Deutsche Heimat in Africa: Ein Bildbuch aus unseren Kolonien.* Berlin: Reichskolonialbund, 1939.

———. "Ein neuer Staat entsteht." *Berliner Illustrierte Zeitung,* 15 May 1941, 550–551. Reprinted in *Konkret* (January 1992): 36–37.

Steinmeister, Nora von. "Aus dem Leben der Kolonialdeutschen." In *Das Buch der deutschen Kolonien,* ed. Anton Mayer, 302–306. Potsdam: Volk und Heimat, 1933.

———. "Jahresbericht des Frauenbundes der Deutschen Kolonialgesellschaft 1929/30." In *Koloniale Frauenarbeit,* ed. Frauenbund der Deutschen Kolonialgesellschaft, 1–8. Berlin: Zentrale des Frauenbundes der Deutschen Kolonialgesellschaft, 1930.

Stengel, Karl. "Zur Frage der Mischehen in den deutschen Schutzgebieten." *Zeitschrift für Kolonialpolitik, Kolonialrecht und Kolonialwirtschaft* 14 (1912): 738–780.

Stephenson, Jill. *The Nazi Organisation of Women.* London: Croom Helm, 1981.

Stern, Fritz. *The Politics of Cultural Despair: A Study in the Rise of the Germanic Ideology.* New York: Anchor, 1961.

Steudel, E. "Deutscher Frauenverein vom Roten Kreuz für die Kolonien." In *Deutsches Kolonial-Lexikon,* ed. Heinrich Schnee, 1:311. Leipzig: Quelle & Meyer, 1920.

Steup, Else. *Wiete erlebt Afrika: Ein junges Mädchen bei deutschen Farmern.* Berlin: Deutscher Verlag, 1938.

———. *Wiete will nach Afrika: Ein Jungmädchen-Buch.* Berlin: Ullstein, 1936.

Stöcker, Helene. "Sexuelle Moral im Reichstag und auf der Bühne." *Mutterschutz. Zeitschrift zur Reform der Sexuellen Ethik* 3 (June 1907): 225–229.

Stoecker, Helmuth, ed. *Drang nach Afrika: Die deutsche koloniale Expansionpolitik und Herrschaft in Afrika von den Anfängen bis zum Verlust der Kolonien.* 2d, rev. ed. Berlin: Akademie Verlag, 1991.

Stoehr, Irene. "Organisierte Mütterlichkeit." In *Frauen suchen ihre Geschichte,* ed. Karin Hausen, 225–253. 2d, rev. ed. Munich: C. H. Beck, 1987.

Stokes, Eric. *The English Utilitarians and India.* Oxford: Clarendon, 1959.

Stoler, Ann Laura. "Carnal Knowledge and Imperial Power: Gender, Race, and Morality in Colonial Asia." In *Gender at the Crossroads of Knowledge: Feminist Anthropology in the Postmodern Era,* ed. Micaela di Leonardo, 51–101. Berkeley: University of California Press, 1991.

———. "Making Empire Respectable: The Politics of Race and Sexual Morality in Twentieth-Century Colonial Cultures." *American Ethnologist* 16 (1989): 634–660.

———. *Race and the Education of Desire: Foucault's* History of Sexuality *and the Colonial Order of Things.* Durham: Duke University Press, 1995.

——— "Sexual Affronts and Racial Frontiers: European Identities and the Cultural Politics of Exclusion in Colonial Southeast Asia." *Comparative Studies in Society and History* 34 (1992): 514–551.

Stoler, Ann Laura, and Frederick Cooper. "Between Metropole and Colony: Rethinking a Research Agenda." In *Tensions of Empire: Colonial Cultures in a Bourgeois World,* ed. Stoler and Cooper, 1–56. Berkeley: University of California Press, 1997.

Streiter, Sabina. "Frieda von Bülow und Ricarda Huch. Briefe aus dem Jahr 1895." *Jahrbuch der Deutschen Schillergesellschaft* 32 (1988): 51–73.

———. "Nachwort." In *Das Haus: Familiengeschichte vom Ende vorigen Jahrhunderts,* by Lou Andreas-Salomé, 239–252. Frankfurt: Ullstein, 1987.

———. "Nachwort." In *Die schönsten Novellen der Frieda von Bülow über Lou Andreas-Salomé und andere Frauen,* ed. Streiter, 236–252. Frankfurt a.M.: Ullstein, 1991.

Stritt, Marie, ed. *Der Internationale Frauen-Kongress in Berlin 1904.* Berlin: Carl Habel, 1905.

———. "Einsame Frauen." *Die Frauenbewegung* 3, no. 11 (1 June 1897): 114–115.

Strobel, Margaret. *European Women and the Second British Empire.* Bloomington: Indiana University Press, 1991.

Summers, Anne. *Angels and Citizens: British Women as Military Nurses 1854–1918.* London: Routledge & Kegan Paul, 1988.

Sveistrup, Hans, and Agnes von Zahn-Harnack, eds. *Die Frauenfrage in Deutschland: Strömungen und Gegenströmungen 1790–1930. Sachlich geordnete und erläuterte Quellenkunde.* Burg b.M.: August Hopfer, 1934.

Teubner, Susi. "Mädel mit 'Kopf fürs Studium.'" *Die Frau und die Kolonien*, no. 12 (December 1937): 179–180.

Theweleit, Klaus. *Male Fantasies*. Vol. 1. *Women, Floods, Bodies, History.* Minneapolis: University of Minnesota Press, 1987.

Thorne, Susan. *Congregational Missions and the Making of an Imperial Culture in Nineteenth-Century England.* Stanford: Stanford University Press, 1999.

Thurnwald, Hilde. *Menschen der Südsee: Charaktere und Schicksale.* Stuttgart: F. Enke, 1937.

——. *Die schwarze Frau im Wandel Afrikas: Eine soziologische Studie unter ostafrikanischen Stämmen.* Stuttgart: Kohlhammer, 1935.

Timm, Uwe. *Deutsche Kolonien.* Munich: AutorenEdition, 1981.

Townsend, Mary E. *The Rise and Fall of Germany's Colonial Empire 1884–1918.* New York: Macmillan, 1930. Reprint, New York: Howard Fertig, 1966.

Twellmann, Margrit. *Die deutsche Frauenbewegung: Ihre Anfänge und erste Entwicklung 1843–1889.* Meisenheim am Glan: Anton Hain, 1972.

Valentin, Veit. *Kolonialgeschichte der Neuzeit. Ein Abriss.* Tübingen: J. C. B. Mohr (Paul Siebeck), 1915.

Vascik, George. "Agrarian Conservatism in Wilhelmine Germany: Diederich Hahn and the Agrarian League." In *Between Reform, Reaction, and Resistance: Studies in the History of German Conservatism from 1789 to 1945*, ed. Larry Eugene Jones and James Retallack, 229–260. Providence: Berg, 1993.

Velten, Carl, ed. *Sitten und Gebräuche der Suaheli: Nebst einem Anhang über Rechtsgewohnheiten der Suaheli.* Göttingen: Vandenhoeck & Ruprecht, 1903.

Verhandlungen des Deutschen Kolonialkongresses 1924. Berlin: Verlag Kolonialkriegerdank "Koloniale Rundschau," 1924.

"Verordnung, betreffend Rechtsverhältnisse in Deutsch-Ostafrika. Vom 1. Januar 1891." *Deutsches Kolonialblatt* 2, no. 2 (15 January 1891): 23–26.

Vicinus, Martha. "Reformed Hospital Nursing: Discipline and Cleanliness." In *Independent Women*, 85–120. Chicago: University of Chicago Press, 1985.

Vietsch, Eberhard von. *Wilhelm Solf: Botschafter zwischen den Zeiten.* Tübingen: Rainer Wunderlich Verlag Hermann Leins, 1961.

Volkmann, Richard. "Generaloberarzt Professor Dr. Kuhn." *Die Frau und die Kolonien*, no. 9 (September 1937): 132–134.

Walby, Sylvia. "Woman and Nation." In *Mapping the Nation*, ed. Gopal Balakrishnan, 235–254. London: Verso, 1996.

Walker, Mack. *Germany and the Emigration, 1816–1885.* Cambridge: Harvard University Press, 1964.

Walkowitz, Judith R. *Prostitution and Victorian Society: Women, Class, and the State.* New York: Cambridge University Press, 1980.

Ware, Vron. *Beyond the Pale: White Women, Racism and History.* London: Verso, 1992.

Warmbold, Joachim. *Germania in Africa: Germany's Colonial Literature.* New York: Peter Lang, 1989.

———. "Germania in Afrika: Frieda Freiin von Bülow, 'Schöpferin des deutschen Kolonialromans.'" *Jahrbuch des Instituts für deutsche Geschichte* 15 (1986): 309–336.

Warneck, Gustav. "Nachschrift." *Beiblatt zur Allgemeinen Missions-Zeitschrift* 13, no. 3 (April 1886): 228–231.

Weber, Marianne. "Beruf und Ehe." In *Beruf und Ehe: Die Beteiligung der Frau an der Wissenschaft. Zwei Vorträge,* 3–18. Berlin: Schöneberg: Buchverlag der "Hilfe," 1906.

———. *Ehefrau und Mutter in der Rechtsentwicklung.* Tübingen: J. C. B. Mohr (Paul Siebeck), 1907.

Wehler, Hans-Ulrich. *Bismarck und der deutsche Imperialismus.* 1969. Reprint, Frankfurt a.M.: Suhrkamp, 1984.

Weiler, Gershon. "Fritz Mauthner: A Study in Jewish Self-Rejection." *Yearbook of the Leo Baeck Institute* 8 (1963): 136–148.

Wer ist's. 2d ed. Leipzig: H. A. Ludwig Degener, 1906.

Wer ist's. 4th ed. Leipzig: H. A. Ludwig Degener, 1908.

Wermuth, Adolf. *Ein Beamtenleben. Erinnerungen.* Berlin: A. Scherl, 1922.

Whitehead, Judy. "Bodies Clean and Unclean: Prostitution, Sanitary Legislation, and Respectable Femininity in Colonial North India." *Gender and History* 7, no. 1 (April 1995): 41–63.

Wild, Inge. "Der andere Blick: Reisende Frauen in Afrika." *Etudes Germano-Africaines,* no. 10 (1992): 119–138.

Wildenthal, Lora. "Mass-Marketing Colonialism and Nationalism: The Career of Else Frobenius in Weimar and Nazi Germany." In *Nation, Politik und Geschlecht: Frauenbewegungen und Nationalismus in der Moderne,* ed. Ute Planert, 328–345. Frankfurt: Campus, 2000.

———. "The Places of Colonialism in the Writing and Teaching of German History." *European Studies Journal* 16 (1999): 9–23.

———. "Race, Gender, and Citizenship in the German Colonial Empire." In *Tensions of Empire: Colonial Cultures in a Bourgeois World,* ed. Frederick Cooper and Ann Laura Stoler, 263–283. Berkeley: University of California Press, 1997.

———. "'She Is the Victor': Bourgeois Women, Nationalist Identities, and the Ideal of the Independent Woman Farmer in German Southwest Africa." In *Society, Culture, and the State in Germany, 1870–1930,* ed. Geoff Eley, 371–395. Ann Arbor: University of Michigan Press, 1997.

———. "'When Men Are Weak': The Imperial Feminism of Frieda von Bülow." *Gender and History* 10 (1998): 53–77.

Winkler. "Aussendung von Frauen und Mädchen nach Deutsch-Südwestafrika." *Deutsche Kolonialzeitung* 28 (1911): 652–653.

———. "Aussendung von Frauen und Mädchen nach Südwest." *Deutsche Kolonialzeitung* 27 (1910): 551–552.

———. "Zur kolonialen Frauenfrage." *Deutsche Kolonialzeitung* 29 (1912): 258.

Wir hatten eine Dora in Südwest. Dir. Tink Diaz. Germany. 1991.

Wittmann, Livia. "Zwischen 'femme fatale' und 'femme fragile' — die neue Frau? Kritische Bemerkungen zum Frauenbild des literarischen Jugendstils." *Jahrbuch für internationale Germanistik* 17 (1985): 74–110.

Wittum, Johanna. *Unterm Roten Kreuz in Kamerun und Togo.* Heidelberg: Evangelischer Verlag, 1899.

Wobbe, Theresa. "Frieda Wunderlich (1884–1965): Weimarer Sozialreform und die New Yorker Universität im Exil." In *Frauen in der Soziologie. Neun Portraits,* ed. Claudia Honegger and Theresa Wobbe, 203–225. Munich: C. H. Beck, 1998.

Wolff, K. F. "Mischehen — Kolonien — deutsches Neuland." *Politisch-anthropologische Revue* 11, no. 10 (January 1913): 534–539.

Wright, Marcia. *German Missions in Tanganyika 1891–1941: Lutherans and Moravians in the Southern Highlands.* Oxford: Clarendon, 1971.

Wülfing, Wulf. "Königin Luise von Preussen." In *Historische Mythologie der Deutschen 1798–1918,* by Wülfing, Karin Bruns, and Rolf Parr, 59–111. Munich: Wilhelm Fink, 1991.

Zache, Hans, ed. *Das deutsche Kolonialbuch.* Berlin: Wilhelm Andermann, 1925.

———. "Deutschland und der Kongress der 'unterdrückten Völker.'" *Koloniale Rundschau,* no. 4 (1927): 97–104.

Zantop, Susanne. *Colonial Fantasies: Conquest, Family, and Nation in Precolonial Germany, 1770–1870.* Durham: Duke University Press, 1997.

Zastrow, Margarete von. "Fortbildung afrikanischer Jugend in Deutschland." In *Koloniale Frauenarbeit,* ed. Frauenbund der Deutschen Kolonialgesellschaft, 31–34. Berlin: Zentrales des Frauenbundes der Deutschen Kolonialgesellschaft, 1930.

Ziemann, Grete. *Mola Koko! Grüsse aus Kamerun. Tagebuchblätter.* Berlin: Wilhelm Süsserott, 1907.

Ziemann, Hans. *Über das Bevölkerungs- und Rassenproblem in den Kolonien: Vortrag gehalten am 31. Oktober 1912 in der Deutschen Kolonial-Gesellschaft, Abteilung Westliche Vororte.* Berlin: Wilhelm Süsserott, 1912.

———. *Wie erobert man Afrika für die weisse und farbige Rasse?* Leipzig: Johann Ambrosius, 1907.

Zieschank, Frieda. *Ein Jahrzehnt auf Samoa (1906–1916).* Leipzig: E. Haberland, 1918.

Gays and lesbians, 11, 65–66. *See also* Homosexuality

German Colonial Congress: in 1910, 171; in 1924, 172

German colonial empire, 83; annexations, 2; area, 1–2; decolonization of, 173; deportation of colonists, 186–87, 189; as mandates, 173, 190; military, 88–91, 94, 132, 138–39, 146, 148–50, 153, 156, 181; occupation of, 186; Pacific colonies, 1, 196; population, 1–2; postcolonial era, 171, 174, 185, 188, 200. *See also* Revisionism, colonial

German Colonial League, 146

German Colonial Society, 50–52, 72, 90, 132–33, 136, 138–39, 144–51, 156, 162–63, 165–66, 169–70, 181, 183

German-Colonial Women's League. *See* Women's League of the German Colonial Society

German Communist Party, 179

German Congo League, 40

German Democratic Party, 179–81

German East Africa, 2–4, 15–16, 19–22, 24–34, 39, 42–44, 47, 52–60, 64, 70–71, 80, 84, 107–21, 125–27, 145, 153, 167–68, 179, 181, 186, 190; coastal war of 1888–1890, 16, 38, 40, 71; Maji Maji uprising, 38, 83, 107, 118, 153; *Tanganyika,* 168, 184, 189–91, 198

German East African Company, 15, 28, 31, 34, 65, 71

German-Evangelical Women's League, 157, 176

German Hospital, 33, 35, 111

German Hygiene Association, 160

German League against Women's Emancipation, 177

German National People's Party, 179, 195

German-National Women's League. *See* German Women's Association for Nursing in the Colonies

German New Guinea, 2, 4, 40, 43, 47–48

German People's Party, 179–82

German-Populist Colonial Association, 146

German Protection League for Borderlands Germans and Germans Abroad, 176

German Samoa, 2, 4, 40, 42–43, 80, 84, 115, 121–29, 154–55, 180, 184; women, 122

German Society for the Protection of Natives, 40

German Southwest Africa, 2, 4–5, 38–44, 47, 64, 80, 82–84, 86–110, 115, 118, 120–22, 127, 132–33, 135, 137, 141, 143–44, 148–49, 152, 158, 162–63, 166–67, 172, 193; Namibia, 8, 23, 86–87, 102; Southwest Africa (mandate), 186, 189, 191, 193, 195–96, 198; Territorial Council, 105–7; war in 1904–1907, 38, 83, 93, 96, 137, 139, 142, 150, 152–54, 157

German Women's Association for Nursing in the Colonies, 13, 15, 37–53, 58, 64, 105, 133, 137, 149–50, 168; conflicts with Women's League of the German Colonial Society, 169; coordination of, 185; German-National Women's League, 21–32, 35–37, 62; German Red Cross, Main Division — Overseas, 185; membership, 41, 48, 169, 183; Women's Red Cross Association for the Colonies, 168, 170–72, 175, 177, 181, 183–84, 191; Women's Red Cross Association for Germans Overseas, 178; youth groups in, 191

German Women's Enterprise, 182. *See also* Nazism

Germans: of colonial descent, 93; of
African descent, 183; German
negroes, 174; of Samoan descent,
183
Gierke, Anna von, 159, 162
Goans, 29, 109
Goering, Heinrich, 86, 88
Going native, 95, 103
Götzen, Adolf von, 108–9, 112–18
Goudstikker, Sophie, 65, 68
Gravenreuth, von, 29, 71
Grevel Wilhelm, 126
Grimm, Hans, 172
Grimm, Karl, 21

Hahl, Albert, 122
Hahn, Diederich, 20
Harem, 29, 110
Hedwig Heyl Housekeeping School,
190
Heligoland-Zanzibar Treaty, 56
Henckel von Donnersmarck (prince),
41
Henckel von Donnersmarck (prin-
cess), 41
Herero: people, 94–95; language, 23
Herrnhuter missionaries, 18
Hertzer, Auguste, 47
Heyl, Eduard, 159
Heyl, Georg Friedrich, 158–59
Heyl, Hedwig, 151, 156–63, 166, 169,
171, 176–77, 183, 189, 192
Hilske, Bertha, 111–18, 120
Hilzebecher, Max, 134
Himmler, Heinrich, 197–99
Hindus in East Africa, 29, 109
Hintrager, Oskar, 94–95
Hitler, Adolf, 182–83
Hoechstetter, Sophie, 65, 67
Hoesch family, 41
Hoffmann, Ottilie, 158
Holocaust, 8–9. See also Anti-Semitism
Holstein, Christine, 196

Home economics. See Housekeeping,
professionalized
Homeland House, 148, 165–66
Homosexuality, 56, 63
Hoppstock-Huth, Magda, 179–80
Household: as locus of German cul-
ture, 7, 193; as locus of colonial revi-
sion, 175; and national economy,
157, 177
Housekeeping, professionalized, 160–
61, 177, 189. See also Domesticity
Hygiene, 157; racial, 148; tropical, 155

Imperial patriarchs, 4, 80–84, 89, 99–
101, 106, 108, 123, 130. See also Masculinity, colonial
Independent Social Democratic Party,
179
India, 28, 105
Indians in East Africa, 29–30, 45, 108
Institute for Maritime and Tropical Diseases, 197
Intermarriage: between German men
and African or Pacific Islander
women, 53, 80, 82, 85–90, 103–5,
109, 115, 119–21, 124–25, 133–34,
154, 165, 174; between German men
and Boer women, 89, 165; between
German women and African men,
110, 115, 121; and divorce, 105;
retroactive invalidation of, in German Southwest Africa, 99, 105
International Women's League for
Peace and Freedom, 179
Inter-Party Colonial Union, 179
Israelite Women's Association, 184
Italy, 98; as imperial rival, 28

Jagodjo, 3, 72–74
Japan, 173
Jews: assimilation of, in Germany, 20,
183; as characters in Bülow's novels,
60; in colonialist movement, 7, 39,

Jews (*cont.*)
181, 183–84; in First World War,
181; as racially different from Christian Germans, 10; as targets of
Nazis, 184; as targets of radical nationalism, 55, 57; women, 184. *See also* Anti-Semitism
Juchacz, Marie, 179
Jugendheim, 162

Kaiserswerth Deaconessate, 18, 25
Kanza, 49
Karow, Maria, 154
Kayser, Paul, 46, 72
Keudell, Else von, 25
Kiao-Chow, 42. *See also* China
Kleinschmidt, Franz Heinrich, 86
Kleinschmidt, Frau, 86
Kleinschmidt, Mathilde, 88
Klotz, Marcia, 58
Knigge, Mathilde, 44
Koch, Robert, 48
Körner, Karl, 198–99
Kühn, Lenore, 194–95
Kuhn, Maria, 148
Kuhn, Philalethes, 148–49, 165, 170
Külz, Agnes, 149
Külz, Erna, 103
Külz, Ludwig, 149
Külz, Wilhelm, 99–106, 148, 181, 183, 195. *See also* Self-administration
Kyffhäuser League, 20

Lange, Friedrich, 17–20, 63, 65
Lange, Helene, 20, 63, 68, 158–59
Lavigerie, Cardinal, 22
League against Colonial Oppression and Imperialism, 180
League of German Housewives' Associations, 160
League of Nations, 173
Ledebour, Georg, 63, 128
Left-liberalism and left-liberals, 1, 7, 10,

83–84, 96, 99–100, 157–58, 176, 179, 184; and women, 184
Leist, Heinrich, 70–74, 82
Lettow-Vorbeck, Paul von, 181–82
Leue, August, 17, 27
Leue, Margarete, 44–47
Leutwein, Theodor, 89–93, 101, 133–38, 143, 156
Lewa plantation, 34, 70
Liberalism and liberals, 98, 104, 183; German Southwest Africa as liberal idyll, 100–101; individualism, 67; liberal feminists, 10, 84, 104
Liberal nationalists, 4, 80, 82–84, 89, 99–100, 103, 120, 123, 129–30, 202. *See also* Masculinity, colonial
Liebert, Governor von, 108
Liliencron, Adda von, 139–50, 156, 158, 163, 165, 169, 189
Liliencron, Karl von, 140
Lindequist, Friedrich von, 94, 99, 116, 126
Lüders, Else, 138, 177
Luise, Queen, 37
Lützerode, Olga von, 42
Lyceum Club, 159, 183

Mabruk, 72–74
MacLean, Eva, 195
Maji Maji uprising. *See* German East Africa
Mandates. *See* German colonial empire
Marriage: civil ceremony, 87, 90, 99, 121; civilized, 126; companionate, 79; law, 89, 115; religious ceremony, 87, 90, 99, 121, 124; restrictions for colonial civil service, 42; rights bestowed by, 87. *See also* Intermarriage
Marx, Karl, 1
Masculinity, colonial, 79, 82, 84, 89, 100, 120, 130. *See also* Imperial patriarchs; Liberal nationalists
Materialism and maternity, 6, 13, 47,

United British Women's Emigration Society, 136

United States, 2, 69, 84, 87, 99, 131, 178, 180, 184; abolition of slavery in, 125; citizens as residents of German Samoa, 123; colonial empire, 2; as mandate power, 173; Reconstruction in, 125; white women in, 70

Velsen, Dorothee von, 180
Velten, Carl, 112 13
Versailles Treaty, 173, 188; Article 119, 176, 179–80; Article 231, 178–79
Victoria, Princess, 161
Victoria Sisters nursing order, 25, 62
Violence, 4, 31, 46–54, 53–54, 69–78, 82, 96, 105, 187–88
Volkmann, Richard, 148
Vollmar, Georg von, 72

Waldersee, Admiral Alfred, 16–17
Waldersee, Countess, 16
Waldersee, Helene, 16
Warfare, in colonies, 4, 38, 46, 151, 153; in Europe, 37, 38. See also Cameroon; First World War; German East Africa; German Southwest Africa; Second World War
Warneck, Gustav, 19–20, 23–24
Wars of Liberation. See Napoleonic wars
Wars of Unification, 13
Weitzenberg, Luise, 130
Wendland, Hans, 20
White supremacy, 94–95, 98, 154
White Women's Protection Ordinance. See Britain
Wilhelm I, Emperor, 41
Wilhelm II, Emperor, 1, 4, 110, 117, 137
Wilke, Bertha, 28, 30, 32, 34–35
Windthorst, Ludwig, 40

Wissmann, Hermann von, 40
Witbooi, Hendrik, 134
Witzenhausen colonial housekeeping school. See Colonial housekeeping schools
Woman Question, 6, 18, 130, 135, 143, 152, 165; in the colonies, 6, 143, 162, 165
Women, African, 4, 71, 74, 77, 79, 82, 84, 106; and interracial sexuality, 143; surveillance of, 105, 120. See also Cameroon; Domestic servants; Men, German; Women of colonial descent
Women, German: acclimatization of, 154–56; as colonists, 5, 129, 134, 154, 172, 191; educated, 136, 162–64; female as such, 135–36, 156, 163; freedom of, 69, 77; independence of, 174, 193–96, 199–200; marriage as goal of, 6, 132, 135; middle-class, 132–33, 136, 161–63, 166–67; non-feminist, 39, 201; rights of, 2, 6–7; as solution to race mixing, 5, 79, 90–91, 102, 121, 143, 145, 149, 170, 202; and suffrage, 172; unmarried, 6, 14, 16, 41, 47, 66, 91, 131, 136, 151, 165, 191; working-class, 133, 136, 161–63, 165, 167. See also Domestic servants; Maternalism and maternity; Race; Settlement; Woman Question
Women of colonial descent, 104; of African descent, 88, 90, 106; Christian, as marriage partners of German men, 82, 87, 109. See also Women, African; Intermarriage; Pacific Islanders
Women's Association for Nursing. See German Women's Association for Nursing in the Colonies
Women's Committee against the Guilt Lie, 180
Women's Leadership of the Warthegau, 199

Women's League of the German Colonial Society, 5, 99, 103, 132–33, 139, 142–72, 175–78, 181–85, 189–93; conflicts with Women's Red Cross Association (*see* German Women's Association for Nursing in the Colonies); Division IV of Reich Colonial League, 185, 197; German-Colonial Women's League, 132, 138–39, 141; membership, 148–49, 156, 169, 183; men in, 148, 150; youth groups in, 190–91

Women's movement. *See* Feminism and feminists

Women's Red Cross Association. *See* German Women's Association for Nursing in the Colonies

Women's Welfare Association, 132, 136–38, 156. *See also* Cauer, Minna

Women, white, 4, 79

Work, women's: on colonial farm, 151–52; paid and unpaid, 5, 13, 25, 53, 77, 130, 133, 136, 157, 161–62, 165, 189

Wrangel, General von, 139

Wunderlich, Frieda, 183

Wunderlich, Georg, 183

Youth groups, colonial. *See* German Women's Association for Nursing in the Colonies; Women's League of the German Colonial Society

Zampa, Paul, 49

Zastrow, Berengar von, 192

Zastrow, Margarete von, 192–93

Zech, Anna von, 166

Zelewski, Emil von, 71

Zepler, Wally, 179

Ziemann, Grete, 155

Ziemann, Hans, 148–49, 155

Zieschank, Frieda, 154–55

Zimmerer, Eugen von, 72

LORA WILDENTHAL is Associate Professor of
History at Texas A & M University.

Wildenthal, Lora.
    German women for empire, 1884–1945 / Lora Wildenthal.
        p. cm. — (Politics, history, and culture)
    Includes bibliographical references and index.
    ISBN 0-8223-2807-0 (cloth : alk. paper)
    ISBN 0-8223-2819-4 (pbk. : alk. paper)
        1. Women—Germany—History—19th century. 2. Women—
Germany—History—20th century. I. Title. II. Series.
HQ1623.W55 2001   305.4'0943'09034—dc21   2001040392